IN THE COMMON DEFENSE

The United States faces the realistic and indefinite threat of catastrophic terrorist attack. Whether the United States is successful in preventing a nuclear, biological, or other security catastrophe depends on how effectively we wield the instruments of national security. It will also depend on how effectively we manage national security processes and whether we apply the law in a manner that both enhances security and upholds our core constitutional values. Therefore, lawyers, not just presidents, generals, and intelligence officers, will decide the outcome of this conflict.

This book is essential for anyone wanting to understand national security law and process. The book includes chapters on constitutional law, the use of force, and homeland security, presented in the context of today's threats and as applied to issues such as rendition and electronic surveillance. Emphasis is placed on national security process and intelligence, as well as the role of the lawyer. Written in a style accessible to both the general reader and the specialist, the book offers a unique inside look at the practice of national security law from the perspective of a president's national security lawyer.

James E. Baker is a judge on the United States Court of Appeals for the Armed Forces and an adjunct professor at the Georgetown University Law Center and University of Iowa College of Law, where he teaches national security law. He previously served as special assistant to the president and legal advisor to the National Security Council, where he advised the president, the national security advisor, and the National Security Council staff on U.S. and international law involving national security, including the use of force, intelligence, and terrorism. Judge Baker has also served as counsel to the President's Foreign Intelligence Advisory Board, an attorney advisor at the Department of State, an aide to a U.S. Senator, and an infantry officer in the United States Marine Corps. He is a recipient of the Colonel Nelson Drew Memorial Award, the National Security Council's highest honor, and co-author of *Regulating Covert Action*, as well as of numerous articles on national security and criminal law. He holds degrees from Yale College and Yale Law School.

In the Common Defense

National Security Law for Perilous Times

James E. Baker

CAMBRIDGE
UNIVERSITY PRESS

32 Avenue of the Americas, New York NY 10013-2473, USA

Cambridge University Press is part of the University of Cambridge.

It furthers the University's mission by disseminating knowledge in the pursuit of education, learning and research at the highest international levels of excellence.

www.cambridge.org
Information on this title: www.cambridge.org/9781107638914

© James E. Baker 2007

First published 2007
First paperback edition 2013

A catalogue record for this publication is available from the British Library

Library of Congress Cataloguing in Publication data

Baker, James E., 1960–
In the common defense : national security law for perilous times /
James E. Baker.
  p.   cm.
Includes bibliographical references and index.
ISBN 978-0-521-87763-3 (hardback)
1. National security – Law and legislation – United States.   2. National security –
United States.   3. Terrorism – United States – Prevention.   4. Civil liberties – United
States.   I. Title.
KF4850.B347   2007
343.73′01 – dc22   2006103441

ISBN 978-0-521-87763-3 Hardback
ISBN 978-1-107-63891-4 Paperback

To my teachers.

Contents

Acknowledgments

National security law combines substance, process, practice, and personality. It also depends on the moral integrity and values of those who wield its authority. My teachers taught moral integrity, self-respect, and values through their example. My educational path included a number of good as well as great teachers. There are too many to identify by name. My list of great teachers includes Gene Pool, Michael Reisman, Mrs. Harrison, Judy Mendelsund, and Bob O'Brien.

No teacher has influenced my life more than Molly Flender, a superb grade-school teacher, librarian, mother, and grandmother. I find her lessons every day, in an inscription discovered, in the remembrance of her humor, and in the daily consideration of her values as I contemplate how she might approach a problem.

Lori, Jamie, and Grant are marvelous teachers as well. Every day, they remind me to look up with hope and happiness rather than down with fear and anger; a wise lesson for the perilous times ahead. For this, and so much more, I love them.

I would also like to acknowledge John Sparks, Melanie Krebs-Pilotti, Adam Smith, Dan Koffsky, Chris Healey, Bob Kimball, and David Koplow, who kindly read portions of the text, except those segments within which the reader might identify any errors. Naturally, they did so without endorsement of what they read, and as each read only a portion of the book, they all may plausibly deny knowledge of any passages with which they disagree. More broadly, I note that the views expressed in this book are my own and do not necessarily reflect the views of any organization with which I have been affiliated or am presently affiliated.

Don Mitchell merits special thanks for his encouragement, and then insistence, that I write a book and keep on writing it until it was done. I would also like to acknowledge John Norton Moore, an anonymous reader, who broke silence to give the book his vote of confidence and to make helpful comments.

Finally, thanks and appreciation go to my chamber's teams and the National Security Council teams with whom I have shared public service, the law, and friendship. Each team has participated in one form or another in the substance, process, and practice reflected in this book.

Abbreviations

APNSA	Assistant to the President for National Security Affairs (also known as the National Security Advisor)
BWC	Biological Weapons Convention
CBP	Customs and Border Protection
CBRN	chemical, biological, radiological, nuclear
CJCS	Chairman, Joint Chiefs of Staff
CWC	Chemical Weapons Convention
DAPNSA	Deputy Assistant to the President for National Security Affairs
DCI	Director of Central Intelligence (now DNI)
DHS	Department of Homeland Security
DNI	Director of National Intelligence
DOD	Department of Defense
EOP	Executive Office of the President
FISA	Foreign Intelligence Surveillance Act
FISC	Foreign Intelligence Surveillance Court
FRCP	Federal Rules of Criminal Procedure
FRP	Federal Response Plan
HHS	Department of Health and Human Services
HSPD	Homeland Security Presidential Directive
HUMINT	human intelligence
IAEA	International Atomic Energy Agency
IC	intelligence community
ICC	International Criminal Court; established by the Rome Treaty
IEEPA	International Emergency Economic Powers Act
IRTPA	Intelligence Reform and Terrorism Prevention Act
JCS	Joint Chiefs of Staff

JTTF	Joint Terrorism Task Force
LOAC	law of armed conflict
IOB	Intelligence Oversight Board
NCTC	National Counterterrorism Center
NEST	Nuclear Emergency Search Team
NIE	National Intelligence Estimate
NIMS	National Incident Management System
NORAD	North American Air Defense Command
NPT	Treaty on the Non-Proliferation of Nuclear Weapons
NRP	National Response Plan
NSA	National Security Agency
NSC	National Security Council
NSPD	National Security Presidential Directive
OHS	Office of Homeland Security
OIPR	Office of Intelligence Policy and Review (at the Department of Justice)
OLC	Office of Legal Counsel (at the Department of Justice)
OMB	Office of Management and Budget
OSD	Office of the Secretary of Defense
OVP	Office of the Vice President
PDD	Presidential Decision Directive
PFIAB	President's Foreign Intelligence Advisory Board
POTUS	President of the United States
PSI	Proliferation Security Initiative
SCI	sensitive compartmented information
SIGINT	signals intelligence
SNS	Strategic National Stockpile
TTIC	Terrorism Threat Integration Center (now NCTC)
UCMJ	Uniform Code of Military Justice
USC	United States Code
WHO	White House Office
WMD	weapons of mass destruction
WPR	War Powers Resolution

Introduction

The United States faces four immediate and potentially catastrophic threats. First, there is the threat of terrorist attack using a weapon of mass destruction (WMD) – a chemical, biological, radiological, or nuclear device. Second, in defending against this WMD threat, the United States may take measures that degrade the quality of our democracy and do so permanently, because the threat from catastrophic terrorism is indefinite. Third, we may not agree as a society on the nature of the threat and therefore on the nature of the response. In failing to agree, we may compromise. If we split the difference, we may fail to fully protect against a WMD attack or to preserve those values that underpin both our security and our liberty. Fourth, in addressing the threat of a WMD attack, and perhaps in coping with the war in Iraq and its consequences, we run the risk that we will degrade our ability to address this century's other certain threats – nuclear proliferation, instability in the Middle East, pandemic disease, environmental degradation, and energy and economic rivalry. This may occur because we are distracted or divided, or because we are exhausted.

National security law, by which I mean the substance, process, and practice of law, is central to addressing each of these threats. First, the tools necessary to provide physical security are defined in law, as is the process of decision-making for using them. Second, law is itself a national security tool. It distinguishes the United States from our opponents and underpins the moral authority to lead in conflict and demand in alliance. Third, the law, and in particular the Constitution, provides a framework for a government that is subject to checks and balances, and therefore a society of security with liberty. If well designed, national security process and law improve security.

This book explains why and how the good faith application of law results in better security at the same time that it honors America's commitment to the rule of law. This theme is introduced in Chapter 3 and followed throughout the remainder of the text. The book starts with the threat, for law is not an abstraction. Rather, law reflects societal values and represents an effort to

1

set substantive and procedural standards for individual and state behavior in context. With national security, context reflects threat. Moreover, sometimes differences in legal outlook in fact reflect differences in perceptions about the threat, and not differences regarding the law.

The book focuses on the risk of a terrorist attack using weapons of mass destruction, in particular a nuclear device. This is not the only threat the United States faces, nor the most certain. But it is potentially the most catastrophic and it is the threat that defines the legal debate over the shape and application of national security law.

The book then explains why this threat presents the prospect of endless conflict and the corresponding pressure such a conflict will place on principles embodied in the concept of liberty and law. Chapter 1 closes by describing how national security law and process can improve national security while at the same time advancing the rule of law. Hence the title: *In the Common Defense.*

The phrase comes from the preamble to the Constitution:

> We the People of the United States, in Order to form a more perfect Union, establish Justice . . . provide for the common defence . . . and secure the Blessings of Liberty to ourselves and our Posterity, do ordain and establish this Constitution for the United States of America.

The phrase captures a number of principles essential to national security law. At the outset, for example, the Constitution is a national security document. Seven of the enumerated legislative powers expressly relate to national security. Many others, such as the authority to raise taxes, indirectly do. The executive's responsibilities start in Article 2, Section 2, with the president's designation as commander in chief followed immediately by the specification that the militia shall serve under the president's command "when called into the actual Service of the United States." The Constitution was forged in conflict, and it has as a principal objective the security of the United States – the common defense.

The phrase also signifies that security is a shared endeavor. The president is the central and in some cases essential national security actor; however, the three federal branches of government share this responsibility. When it comes to terrorism or pandemic disease, state and local governments share this responsibility as well. Just how this responsibility is divided is a critical constitutional question discussed in Chapters 4 and 9.

Two additional principles are evident. First, national security has as a goal the defense of liberty as well as of our physical security. This commitment is evident in the preamble, and it is affirmed in the oath government lawyers take "to uphold and defend the Constitution." Second, as the preamble recognizes, the Constitution is a compact among the states established by the people for specific purposes. Consistent with the principle of federalism, the states have retained the police power under the Tenth Amendment. Thus, in homeland security context, the states share responsibility for the common defense.

Having framed the immediate threat and described the importance of law to security as well as to liberty, Chapter 2 steps back and considers the meaning of "national security." Within the law, invocation of the phrase carries important normative and procedural implications. "National security," for example, is the predicate for many of the president's security tools, including the intelligence, military, and homeland security instruments. A "national security" designation also determines the process of analysis and decision. What should qualify for such treatment and who should determine if it qualifies for such treatment? The chapter concludes with consideration of a working definition of "national security" that comprises an objective element, physical security, and a subjective element, liberty – by which I mean the rule of law founded on respect for constitutional values.

The book then turns to the constitutional framework for national security. The nature and scope of the executive's constitutional authority form *the* question in national security law today. Foremost, is the president's commander-in-chief authority subject to meaningful constitutional check and balance, or is it in some sense inherent? The chapter reviews the sources of constitutional law, including text and case law. Certain framework statutes, such as the National Security Act, also reflect constitutional law, or at least rapprochements among the political branches, defining constitutional expectations and limits.

However, for a number of reasons constitutional law is often indeterminable. The application of constitutional law entails a significant amount of choice. There are few agreed upon statements of black-letter (settled) law. For example, although it is settled that the president is the commander in chief – the Constitution expressly states so – lawyers do not agree on what authority is derived from the commander-in-chief clause. That is a matter of interpretation, which necessarily reflects constitutional theory, historical perspective, and, ultimately, the values practitioners believe should inform the interpretation of constitutional authority. Finally, where national security is concerned, the courts are unlikely to resolve core constitutional questions, deferring instead to the political branches, unless, perhaps, such questions arise during the adjudication of specific cases involving tangible individual rights.

The substance and practice of constitutional law is illustrated with reference to electronic surveillance. Chapter 5 reviews the legal and policy background relevant to electronic surveillance as a domestic intelligence instrument. It then uses that background to illustrate how lawyers might apply the tools of constitutional law – text, theory, gloss, and historical practice – to shape arguments affirming or rejecting the president's authorization of surveillance outside the Foreign Intelligence Surveillance Act framework. The illustration also serves to identify the importance of legal policy and values to the practice of national security law.

As electronic surveillance illustrates, the meaningful application of law requires that lawyers (and those who evaluate and apply their judgments) understand where, how, and when legal decisions might be taken, and not just where they are recorded. Moreover, the central national security laws, like the National Security Act, are procedural rather than substantive. They are intended to encourage deliberation at the same time that they provide for timely decision. But they do not guarantee a favorable substantive result or outcome. Without knowledge of the process of national security, one cannot appraise whether the law has been applied and is guiding decision-making to lawful result as well as whether it has been applied in a manner that contributes to positive national security impact. The focus in this book is on the process of presidential decision-making and identification of those factors that distinguish effective process from the merely bureaucratic process.

National security decision-making gravitates to the president for legal, policy, and functional reasons. This focus is magnified during wartime. We know this. James Madison knew this. Less understood is the degree to which the practice of national security law is informal, undocumented, and dependent on the moral integrity of the government's officials. The national security lawyer may operate under great pressure. He or she may find a tension between the duty to apply the law faithfully and the duty to enable decisionmakers to protect U.S. security. As the book articulates, the president's foremost duty and focus is on protecting the nation. That means that the lawyer bears primary responsibility for ensuring that the law is applied and that constitutional values are preserved in the context of national security practice.

This tension is emblematic of the tensions endemic to national security process: between speed and accuracy, between secrecy and accountability, between headquarters and the field, and ultimately between security and liberty. This book considers how these tensions are addressed in three contexts: the National Security Council process (Chapter 6), the military chain of command (Chapter 8), and the Homeland Security Council process (Chapter 9). Whether these tensions are addressed effectively will determine whether the United States identifies the intelligence indicators before the next 9/11, or not, or prevents states such as North Korea and Iran from developing, exploiting, or sharing nuclear weapons.

The book next turns to the national security tools in the policymaker's kit. Intelligence, meaning the sources and methods of gathering, analyzing, and using information relevant to national security, is the predicate that informs (or is supposed to inform) whether and how the other national security tools are used. Intelligence is our early warning radar. Intelligence is also our most agile offensive weapon in a global campaign to counter terrorism. Nonetheless, the legal and bureaucratic structure of U.S. intelligence incorporates two misunderstandings regarding the U.S. response to 9/11. First, law can help to bridge the historic divisions in intelligence function, between national intelligence and military intelligence, between foreign and domestic intelligence, and between the CIA and the FBI; however, in the end, the law cannot solve what is essentially a leadership and intellectual challenge. Second, a director of national intelligence (DNI) may well assist the president (and permit the director of the Central Intelligence Agency to focus on the human intelligence mission). But as a matter of constitutional law, policy, and process, the president remains the central and essential intelligence actor, regardless of bureaucratic template or statutory framework.

The book next considers the five intelligence functions – collection, analysis and dissemination, covert action, liaison, and counterintelligence – in the context of a second overriding intelligence issue: How should a democracy in conflict modulate and appraise the efficacy, legality, and allocation of risk in performing the intelligence functions? These issues have bedeviled the political branches since the advent of congressional intelligence oversight in the 1970s. This suggests that the answer to the question is not found in legal prescript, but in a process of proactive internal appraisal that places emphasis on efficacy as well as legality.

The importance of the appraisal function is illustrated through consideration of the process and law applicable to rendition. Rendition also conveys some of the texture of national security legal practice, describing the questions raised, the nature of informal as well as formal practice, and the pressures brought to bear on the lawyer to "get it right."

Lawyers and intelligence analysts play parallel roles in the national security process – they are supporting actors to policymakers and often operate under the same client pressures. Thus, if you want to know what sort of pressure intelligence analysts encounter, ask a lawyer. Lawyers, like analysts, understand that "law," like "intelligence," rarely answers the policy question. Law and intelligence guide and inform.

The book next addresses three issues involving the use of military force. Question one: When may the president resort to force unilaterally? In the domestic context, this is a constitutional war powers question. The issue: When can the president use force without congressional authorization, concurrence, or even knowledge? The answer starts and ultimately ends with the plain text of the Constitution. But constitutional text is not definitive. As a result, the law remains unsettled, and the answer to most war power questions depends on the constitutional theory applied. Theory in turn depends on personality, which is to say, the views and legal values of the person interpreting the constitutional text.

Question two: Under international law, when can a state use force? The answer may determine whether the United States acts alone or in alliance, as well as the ramifications of action or inaction. In contemporary rhetoric and, what is more important, in contemporary practice, the debate quickly zeros in on the concept of anticipatory self-defense and preemption, and on whether there is a distinction between the two in law or policy.

Question three: What law pertains to the conduct of military operations – the methods and means of warfare? Is the law of war outdated in the context of a conflict against nonstate actors? Do the core concepts of proportionality, necessity, discrimination, and military objective offer continuity and guidance? How is the law of armed conflict applied in U.S. practice, who are the critical actors, and what methodology is used?

The U.S. response to terrorism must include three elements: offensive military and intelligence operations; preventive diplomacy, to stem the tide of recruitment and facilitate allied response; and defense, known today as homeland security. Chapter 9 introduces the bureaucratic structure, legal framework, and decision process applicable to homeland security. To an outside observer, homeland security looks like children's soccer. The players tend to surge toward the ball and do not hold their positions. When the ball is kicked, the players surge anew to convene en masse at the new location, identified perhaps as aviation security, port security, or New Orleans. Similarly, the parents seem more intent on arguing with the referees or with each other, to gain tactical advantage, than they do on investing in the benefits of long-term training and practice (this might be unfair to a majority of soccer moms and dads and dedicated public servants). There has been progress, but there is yet room, through the informed use of law and policy, to better harness the courage and dedication of "first responders" to protect America, and, if attacked, to respond. This chapter introduces the reader to the substance, process, and practice of law in this area so that they are not distracted by the soccer play. However, the law is evolving in this area, as illustrated with reference to two topical regimes, maritime security and public health.

Special emphasis is placed on nonproliferation. The subject might fit within any of the preceding headings, for nonproliferation fuses all the national security tools, including diplomacy, intelligence, and military force. However, given its centrality to the physical safety of the United States, it occupies (or should occupy) the center of the homeland security stage.

We are on borrowed time. Essential resource gaps persist in the homeland security regime. Differences in legal perspective persist regarding two essential areas of law involving federalism and the use of the military in the civil context. Both issues are new to national security law. Both warrant development. Although the principles of the vertical separation of powers, or federalism, may be apparent, they remain uncertain in application to the relationships among federal, state, and local authorities and private entities. With respect to the military, the law contains permissions and prohibitions relating to the domestic use of the armed forces. Ultimately, the law is permissive; however, political, policy, and cultural barriers cloud expectations as to how the law will or should be applied. The prospect of critical error or delay remains.

As the book stresses throughout, national security law is dependent on the moral integrity of those who wield its power. As a result, Chapter 10 addresses the roles and duties of the national security lawyer. Some scholars argue that the lawyer's role depends on identification of the "client," with candidates including the president, federal agencies, and the public. Other scholars find the answer in identifying the contextual role of the lawyer, as advisor, advocate, counselor, or judge.

National security lawyers should play all of these roles. The key is in determining the appropriate role at the appropriate time and in gaining the confidence of the decisionmaker in order to do so. The duty of the national security lawyer is not based on identification of the client. It is based on the Constitution. National security lawyers swear an oath of loyalty to the Constitution. In some cases the oath is itself required by the Constitution; in other cases it is a product of statute. Constitutional fidelity requires faithful legal analysis. That means good faith application of the law, including good faith application of constitutional structure and principle.

In summary, this book intends to make the substance, process, and practice of national security law accessible to decisionmakers and lawyers. It is also intended for the public. Understanding the law and its role, each of these actors might better perform the duty to appraise the efficacy of U.S. policy in upholding our physical security and in protecting our liberty. We need not choose between the two. That is a false choice. Security is a predicate for liberty, not an alternative to liberty. The Constitution is intended to provide for the common defense of both.

1 Perilous Times: Describing the Threat

Al Qaeda has tried, and is trying, to obtain weapons of mass destruction (WMD). Al Qaeda's leadership has said so, and this intent is documented in materials obtained in Afghanistan and elsewhere. Like-minded groups and individuals inspired or informed by Al Qaeda, which also use terrorism as a tactic, are trying to do the same. States such as Iran and North Korea are also in the nuclear arms hunt. Iran's present weapons capacity is uncertain; its intention to obtain nuclear status and its link to a global terrorist network are not. North Korea's status as a nuclear state is certain; its stability and longevity are uncertain.

The jihadists'[1] tactical objectives likely include the physical destruction of New York City and Washington, D.C., and, in the interim, the conduct of symbolic and mass casualty events. For those actors who are not just expressing anger or despair, their strategic objectives likely include the diminution of democracy as a symbol of transitional hope in the Middle East, South Asia, and Africa as well as the diminution of American cultural influence in the Islamic world.

With nuclear weapons as the backdrop, this contest *is* potentially about the survival of the state, as we know it today, its core security and values. The United States has fought for its survival and soul before, in 1812 and during the Civil War, for example. But this conflict is different. Indeed, it is not a conflict so much as it is a threat. Success is not defined militarily by territory seized and held, as in World War II. And, while the capture or death of the opponents' leaders and individual combatants matters, this is not a threat that can be addressed through attrition alone because it requires only a handful of dedicated individuals to sustain. Moreover, the opponent does not need territory, armies, or a chain of command to fight this conflict. Unlike the Cold War or even World War II, the logic of rational deterrence against the use of WMD does not pertain to the nonstate jihadist. Indeed, we do not face an opponent, but a threat from a wide swath of organizations and individuals unified in their hatred and their tactics.

Choose your word. The threat is perpetual, indefinite, endless, and not just long. That, too, makes this conflict different. So long as there is a supply of precursors for WMD in the world's arsenals, laboratories, and power plants, the jihadists will seek to obtain them. So long as there is a supply of young, disgruntled men and women in the world, the jihadists will retain an apparent capacity to deliver them. There is such a source. Indications are that it is growing. Global polls reflect widespread support for jihadists like Osama Bin Laden.[2] Moreover, the war in Iraq has produced at least a generation – the next generation – of jihadists, as Afghanistan produced the generation before. The generation beyond, one suspects, is at work in madrasahs throughout South Asia and elsewhere. As Arnaud de Borchgrave points out, there are 10,000 madrasahs on Mindanao alone; before 9/11 there were a handful of jihadist websites; there are now more than 5,000.[3]

Finally, this conflict is different because for the American public, but not its national security services, this is an intermittent conflict. It requires inconvenience, and for some sorrow and fear, but not to date the sort of societal sacrifice commensurate with the threat. For example, as commentators such as Thomas Friedman argue, we have not taken basic steps to curtail our dependence, and thus the influence of foreign oil, on U.S. policy and U.S. security. Reasonable people might disagree on whether we might better focus on improving vehicle mileage, adopting alternative energy sources, or developing additional reserves, or all three. But are there really divergent views on the national security impact and benefit of doing so? What of port security, public health, and the tax base to pay for them? Clearly, we lack a consensus in all but rhetoric regarding the costs and benefits of response.

Although we might contain the threat from this conflict with sustained commitment, we can lose this conflict in a day. The jihadist may need to get through only once with a WMD weapon to deeply change the nature of American society – its optimism, its humanity, its tolerance, and its sense of liberty. Thus, even if we succeed in deterring an attack over time, we cannot ever know if we have "won." Nor can we ever assume that we have "won," because we cannot ignore a threat that can kill thousands, perhaps millions, and undermine our way of life with a single successful attack. Of course, this judgment depends on one's views about the WMD threat and the probability of its fruition.

The historian Joseph Ellis argues that it is not too soon to debate the meaning of 9/11 and its place in history. Ellis writes:

> Where does Sept. 11 rank in the grand sweep of American history as a threat to national security? By my calculations it does not make the top tier of the list, which requires the threat to pose a serious challenge to the survival of the American republic.[4]

Such discourse is part of the process of finding our constitutional equilibrium after 9/11. But Ellis is wrong. September 11, 2001, was not the beginning of the conflict, nor was it the entirety of the conflict. It was a defining moment, but a moment nonetheless in an ongoing and open-ended conflict. Churchill might have called it the end of the beginning. On 9/11, the jihadists realized that the grand attack works, at least on a tactical level. For our part, we realized that the jihadists have the wherewithal to attack America and do so in sophisticated fashion. On 9/11, the threat of a WMD attack in the United States morphed from a tabletop security scenario to a daily security reality.

Most alarming is the threat of a nuclear attack. Harvard's Graham Allison explains in his book *Nuclear Terrorism* that it does not, in fact, take a rocket scientist to make a nuclear weapon. It takes fissionable material. Indeed, the International Atomic Energy Agency (IAEA), the United Nation's global watchdog for nuclear proliferation, documented at least 175 instances from 1993 to 2001 involving trafficking in nuclear material; 18 of these cases involved weapons-grade fissionable material. Media and IAEA reports indicate that this trend continues five years after 9/11.[5] According to Department of Homeland Security (DHS) officials, "incidents tracked by the Department average about twice the number made public by the IAEA...reports of nuclear and radioactive materials trafficking have ranged from 200–250 a year since 2000."[6] Moreover, if a jihadist network cannot find material on the black market, it might find a state sponsor willing to share nuclear technology or know-how. Alternatively, a terrorist network might find itself in transitory alliance with a dying or desperate regime like North Korea, or a regime under military attack and intent on survival.

The potential is there for a catastrophic attack. Whether jihadists will connect the WMD dots and whether they will successfully deploy a weapon into the United States is uncertain.

This threat means that if we value our physical safety we must remain in that state of "continual effort and alarm attendant on a state of continual danger" that James Madison described and feared. There is danger that in facing this threat, presidents and their lawyers may conclude that (1) the process due is no process at all; (2) that every search or seizure is reasonable; and (3) that extraordinary circumstances negate the necessity for meaningful checks and balances on the president's use of the military and intelligence instruments. But there will be no respite, nor return to peace, to reestablish our constitutional equilibrium. Changes in constitutional interpretation today may persist past tomorrow. Thus, assertions of constitutional authority may serve, in effect, as silent and sometimes secret constitutional amendments.

Focused on the terrorist threat, we may fail to realize, or fail to care, that physical security is a means to obtain "the blessings of liberty," not the objective itself. As important, we may fail to appreciate the extent to which constitutional checks and balances and the process of decision presently embedded in law enhance security and not just our sense of moral accomplishment. In short, we cannot hold our constitutional breath if we wish to guard our liberty at the same time that we guard our physical security. We must continuously strive to find a lasting architecture that provides physical security and the sorts of checks and balances that serve as the hallmark of the rule of law.

The difficulty in finding the correct equilibrium of security and liberty is compounded because national security law is more dependent than any other area of law on the moral integrity of those who wield its power. That is because there are fewer mechanisms for evaluating and validating claims of legal authority than with other policy disciplines. Similarly, there are fewer external mechanisms for appraising the efficacy of policies and the manner of their implementation.

Most national security law is practiced informally and almost always in secret. Heretofore, doctrines of judicial, legislative, and political deference also come into play in minimizing review of executive action. Limits on external appraisal also derive from certain functional and structural aspects of national security decision-making and the presidency, especially during conflict. For example, where national security is concerned, the policy pressure to succeed, perhaps at the knowing or unknowing expense of law, is at its greatest. Safety from external danger, as Alexander Hamilton observed, is indeed the most powerful director of national conduct.

Presidential focus on the safety of Americans is not new, and in my observation it is sincere. Whatever aides might say and do, presidents know this responsibility. They feel it. President Clinton and President Bush have described protecting the safety of Americans as their foremost duty. For my part, I never felt so much pressure as a lawyer "to get it right" as when I was reviewing military or intelligence options for deterring and responding to terrorism. As Justice Jackson observed during a different war, "[t]he tendency is strong to emphasize transient results upon policies . . . and lose sight of the enduring consequences upon the balanced power structure of our Republic."[7]

Further, for a presidency conditioned to crisis and command, which is to say the modern presidency, appraisal is a difficult function to implement. Policymakers tend to move from crisis to crisis. They must. After 9/11, the national security apparatus must remain at a crisis level of commitment and care. Where real-world deadlines are constant, opportunities to reflect are few. In this context, policymakers are less likely to appraise policy effect and legal implementation. They don't have the time. Moreover, "steady" and "strong" are perceived as policy virtues in an indefinite conflict. In addition, as the Supreme Court observed with respect to the Fourth Amendment, "after-the-event justification . . . is [a] far less reliable procedure for [it is] . . . too likely to be subtly influenced by the familiar shortcomings of hindsight judgment."[8] This makes a process of rigorous proactive executive appraisal embedded in law essential.

Finally, there may be less opportunity for appraisal because where national security is concerned the Constitution is open to varied, and in some cases, broad assertions of authority. Taken to their extremes, some constitutional theories effectively preclude external checks and balances. Take, for example, the commander-in-chief clause: "The President shall be Commander in Chief of the Army and the Navy of the United States. . . ." "Just what authority goes with the name commander in chief – these cryptic words – has plagued presidential advisors who would not waive or narrow it by nonassertion yet cannot say where it begins and ends."[9] As Chapter 4 explains, the answer has as much to do with theory as text, and theory involves choice.[10] Theory and choice mean that national security law necessarily entails the application of constitutional values, nonbinding principles that should inform how we apply law and which values we emphasize in doing so. In short, the law, and the rule of law, is dependent as much on who applies it as on the law itself.

For these reasons, the United States is as much a nation of men and women as it is a nation of laws. Where national security is concerned, the good faith application of law depends on the lawyers and policymakers who wield the law in secret and with few, if any, external checks. The faithful execution of the law requires lawyers, and, as important, the policymakers who choose the government's lawyers and then decide whether to implement their advice, to advance both the Constitution's promise of security and its promise of liberty. Such commitment requires an understanding that national security is defined by our physical safety and by our commitment to the rule of law. Indeed, as Chapter 3 elaborates, law contributes to our physical safety as well as our liberty.

2 The Meaning of National Security

A. INVOKING NATIONAL SECURITY

There is no more important assertion of policy validation than an assertion of national security. Within the law, invocation of the phrase carries important substantive and procedural implications. Where the president acts in the interest of national security, he can assert the constitutional authority to do so as chief executive and commander in chief and with all the authority the president possesses over the conduct of foreign affairs. This has obvious ramifications in a constitutional climate where presidents have long asserted authority to use force as commander in chief, without express congressional authorization, and to employ the instruments of intelligence without legislative or judicial review.

Like the president, the Congress also acts with additional constitutional authority in the area of national security. Thus, in addition to the power of the purse, the take care clause, and the "legislative Powers," the Congress has express authority to "declare war," "to lay and collect taxes . . . to . . . provide for the common Defense," "to raise and support Armies," and "to provide and maintain a Navy." From a lawyer's perspective, this means that invocation of national security will often put questions of law into that often indeterminate twilight of constitutional law involving the separate and shared powers of the political branches.

Invocation of national security also increases the statutory instruments available to the president. "National security" is the substantive threshold for many, if not most, of the statutorily authorized national security tools. By example, resort to covert action requires the president to determine that an activity "is necessary to support identifiable foreign policy objectives of the United States and is important to the national security of the United States." Similarly, the International Emergency Economic Powers Act (IEEPA) requires a presidential declaration of national emergency finding an "unusual and extraordinary threat to the national security, foreign

policy, or economy of the United States." Whether these substantive thresholds are meaningful or malleable depends, in part, on how broad a definition of national security the president and executive branch lawyers apply
to each statute. However defined, the president's authority emerges through
the national security door.

National security is also among the most effective of the president's tools
for rallying the nation to action, engaging what President Theodore Roosevelt called "the bully pulpit." The public can expect, debate, and prepare
for a full range of policy options when national security is invoked. "National
security" reaches a vein of American patriotism, commitment, and sacrifice that is not tapped through other means. This is not a phenomenon of
the communications age. Alexander Hamilton recognized as much when
he wrote in *Federalist 8*: "Safety from external danger is the most powerful
director of national conduct."[1] But in a modern age, the bully pulpit is a
press conference or sound-bite away during a 24-hour news cycle; and in a
global age, the pulpit is worldwide in dimension. This gives the president
a powerful tool of persuasion. But it also magnifies the effect of error or
change, and makes it harder to modulate and distinguish a message for a
domestic or international audience.

The invocation of national security also influences the process and
bureaucratic content of decision. Will a decision come to the president
through the National Security Council process, the Homeland Security
Council process, the military chain of command, or the domestic policy
staff? Who will be invited to meetings? Who will be excluded? In other
words, "national security" will determine whose views will be considered
before decision and whose views will be excluded.

National security also means that the budgetary and personnel resources
of the Department of Defense are available to the president for noncombat
missions. Because this department is well funded in comparison with other
national security agencies, this creates a bureaucratic incentive for agencies
to cast their policy objectives in national security terms, even where such
claims are marginal. The Department of Defense, in turn, has an antonymous
incentive to define national security narrowly to preserve its assets for its core
war-fighting missions. However, where the Department of Defense may resist
a request for assistance from an agency, as a matter of constitutional law, it
may not do so if the request is from the commander in chief and expresses
a colorable national security goal, however broadly defined. This can result
not only in broad claims of national security, but in the absence of policy
or legal consensus, it may drive relatively routine decisions to the president
for decision. For example, a decision as simple as providing blankets to
hurricane victims overseas can become presidential in nature if the Defense
Department demurs as a matter of law or policy.

Within the Congress, "national security" designation drives issues to the leadership. As a matter of both practice and law, the so-called Gang of Eight (or in some cases Four) may be the only members of Congress aware of key intelligence information or decisions (see Chapter 7). National security designation also dictates committee referrals and, in times of crisis, affords certain committees increased influence, in particular those dealing with the armed services, intelligence, and appropriations. However, unlike the president's bully pulpit, the legislative pulpit is not voice activated, but requires active and repetitive engagement to reach above the din of voices.

National security also serves as an important influence on the budget process as both a rhetorical device and a funding vehicle. Hence, lawmakers will seek opportunities to cast favorite projects as "national security" necessities or append such projects to national security bills, knowing that such travel arrangements increase the odds of arrival. Not surprisingly, national security has been invoked to garner support not only for military operations and foreign policies but also to support beef subsidies, the breakup of Microsoft, and improvements to Medicaid.

For the judiciary, the invocation of national security implicates doctrines of judicial deference to the executive branch. This can have significant ramifications in defining the qualitative and quantitative nature of judicial participation in the national security process. (See Chapter 4.)

Where national security is at stake, some also argue, nonpartisan principles should prevail, as captured in the cliché "politics stops at the water's edge." Both political parties have spoken of a tradition of limiting criticism of a president and his foreign policies while he is abroad. Lawyers might say that this principle has fallen into desuetude (legalese for disuse), if it ever truly was embedded in the psyche of the national security framework. An international lawyer might say that the norm is more aspirational than operational. But the concept is more than a talking point where there is agreement that core national security interests are at stake. In many cases politicians do feel constrained and do run the risk of political sanction for appearing to depart from a spirit of nonpartisanship or for failing to support the president at times of perceived or real national security urgency. One detects a parallel public deference to the government, and particularly the president, when national security is invoked. The public, for example, may assume the government is privy to relevant information that the public is not, at least until this presumption is proven false.

National security is also a compelling source of political motivation. However, overuse of the term can debase its value. If overplayed, the broader audience may discount real and legitimate assertions of security necessity as political slogans. They may be both. Such a perception may appeal to the political base, but degrade popular support for essential actions, with damaging results when facing an indefinite threat requiring generational commitment and continuity in response. Core definitions of security can help, giving observers a consistent measure against which to evaluate national security claims.

These are some of the substantive, procedural, and political ramifications of invoking national security. As a result, it is not surprising that decision-makers, commentators, and politicians debate the meaning of the term. It is also not surprising that definitions of national security are often contextual, designed to open the security tool box to favored policy positions, or to cloak a political position or party in a favored mantle. But if it is easy to agree that national security bears significant normative and procedural implications, it is not as easy to define what it means.

B. DEFINING NATIONAL SECURITY

Definitions of "national security" abound.[2] Statutory definitions tend to include "foreign affairs" and "defense," without defining those terms in detail, if at all. Such a definition, for example, is found in the Classified Information Procedures Act, which states "'national security' as used in this Act, means the national defense and foreign relations of the United States."[3] In contrast, the National Security Act does not define "national security." Neither does the PATRIOT Act.

Within the executive branch, "national security" has been defined broadly, as in the case of President George W. Bush's directive, "Organization of the National Security Council System," which states:

> National security includes the defense of the United States of America, protection of our constitutional system of government, and the advancement of United States interests around the globe. National security also depends on America's opportunity to prosper in the world economy.[4]

In "A National Security Strategy for a New Century," President Clinton stated: "Protecting the security of our nation – our people, our territory and our way of life – is my foremost mission and constitutional duty."[5] The "advancement of United States interests" and "the protection of our way of life" are, of course, broad statements of national security.[6]

Executive definitions are equally likely to return to the generic statutory elements of foreign affairs and defense. Thus, Executive Order 12958, addressing "Classified National Security Information," adopts the more succinct reference to defense or foreign relations of the United States,[7] as does the Joint Chiefs of Staff *Dictionary of Terms* in defining the term.[8]

Judicial treatments of "national security" also vary, in part, because courts tend to be guided by the specific case or controversy presented rather than a desire to find central and lasting constitutional constructions. When given the opportunity to define national security, the Supreme Court has spoken with disparate voices. In *New York Times v. United States*, for example, the Supreme Court declined to enjoin *The New York Times* and *The Washington Post* from publishing the "Pentagon Papers," a classified account of the policy process leading to America's involvement in Vietnam. The Court concluded that the government had not met its burden of demonstrating national security harm. While colored by the First Amendment context, the case illustrates the difficulty of fixing a constitutional definition of national security. The case fostered six concurrences and three dissents. In Justice Black's view, "the word 'security' is a broad, vague generality whose contours should not be invoked to abrogate the fundamental law embodied in the First Amendment."[9] Justice Brennan equated the government's claim of national security with "national interest," and argued that only "the occurrence of an event kindred to imperiling the safety of a transport already at sea can support even the issuance of an interim restraining order."[10] Justice Marshall associated national security ("however that term may be defined") with the president's authority to conduct foreign affairs and as commander in chief. In short, one finds in *The New York Times* case the same range of national security perspectives reflected in executive and legislative definitions of the term without ultimate agreement on a definition.

Academics and commentators offer a greater range of views on the meaning of national security. Harold Lasswell, one of the twentieth century's leading sociologists and political scientists, defined national security narrowly in terms of foreign threats and military preparedness. "The distinctive meaning of national security is freedom from foreign dictation. National security policy implies a state of readiness to use force if necessary to maintain national independence."[11] The commentator Walter Lippman enjoined the concepts of national interest and physical force: "A nation has security," Lippman wrote in June 1943, "when it does not have to sacrifice its legitimate interests to avoid war and is able, if challenged to maintain them by war."[12] Other authors return to themes found in Lippman's concept of national interest and in President Clinton's "way of life," arguing that national security is measured by the advancement of certain societal values, as well as security. Professor Frederick Tipson, for example, argued that

> For the leaders of the founding generation, principles of constitutional structure and procedure and ideals of political and civil liberty were dominant motivations. The Founding Fathers were as concerned with threats to such principles from within the nation – from factionalism, separatism, and tyranny – as with threats from without. To them, the 'safety of the people' referred to the safety of a political way of life.... The pursuit of national security is hardly meaningful if it is achieved at the expense of the values comprising the nation itself.[13]

The end of the Cold War generated interest in new definitions of national security correlated against new and emerging threats. The sometime government official and energy expert Joseph Romm, for example, argues that national security should not only address military security, but also other

> action[s] or sequence[s] of events that (1) threaten drastically and over a relatively brief span of time to degrade the quality of life for the inhabitants of a state, or (2) threaten significantly to narrow the range of policy choices available to the government of a state or to private nongovernmental entities (persons, groups, corporations) within the state.

Notably, Romm does not define security in terms of external coercion, or human threat, but by the impact an action or event might have on the quality of life and on policy choice. Consequently, Romm includes on the national security agenda issues of global warming, energy security, and economic security, with all the focus and authority such invocation brings. "With respect to military threats to our national security, we routinely plan for worst-case scenarios," Romm argues, "but we are not planning in a similar manner or with similar urgency for some of the worst case scenarios involving global warming that could impact one-third of the world's people living within 40 miles of the coast (and half of the U.S. population) and cause 200,000 skin cancer deaths per year."

In a 1994 *Atlantic Monthly* article, journalist Robert Kaplan argued that demographic, environmental, and societal stresses such as crime and poverty could lead to an increasing erosion of nation-states and international borders, and engender private armies that would fill the void. "These forces," Kaplan argued, "are now most tellingly demonstrated through a West African prism."[14] Elsewhere in Africa AIDS is surely a national security issue where it threatens to undermine the stability of the state and its economic capacity. In turn, failed states are fertile ground for the nurture of local and international sources of terrorism.

This sketch suggests that no single definition of national security is recognized in law or as policy predicate. Within the government, this in part reflects function. The reality is that the executive branch employs, and the Congress creates, different definitions for different purposes. An executive order covering classified information must be broad and flexible in scope if it is to reach the different forms of information that could legitimately warrant protection from public disclosure, which is to say disclosure to our enemies. The rubric for doing so is "national security," in part because the president's authority to classify information is based on the state secrets privilege (discussed in Chapter 4). So too, one would expect a different characterization of national security to define the bureaucratic reach of the president's national security staff than that defining the predicate for resorting to military force. One might expect the former to be broad, especially if drafted by the National Security Council (NSC) staff; one might expect the latter to be less so.

Notwithstanding the absence of a common definition of national security, common themes are evident. Most definitions include an element of physical security, or freedom from coercion, both for the individual and the state. Most definitions also reference the preservation of a value system (e.g., "way of life"). Of course, where values are directly invoked (human rights) or indirectly invoked (way of life), these definitions are inherently subjective.

Further, definitions of national security are colored by a temporal component. In the United States, immediate threats are more likely viewed as national security problems than those posing equal potential for harm over an extended period of time. So too, human threats are more likely to be viewed through a national security lens than natural threats. The prospect of global warming is a case in point. If the government's own projections are accurate, the effects of global warming could transform our way of life, including the viability of many cities on the coast.[15] A comparable, even hypothetical, threat of foreign invasion leading to the occupation of the same territory would receive immediate national security treatment and likely the mobilization of the nation to defeat the threat.

This disparate treatment may also reflect that national security, as the phrase implies, remains a concept founded in national sovereignty. As a result, most definitions of national security coalesce around concepts of foreign affairs and defense, arguably the two central functions of the state. Within this class there will remain core issues that will always warrant national security treatment regardless of immediacy or location, such as those involving terrorism, nuclear weapons, and conventional attack. Such issues will rise to the top of the national security agenda because they are generally recognized national security threats.

These definitions – with their focus on immediacy, coercion, and human actors – make it harder for the "soft" issues like pandemic disease and global warming to break into the national security hierarchy. To be clear, some experts like Romm and some officials recognize these issues as national security threats. Both AIDS and climate change are cited in the National Security Strategies of President Clinton *and* President Bush. In U.S. practice, however, they remain on the national security periphery. Overshadowed by more immediate and potentially catastrophic threats such as terrorism, such problems are unlikely to penetrate the upper tier of national security agenda, *except* to the extent they are perceived as essential to combating terrorism. The problem is that such issues do not lend themselves to immediate solutions; rather, they take sustained effort over years to manage, but with a national security level of commitment.

C. SECURITY, THE RULE OF LAW, AND CONSTITUTIONAL VALUES

Defining national security is more than an academic exercise. Terminology matters. It matters to policy, to process, to the law, and to the application of legal values to all three. Core definitions of national security inform how policymakers and lawyers interpret the application of specific statutory definitions tied to national security. Policy definitions of national security are also used to calibrate when and where military force and other forms of coercion may or should be used. In less dramatic manner, national security determines the extent of U.S. investment in foreign policy endeavors. Policy definitions of national security also drive the formation of doctrine, which both informs and confines policy options. If states are presumed to act in their national security interest, clear definitions can help states predict behavior and avoid unintended signals and consequences. Doctrines that are vague or invoked irregularly serve less well as gauges of conduct, although they may serve to keep the opponent off balance.

In addition, while national security policy options are shaped by the law, doctrines also shape the law. States generally follow international law to settle international commercial disputes, to arrange for diplomatic discourse, and to deliver the mail, even when they do not agree with or dislike a particular application of the law. As a result, in these fields changes in customary law tend to be gradual and or settled through diplomatic discourse. International law helps create expectations and defines rules of the road for state and nonstate behavior. But that is not necessarily the case where states believe core national security interests are at stake. As President Truman's Secretary of State, Dean Acheson, said, "[t]he survival of states is not a matter of law." Therefore, whether lawyers like it or not, core national security interests are as likely to shape international law as take shape from it. One can see this process in the U.S. government's evolving articulation of the right of self-defense from the *Caroline* incident, to the 1981 Israeli raid on Iraq's Osirik nuclear reactor, to the *Nicaragua* case, to the U.S. strike on the Al-Shifa plant in Sudan, and subsequently to 9/11 consideration of a "preemption doctrine." (See Chapter 8.)

Finally, if we cannot define national security, we are less apt to uphold and defend it. We will be less able to identify whether differences in policy, for example, reflect different views on the nature of the threat, differences in how to address the threat, or differences in values. Intentionally, or unintentionally, policymakers and commentators may talk past each other, diverting energy, resources, and time. Further, we will be unable to effectively set criteria to measure success, or at least progress.

In my view, there are two essential elements to a meaningful definition of national security: a physical element, and a values element, referred to in sound-bite debate by the catchall "liberty."

1. Physical Security

As we now sense, feel, and know national security is in its most fundamental sense freedom from external coercion, as Lasswell and Lippman argued, in particular, freedom from physical threat to our homes, workplaces, and to our persons. As a measure of consequence divided by likelihood, the gravest national security threat our nation faces into the indefinite future is the threat of a WMD attack in the United States. Likewise other acts or events that threaten the physical security of the national infrastructure (legal, political, economic) or the physical security of the people are also threats warranting national security response drawing from the full spectrum of available policy tools. Such threats may indeed emerge from nontraditional sources, such as economic crisis, disease, and climate change. We discount such unconventional threats at our peril even as we mobilize to address the hard known threats from state and nonstate sources.

2. Constitutional Values and the Rule of Law

But physical security is not the end, but the means of securing a way of life. As the preamble to the Constitution suggests, common defense and the blessings of liberty walk hand in hand. But liberty is an amorphous concept that loses meaning and effect without content. Liberty, "way of life," and "U.S. interests" can mean everything from access to consumer goods to the preservation of specific cultural values. In my view, way of life should be defined "narrowly" as a system of constitutional values, from which flow the structural opportunities of constitutional democracy. More than anything else this means a society and a government bound by law, and respect for law, which is to say, bound by the Constitution with its Bill of Rights, checks and balances, and principle of federalism. There is room to debate what we mean by constitutional values, and more to the point, which values to emphasize in national security context. For example, emphasis on the separation of powers to some is code for a theory of a unitary executive and a president free from meaningful external oversight. For others, shared powers means active and coordinated congressional participation in the policy function, at the expense of presidential authority. Indeed, freedom to openly debate these points is among the constitutional values central to national security.

This is admittedly a subjective element to national security. As a result, there is less consensus on this element of national security than on threats to physical security. Thus, following 9/11 there was immediate popular and political consensus to take the fight to Afghanistan, but there was a rigorous debate over what to do with detainees in a "global war on terrorism," a question presenting both questions of security as well as legal values. The debate continues.

Another problem with this definition is balance. Security is concrete. Rule of law is an abstraction, a term that is easy to employ in rhetoric, but hard to measure in result. Take the debate over interrogation, for example. Putting aside arguments about the reliability of coerced information, the information garnered from interrogation is generally tangible in nature – names, actions, locations. Intelligence is needed to prevent attacks. Intelligence has prevented attacks. In contrast, the impact of U.S. interrogation practices (authorized and unauthorized) on U.S. public diplomacy, jihadist recruitment, or U.S. standing as an alternative to jihadism is harder to measure and is less immediately tangible. Indeed, there may be arguments that tough tactics deter recruitment, an argument that is equally hard to measure. Alternatively, there may be arguments that U.S. conduct has spurred the jihad movement.

In legal interpretation, rules of construction invite courts to read competing statutes in a manner that affords internal consistency and that recognizes that specific language controls general language.[16] Thus, in *Youngstown*, Congress's enactment of a specific statute addressing price controls and labor disputes prevailed over the president's assertion of a general and inherent constitutional authority as commander in chief.[17] Similarly, where a constitutional balancing test is applied to constitutional or common law privileges, as in *Nixon*[18] or *Miller*,[19] the specific need – grand jury access to facts in a criminal case – invariably prevails over the generalized projection of harm to the president's deliberations or First Amendment freedom of the press.

This is generally true with national security as well. Faced with a choice between the concrete necessity of security and the abstract preservation of "liberty," policymakers tend to choose security. Counterintelligence specialists err on the side of investigating innocent persons rather than taking the risk of overlooking hostile foreign agents. If I were a counterintelligence specialist, I would too. The enduring consequences to "liberty" are harder to identify, uncertain, and thus certainly harder to frame and argue. Moreover, the risks in not favoring security are immediately apparent in lives lost. Nor do many policymakers perceive that liberty is at risk in their good hands, when they opt for one legal strategy over another. Nonetheless, a national security policy that does not include the rule of law as a core element will diminish not only our liberty but also our security. That is because good process, founded in law, including good legal process, as well as good faith adherence to the law, produces better security results.

3 National Security Law

Law is essential to national security in three ways. Law enables our security. It shields our liberty. And it provides the process and framework within which to evaluate the efficacy and legality of our efforts.

A. LAW AND SECURITY

The United States may not stop "the next attack." We may be unable to stop the next attack, even if we were better prepared to do so; even if we made the societal shifts necessary to do so. If we do prevent a catastrophic attack, it will be through the effective, hard, and creative use of the national security tools – intelligence, the military, law enforcement, and diplomacy.

Each tool is a product of law. The law defines the thresholds for their use, and the process, if any, predicate to their use. These are, of course, the same tools available for addressing the daily grist of national security: nonproliferation, Middle East stability and peace, great power rivalry, and disease epidemics.

Some national security law permits, by authorizing the president to take certain actions. The International Economic Emergencies Act (IEEPA),[1] for example, authorizes the president to freeze and seize financial assets in response to threats to the national security, as well as to regulate financial transactions with foreign states and entities, such as North Korea, Iran, and Syria, or individuals associated with terrorism. Other laws prohibit conduct. For example, the National Security Act prohibits the Central Intelligence Agency from undertaking internal security functions.

However, most national security law is procedural. In the case of foreign assistance, for example, in almost every case where there are substantive legislative restrictions on assistance, those restrictions are subject to a process of waiver. Likewise, two critical national security tools, covert action and electronic surveillance, are primarily regulated by procedural statutes. In the case of foreign intelligence surveillance, the substantive threshold to initiate surveillance is low – "reason to believe that the target is an agent of a foreign power." But the procedural mechanism is high; heretofore, the warrant request must be signed by the attorney general or deputy attorney general and must include certifications from additional senior officials.[2] An independent judge must then concur in the government's certification by finding that the government has met this standard of probable cause. By further example, the National Security Act expressly authorizes covert action, and prohibits activities with intended effect in the United States. However, the majority of the statute regulates use of the instrument, creating substantive thresholds that trigger statutory and executive processes of review and specifies aspects of covert action the president is required to address in authorizing activities, such as risk and the role of third parties.

With executive process comes accountability. Process identifies the official responsible for the decision and for the outcome, as well as the criteria to measure effect. Without such legal process, national security decision-making might be all speed, secrecy, and silence. To be clear, process is a neutral term. Some commentators, like 9/11 Commissioner John Lehman, equate process with bureaucracy (pejorative meaning intended).[3] In context, Lehman is correct. Consider General Wayne Downing's 2006 description of the process for reviewing Special Forces Operations against terrorists, a process we will stipulate that must be nimble, secret, thorough, and accountable.

> Over the years, the inter-agency system has become so lethargic and dysfunctional that it materially inhibits the ability to apply the vast power of the U.S. government on problems.[4]

But note, General Downing is bemoaning the failure of process, not advocating its absence. What type of process is the question.

Good process generally leads to better results. Good process provides for rapid decision and the clear communication of decision. Good process drives issues up for resolution, or out for implementation. Good process, for example, is also more likely to "fuse" all sources of intelligence. Good process might have drawn critical information from the bureaucracy before 9/11 that we now know was present, such as knowledge of Zacarias Moussaoui's flight training in Minneapolis. Good process helps to ensure that policy dissent is identified to decisionmakers before decisions are taken. Dissent and discussion may change views. Just as important, it may identify weaknesses in the prevailing position and thereby improve mitigation strategies in implementation. Where secrecy is warranted, process helps to channel classified debate to the White House Situation Room and away from the Press Room by offering alternative avenues for rigorous debate and presidential appeal.

Good process also helps policymakers juggle multiple issues and crises. It is hard to imagine that the prospect of North Korea or Iran developing, and possibly using or trading nuclear weapons might be only one and not *the* national security priority of our time. Consider as well that the U.S. relationship with the People's Republic of China (PRC) is overshadowed by the conflict in Iraq and the threat of terrorism. The hard reality is that for the future there is not one definitive threat to national security, but multiple paramount threats. Good process ensures that multiple crises are handled concurrently, rather than consecutively, or perhaps, not at all.

Process becomes substance when participation, or its absence, results in the exclusion of critical views and critical facts. Substantive policy resistance is also sometimes nurtured through exclusion. Consider, for example, a hypothetical executive process for reviewing extraordinary renditions. One can imagine that whether and how issues of public diplomacy and humanitarian protections are addressed depends in part on who participates in the review. A process conducted solely by intelligence operatives is likely to yield one result, just as a process conducted solely by human rights advocates will predictably yield a different result. The question is: are both views present and is someone playing the role of devil's advocate to test factual assumptions, test assurances, and evaluate the public policy implications of particular transfers?

By further example, and without addressing the merits, consider the process resulting in the president's promulgation of an executive order in October 2001 establishing military commisions to try unlawful combatants for violations of the law of armed conflict. Numerous issues were left unanswered, suggesting fairly or unfairly that the proposal was half baked and ill advised. Nor could the experts in those omitted areas field the questions, for they were not included. As is now widely known, the initial order was drafted by a handful of lawyers without the input of military lawyers or even the national security advisor.[5] Might a more inclusive process have led to a different result with less cost to public diplomacy and more rapid implementation?

Process also conveys validity. In a constitutional democracy, who makes the decision can be as important as the substance of the decision. This is necessarily the case if the decision requires the constitutional authority of the president or the statutory authority of a department secretary. Where the capacity to decide is discretionary, good process guides decisions to appropriate actors, who are accountable and who may invoke electoral or appointive legitimacy and credibility. Alternatively, process may direct decision away from such actors, where for example, partisan factors may color, or perceive to color, the exercise of intelligence judgment or prosecutorial discretion. In short, for lawyers understanding process can be as important as understanding substance, in guiding national security policy, appraising the result, and in meaningfully applying the law.

Understanding process also entails an appreciation as to how to effectively engage the constitutional process between branches. Unilateral executive action has advantages in surprise, speed, and secrecy. In contrast, it is also functionally imperative. As discussed in Chapter 8, for example, military command could hardly function if it were subject to interagency, let alone, interbranch application. Unilateral decision and action have other advantages. Advantage comes in part from the absence of objection or dissent and in the avoidance of partisan political obstruction. In the view of some experts, during the past fifteen years, "party and ideology routinely trump institutional interests and responsibilities" in the Congress.[6] These years coincide with the emergence of the jihadist threat.

However, there are also security benefits that derive from the operation of external constitutional appraisal. These include the foreknowledge of objection and the improvements in policy or execution that dissent might influence. Chances are, if the executive cannot sell a policy to members of Congress, or persuade the courts that executive actions are lawful, the executive will not be able to convince the American public or the international community.

A sustained and indefinite conflict will involve difficult public policy trade-offs that will require sustained public support; that means support from a majority of the population, not just a president's political base or party. Such support is found in the effective operation of all the constitutional branches operating with transparency. Where members of Congress of both parties review and validate a policy, it is more likely to win public support. Likewise, where the government's legal arguments and facts are validated through independent judicial review, they are more likely to garner sustained public support. Thus, where there is more than one legal and effective way to accomplish the mission, as a matter of legal policy, the president and his national security lawyers should espouse the inclusive argument that is more likely to persuade more people for a longer period of time. The extreme and divisive argument should be reserved for the extraordinary circumstance. In short, congressional and judicial review, not necessarily decision, offers a source of independent policy and legal validation that is not found in the executive branch alone.

Further, while the president alone has the authority to wield the tools of national security and the bureaucratic efficiencies to do so effectively, that is not to say the president does not benefit from maximizing his authority through the involvement and validation of the other branches of government. Whatever can be said of the president's independent authority to act, as the Jacksonian paradigm recognizes, when the president acts with the express or implied authorization of the Congress in addition to his own inherent authority, he acts at the zenith of his powers. Therefore, those who believe in the necessity of executive action to preempt and respond to the terrorist threat, as I do, should favor legal arguments that maximize presidential authority. In context, this means the meaningful and transparent participation of the Congress and the courts.

Risk-taking in the field also increases where the government exercises shared authority. For sure, this statement is hard to demonstrate. The concept is nonetheless real. We know, of course, that Armed Forces' morale improves with the knowledge of public support. But I am talking as well about the intelligence instrument, and specifically, risk-taking. As reflected in statements made to the National Commission on Terrorist Attacks Upon the United States (9/11 Commission), there is a cultural perception in the intelligence community that there is danger in acting too aggressively when the authority to do so is unclear or subject to political change. Where authority is embedded in statute, intelligence actors are on their surest footing. There can be no legitimate debate as to what was or was not authorized and therefore no excuse for not leaning forward in execution (unless the law itself is written with intentional or inadvertent ambiguity). As President Carter stated when he signed the Foreign Intelligence Surveillance Act (FISA) into law, "it assures that those who serve this country in intelligence positions will have the affirmation of Congress that their activities are lawful."[7]

The inclusion of independent checks on executive action also reduces the potential for mistake because the executive takes particular care in what it tells the Congress and what it says in court. War powers reports, for example, may be bland, but they necessitate an internal process before they are submitted that causes senior officials to check their assumptions and their arguments before they send the report to the president and then to the Congress. More generally, the executive process of review tends to be more rigorous and more inclusive of views than when a decision is taken unilaterally, just as an inter-agency review is more inclusive than single intra-agency review, within the executive branch. That does not mean mistakes are frequent, but they tend to be devastating to public diplomacy, and create lasting and sometime erroneous impressions when they do occur, as in the case of the erroneous bombing of the Chinese Embassy during the Kosovo conflict or the rendition of an erroneous subject. Additional checks do not necessarily eliminate mistakes; they diminish the potential for error. And they demonstrate confidence in policy choice and legal arguments and a willingness to account for effect.

Nor does the inclusion of the legislative or judicial branches necessarily undermine the national security requirements for speed and secrecy. The FISA court has demonstrated that the government's most sensitive secrets can be subject to external judicial validation without disclosure. Likewise, it is noteworthy that one of the most significant intelligence secrets briefed to the Gang of Eight prior to 9/11 – the U.S. effort to kill or capture Osama Bin Laden in the late 1990s – did not leak.

Moreover, where secrecy is paramount, there is usually a lawful means to follow the statutory framework and preserve secrecy. In a criminal context, for example, there is the Classified Information Procedures Act. In the War

Powers reporting context, the executive can file a classified report. In the covert action context, the law provides three reporting mechanisms, including notification to just eight senior members of Congress or in the rarest case, post-facto notification. In addition, where it is important to enact legal policy to protect those in the field, or to validate controversial or dangerous initiatives, statutory documentation can occur in classified form. This is done frequently with budgetary matters in the classified annexes to the intelligence and defense bills. In other words, there is usually a means to make constitutional and procedural checks and balances function in the national security context, so as to appraise the efficacy of policy and to ensure policy is implemented consistent with the rule of law.

B. LAW AND LEADERSHIP

Law is itself a national security tool. The moral imperative and relevance of law is more apparent today than before 9/11. Law distinguishes democratic societies from the states and nonstate actors that employ tactics of terrorism; nowhere is this more apparent than in the methods and means of warfare. Indeed, part of our revulsion and contempt for terrorism derives from the terrorists' indiscriminate, disproportionate, and unnecessary violence against civilians; in other words, the terrorists' disdain for the legal principles of discrimination, proportionality, and necessity.

Faithful adherence to U.S. constitutional law underpins the moral authority of the United States to insist on the application of democratic principles abroad. Democracies are less likely to engage in armed conflict with each other, the argument goes, because empowered voters are less likely to tolerate the loss in lives and national treasure from frivolous, unwarranted, or wasteful conflicts.[8] So too, because they share the same benefits and risks of transparent and open societies, democracies are more likely to ally in preventing the use of their territories for illicit purposes and to share in the commitments necessary to combat the proliferation of WMD weapons. This is reflected in the membership of the Proliferation Security Initiative (PSI), and the other proliferation compacts of like-minded states, which are intended to present united fronts in denying technology to rogue actors.

Further, as those who have served in the military will know, there is no more persuasive form of leadership than leadership by example: *ductus exemplo*. Conversely, there is no more demoralizing brand of leadership than that of the leader who does not practice what he preaches. This leader wields the influence of superior power, but not the additional, and sometimes compelling, influence of moral authority.

The conflict against jihadist terrorism is a conflict fought over values with words and not just territory with weapons. That means that the United

States may do harm to its physical security when it employs arguments and means that address safety, but otherwise undermine U.S. efforts to present an alternative to the jihadist view. The opponent will distort almost any Western action or mistake. Witness the capacity of the jihadists to magnify and manipulate the publication of cartoons in Denmark or a papal speech through skillful use of the Internet, the mosque, and the madrasah. However, in this contest over values, whether we face thousands, hundreds, or handfuls of jihadist recruits may depend on how effective we are in conveying a consistent moral image, in voice and in practice. Adherence to legal values may dissuade the fence sitter, buttress the modernist, and isolate the jihadist. This means that when choosing between lawful options, we should consider not only which alternative provides the most efficient means, but which alternative is most likely to resonate in U.S. legal practice, and bear greatest moral and persuasive impact overseas. In an indefinite conflict, we cannot damn the torpedoes at every turn, but must advance on numerous fronts at once, including through consistent presentation of the rule of law.

C. LAW AND LIBERTY

Finally, and most apparent to those outside the law, law is essential to "the blessings of liberty." The point bears brief identification. The Constitution provides the structure for a government of the people and subject to law. Thus, much of the text is dedicated to the process of election and the peaceful transition from one administration or Congress to the next.

The Constitution also incorporates a structural framework designed to permit effective government, but guard against abuse of authority. Thus, the powers of the federal government are divided among separate and independent branches to avoid accumulation of too much power in too few hands. For this reason, Chief Justice Roberts has identified the separation of powers as the most important of the Constitution's liberty guarantors.[9]

However, the powers of the three branches of government reflected in Articles I, II, and III are also interlocking, or shared. In the case of the elected political branches, responsibility is shared to ensure that more than one voice is heard and that one person cannot exclusively control the instruments of power. The Constitution also provides through interlocking authority a system of checks and balances. The Congress, for example, has authority to make rules and regulations for the armed forces as well as raise and fund the military, while the president is commander in chief. Thus, neither political branch has sole responsibility for the military instrument. Congress has as well authority to make those laws "necessary and proper" to oversee executive branch implementation of the law. At the same time, while the speech and debate clause protects members in the execution of their core legislative duties, it does not otherwise place them above the law, which the executive may enforce as the president "take[s] Care that the Laws be faithfully executed."

Article III, of course, creates an independent judiciary, but at the same time, it delimits the reach of the life-tenured bench by limiting the jurisdiction of Article III courts to "cases or controversies" arising under the Constitution and laws of the United States.[10] Ultimately, the courts are guardians of the Constitution, ensuring that in times of stress or political demand, the political branches are free to express the popular will, but not free to undermine the Constitution through legislative enactment. To paraphrase *Youngstown*, it is the duty of the courts to be last, not first, to give up the institutions of democratic government.

The vertical separation of powers is founded in the concept of federalism. The Constitution enumerates certain authorities to be exercised by the federal government. The remaining governmental authority is reserved to the states, including the police power, derived from the language and intent of the Tenth Amendment. Thus, in theory, those officials closest to the people in everyday life wield the majority of power directly relevant to their welfare, while the federal government is responsible for matters that necessarily require uniform application to all the states.

Finally, the Bill of Rights, the first ten amendments to the Constitution, defines a zone of individual liberty for each citizen within which the government acts with prescribed and, in some cases, limited authority. These rights, like those requiring due process in the Fifth Amendment, provide the ingredients that underpin a society of liberty and justice. Additional joints and joists are found throughout the text; for example, the document's clauses pertaining to the regulation of commerce, the full faith and credit clause, and the takings clause all help undergird a free market economy.

The Constitution is a short document. It is also short in substance. But it is long in process. Whether one is informed by a theory of original intent, or one based on a living view of the law, the document's focus on process has allowed the Constitution to apply in a timeless manner. The Constitution rarely answers the national security question; rather, it provides each generation the procedural means to do so.

Through the Constitution comes the rule of law, an expectation that each branch of government, and each person within each branch, will comply with its structural, substantive, and procedural requirements and that the other branches will verify that this is done. This was not always so and there is nothing automatic about it remaining so. President Jackson is said to have remarked, after the Supreme Court ruled against him in the Cherokee cases, "Justice Marshall has made his law, now let him try to enforce it." The law was not enforced. Rule of law, and respect for the law, has come over time through practice and education and the hard daily adherence to principle.

But where some may have thought such constitutional principles were fixed, they may yet come unhinged under the pressure of indefinite threat.

Liberty is a security value because where national security puts exceptional stress on constitutional values, both internal and external to the executive branch, the rule of law helps to regulate that stress through the faithful execution of the constitutional structure and statutory procedure. In turn, these internal and external mechanisms of preview, review, and validation generally produce improved security results by generating better intelligence and better security choices, not just more liberty. In other words, the rule of law provides for the common defense of liberty and security.

4 Constitutional Framework

The Constitution incorporates three structural limitations, or checks, on the exercise of the executive's national security authority. First, the political branches share national security power and they each exercise separate powers as reflected in Articles I and II. Second, the vertical separation of powers, or principle of federalism, divides governmental responsibilities between the federal government, which exercises enumerated constitutional authorities, and the states, to which are reserved the remaining or residual authorities, including, most notably for national security, the police power. Third, the Bill of Rights, the first ten amendments to the Constitution, defines a zone of individual liberty within which the government acts with prescribed and, in some cases, limited authority.

This chapter addresses the separate and shared national security powers of the federal government. There are many books on this topic. Indeed, for some lawyers the study of the separation of powers is the study of government. My objective is to convey the essential ingredients of the law. If I have found new ground, it is in recognizing the role of informal practice in defining the substance, process, and practice of constitutional law. The successful national security lawyer must meaningfully participate in this informal practice as much as he or she participates in the formal practice of constitutional law.

I also recognize (acknowledge may be more accurate) that when the Constitution addresses national security, black-letter law is elusive and constitutional theory pervasive. By "black-letter law" I mean statements of law that lawyers generally agree are binding and enforced through effective political, administrative, or criminal sanction. Nonetheless, where national security is concerned, scholars and government practitioners often present theory as if it were black-letter law. This chapter and this book are intended to assist the reader in distinguishing between agreed "law" and constitutional theory and assertion.

The chapter starts with the sources of constitutional law, including the legal benchmarks that inform the operation of the separation of powers between the political branches. Constitutional analysis starts with the text of the Constitution. The chapter then addresses supplementary sources of law, including case law, and legislation that reflects the constitutional views of one or both political branches, at least at a moment in time. The discussion of case law focuses on two enduring Supreme Court cases addressing the separation of powers, *Curtiss-Wright* and *Youngstown*. In *Youngstown* alone, one finds many of the principles of constitutional analysis, such as Justice Frankfurter's "gloss" and the ageless tension between plain text and evolving context. In Chapter 5, which deals with electronic surveillance, the reader will see how these principles might resonate in practice.

Readers will recognize that these are but two cases out of the roughly ten Court cases that, in context, should be part of the standard national security kit.[1] Collectively, this material represents the body of case law with which every national security generalist should be familiar. However, for reasons I explain, definitive constitutional cases are rare. *Totten*, for example, an 1875 case, remains good law and is frequently cited, as is the 1901 case involving the seizure of a fishing vessel during the Spanish-American War, the *Paquette Habana*.

The second half of the chapter observes the operation of the separate and shared powers in practice. How does constitutional law actually function? What lessons and principles can we extract from this practice? Here, the book identifies the importance of the informal operation of law, unseen and often undocumented, but critical to the fabric of constitutional law. The chapter considers as well the role of history and theory in constitutional interpretation, and the importance of moral integrity in upholding the rule of law.

The Constitution offers opportunity, not guaranty. Because much is unsettled in this area, and intentionally so, and because the legal landscape permits broad, even unchecked, claims of constitutional authority, legal values as much as the law govern the practice of national security law.

A. SEPARATE AND SHARED POWERS: SOURCES OF CONSTITUTIONAL LAW

1. Text

As the president's national security lawyer, I was initially surprised how often my legal analysis started, and often ended, with the text of the Constitution. This reflected the vitality and foresight in the drafters' choice of text. However, it also reflected a dearth of accepted and binding sources of constitutional interpretation. Whereas, for example, the Supreme Court has issued multiple opinions interpreting the Fourth Amendment, there are far fewer opinions addressing specific applications of national security law. Thus, where the president's authority to place U.S. forces under foreign operational control was at issue, it was the president's constitutional designation as commander in chief that was cited, along with 200 years of historical practice involving Lafayette, Foch, and Mountbatten.[2] Where the president sought to appoint a sitting member of Congress as U.S. ambassador, the legal issue presented revolved around the ineligibility clause. Could the president appoint a sitting member of Congress as an ambassador during a congressional term in which the member had voted to increase the salary, or emolument, of ambassadors?[3] In both cases, the essential law was found in the Constitution.

In the first instance, the drafters anticipated the potential for disputes regarding the president's authority to command troops in defense of the nation absent congressional authorization. Thus "make war" was changed to "declare war" in describing Congress's war power. This left the president, as commander in chief, free to make war in defense of the country, as well as to exercise whatever additional and inherent authority that clause might provide. Many of the drafters served in the military during the Revolutionary War, or oversaw military operations as members of the Congress, and surely understood the role that foreign commanders – Lafayette, Rochambeau, and von Steuben, for example – played in the conflict while commanding colonial troops.

With respect to the ineligibility clause, commentators generally agree that the Constitution's drafters were contemplating an English practice where members of Parliament might create and accept lucrative appointments from the king while serving as members of Parliament, an obvious threat to the independence of the Parliament. However, in addressing the practice of kings, the drafters anticipated a range of potential conflicts that might occur centuries later. Thus, whether the drafters could have foreseen the specific instance that arose, they furnished the applicable law in the Constitution. It was the Constitution, therefore, that prompted the president (along with his senior advisors) to ask first, and appoint second.

The first source of U.S. national security law, therefore, is the text of the Constitution. One need read no further than the preamble to appreciate that national security is a paramount constitutional function and a shared function. Thus, it is the "people of the United States, [who] in order to provide . . . for the common defence . . . do ordain and establish this Constitution for the United States of America." Enumerated responsibilities to accomplish this common goal follow in the subsequent Articles.

Article I sets out "the legislative Power." Section 8 states *inter alia* that "Congress shall have power":

"To declare War, grant Letters of Marque and Reprisal, and make Rules

"To lay and collect Taxes . . . to . . . provide for the common Defence;"

"To define and punish . . . Offenses against the Law of Nations;"

"To raise and support Armies;"

"To provide and maintain a Navy;"

"To make Rules for the Government and Regulation of the land and naval Forces;"

"To provide for calling forth the Militia to execute the Laws of the Union, suppress Insurrection and repel Invasions;"

"To provide for organizing, arming, and disciplining, the Militia, and for governing such Part of them as may be employed in the Service of the United States;" and

"To regulate Commerce with foreign Nations, and among the several States, and with the Indian Tribes."

Congress has as well the more general enumerated power to raise taxes and appropriate money and to pass such laws as are "necessary and proper" to effectuate its enumerated authorities. This latter power, for example, is cited as a constitutional basis for the War Powers Resolution.

The president's enumerated powers include those as commander in chief and chief executive as well as those express authorities dealing with foreign affairs, such as the power to appoint ambassadors, receive ambassadors, and to make treaties, with the advice and consent of the Senate. The president is also charged "to take care that the laws be faithfully executed."

From enumerated text national security lawyers, judges, and academics identify derivative or implied authorities. For example, from the commander-in-chief clause, the chief executive clause, and the president's foreign affairs powers derives the president's authority over the intelligence instrument as well as his authority not only to command the armed forces in times of conflict, but arguably as well, authority to initiate conflict. From these same authorities, the argument progresses, comes the president's plenary (meaning exclusive in this context) authority over state secrets. For without state secrets the president could not effectively command the armed forces, engage in diplomacy, or conduct intelligence.

In the legislative realm, from Congress's express and plenary authority to raise revenue ("such bills originating in the House") derives the power to authorize and then oversee the manner in which the money is in fact spent. A broad textual underpinning for derived authority is found in Article I's threshold sentence creating the "legislative Powers" and in the necessary and proper clause, which grants to the Congress the power "to make all laws which shall be necessary and proper for carrying into Execution the foregoing Powers." However, as the War Powers Resolution illustrates, what qualifies as a "proper" exercise of such authority is the subject of debate

More generally, how much authority may or should in fact derive from particular clauses remains a source of ongoing tension between the branches. The tension is intentional. The drafters created a system of separate powers as a mechanism to discourage and, one hopes, prevent one branch from accumulating too much control or even absolute control over the instruments of authority. But at the same time, the drafters created shared or interlocking powers as a mechanism to encourage each political branch to check and balance the authority asserted by the other.

2. Statutory Gloss and Interpretation

Constitutional law in the form of constitutional interpretation is also found in statute. For example, laws such as the War Powers Resolution, the National Security Act of 1947, as amended, and the Foreign Intelligence Surveillance Act (FISA) reflect legislative (and in some cases executive) views regarding the allocation and reach of constitutional powers, at least at the time of passage. This reflection may come in the form of positive recognition of an executive power to act. Or, it may come in the form of language delimiting by substance or process the executive's discretion. One need not agree, or concede, that such statutes accurately portray constitutional law. Each act is the product of constitutional compromise and conflict and in most cases expresses the truism that each should be read consistent with the Constitution. But they do offer insight, in the absence of other vehicles, into constitutional perspectives.

The most controversial of these statutes is the War Powers Resolution (1973), which purports to regulate the president's use of the military instrument through prospective exercise of Congress's "war power." In theory, the Resolution is procedural, intending to "fulfill the intent of the framers ... that the collective judgment of both the Congress and the president will apply to the introduction of the United States Armed Forces into hostilities." By definition, the statute could not create constitutional authority that did not already exist nor terminate authority that did exist. Nonetheless, the Resolution's sixty-day clock suggests that the president possesses some degree of independent constitutional authority to resort to force, at least for sixty days.[4] Of course, this same language purports to constrain whatever authority the president has, by requiring the withdrawal of U.S. armed forces from hostilities after sixty days, absent express congressional authorization (ninety days if it is impracticable for the president to safely withdraw troops at the sixty-day mark).

The Resolution's proponents argue that the sixty-day clock is a "necessary and proper" exercise of congressional authority to create the conditions for Congress to affirmatively exercise its authority over decisions of war and peace. Although the president may have broad authority to engage in emergency hostilities, the argument goes, surely that authority does not extend past sixty days absent some affirmative exercise of Congress's own authority. Opponents return fire, noting that the Resolution cannot otherwise alter the Constitution's allocation of inherent authority, which is found in the commander-in-chief clause among other places, and is evidenced in long-standing unilateral executive resort to the military instrument. The Resolution was passed over the president's veto, and practitioners and scholars have debated the constitutional validity of the sixty-day clock ever since.

In contrast, lawyers no longer seriously debate the constitutionality of the requirement that the "President in every possible instance shall consult with Congress before introducing United States Armed Forces into hostilities."[5] This language recognizes, without defining its scope, that the decision to resort to war in some manner implicates shared responsibility. But it also contains its own constitutional trap door, which may account for the executive's acceptance of its terms. This same language is also a good example of how lawyers may agree on constitutional principle, but not on constitutional fact. The president must consult "in every possible instance." Through a legislative lens, this language might suggest consultation in every instance short of a surprise nuclear exchange. But through an executive lens, it might reflect exception in instances in which secrecy and surprise are paramount to military success. Indeed, that is how it has been applied. Likewise, to a member of Congress wearing his constitutional rather than political hat, "consult" may imply a sharing of views before a decision is taken, while to a president it means little more than a notification with opportunity to comment. (These arguments are explored further in Chapter 8.)

In contrast to the War Powers Resolution, a different constitutional approach is found in the National Security Act's covert action reporting provisions. In response to competing executive and legislative positions, the National Security Act contemplates three separate reporting scenarios, including (1) written notification to the full committees prior to initiation of an activity; (2) limited and oral notification to eight or more congressional leaders in "extraordinary circumstances"; as well as, (3) the prospect of retroactive notification in undefined, but rare circumstances, presumably exceeding "extraordinary circumstances." In other words, the branches agreed to disagree and to work out their differences in context.

In summary, one should not overlook that statutes reflect constitutional views and not just legislative law. But where there are disputes over the meaning of constitutional text, these disputes tend to migrate into statute. In the case of covert action this was accomplished through compromise – with each branch agreeing to disagree on fundamental positions and agreeing to address constitutional issues in political and policy context. In the case of the War Powers Resolution, the law incorporates only one view, the legislative view of the 93rd Congress, which has been met with sustained executive opposition.

3. Case Law

Constitutional law is also found in case law. The two most important structural cases remain *Youngstown* and *Curtiss-Wright*. The specific holdings of these cases have long been overtaken by the ascension to constitutional doctrine of what would be viewed as dicta in other cases (those portions of opinions that are viewed as nonbinding commentary as opposed to binding statements of law). The cases are significant in locating and defining constitutional perspective. They also illustrate recurring facets of constitutional analysis and interpretation.

In 1936, the Curtiss-Wright Export Corporation was prosecuted for selling fifteen machine guns to Bolivia in violation of an executive proclamation proscribing such transfers. At the time of the sale, Bolivia was engaged in a conflict with Paraguay over control of the Chaco Boreal, a swampy region abreast the Paraguay River. Land-locked Bolivia had sought control of the contested region in an effort to gain access to the Atlantic Ocean along the Paraguay River. The Chaco was also (erroneously) thought to hold substantial oil reserves. The three-year war resulted in the loss of more than 100,000 lives to combat and disease, representing a substantial proportion of the male populations in each country.

As a result, in 1934, Congress passed a Joint Resolution authorizing the president to embargo arms shipments to the region

> if the president finds that the prohibition of the sale of arms and munitions of war in the United States to those countries now engaged in armed conflict in the Chaco may contribute to the reestablishment of peace between those countries.[6]

The Joint Resolution provided for fines and imprisonment for whoever violated such a prohibition. That same day, President Roosevelt issued a proclamation giving effect to the law and delegating to the secretary of state the power of proscribing exceptions and limitations to its application. The Curtiss-Wright Corporation soon found itself on the wrong side of the law.

The company challenged its conviction on among other grounds that the Joint Resolution constituted an invalid delegation to the president of the legislative power to define the criminal law. The Court disagreed, concluding that

> there is sufficient warrant for the broad discretion vested in the president to determine whether the enforcement of the statute will have a beneficial effect upon the reestablishment of peace ... whether he shall ... bring the resolution into operation; ... when the resolution shall cease to operate; and to prescribe limitations and exceptions. ...

The Court further noted,

> It is important to bear in mind that we are here dealing not alone with an authority vested in the president by an exertion of legislative power, but with such an authority plus the very delicate, plenary and exclusive power of the president as the sole organ of the federal government in the field of international relations – a power which does not require as a basis for its exercise an act of Congress, but which, of course, like every other governmental power, must be exercised in subordination to the applicable provisions of the Constitution.[7]

Today this might seem a straightforward analysis fitting within the paradigm subsequently stated and celebrated in Justice Jackson's *Youngstown* concurrence. In the first sentence above, the Court recognizes that the president is acting pursuant to delegated congressional authority to proscribe. In other words, the president is acting pursuant to both legislative and executive authority. In present context the president does this all the time. In the case of the International Economic Emergency Powers Act (IEEPA), for example, presidents almost routinely declare "emergencies" pursuant to Congress's delegated authority to criminally proscribe transactions with designated countries or entities.

However, in the second sentence, the Court also recognizes that the president is exercising a measure of independent – exclusive – authority in the field of foreign relations. Both powers are subordinate in some manner to "applicable provisions of the Constitution." Note that the Court does not hold that the president can proscribe federal criminal law in the absence of an affirmative congressional authorization setting out the parameters for executive action.

This might have been the last heard of *Curtiss-Wright* and fifteen machine guns; however, the case is identified with Justice Sutherland's broad theory of executive authority over foreign affairs, which he suggests is derived from the nation's sovereignty and not enumerated constitutional authority. The opinion offers ample quotation for the executive branch brief. First, the president is "the sole organ of the federal government in the field of international relations." Justice Sutherland continues,

> he, not Congress, has the better opportunity of knowing conditions which prevail in foreign countries and especially is this true in time of war. He has his confidential sources of information. He has his agents in the form of diplomatic, consular, and other officials.

This is powerful language if you advise the president on foreign relations or intelligence law. This language represents a rhetorical zenith in Court rulings interpreting the executive's foreign affairs power. But read on to the second point.

> The investment of the federal government with the power of external sovereignty did not depend upon affirmative grants of the Constitution. The powers to declare and wage war, to conclude peace, to make treaties, to maintain diplomatic relations with other sovereignties, if they had never been mentioned in the Constitution, would have vested in the federal government as necessary concomitants of nationality.

Is the power of the executive to conduct foreign relations and wage war extra-constitutional?

On the one hand, the attraction of this theory is apparent, at least to executive lawyers. If the president's authority as the sole organ of the nation in external affairs is derivative of the nation's sovereignty and not the Constitution, then arguably the president's exercise of this authority is outside the reach of congressional or judicial checks and balances. This is particularly so if one places theoretical emphasis on the *separation* of powers among the branches rather than on the interlocking nature of the branches' responsibilities.

On the other hand, this same text can be read as a legal truism. "Under international law, a state is an entity that has a defined territory and a permanent population, under the control of its own government, and that engages in, or has capacity to engage in, formal relations with other such entities."[8] Thus, for the United States to qualify as a state, its national government would have to hold the capacity to conduct international relations, including the making of treaties, and the conduct of war. This principle is indeed extra-constitutional. In international law, external sovereignty does not depend on internal governing mechanisms, unless the internal organ asserting the capacity to conduct foreign relations does not in fact possess the domestic constitutional wherewithal to do so. But Justice Sutherland was addressing the federal government generally. Moreover, by definition, the federal government's competence to conduct foreign affairs is necessarily subject only to the *applicable* provisions of the Constitution.

In *Youngstown*, the Court left no doubt as to the Constitution's applicability. In 1952, during the Korean conflict, President Truman ordered the attorney general to seize U.S. steel mills in response to an impending labor strike. The president defended his decision on the ground that steel was an essential commodity on which the war effort depended. The commander in chief, the government argued, possessed inherent authority to ensure its supply. The Youngstown Sheet and Tube Company and other affected industry members sued Secretary of Commerce Charles Sawyer, seeking a judicial bar to enforcement of the order.

The Court ruled against the president, holding that the president could not, as a matter of military authority, take possession of private property in order to keep labor disputes from stopping steel production. Justice Black, writing for the Court, stated

> Even though "theater of war" be an expanding concept, we cannot with faithfulness to our constitutional system hold that the Commander in Chief of the Armed Forces has the ultimate power to take possession of private property in order to keep labor disputes from stopping production.[9]

Justice Black also noted that Congress had passed two statutes that would authorize the president to take personal and real property under certain conditions. But the president had not relied on these statutes and could not be said to have exhausted his remedies.

More so than *Curtiss-Wright*, *Youngstown* is a primer on constitutional interpretation and a reservoir of quotation. There are five concurring opinions to Justice Black's short lead opinion as well as Chief Justice Vinson's dissent joined by Justices Reed and Minton. These opinions spill with the principles of analysis familiar to the separation of powers debate. Justice Jackson, for example, zeros in on the executive's reliance on the commander-in-chief authority to derive a broad range of implied authorities.

> The Constitution did not contemplate that the title Commander in Chief of the Army and Navy will constitute him also commander in chief of the country....[10]

Justice Jackson also sounds a familiar refrain from the war powers debate – the Congress has ample authority to act in the realm of national security; however, the existence of Congress's authority does not demonstrate the absence of executive authority. The Congress must act to preserve its role in national security matters. Thus,

> We may say that power to legislate for emergencies belongs in the hands of Congress, but only Congress itself can prevent power from slipping through its fingers.[11]

Also found are many of the traditional tools of constitutional analysis. For example, Justice Clark describes the relationship between a specific and a generalized exercise of authority.

> That where Congress has laid down specific procedures to deal with the type of crisis confronting the president, he must follow those procedures in meeting the crisis; but that in the absence of such action by Congress, the president's independent power to act depends upon the gravity of the situation confronting the nation.[12]

Justice Frankfurter, in turn, introduces the concept of a constitutional gloss on executive power, often cited by executive lawyers in national security debates involving the military and intelligence instruments. One sees as well in Frankfurter's concurrence the importance of practice in constitutional analysis.

> It is an inadmissibly narrow conception of American constitutional law to confine it to the words of the Constitution and to disregard the gloss which life has written upon them. In short, a systematic, unbroken, executive practice, long pursued to the knowledge of the Congress and never before questioned, engaged in by Presidents who have also sworn to uphold the Constitution, making as it were such exercise of power part of the structure of our government, may be treated as a gloss on 'executive Power' vested in the president by s 1 of Art. II.[13]

In *Youngstown*, one also feels the ageless tension between those jurists and scholars who find the source and check on governmental authority in the plain text of the Constitution, and those who interpret the Constitution as a living or evolving document. Justice Douglas, usually associated with the latter view, cautions that the government's authority flows from the Constitution and the law, not from the necessity of response.

> But the emergency did not create power; it merely marked an occasion when power should be exercised.

> The doctrine of the separation of powers was adopted by the Convention of 1787 not to promote efficiency but to preclude the exercise of arbitrary power.[14]

Justices Vinson and Jackson respond, stressing that the meaning of the Constitution is found outside its text and is derived in part from the reality of circumstantial interpretation.

> Subtle shifts take place in the centers of real power that do not show on the face of the Constitution.[15]

> ... the Constitution is 'intended to endure for ages to come, and consequently, to be adapted to the various crises of human affairs' and that '[i]ts means are adequate to its ends.' Cases do arise presenting questions that could not have been foreseen by the Framers. In such cases, the Constitution has been treated as a living document adaptable to new situations.[16]

Justice Jackson's warning to the Court appears addressed not just to his brethren, but to future generations.

> Such institutions [of free government] may be destined to pass away. But it is the duty of the Court to be last, not first, to give them up.

One feels as well the pressure placed on the Constitution and those who wield its authority when national security is at stake. Justice Jackson, recalling his experience as President Roosevelt's attorney general, describes it well.

> That comprehensive and undefined presidential powers hold both practical advantages and grave dangers to the country will impress anyone whom has served as legal adviser to a President in time of transition and public anxiety.... The tendency is strong to emphasize transient results upon policies – such as wages or stabilization – and lose sight of enduring consequences upon the balanced power structure of our Republic.[17]

This tension is greatest when U.S. lives are directly at risk. *Youngstown* involved the seizure of steel mills, presenting questions about the taking of private property. Imagine these same tensions played out in a scenario involving a more imminent and direct threat to the physical safety of Americans, like the possible introduction of a pathogen into the U.S. food supply.

Justice Jackson also identifies and describes the tension presidential lawyers feel to apply the law in good faith, but not to concede an argument, and thus an authority, the president may need later.

> The president shall be Commander in Chief of the Army and Navy of the United States...These cryptic words have given rise to some of the most persistent controversies in our constitutional history. Of course, they imply something more than an empty title. But just what authority goes with the name has plagued presidential advisors who would not waive or narrow it by nonassertion yet cannot say where it begins and ends.[18]

Finally, Justice Frankfurter demonstrates his own humorous knowledge of government. He notes that government is far more complex than most realize. (And he was writing before the Department of Homeland Security was established.) He also suggests that where government is concerned one ought to check one's facts for they may not always prove as advertised.

> Before the cares of the White House were his own, President Harding is reported to have said that government after all is a very simple thing. He must have said that, if he said it, as a fleeting inhabitant of fairyland.[19]

Notwithstanding this reservoir of constitutional wisdom about the practice of government, *Youngstown* is best known for Justice Jackson's concurrence in which he presents an essential paradigm of separation of powers law.

1. When the president acts pursuant to an express or implied authorization of Congress, his authority is at its maximum, for it includes all that he possesses in his own right plus all that Congress can delegate. In these

circumstances, and in these only, may he be said (for what it may be worth), to personify the federal sovereignty.

2. When the president acts in absence of either a congressional grant or denial of authority, he can only rely upon his own independent powers, but there is a zone of twilight in which he and Congress may have concurrent authority, or in which its distribution is uncertain.

3. When the president takes measures incompatible with the expressed or implied will of Congress, his power is at its lowest ebb, for then he can rely only upon his own constitutional powers minus any constitutional powers of Congress over the matter.[20]

This is not a remarkable statement of law; arguably it merely echoes the eloquent balance found in the Constitution itself. The text describes the legal relationship between the political branches, as applied everyday by executive, congressional, and judicial actors. But the paradigm is important because it is presented in Supreme Court case law, giving lawyers something to cite along with the apparently familiar comfort of black-letter law. And, the paradigm is presented with clarity and eloquence. But note that Justice Jackson's third category leaves the constitutional door ajar, stating that the president's power is at its lowest ebb, not necessarily that it is extinguished, as the Court actually held in *Youngstown*.

Youngstown and *Curtiss-Wright* are often presented as bookends. To the extent one case recognizes presidential power and the other limits it, this is accurate. But they might better be viewed on a continuum with two axes, one moving from the solely external to the solely internal, and one moving from a president acting pursuant to legislative as well as executive authority to a president relying solely on executive authority in the face of a contrary legislative view. Thus, the Court recognized, in the context presented, that the president's authority is at its zenith not just when he acts consistent with the express will of Congress, but when he acts in the realm of external relations *overseas*. Conversely, the president's authority ebbs when he acts contrary to legislative pronouncement *and* when he is exercising his authority within the United States to effect national security ends. The Court itself has recognized that the Jackson paradigm is not a rigid set of analytic chimneys, but rather occurs along a continuum of factual and constitutional contexts.

'[t]he great ordinances of the Constitution do not establish and divide fields of black and white.' Justice Jackson himself recognized that his three categories represented 'a somewhat over-simplified grouping,' and it is doubtless the case that executive action in any particular instance falls, not neatly in one of three pigeonholes, but rather at some point along a spectrum running from explicit congressional authorization to explicit congressional prohibition. (Citations omitted.)[21]

In the summer of 2006, the Court revisited the *Youngstown* paradigm in *Hamdan v. Rumsfeld*. The immediate question presented was whether the president had the authority to try Salim Hamdan before a military commission established by the president at Guantanamo, Cuba. Hamdan, a Yemeni national, was captured in Afghanistan by militia forces and turned over to the United States during hostilities between the Taliban and the United States in November 2001. Hamdan challenged the authority of the military commission on two grounds.

> First, neither congressional Act nor the common law of war supports trial by this commission for the crime of conspiracy – an offense that, Hamdan says, is not a violation of the law of war. Second, Hamdan contends, the procedures that the president has adopted to try him violate the most basic tenets of military and international law, including the principle that a defendant must be permitted to see and hear the evidence against him.

A five-judge majority of the court concluded that the commission "lacks power to proceed because its structure and procedures violate both the UCMJ [Uniform Code of Military Justice] and the Geneva Conventions." The separation of powers question therefore was whether the Congress had authorized such a commission pursuant to the UCMJ, and in particular through operation of Articles 21 and 36. If not, could the president, pursuant to his authority as commander in chief, et al., nonetheless establish such a commission?

In this context, the case is significant for three reasons. First, the Court addressed the substantive question presented, rather than applying doctrines of national security deference, avoidance, or by addressing the case on the ground that appellant lacked standing, as the three justices in dissent urged.

Second, the Court applied the *Youngstown* framework, validating that framework fifty years later and in a new and challenging context. Moreover, in doing so the Court appeared to repudiate the line of emphasis in *Curtiss-Wright* dicta regarding the president's inherent powers. The Court left little doubt where it stood on the concept of extra-constitutional authority. The Court emphasized the shared and interlocking relationship among the powers of the political branches rather than the separate nature of those powers.

> Exigency alone, of course, will not justify the establishment and use of penal tribunals not contemplated by Article I, section 8 and Article III, section 1 of the Constitution unless some other part of that document authorizes a response to the felt need.
>
> ...*see also Quirin*, 317 U.S., at 25 ("Congress and the president, like the courts, possess no power not derived from the constitution"). And that authority if it exists can derive only from the power granted jointly to the

president and Congress in time of war. *See* id. at 26–29; *In re Yamashita*, 327 U.S. 1, 11 (1946).[22]

Third, the Court opened the door to the possibility that in applying *Youngstown*, the Court had adjusted the paradigm. Recall, that in Justice Jackson's three circumstances, the third states:

> When the president takes measures incompatible with the expressed or implied will of Congress, his power is at its lowest ebb, for then he can rely only upon his own constitutional powers minus any constitutional powers of Congress over the matter.

In *Hamdan*, the Court states in footnote 23:

> Whether or not the president had independent power, absent congressional authorization, to convene military commissions, he may not disregard limitations that Congress has, in proper exercise of its own war powers, placed on his powers. *See Youngstown*. The Government does not argue otherwise.

This language can be read as a restatement of *Youngstown*, as suggested by the citation. But it can also be read to signal a subtle shift in the Court's constitutional analysis. To the extent it represents a shift, it is not clear whether the shift is strictly contextual, that is applying only to military commissions, or whether this represents a shift to the *Youngstown* paradigm generally. On the one hand, Congress possesses a number of enumerated Article I powers applicable in the commission context that might not apply elsewhere, just as Congress's commerce power was specially implicated in *Youngstown*. Among other things, the Congress shall make rules and regulations for the Armed Forces, define the law of nations, and establish inferior courts. Thus, the *Youngstown* balance might be struck in a particular manner here, but not elsewhere. On the other hand, the Court has relied on the congressional war power in its footnote. In the end, we do not know whether the author lacked the votes to develop the note, was applying "case or controversy" principles, or adopted the language for other reasons.

The bottom line remains. The *Youngstown* paradigm remains the essential structural framework in today's perilous context. Whether the president will in the future find himself at a low ebb, or out of the water altogether, when confronting Justice Jackson's third paradigm will depend on the legal and ground facts presented. It will also depend on whether there is an available and effective means to adjudicate the question.

B. COURTS AND CONSTITUTIONAL LAW

That *Youngstown* and *Curtiss-Wright* remain the lead "structural" cases suggests the scarcity of controlling case law generally, and in particular with respect to questions involving the separate and shared national security powers. As Justice Jackson himself noted in *Youngstown*, "a judge...may be surprised at the poverty of really useful and unambiguous authority applicable to concrete problems of executive power as they actually present themselves."[23] There are varied reasons for the absence of national security precedent.

1. Legal Limits on the Exercise of Jurisdiction

As in other jurisdictional contexts, there are legal hurdles plaintiffs must overcome before courts will hear and decide constitutional questions. As a threshold, plaintiffs must have standing to challenge a governmental exercise of constitutional authority. "Whether a party has a sufficient stake in an otherwise justiciable controversy to obtain judicial resolution of that controversy is what has traditionally been referred to as the question of standing to sue."[24] Among other things, standing requires that a party have suffered a cognizable harm, as opposed to a generalized harm, and that the harm can fairly be traced to the matter in dispute. By example, dissatisfaction with the manner in which the government spends tax dollars is a generalized harm. A government order to impose a lien on your house for tax purposes is a specific cognizable harm.

In national security context, standing often proves a high barrier to individual plaintiffs who might, for example, wish to challenge the president's exercise of his commander-in-chief authority or the manner in which he has collected and applied intelligence. Such exercise of this authority rarely reaches the specific concrete rights of individuals. Courts have generally and consistently held that dissatisfaction with the manner in which the president exercises his constitutional authority, without some more concrete harm, does not give rise to a right of the citizenry to sue the president.[25]

The flip side of standing is found in Article III's limitation on the exercise of Article III (judicial) jurisdiction to cases or controversies arising under the Constitution and enumerated areas of law.[26] As a result, Article III courts may not issue advisory opinions. If honored, this means a court should not dismiss a case on standing grounds, but nonetheless offer an opinion on the constitutional authority of the president or the Congress. Where this occurs, the opinion is clearly dicta and not binding law.

In addition, a plaintiff must show that an issue is ripe for decision. For example, the plaintiff that sues the government based on the possibility that the president will do something or that the plaintiff *may* be specifically harmed by an exercise of prospective authority will likely find his suit dismissed on the ground that it is not ripe, or ready for decision, because the harm has yet to come to pass and an actual case or controversy is therefore not at hand. Alternatively, where an event has already occurred and is complete, for example, the president has sent armed forces into hostilities and withdrawn them, courts may find a constitutional challenge moot, meaning overtaken by events and no longer necessitating resolution. Of course, because we are dealing with the law, there are exceptions to the standing rule, most notably for matters that are capable of repetition but that otherwise are likely to escape review, perhaps because of the time necessary to litigate the issue. The classic example of such an exception relates to whether a woman does or does not have a constitutional right to have an abortion. To prevail on such an argument in the national security context, a plaintiff likely would have to show that the factual predicate is indeed subject to repetition and not a singular course of action based on particular world events. A case that passes over these various hurdles is said to be justiciable (subject to judicial resolution).

However, in national security context, the government may assert the state secrets privilege in what might otherwise be a justiciable case. The privilege finds its roots in the common law and in the president's constitutional authorities over national security.[27] Thus, the lead cases addressing or applying the privilege blend both constitutional and common law principles. *Reynolds* (1953) involved a Federal Torts Claim Act suit arising from a fatal crash of an Air Force plane engaged in testing equipment. The government blocked discovery of the accident report based on a State Secrets Declaration from the secretary of the air force. The Supreme Court upheld the claim of privilege ruling:

> In each case, the showing of necessity which is made will determine how far the court should probe in satisfying itself that the occasion for invoking the privilege is appropriate. Where there is a strong showing of necessity, the claim of privilege should not be lightly accepted, but even the most compelling necessity cannot overcome the claim of privilege if the court is ultimately satisfied that military secrets are at stake.[28]

Nixon involved an assertion by the president that, under separation of powers doctrine and based on his need for confidential advice, the powers of the president provided an absolute privilege against enforcement of a subpoena for documents in a criminal case (arising out of the Watergate break-in). Responding, the Court pointed out that

> He [President Nixon] does not place his claim of privilege on the ground they are military or diplomatic secrets. As to these areas of Art. II duties the courts have traditionally shown utmost deference to presidential responsibilities.[29]

In *Totten*, as reaffirmed in *Doe* (discussed in Chapter 7), the Court moved beyond "utmost deference" and held the privilege absolute with respect to the

the Court's interpretation is rooted in common law or the president's constitutional authority, the state secrets privilege has been generally upheld to apply in three circumstances. First, when the subject matter of the suit is itself a state secret (e.g., the existence or lack of existence of an intelligence relationship); (2) when the plaintiffs cannot make out their threshold claim without disclosure of the secret (e.g., *Reynolds*); and, (3) when the defendants cannot fairly defend the suit without disclosing the state secret in question (e.g., so called Iran-Contra claims, where the plaintiffs assert that they were acting on behalf of the government, and the government would need to state on the record that the individuals were not government agents, raising an inference of silent affirmation when it does not do so). In civilian criminal context, the Classified Information Procedures Act[30] is applied in balancing the government's interest in preserving state secrets against the defendant's constitutional rights to put on a defense, to be informed of charges against him, and to confront witnesses. In short, under the trial court's supervision the law seeks to protect the government's secrets while placing the defendant in the same position he would be in with the benefit of the classified material.

In each instance, the national security lawyer will be asked to identify, and, if necessary, draft, relevant declarations focusing a court's attention on what the actual and necessary secret(s) is. Here too the moral integrity of the government (collectively), the agency head or president, and the lawyer all come into play. The lawyer has an additional duty to test that the information is in fact secret and properly designated so. In one circumstance, for example, I was requested to validate personally that a subject matter was appropriately classified and to document the harm that would accrue if the secret were disclosed.

2. Legal Policy and the Exercise of Jurisdiction

In addition, the judiciary has historically deferred to the executive (and to a lesser degree the Congress) on matters of national security. The courts have done so through application of a variety of "abstention doctrines," most notably the political question doctrine, which is grounded in legal policy as well as constitutional text. The political question doctrine posits that courts should eschew deciding questions of law in three circumstances:

- First, where the question presented hinges on a grant of authority that is textually assigned to one or both political branches; for example, whether the United States should resort to war, which power is committed to the political branches.
- Second, where the matter raised is incapable of discoverable or manageable standards of judicial review. This might be the case, for example, where the president's use of force is challenged on the ground that the force was not "vital to national security."[31]

- Third, where the matter is really one of policy disagreement and not law; for example, whether the president was correct to conclude that the intelligence predicate warranted the use of force.

As a general matter, the doctrine is based on the view that political questions are more appropriately treated as matters of policy dispute and resolution than as justiciable questions and therefore ought to be resolved through the electoral process, representational government, and the popular will. Of course, parties to litigation often do not agree as to whether their issues are in fact "political." Indeed, my examples are generally illustrative, but in a specific context with the addition of facts, a court might conclude that such matters are subject to judicial review and determination. For these reasons, courts tend to follow a general rule that constitutional questions should be avoided where a case can be resolved on other grounds.

In application, these doctrines have been called "avoidance mechanisms." Others argue that in application courts are in fact creating substantive law by leaving in place the constitutional status quo. In other words, they are implicitly recognizing the constitutional validity of the status quo, when they decline to decide and leave the parties as they are. However, one should not reach too far with this argument. Where courts in fact defer on political question grounds, they may do so on the basis of the facts as presented, and not as adjudicated. They also will often do so based on allocations of burden, the moving party usually carrying the burden of proceeding. Thus, a decision may do no more than acknowledge a party's failure to carry its burden to establish standing, as opposed to a validation of the constitutional status quo.

3. Institutional Limitations

Courts are also inherently cautious institutions. As Learned Hand observed, the common law moves in small steps. Constitutional "common law" operates in the same manner, with courts biting off only what they view as necessary to resolve the immediate case or controversy. In part these small steps reflect the reluctance of courts to make broad pronouncements that may unwittingly reach cases not yet heard, raising distinguishing facts not yet known. As Justice Jackson wrote: "Court decisions are indecisive because of the judicial practice of dealing with the largest questions in the most narrow way."[32]

This reluctance also reflects the institutional difficulty of appellate courts, composed as they are of multiple members, personalities, and views, to speak definitively and clearly with one voice. Moreover, until the Supreme Court speaks, if it speaks at all, the judiciary speaks with up to thirteen, often competing, voices representing each of the federal circuits. In contrast, while the

Congress may consist of 535 secretaries of state or 535 attorneys general, ultimately the Congress can speak with the singular voice of a joint or concurrent resolution. The executive branch ultimately speaks with the voice of the president.

With this backdrop, it is not surprising that where the political branches seem prone to broad prescriptive assertions of authority – let's say regarding the president's commander-in-chief authority – judicial pronouncements are generally limited in their reach.

4. Contextual Application of Law

Courts are also prone to small steps because the application of constitutional law, like other law, is often contextual, even where principles of black-letter law apply. The sweeping opinion offers clarity, but few judges escape the experience of having a case written early in their career come back in different context to catch a long statement of the law short in application.

The case of the *Mayaguez* rescue illustrates the contextual point. In May 1975, the U.S. merchant vessel *Mayaguez*, with a crew of eighteen, was seized in international waters in the Gulf of Cambodia by Khmer Rouge fast boats. At the time, there was a funding rider, or statutory restriction, precluding the expenditure of appropriated funds for military operations in the Gulf of Cambodia and elsewhere in Southeast Asia. Exercise of the funding power was, after all, one of the arguments cited for implied congressional support or acquiescence in the Vietnam War.

The exclusive power to raise, authorize, and appropriate moneys – the power of the purse – is Congress's constitutional cannon in the war power debate. Where the president might challenge a competitive claim of authority, like the War Powers Resolution, the president cannot as a practical matter ignore an exercise, or lack of exercise, of the spending power. Moreover, even ardent executive branch advocates concede that Congress can ultimately cut off future funding for military operations, so long as it does so in a manner permitting the safe withdrawal of U.S. armed forces. But in constitutional law one should take care never to say never...*and* never to say always.

The funding rider notwithstanding, as commander in chief President Ford ordered military action to rescue the *Mayaguez* hostages. Although much was subsequently written on the ensuing military operation, no serious debate ensued regarding the president's constitutional authority to rescue Americans in harm's way regardless of the appropriations prohibition in place.

The contextual application of constitutional law is also seen in the pre-9/11, pre-PATRIOT Act, treatment of grand jury material. As a general matter, under Section 6(e) of the Federal Rules of Criminal Procedure (FRCP), material presented to a federal grand jury may not be disclosed by members of the grand jury or government attorneys appearing before the grand jury except for certain specified purposes or when authorized by the court overseeing the grand jury. The rule is intended to protect the integrity of the government's investigation and provide for the security of witnesses. It is also intended to safeguard the privacy of persons who are subjects, targets, or witnesses appearing before grand juries, in keeping with the principle that the accused, or in 6(e) context the suspected, are presumed innocent until proven guilty. In 1993, however, the Office of Legal Counsel (OLC) advised the attorney general that

> there are circumstances where the president's constitutional responsibilities may provide justification for the Attorney General to disclose grand jury matters to the president independent of the provisions of Rule 6(e). Such circumstances might arise, for example, where the Attorney General learns through grand jury proceedings of a grave threat of terrorism, implicating the president's responsibility to take care that the laws be faithfully executed.[33]

Where the president's core national security responsibilities were implicated by the information in question, a congressional statute, that is, FRCP 6(e), could not constrain the president (and the immediate staff assisting the president) from performing his core security functions.[34] But, the opinion cautioned that this constitutional exception was not a blank check, but rather "in the absence of judicial precedent on this point . . . disclosure . . . should be cautiously undertaken and reserved for matters of clear executive prerogative in areas where the Rule 6(e)(3)(A)(i) exception could not be used."

Of course, the fact that lawyers can assert an argument doesn't mean that they should. For instance, take the hypothetical case involving grand jury secrecy suggested above. The president and attorney general might yet adhere to the statutory process as a prudential matter if in their judgment doing so would garner confidence in the basis for the request and otherwise not impede a core presidential responsibility. Of course, as discussed in the next chapter, the PATRIOT Act subsequently provided a blanket 6(e) exception for national security information. The hypothetical is presented here as an example of narrowly tailored contextual constitutional analysis.

C. OBSERVATIONS ON THE PRACTICE OF CONSTITUTIONAL LAW

So far this chapter has explored formal textual elements of the law – text, statute, and cases. This section of the chapter is intended to convey a feel for the texture of constitutional practice through consideration of five observations.

- First, in the absence of definitive black-letter text or case law, historic practice takes on added, even controlling, importance.
- Second, the same is true of constitutional theory. Historic practice and theory are particularly relevant to national security, where legitimate and intended textual tensions persist. Thus, terms such as "commander in chief" are subject to both narrow and expansive interpretations depending on one's constitutional perspective. Such interpretations, in my view, are legitimate if they are fairly founded on text and case law interpretation and do not stray from the structural principles identified in Chapter 3, including the operation of checks and balances, the Bill of Rights, and the recognition of shared and separate authorities.
- Third, the volume of constitutional decision flowing to and from the chief executive can be extraordinary, depending on the role assigned to lawyers and the manner in which the president defines his constitutional duties. The U.S. Constitution is not a prop, as constitutions are in totalitarian societies; it is indeed the daily foundation of U.S. national security government.
- Fourth, at the highest levels of government much of constitutional practice is informal; that is, it is based on informal contacts within the executive branch and between the executive and legislative branches. The results rarely take on the shape of formal constitutional law and are rarely documented. However, many of the most important constitutional issues are addressed using informal processes, such as a letter from the president to members indicating how he will interpret a statutory provision.
- Finally, and most important, there is nothing automatic about constitutional government, if constitutional government means government conducted with respect for, and subject to, law, including constitutional law. We are more dependent on the integrity of the men and women who wield constitutional authority than most people realize. Indeed, as discussed in Chapter 3, with national security, the rule of law depends entirely on the good faith application of law by a few actors, operating in secret and under pressure not to apply the law in a manner that might constrain national security. Further, there is less internal and external appraisal of legal reasoning than is usual in other areas of practice.

For the constitutional practitioner, there is satisfaction in the daily discovery that the Constitution is a living document that encourages "good government" through internal and external checks and procedural safeguards. There is also ample frustration in the lesson that political alliance can count more than constitutional or statutory text, and that not everyone in government works forward, applying law to fact; the reality is that some lawyers work backward, finding or interpreting law to justify results or policy choices already made. That magnifies the importance of the moral and legal integrity of national security lawyers.

These observations have two immediate results for lawyers as well as for those who would observe and evaluate their performance. First, lawyers must learn to practice where constitutional authority is in fact exercised – at the points of policy inception and decision, and not just after the fact, at the moment of formal documentation. Second, where there is an absence of hard law, or agreed law, constitutional government depends on the exercise of constitutional values.

1. Practice as Precedent

In the absence of case law, historic example takes on added weight in illuminating the Constitution's national security authorities, particularly with regard to use of the military and intelligence instruments. Practice in effect becomes constitutional common law. Thus, executive lawyers not only cite to *Curtiss-Wright* when addressing the president's commander-in-chief authority, but they also place emphasis on prior instances where presidents have acted unilaterally. This is reflected in the Office of Legal Counsel opinions of attorneys general who advocated an expansive view of presidential authority as well as those more cautious in approach. The legal premise is clear. If the president had the authority to act in a comparable manner then, he must retain the authority to do so now, absent perhaps a change in statutory overlay. This is the *Youngstown* gloss.

> A systematic, unbroken, executive practice, long pursued to the knowledge of the Congress and never before questioned, engaged in by Presidents who have also sworn to uphold the Constitution, making as it were such exercise of power part of the structure of our government, may be treated as a gloss on 'executive Power' vested in the president by section 1 of Art. II.[35]

Of course, executive lawyers place emphasis on the continuity of practice, not necessarily the meaning of Justice Frankfurter's caveat that a practice was "never before questioned."

The degree to which one finds in historic gloss a "winning" constitutional hand may depend on one's view of negative law. That is, does congressional inaction reflect affirmative recognition that an exercise of executive authority is constitutional? Or might it be more reflective of political avoidance, or perhaps a failure on the part of those with a different legal view to garner enough votes to say so legislatively? Moreover, the lack of exercise of an authority does not necessarily demonstrate its absence as the *Youngstown* Court noted. But as seen in Chapter 5, this argument cuts both ways. The fact that the president, and not just the Congress, has not previously exercised an authority does not necessarily demonstrate its absence.

Historic precedent is of equal importance, if not more, in intelligence law. This is expressly recognized in statute. For example, the definition of covert action found in the National Security Act exempts "traditional" counterintelligence, diplomatic, law enforcement, and military activities from the substantive and procedural requirements of the law. The legislative history goes further, stating:

> It is not intended that the new definition exclude activities which were heretofore understood to be covert actions, nor to include activities not heretofore understood to be covert actions.[36]

One can see immediately the difficulty in applying this law, or evaluating the manner in which others do, without in fact knowing what has occurred before. Unlike military action, which is generally recognizable and documented, at least after the fact, one is harder pressed to document, and certainly to document definitively, U.S. intelligence practice, or for that matter clandestine but traditional military or law enforcement practice. Even within the executive branch the evidence tends toward the anecdotal – there being few central depositories of state secrets – relying heavily on the personal recollection and knowledge of the operatives and lawyers involved.

Certainly, covert actions must be authorized in written presidential findings and Memoranda of Notification (MONs) – but if they are "extraordinary" in nature, they may be known to only a handful of officials outside (and inside) the Central Intelligence Agency (CIA). Traditional liaison activities may not be documented at all. Evidence of traditional or historic practice is thus subject to the intentional and unintentional variances in recollection that sometimes reflect where one sits, as well as what one remembers. Policy proponents of immediate action and operators generally tend to recall that most of what they do is traditional in nature and therefore not subject to covert action process and appraisal; whereas policy opponents or operators with reservations tend to draw inapposite conclusions from practice. The wise presidential lawyer will find it prudent to check the written record, if it exists.

2. Theory as Law

In the absence of binding constitutional law and interpretation, theory, like historical practice, takes on critical and often controlling importance. By theory, I mean one's methodology for addressing and interpreting constitutional text. For example, some scholars and judges believe constitutional meaning is found only in the document's plain and literal text, and/or by limiting the words to their meaning at the time the Constitution was ratified. Others argue that constitutional law is found in context by giving constitutional words their implied and evolving meaning. This tension is epitomized by the debate between Justice Scalia and Justice Breyer in their speeches and books, *A Matter of Interpretation* and *On Liberty*. This tension is also recognizable to some from the Court's cases discussing the meaning of liberty. As *Youngstown* illustrates, this tension is not new, nor is it confined to cultural and social issues, where it may be cast in "conservative" or "liberal" hues, as opposed to one of interpretive theory that may transcend political viewpoint. Recall that in *Youngstown* it was the "liberal" Justice Douglas limiting the president to the plain text of the Constitution, and the "conservative" Justice Vinson resorting to "living" text.

Depending on one's view, theory as much as hard sources of law or fact can control constitutional analysis and outcome. For example, if one believes as a matter of constitutional law that the authority to conduct covert action is derived exclusively from the president's enumerated authorities, or perhaps from the nation's sovereignty, then there is not much legal analysis required to determine whether the president can withhold notification to the Congress of a covert action. The argument might be framed as follows:

- The president is commander in chief, chief executive, and the nation's sole organ in external affairs. *See, Curtiss-Wright.* Covert action is an extension of the diplomatic and military instruments through clandestine intelligence means.
- Pursuant to these authorities, the president long authorized covert action without independent congressional authorization, restriction, or notification.
- This practice was not challenged by the Congress until the 1970s, and thus longstanding practice and the constitutional perspective it reflects provide a further gloss on the president's constitutional authority.
- Moreover, unlike the military instrument, Congress's authority in this area is textually weak and must derive from implied legislative authority. This view is recognized by Congress itself in the Act's third reporting provision, which contemplates post facto notification, if notification is given at all.

With such a legal view, the question is solely one of legal policy. What are the policy and political costs and benefits of asserting such a legal position, and doing so in the circumstances presented?

Alternatively, if one believes this intelligence function is subject to the exercise of shared constitutional powers, then the executive lawyer will need to consider whether a proposed action falls within the statutory definition of covert action, and, if so, whether the action is within a statutory category for which the president may limit notification ("to meet extraordinary circumstances affecting vital interests of the United States") or withhold notification altogether ("whenever a finding is not reported pursuant to paragraph (1) or (2) of this section, the president shall fully inform the intelligence committees in a timely fashion and shall provide a statement of the reasons for not giving prior notice"). Such an argument might incorporate the following elements:

- The Congress shares with the executive constitutional authority over the national security function, including the intelligence instrument.
- This shared authority is found textually in Congress's general legislative authority, the "take care clause," Congress's plenary authority to authorize and appropriate monies, including for the purpose of conducting intelligence activities, as well as all that Congress possesses in authority over the war power.
- With respect to longstanding practice and the absence of congressional authorization or express oversight prior to the Hughes-Ryan Amendment of 1974, the lack of exercise of an authority does not demonstrate its absence. Rather, in the wake of the Church and Pike Committees' revelations and those of the Rockefeller Commission, as well as the Iran-Contra Affair, Congress found it necessary and proper to exercise its authority over the intelligence function, first with the Hughes-Ryan Amendment, then by establishing select oversight committees in 1978 and then by defining covert action and formalizing the practice for authorizing and reporting findings in 1991.
- Moreover, covert action is essentially a modern national security tool, an instrument of the Cold War. Thus, the importance of historic practice is minimized. Moreover, the Congress may not have asserted an oversight role prior to the 1970s, but it legislatively authorized covert action in the National Security Act of 1947, authorizing CIA to engage in "such other activities as the president may direct." This term was understood at the time as a euphemistic placeholder for covert action.

Under this alternative theory of shared powers, the issue of covert action notification presents questions of law as well as of policy and legislative tactics.

As noted earlier, it happens that in the area of covert action the political branches have (for now) reached a constitutional rapprochement, with the relevant statute recognizing a legislative view that notification, but not consultation or approval, is required to the Congress prior to initiation, and an executive view that either as a general matter, or in context, the president may engage in covert action without prior congressional notification. In short, in 1991, at least, the president (and his lawyers) and the Congress (and its lawyers) agreed to disagree. As a result, the National Security Act fairly frames the constitutional positions, and in practice the political branches (to our knowledge) have found it advantageous not to force the issue.[37] The same cannot be said of the war power, discussed in Chapter 8. As the reader will see, with the war power more than any other area of national security law, theory and history are at the core of the constitutional debate.

3. The Volume of Constitutional Decision

The volume of presidential decision, much of it a product of constitutional responsibility, is staggering. True, the president has discretion to regulate the volume of material he sees by delegating certain constitutional functions. For example, as commander in chief, the president may choose to approve the "concept of military operations" but then defer to the secretary of defense or field commanders on execution, tactics, and specific rules of engagement. In other contexts, the president may be involved solely as a matter of policy choice and discretion. The manner in which the president exercises his decisional discretion will depend on, among other factors, the mission, the policy context, the legal context, as well as presidential personality and style.[38]

However, in many circumstances the president alone must personally exercise the constitutional authority in question. For example, in some cases the decision to use force will encompass the tactical method of attack as well, for example, a missile strike. In such a case the president must approve both the resort to force and the specific method of force. Likewise, the attorney general might assert that a document is subject to executive privilege, but where such a document is in fact subpoenaed, the president alone can exercise the actual privilege. In like manner, the president alone has the power to pardon. The president alone can nominate for Senate advice and consent candidates to serve as ambassador. Where the Congress has statutorily given the director of national intelligence (DNI), the secretary of defense, and the director of the CIA authority over sources and methods of intelligence, the president alone can direct the exercise of this statutory authority in his capacity as chief executive. He alone wields the constitutional authority over state secrets to do so. (Here the president's lawyer would cite to the president's textual authorities as commander in chief, chief executive, and in the area of foreign relations as well as to *Totten, Doe, Egan*, and *Curtiss-Wright* in support of his argument.)

As these examples illustrate, questions of constitutional law arise in myriad contexts. This is part of the challenge and fun of the practice. Of course, the texture of constitutional practice is highly dependent on the personalities and outlook of the participants. In general, the central national participants will include the president, the vice president, the national security advisor, the attorney general, the assistant attorney general for the Office of Legal Counsel, the counsel to the president, and the legal advisor to the National

Security Council (NSC). However, in any given administration, other actors – based on access, personality, background, and, of course, the desires of the president – will play central roles. For example, the counsel to the vice president in the Clinton administration did not play an active role in national security practice; however, in the Bush administration the vice president's counsel has played a, and some argue the, central role in shaping the administration's constitutional perspective on national security law.

Other counsel, including the agency general counsel and line counsel at the Departments of State and Defense, the Joint Chiefs of Staff, the Department of Homeland Security, the Central Intelligence Agency, the Federal Bureau of Investigation, and the National Security Agency (to identify just a few), of course play critical internal roles within their agencies and in advising their departmental representatives on the NSC, on the Principals Committee, and the Deputies Committee. They also play an important role in advising the president to the extent that the NSC legal advisor and the counsel to the president run an inclusive interagency process for generating legal advice for the president. Personality, as well as the manner in which each counsel defines his responsibilities, and not the law, will determine which lawyers participate and whether they play a proactive role or a passive role; these roles are also highly dependent on the relationship between lawyers, and between lawyers and policymakers. If the national security advisor wants his counsel to participate or see something, then he will. If the national security advisor does not, he will not.

For the president's national security lawyers, constitutional matters generally arise in four areas. First, the identification of policy options for Deputies Committee, Principals Committee, and ultimately presidential consideration invariably raises questions of constitutional law and policy. In particular, lawyers will have to verify that the president has the constitutional or statutory authority to direct implementation of each policy option presented. That means, for example, that if the Deputies Committee is considering all the options in each context, as surely it should, before presenting preferred options up the chain of command, counsel will consider a wide range of questions that will never make it out of committee. Counsel will also have to advise as well on the implementation of the selected policy options, including on whether the Congress must or should be consulted or notified. If there is a public dimension to the policy, counsel will need to participate in the articulation and presentation of the government's legal views.

In my view, the most effective way to address these questions is through prior interagency review of the policy options. This allows for identification and satisfaction of legal issues in advance of policy consideration so that Principals, and certainly the president, are not spending their time considering unavailable options or unavailable means of implementation. Of course, the sensitivity of the issue presented may limit the opportunity for intera-gency consultation. In context, the lawyer may find he is working alone, in which case he must determine whether he should insist on widening the circle as a matter of good government, expertise, or law.

Second, presidential counsel will routinely address procedural questions of constitutional law involving the separation of powers; for example, the who, when, where, and what of NSC staff briefing the Congress, or the con-trol and distribution of national security information. From an executive perspective, the constitutional question is whether Congress (e.g., a con-gressional committee) can compel the president's immediate senior staff to testify if the Congress could not compel the president, as head of a coequal branch, to testify. In this context, the lawyer may find himself explaining how the immediate policy and political benefits of acquiescing to congressional requests may be outweighed by the enduring consequences to the president's national security process. On the one hand, a well-timed appearance by the national security advisor may clinch support for a presidential position or eliminate the appearance that the president is "covering up." On the other hand, variation from the no-testimony norm will in the longer run make it harder to resist comparable requests where the president's interests are not aligned with an appearance. Before long the president may find his immedi-ate staff is spending its time addressing congressional requests rather than advising and assisting the president in executing his immediate national security responsibilities.

Where deliberative presidential documents are in play, counsel must also take appropriate measures to ensure that communications to and from the president to cabinet officers, for example, receive comparable constitutional treatment, as opposed to ad hoc or haphazard treatment, which makes it harder to draw and hold constitutional lines. Counsel are also responsible for identifying ongoing litigation that implicates the president's constitu-tional national security authorities and ensuring that agencies, and in par-ticular the Department of Justice litigators representing those agencies, take positions consistent with the president's constitutional views.

Third, counsel routinely comment on the constitutional implications of pending legislation. This occurs formally and daily through the legislative comment process run by the Office of Management and Budget (OMB). OMB circulates to government agencies legislation that is pending on Capitol Hill or that the executive will present to the Congress. Agencies are then given a period of time to comment, resulting in Statements of Administration Posi-tion (SAPs) (here, too, an informal and parallel process may apply). As often, and not infrequently concurrently, counsel will comment on legislation or participate in negotiations regarding constitutional issues identified on fast-moving or high-tension legislation. This is done on the fly and often without the formal validation of an OLC or attorney general concurrence. Backroom legislative drafting places a premium on prior preparation and review. Signing statements, in which the president may signal constitutional concerns with particular provisions, are drafted and circulated in similar manner.[39]

A fourth category of constitutional questions might be dubbed "pop-ups," one-time questions arising outside normal paper and meeting flow. Such a question might arise in the form of an inquiry from the Joint Staff as to whether the president is required to review and approve a particular matter. Counsel might have occasion to consider whether Fifth Amendment rights advisement is necessary in the context of an administrative inquiry. Lawyers may also have to respond to a document request from a hybrid form of committee like a commission or perhaps address a question involving the appointments clause as the president considers filling a particular post or perhaps creating a special envoy. Of this lot, one or two a day might raise new constitutional questions requiring deliberation and coordination with a relevant agency counsel. Usually such questions entail some degree of consultation with the Department of Justice or the counsel to the president (commonly known as the White House counsel).

Form and context can be as important as content, for the lawyer needs to understand the bureaucratic context in which questions arise if he is to apply the law meaningfully. To illustrate, during my watch at the National Security Council, the legal team might receive 100 to 300 e-mails a day, many conveying documents for review, such as memoranda for the president and papers for Deputies and Principals meetings. In addition, the legal advisor would likely attend at least one scheduled meeting with the national security advisor (formally the assistant to the president for national security affairs or APNSA) each day. This might be an 8:00 A.M. full senior staff meeting in the Situation Room on Tuesdays and Fridays or a "small staff" meeting in the APNSA's office on the other days. There might also be, on average, one to three scheduled or unscheduled meetings to discuss matters such as a particular memorandum, a comment to a memorandum, an emerging issue, or a personnel or legislative matter. In addition, there are daily interagency meetings at the Principals, Deputies, or working group level, as well as bimonthly meetings with the attorney general, which the NSC counsel would staff. There were also one to five interagency legal and policy meetings a week. Of course, for each "event" there were numerous telephone calls and side conversations with the national security advisor, deputy national security advisors, among staff, with the counsel to the president, or between agency actors.

An estimated 10 percent of the paper that transited the office raised constitutional considerations warranting comment or review (in theory, 100 percent of the president's national security acts implicate the Constitution). It is harder to quantify the number of constitutional issues that might arise in a meeting format; meetings often entail issue spotting, as policy discussions range, as opposed to defined agendas and predictable legal questions. For example, at the morning staff meeting the NSC lawyer would listen to the other presentations involving the geographic and functional disciplines at the NSC, and if necessary raise legal considerations of which the national security advisor or the larger audience ought to be aware. On occasion, constitutional issues might arise, at which point counsel would spot the issue and either offer to learn the facts and address the issue off-line, or offer an opinion on the spot. In some cases, counsel might spot the issue, even if it was already on track, so as to identify the issue for the larger audience, for example, the NSC policy on responding to congressional requests for NSC documents or testimony, or the authority (or lack of authority) of NSC staff to direct agency action. Otherwise, individual staff might take it upon themselves based on their own assessment of the policy benefits and pressures to devise their own constitutional arrangements with congressional committees of interest.

In the examples given at the outset of this chapter, involving U.S. armed forces under foreign "command" and the appointment of a member of Congress as ambassador, the definitive executive view was ultimately expressed in an opinion from the Office of Legal Counsel (OLC) at the Justice Department. But these opinions were drafted after the fact to document and cement advice already rendered at the critical legislative moment – when the call came from the congressional mark-up session – in one case, and based on a late night conference call at the moment the president took the initial decision to appoint the ambassador the following morning.

It was the national security line attorneys at the point of legislative and personal contact who had to spot, identify, and frame the questions in the first instance and then drive the process of review to a timely conclusion. This required that the legislative team on Capitol Hill have an ear, an eye, and a nose for the sort of constitutional concerns that might arise. And, it required a commitment on the part of the lawyers "to be in the room" when the call came or, to be in the room and be willing to speak up when the president's nominee was mentioned in passing at a staff meeting. Ed Cummings, a career national security lawyer with the State Department, called this "the importance of being there"; not giving anyone an excuse to avoid asking the legal question or, as important, being on hand to spot the issue oneself. In both cases, the staff actors had to address the problem on a timeline that would meet legislative and executive deadlines, and in a manner consistent with the president's view of his constitutional responsibilities.

4. Institutional and Political Oversight

The texture of constitutional practice is also dependent on politics or, more precisely, whether the president's political party controls one or both houses of Congress. For better or for worse, this is true in the area of national security as well as domestic policy. However, unlike domestic matters that may yet be exposed to the press, many national security decisions if not validated by the legislative branch will be subject to internal executive scrutiny alone. The reality is that the president's constitutional views will not receive the same degree of scrutiny from the same party as they do when the opposite party controls the "legislative power." This is illustrated anecdotally. Having served as an executive lawyer during periods of same-party and opposite-party control, the measure of oversight was night and day in volume and intent. The measure of institutional vigilance seemed to parallel political vigilance. The means would also vary, being more informal in nature, if at all, during same-party control and more formal in nature with the opposite party. The same point is also illustrated empirically with measures like the number of subpoenas issued as part of the oversight process. From 1997 to 2002 the House Government Reform Committee alone issued 1,052 subpoenas regarding the Clinton Administration or Democratic National Committee, compared with 3 during the first three years of the George W. Bush Administration.[40] That is not to say party loyalty is the only factor, only that for some members of Congress it surely is a factor.

Thus, in practice, the lawyers will spend far less time on issues involving separation of powers along with "scandals" real, perceived, and political, when the same party controls the operative house of Congress. It follows that there is less challenge to the assertion of executive authority as well. At the same time, one must not overlook that political affiliation also serves as a potential source of constitutional check on the exercise of presidential authority as does the electoral process itself. A president and his lawyers asserting authority in one administration must be prepared to see a subsequent president from a different party assert a comparable authority. Of course, elected and political officials in both branches and in both parties may place political affiliation ahead of consistency. Constitutional values inform whether and how elected officials weigh their constitutional and institutional responsibilities with their political loyalties. Thus, this is just one more area in which moral integrity as much as the law will determine the application of national security law.

5. Formal and Informal Practice

Lawyers tend to focus on the formal aspects of constitutional government – legislation, the oversight hearing, the Justice Department opinion, and presidential statements. For sure, these legal events dominate constitutional history and precedent. However, much of constitutional practice within each branch, and between each branch, is informal in nature, outside public view, and without documentation. Moreover, for each formal constitutional act there is usually a longer informal tail. This is intuitive in the area of legislation. It is obvious, if not always transparent, that between the committee hearing, the "dear colleague" letter, and the floor vote, there may be a significant amount of side discussion between members, between the executive branch and key committee personnel, and between congressional members, their staff, lobbyists, and the public.

Within the executive branch, it is less apparent that for each formal Justice Department legal opinion, there may be ten times the number of less formal telephonic inquiries and responses. Such responses may be documented in e-mail, in a one-line sentence in a policy memorandum (e.g., "Justice advises that the president has authority to..." "OLC is of the view..." "You may take this action pursuant to your authority as..."), or simply conveyed by telephone. However, more often than not these exchanges are not documented. They may be intended as "just checking" calls, or to ensure that the Justice Department will not undercut a White House or agency position on legal grounds. Moreover, when there is a formal legal opinion, the outside observer may only see the result, not the meeting that informed the result or the presentation of facts that shaped the analysis.

Let me illustrate. When the NSC first considered the emerging threat posed by Osama Bin Laden and Al-Qaeda, the NSC legal advisor asked the head of CIA's Bin Laden or "Alec" station to brief a select group of national security lawyers on the nature of the threat. This occurred before the Kenya and Tanzania embassy bombings of August 1998. The briefing was intended to allow the lawyers to work from a common base of knowledge and better respond to pop-up questions arising in operational context. The briefing was also intended as an opportunity to evaluate the underlying legal paradigm for combating terrorism. The conclusion: the United States could, and as a matter of legal policy should, lawfully respond to the threat within the framework of the Law of Armed Conflict (LOAC). In other words, the United States faced an imminent threat of attack and might appropriately respond in anticipatory self-defense using the full array of military and intelligence instruments available to the president as commander in chief. That meant that Osama Bin Laden (then referred to as UBL) and his organization were legitimate military targets. It also meant that in combating this enemy the United States must otherwise adhere to the law of armed conflict including the principles of necessity and proportionality in the use of force. The attorney general agreed.

This represented a significant shift in the U.S. legal posture. However, the shift occurred following informal consultation within the executive branch and without formal documentation, but rather through the rendering of confidential legal advice within the NSC process. To outside observers this conclusion was not evident until U.S. missile strikes of August 1998 were launched with the express purpose of killing the leadership of Al Qaeda, including Bin Laden, if it was evident then. In the context of intelligence operations, this paradigm shift was not apparent until the 9/11 Commission indicated in its report that the United States had sought to kill or capture Bin Laden using covert intelligence action as well as overt military force. Had 9/11 not occurred, this shift in legal paradigm may not have been disclosed at all.

There are often good national security reasons to seek informal legal advice. Operational deadlines may require immediate input, input that will only occur if the lawyer is on site. There may also be good bureaucratic reasons to avoid definitive opinions. The facts may be shifting or unknown. Or, perhaps, the policymaker wants a sense of the answer before receiving a document that might reach unintended contexts. Critical in these exchanges is an understanding on both sides of the discussion as to whether the advice rendered is informal or formal, preliminary or binding. It is also useful for the lawyer to confirm his or her understanding whether the policymaker will or must return for contextual application of advice rendered.

If lawyers insist on knowing all the facts all the time, before they are willing to render advice, or, if they insist on preparing a written legal opinion in response to every question, then national security process would become dysfunctional. The delay alone would cause the policymaker to avoid, and perhaps evade, legal review. Where lawyers let this happen, "process" is not understood as an essential component of rational decision, but a bureaucratic euphemism for delay and obstruction. At the same time, lawyers cannot effectively function if they are always on the spot without an opportunity to identify the issue that requires research, resort to higher authority to resolve issues, or caveat where facts are unknown or emerging. The art of lawyering in such context lies in spotting the issue, accurately identifying the timeline for decision, and applying a meaningful degree of formal or informal review in response.

The Office of Legal Counsel has traditionally addressed this tension with a "two deputy rule." When advice is requested informally, but is intended to bind the future view of the department, then two deputy assistant attorney generals (or, of course, the attorney general or deputy attorney general) must concur in the advice. This has the benefit of cross-checking advice, but also may serve to test whether the action lawyer has been "captured" by the client or succumbed to the pressure of the moment. It also has the intended effect of ensuring that any advice rendered by the office that is binding has been cleared at the political appointee level.

Departmental lawyers address the same tensions through the provision of caveats in informal advice rendered, or through adoption of rules that binding legal advice must be cleared by "the front office." However, lawyers must also take care that in rendering informal advice, necessary nuance, so carefully applied to written work, is not lost in informal dialogue, or surrendered to policy cross-examination. The "yes . . . but" cannot become just "yes;" the "no . . . but," just "no." Much of this informal advice is not transparent, covered as it is by three opaque lenses: security classification, the deliberative process, and the attorney-client privilege, all of which in the case of presidential practice coalesce around the rubric of executive privilege.

Hardest of all to find is the dog that didn't bark, but may nonetheless bare the largest constitutional teeth. Again, from the war power context, the president's lawyers may advise the president on the legal availability of military or intelligence options, but not commit their advice or constitutional positions to formal or public documentation. This may occur if the facts are shifting or unknown and the lawyers do not want to unwittingly bind the president's hands or conversely give a blanket concurrence without first fixing the facts and understanding the policy intent. The press of business may also genuinely deter participants from recording advice. And yet, the most significant constitutional moment may come and go without written documentation that might serve to accurately document precedent and fix accountability.

In my view, on issues of importance, even where the law is clear, as well as situations where novel positions are taken, lawyers should record their informal advice in a formal manner so that they may be held accountable for what they say, and what they don't say. The president can be held accountable as well for the advice he adopts, or chooses not to adopt. Nonetheless, some executive lawyers eschew the documentation of advice out of concern that it will bind the policy or legal hand.

Between the branches, the qualitative and quantitative volume of constitutional practice is also largely informal. If a congressional committee chairman is not satisfied with the nature of the executive's response to requests for information, he might telephone a senior official or tell the press, in the hopes of creating a public cost for not responding. A member might also pressure the executive more directly by threatening to hold a hearing if he or she is a committee chair. A senator might place a hold on a nomination until some unrelated action is taken by the executive. This is not constitutional law, but it is constitutional practice and interplay.

Let me illustrate the formal-informal observation with the war power. The formal mechanisms are evident. From an executive perspective, there must be a presidential decision – the actual exercise of constitutional authority. This will take the form of a presidential memo or verbal order followed, in both cases, by a military execute order. The decision may, or may not, be preceded by formal consultations with the Congress – perhaps hearings or letters inviting congressional authorization. Within forty-eight hours the president will also submit a "War Powers" report to the Congress, "consistent" with the Resolution. (In cases where the United States is asserting the right of self-defense, the United States will also submit an Article 51 report to the Security Council.)

From a congressional perspective, the formal mechanisms of constitutional practice may consist of hearings, floor debate, and the passage of binding or nonbinding resolutions. But this may reflect just the surface of the constitutional play. Beneath the surface may rest a larger iceberg of constitutional consultation, debate, and validation. In the case of the Kosovo conflict, for example, the president "invited" the Congress to authorize U.S. military action against Serbia. Congress "responded" by voting on three contradictory concurrent resolutions. These constitutional acts were in writing and subject to public and historical inspection. Unseen were the hundreds of phone calls within each branch and between each branch debating the merits of policy action and the limits, if any, on the president's discretion to act. Likewise, there is no formal record of the fifty plus separate informal briefings on the Hill by members of the administration. These were informal because they bore no indicia of hearings, that is, testimony, the taking of an oath, creation of a transcript, and committee hearing setting. And, of course, the concurrent resolutions themselves were "informal" in the sense that they were politically, but not legally binding. (Joint Resolutions are presented to the president for signature and become law; concurrent resolutions are not presented to the president, and bear persuasive authority.)

Of course, the decision to resort to the military instrument is not always preceded by overt debate or even genuine consultation. Some missions arise suddenly, either because the threat emerges suddenly (a hostage is seized, an embassy threatened), or the target pops up (e.g., a terrorist target emerges through intelligence). Further, even when pre-planned, discrete military operations, like rescues, snatches, and strikes, simply would not work with advance public consideration of specific proposals. Such debates either occur in the abstract, in secret, or not at all. In these contexts, the constitutional moment between the branches may occur entirely in informal context, a telephonic consultation, during which the parties might agree that the president can act or the member decides not to raise legal objections.

In the case of a clandestine or surprise military operation, congressional consultation will usually occur with the leadership alone. Generally, the national security advisor and the NSC staff take the lead in briefing the congressional leadership, and the Department of Defense and Department of State take the lead in briefing "their" relevant authorizing and appropriating committees, in the event that consultation or notification is not limited. Consultation may not occur at all. For example in the case of the 1980 Iran rescue mission members of Congress, including the leadership, were not consulted or informed in advance of either the preparatory activities or the mission itself.[41] In such a context, the constitutional moment occurred when the president considered and decided not to consult or advise the Congress of these actions.

In contrast to the war power, where some measure of inter-branch consultation qua notification is the norm, intelligence activities are largely conducted without informal prelude. Notice to the Congress, if given at all, tends to occur exclusively through formal mechanisms, namely notification to the intelligence committees, or certain congressional leaders designated in the National Security Act. This reflects historic practice, the legitimate secrecy of many of these operations, and a different level of acceptance within the executive branch (at least) as to the relative constitutional authority and role of each branch.

However, while members of Congress may wield comparatively little formal authority in the area of intelligence, they may yet wield substantial informal constitutional influence behind the scenes. As a matter of law, for example, they may receive notification of an action, but informally they can express their views through use of the funding instrument relative to the action in question or in some other area. They might also request a hearing or send a letter to the president or pull aside the DNI or national security advisor to express their views. Less scrupulous players might also threaten to leak information to effect the same end.

In each of these contexts, national security lawyers should look beneath the formal surface to ensure they are not just rationalizing decisions already made. They must get to the practice point, the point at which the constitutional decision is considered and made – the presidential meeting, memo, or telephone call – and not just the point at where constitutional decision is recorded; for example, the war powers report, the post-strike media talking points, and the congressional briefing points.

The lawyer must also distinguish between that which is hard law and that which is informal practice. With reference to congressional resolutions passed on the eve of military operations against Serbia, for example, the lawyer must distinguish between that which is binding law – a joint resolution – and a concurrent resolution, which is not law. That is not to say, however, that as a matter of legal policy, a concurrent resolution will not bind as a political act. But one is legal authority and the other is "persuasive" authority. The president might still consider legal arguments for acting pursuant to his own constitutional authority albeit with an appreciation that as a practical and political matter he is leaning in the direction of Justice Jackson's third diminished state of authority.

By further example, within the Foreign Assistance Act there are provisions that require prior notice to designated committees, usually the authorizing and/or appropriating committees, before the president or secretary of state may utilize a particular authority or waiver. Over time, practices emerge that bear the semblance and lore of constitutional law, accepted by both branches as conditions precedent to the use of particular authorities. For example, a department legislative aide may agree with committee staff that the chairman and ranking member on a committee "must" receive notification before an authority is used. Alternatively, chairmen may place holds on certain funds being expended unless they are used in a particular manner, or reported in a particular way.

Such practices are an integral part of informal constitutional practice, but they are not law. They cannot be. They are not found in statutory text and they are not derived from constitutional text. The president did not sign such text into law, nor was such language passed over a presidential veto. (Here we do have constitutional case law to apply, *Chadha*, holding the one-house legislative veto unconstitutional, which principle surely extends to the one-chairman legislative veto.) Nonetheless, many such informal practices are followed like law, because the consequences of not doing so are severe. In international law, lawyers distinguish between operational law and aspirational norms by distinguishing between prescripts that are enforced and sanctioned and those that are merely exhorted. In my example, we have effective sanction, an angry member of an appropriations committee who may block future money, or seek changes to existing law, but that does not make the informal practice law. In short, lawyers should take care to distinguish between that which is law, and that which is prudential, but does not have the force of law. In this role, the lawyer as counselor may then advise his policy client on the ramifications and risks of acting in a manner contrary to practice or expectation, while at the same time accurately identifying those options that are lawful, even if risky.

6. A Few Good Men and Women

Paraphrasing Madison, if men were angels we would not need laws. And so we are taught from an early age that we are a nation of laws and not of men. From law come stability, predictability, and the substantive and procedural processes that constitute democracy. It is not by chance that those who drafted the Constitution dedicated four of the first five sections of Article I, and the first section of Article II, to the requirements for elected office and the process of electoral transition. However, one must not underestimate the extent to which the practice of government depends on lawyers and policy-makers to trigger the constitutional and democratic principles embodied in the phrase "rule of law." As Professor Whitney Griswold wrote, we may be a government of laws, but "laws are made by men, interpreted by men, and enforced by men, and in the continuous process, which we call government, there is continuous opportunity for the human will to assert itself."[42] This statement has both positive and negative potential.

Government in accordance with law, and in particular in accordance with the principles identified in Chapter 3, does not happen automatically. The Constitution does not cause them to happen. Rather, it provides a framework within which there are structural incentives to provide for checks and balances and an expectation that they will be used. But it is people, and often lawyers, who in the final analysis act, or fail to act, to uphold the spirit and letter of the Constitution.

In short, the Constitution is a framework that guides men and women in the manner in which they conduct government. It is a road map. In this analogy, the vehicles are the governmental branches, and the drivers are the men and women who wield constitutional authority in government. These men and women may be fueled with the moral integrity to interpret the Constitution in good faith, or they may be fueled by political expedience or a view that the law is whatever we might need or want it to be at a given time, particularly when national security is at stake.

Those who have studied or experienced fascist, communist, and other totalitarian regimes know this. Almost all were draped in the appearance of law. And many purported to be subject to constitutional documents delimiting governmental authority and preserving the rights of the people. It is useful to remember that it was prosecutors and judges in the early days of the Weimar Republic who did not enforce the law who allowed a fledgling fascist movement to take hold in Germany in the 1920s, even as that movement sought to violently overturn the elected government and the courts that sat in judgment of their actions. And it was the Nazi prosecutors and judges who did enforce the law, Nationalist Socialist law from 1933 to 1945, so that Adolf Hitler might claim to act "in accordance with law."

To be clear, U.S. constitutional government is not fragile, as the Weimar Republic was fragile. The example is used to illustrate that law depends on the moral integrity, values, and courage of the men and women who wield it. But unlike in the totalitarian context, what gives the U.S. Constitution value and life is the additional sense of legal obligation, permit, and constraint that most lawyers and decisionmakers accept as derivative of its text, its history, and our practice even if they disagree on the reach of a particular clause or application. But not all officials feel the same sense of obligation, nor derive the same principles from practice and text. Moreover, constitutional law, like customary international law, or common law, evolves with every act and decision. Constitutional law is not static; therefore, even if lawyers start at the same point, they may reasonably disagree on where they end up. The president's terrorist electronic surveillance program is a case in point.

5 Electronic Surveillance: Constitutional Law Applied

A. LEGAL AND HISTORICAL BACKGROUND

Presidents have engaged in the practice of domestic and foreign intelligence collection since the advent of the United States. The colonies' envoy to France, for example, was America's first great, and perhaps its greatest, intelligence officer: Benjamin Franklin. At home, as Geoffrey Stone has illustrated, presidents authorized all measure of intrusion to identify persons engaged in espionage as well as to deter internal dissent.[1] Electronic surveillance would come later, during the Civil War with the tapping of telegraph lines, and then in earnest following Alexander Graham Bell. But the concept of eavesdropping was clearly not new to the telephonic, electronic, computer, or Internet age. The term "eavesdropping" derives from agents standing under the eave of a house to listen to the conversations taking place within.

As historians have documented, in the landline age, presidents routinely authorized electronic surveillance (wiretapping) to collect foreign intelligence. In 1996, for example, the government declassified and released a history of its eavesdropping efforts on Soviet targets within the United States, known by the program name of Venona.[2] In 1978, the Church Committee also revealed that

> Since the 1930's, intelligence agencies have frequently wiretapped and bugged American citizens without the benefit of judicial warrant ... past subjects of these surveillances have included a United States Congressman, Congressional staff members, journalists, newsmen, and numerous individuals and groups who engaged in no criminal activity and who posed no genuine threat to the national security, such as two White House domestic affairs advisors and an anti-Vietnam War protest group.[3]

Eavesdropping reached across the political spectrum; the committee also revealed that Attorney General Ramsey Clark had authorized surveillance of Claire Chennault during Nixon's 1968 presidential campaign.[4]

What law applies? As with any other constitutional question, the starting point is the text of the Constitution. The word "intelligence" is not found in the text. The president's intelligence authority is derived from his enumerated authorities as commander in chief and chief executive, as well as his collective authority over foreign affairs, and to take care that the laws be faithfully executed. As intelligence is an integral function of military command and the conduct of foreign affairs, as a general matter the president has broad derived authority over the intelligence function.

Congress has recognized as much in statute. The National Security Act, as amended, for example, charges the head of the CIA with "perform[ing] such other functions and duties related to intelligence affecting the national security as the President or the Director of National Intelligence may direct."[5] And, the president and not just the DNI is responsible for "ensuring that the intelligence committees are kept fully and currently informed of the intelligence activities of the United States."[6] Moreover, while negative legislative history[7] is disfavored as a source of law, it is noteworthy that President Roosevelt established a wartime intelligence agency, the Office of Strategic Services (OSS), absent statutory authorization or overlay. More significantly, President Truman established the National Security Agency (NSA) with the mission of collecting signals intelligence and to provide for communications security, pursuant to executive order and internal Department of Defense memoranda.[8] The president did so outside a wartime context, or at least a hot war context. The NSA has continued to operate absent an express legislative charter or enabling legislation ever since. Indeed, it was not until 1978 that Congress legislated in the specific area of electronic surveillance for foreign intelligence purposes.

In contrast, the Supreme Court had addressed both the president's inherent intelligence authority as well as electronic surveillance. In 1875, the Court dismissed a lawsuit brought by the administrator (Totten) of the estate of a William A. Lloyd who had sued in Claims Court to recover payment on a wartime contract between Lloyd and President Lincoln to engage in espionage behind Southern lines. (Note here how Totten initially succeeded in establishing standing before the lower court; Totten was not challenging the president's authority, but rather he was seeking to enforce a specific contract). The Claims Court found that Lloyd had a contract with President Lincoln under which he was to be paid $200 a month. However, the lower court dismissed the suit on the ground that the president did not have authority "to bind the United States by the contract in question."[9]

At the Supreme Court, Totten lost again. However, the Court did not question the president's authority to engage agents, nor find it incredible that President Lincoln might have personally hired agents to spy in the South. To the contrary, the Court determined that the president could not be compelled to confirm or deny the existence of his intelligence agents. In a succinct, almost crisp, two-page opinion the Court wrote:

> We have no difficulty as to the authority of the president in the matter. He was undoubtedly authorized during the war, as commander-in-chief of the armies of the United States, to employ secret agents to enter the rebel lines and obtain information respecting the strength, resources, and movements of the enemy.... Our objection is not to the contract, but to the action upon it in the Court of Claims. The service stipulated by the contract was a secret service; the information sought was obtained clandestinely, and was to be communicated privately; the employment and the service were to be equally concealed.[10]

Totten, as lawyers say, remains good law. In 2005, the Supreme Court affirmed the essential principle again. Thus, in *Tenet v. Doe*, the court stated, "[n]o matter the clothing in which alleged spies dress their claims, *Totten* precludes judicial review in cases such as respondents' where success depends upon the existence of their secret espionage relationship with the government."[11] (Note here, the closing of the standing door behind the state secrets privilege.)

Consideration of the president's intelligence authority should, of course, also account for *Curtiss-Wright* with its reference to the president as the "sole-organ" in U.S. foreign affairs, but more particularly, the Court's recognition that this authority encompasses an intelligence function:

> He, not Congress, has the better opportunity of knowing conditions which prevail in foreign countries and especially is this true in time of war. He has his confidential sources of information. He has his agents in the form of diplomatic, consular, and other officials.

The Court has addressed the intelligence function in other cases as well, such as *Chicago & Southern Airlines*,[12] but never as directly as it did in *Totten*.[13]

Thus, unlike some areas of national security and separation of powers law, there *is* case law to cite on the general subject of the president's intelligence authority. However, it should also be noted that these cases address the president's authority where it should be at its broadest – in the case of *Curtiss-Wright* and *Doe* in overseas and foreign context, and in the case of *Totten* during wartime with the United States the site of military conflict.

In addition to addressing the president's general authority in the area of intelligence the Supreme Court has addressed electronic surveillance. The Fourth Amendment states:

> The right of the people to be secure in their persons, house, paper, and effects, against unreasonable searches and seizures, shall not be violated, and no Warrants shall issue, but upon probable cause, supported by Oath

of affirmation, and particularly describing the place to be searched, and
the person or things to be seized.

Until 1967, the application of this limitation on the exercise of governmental
power was limited in case law to instances of physical invasion (the *Olmstead*
trespass doctrine),[14] particularly invasions of the home. However, in *Katz*,
the Supreme Court held that the Fourth Amendment warrant requirement
applied to electronic surveillance for law enforcement purposes and not just
instances of physical intrusion.[15]

By today's standards, the case is almost nostalgic in character.[16] Katz was
not trying to blow up something. He was a bookie placing bets from inside
a telephone booth. The FBI was on the outside clandestinely listening to
Katz's side of the conversation. Katz was charged with, among other crimes,
using a wire communication in interstate commerce to place bets or wagers.
When the government offered evidence of Katz's side of the conversation at
trial, Katz objected and sought to suppress the evidence.

Before *Katz*, the government would have been free to listen. Indeed, the
trial court and the Ninth Circuit held for the government and affirmed the
conviction. However, the Supreme Court reversed, noting that while "it is
apparent that the agents in this case acted with restraint" they were not
required, before commencing the search, to present their estimate of probable cause for detached scrutiny by a neutral magistrate.

> Once it is recognized that the Fourth Amendment protects people and
> not simply "areas" against unreasonable searches and seizures it becomes
> clear that the reach of that Amendment cannot turn upon the presence
> or absence of a physical intrusion into any given enclosure...The gov-
> ernment agents here ignored "the procedure of antecedent justification
> * * * that is central to the Fourth Amendment," a procedure that we hold
> to be a constitutional precondition of the kind of electronic surveillance
> involved in this case.[17]

The Court also noted the advantages of proactive rather than reactive
appraisal. Thus, in response to the government's argument, the Court stated
"the far less reliable procedure of an after-the-event justification for the ***
search, [was] too likely to be subtly influenced by the familiar shortcomings of hindsight judgment."[18] In this way, proactive appraisal protects the
law-abiding citizen from unreasonable interference and tests the balance
between individual and public interests that the Fourth Amendment was
intended to foster. It also better marshals finite law enforcement resources,
a point that is especially true with respect to real time or language specific
capacities.

Congress followed *Katz* in 1968 with passage of the Omnibus Crime Control and Safe Streets Act. As codified in Sections 2510–2522 of Title 18,

Title III of the Act addresses electronic surveillance for law enforcement purposes.[19] Hence, the colloquial reference to "Title III" orders. As a general matter, law enforcement officers use six basic tools of surveillance: electronic surveillance, pen registers,[20] trap-and-trace devices,[21] consensual monitoring,[22] physical searches, human surveillance, and informants. Title III places the first of these tools under statutory regulation applying the constitutional framework of *Katz* and its progeny. Specifically, under section 2518, a Title III search requires a judicial finding in the form of an order that "there is probable cause for belief that an individual is committing, has committed, or is about to commit a particular offense enumerated in section 2516 of this chapter." The section also requires specificity as to the time and place subject to surveillance as well as a determination that normal investigative procedures have been tried or appear unlikely to succeed. Consistent with this "exhaustion" requirement, the authorization to intercept shall be conducted as soon as practicable, minimize the interception of communications that are not otherwise subject to interception, and must "terminate upon attainment of the authorized objective."[23]

"Probable cause" is subject to evolving case-law adjustments, but at its core, it requires a factual demonstration or reason to believe that a crime has or will be committed.[24] As the term implies, probable cause deals with probabilities. "These are not technical; they are the factual and practical considerations of everyday life on which reasonable and prudent men, not legal technicians, act." Probable cause requires more than bare suspicion, but something less than a preponderance of evidence. "'The substance of all the definitions of probable cause is a reasonable ground for belief of guilt,'" based on "reasonably trustworthy" information that would "warrant a man of reasonable caution to believe an offense has been or is being committed."[25]

The law does not require probable cause in the case of pen registers and trap-and-trace devices, which do not capture communication content, but rather tones or signaling data keyed in or out of the target device. Rather, "the court shall enter an ex parte order authorizing installation . . . if the court finds that the attorney for the Government has certified to the court that the information likely to be obtained by such installation and use is relevant to an ongoing criminal investigation."[26] Of course, cell phones communicate other data as well, such as location. Prosecutors, and hence courts, are testing new applications of old law.[27]

In summary, after *Katz*, electronic surveillance directed at persons within the United States for law enforcement purposes is subject to Fourth Amendment review. That means that where individuals have a subjective expectation of privacy in their communications that is objectively reasonable, the Amendment's warrant requirement applies, unless an emergency situation exists as defined in section 2518(7) of Title III. Further, the order must issue from a neutral and detached judge or magistrate prior to initiation of surveillance.

Five years later the Court addressed electronic surveillance in a domestic security context. In *United States v. United States District Court*, ("the Keith case") the Court held that the Fourth Amendment's warrant requirement applied to electronic surveillance for domestic security purposes.[28] Lawrence Plamondon was charged with the destruction of government property for setting off an explosive in the CIA recruiting office in Ann Arbor, Michigan. During the pretrial stage, Plamondon petitioned the court for an order requiring the government to disclose any records in the government's possession of the monitoring of his telephone calls. The government declined. The government further declined to produce the records to the district court, Judge Keith, for *ex parte in camera* (with one party in the judge's chambers) examination on the ground that national security surveillance was not subject to a warrant requirement and therefore outside the reach of judicial review. Specifically, the attorney general of the United States submitted an affidavit to the court stating

> that he had approved the wiretaps for the purpose of "gathering intelligence information deemed necessary to protect the nation from attempts of domestic organizations to attack and subvert the existing structure of government." On the basis of the affidavit and surveillance logs (filed in a sealed exhibit) the Government claimed that the surveillances, though warrantless, were lawful as a reasonable exercise of presidential power to protect national security.

The Court disagreed, stating: "We recognize, as we have before, the constitutional basis of the President's domestic security role, but we think it must be exercised in a manner compatible with the Fourth Amendment. In this case we hold that this requires an appropriate prior warrant procedure." As in *Katz*, the court took care to limit its holding to the circumstances presented.[29] Nonetheless, the Court's reasoning is instructive and seemingly ageless.

> But we do not think a case has been made for the requested departure from Fourth Amendment standards. The circumstances described do not justify complete exemption of domestic security surveillance from prior judicial scrutiny. Official surveillance, whether its purpose be criminal investigation or ongoing intelligence gathering, risks infringement of constitutionally protected privacy of speech. Security surveillances are especially sensitive because of the inherent vagueness of the domestic security concept, the necessarily broad and continuing nature of intelligence gathering, and the temptation to utilize such surveillances to oversee political dissent.[30]

In addition to foreshadowing the disclosures to come three years later before the Congress, the Court identifies some of the inherent tensions in the domestic security field. For example, the Court recognizes the necessity of domestic intelligence gathering including sustained monitoring, but also the risk of abuse. Lurking is the pressure – the weight – upon those in the security bureaucracy to protect. This results in a default or bias to err on the side of caution, which is to say on the side of collecting intelligence. This pressure is (and should be) strongest where the stakes are highest. That is certainly the case with respect to efforts to counter the terrorists' threat of using weapons of mass destruction in the United States.

While it seems intuitive that national governments might read each other's mail (even if gentlemen would not), or that the U.S. government might monitor persons wanting to blow up government offices, the extent to which the U.S. government listened to its own citizens for security (and political) purposes did not become apparent until hearings held by the legislative and executive branches in the 1970s. The hearings are known colloquially by the names of their chairpersons, Senator Church, Congressman Pike, and in the executive branch, Vice President Rockefeller.[31] All three bodies determined that the executive branch had engaged in a long and continuous practice of domestic eavesdropping for security as well as for political purposes, without warrant, and in many cases without security cause, probable or otherwise. As noted earlier, the Church Committee concluded "[s]ince the 1930's, intelligence agencies have frequently wiretapped and bugged American citizens without the benefit of judicial warrant." Thus, in addition to legitimate targets like the Weathermen, or Plamandon's "White Panther Party," which were engaged in plots to attack government facilities, the government had also "tapped" figures like Martin Luther King, Jr., Dr. Spock, and Joan Baez on account of their civil rights or anti-war views. The government might have gone farther had officials, like General Vernon Walters, while serving as the deputy director of intelligence, not refused requests from the White House to monitor political opponents.[32]

As documented in declassified memoranda written to President Ford by his counsel, Philip Buchen, the executive branch responded to the *Keith* case and the intelligence hearings with internal debate over whether to support legislation authorizing electronic surveillance for foreign intelligence purposes and whether to subject such surveillance to "an appropriate prior warrant procedure." Internally, as well, the attorney general advised the director of the NSA that in light of *Keith*, there had to be a foreign intelligence nexus to conduct electronic surveillance absent a warrant. "What is to be avoided," Attorney General Richardson wrote, "is NSA's responding to a request from another agency to monitor in connection with a matter that can only be considered one of domestic intelligence."[33]

As in the case of possible legislation prohibiting "assassination," the debate highlighted the tactical merits of supporting legislation or heading off legislation through the promulgation of internal executive standards.

Memoranda to the president at the time reflect many of the same constitutional and tactical concerns expressed in the later 2006 debate regarding electronic surveillance without FISA orders. The "pros" identified for the president, for example, included the benefits of providing statutory protection to communications carriers, "eliminates question of validity of evidence obtained," and "the stated tests are not of a kind which will materially inhibit surveillance." The "cons" included "unnecessarily requires resort to the judiciary for exercise of an inherent executive power" and "could result in troublesome delays or even a denial of authority in particular cases." Indeed, as some of the arguments were the same, some of the executive players were constant as well, including Donald Rumsfeld who was President Ford's secretary of defense and Richard Cheney, who was President Ford's chief of staff.[34]

The available declassified memos reflect that it was Attorney General Levi, White House Counsel Buchen, and Counselor Jack Marsh who were strongest in advocating a legislative framework. In the end, the president supported (and therefore) sought to influence the shape of legislation. In contrast, where Congress was contemplating legislation to prohibit "political killing," President Ford took a different tack, heading off legislation by promulgating an executive prohibition on assassination. In this latter endeavor the president was supported by Senator Church, who expressed concern that criminal legislation prohibiting assassination might limit the president's options, as a matter of law or legal policy, in circumstances involving another Adolf Hitler.[35]

B. THE FOREIGN INTELLIGENCE SURVEILLANCE ACT, AS AMENDED

Intelligence actors, whether law enforcement officers engaged in domestic security or intelligence operatives seeking positive foreign intelligence information, also rely on an array of electronic surveillance. As in law enforcement context, such surveillance may not be "real time"; that is, retrieved, evaluated, and disseminated at the time of actual discourse.[36] The volume of communications subject to potential intercept is staggering, as is the volume of material actually intercepted and subject to review. According to NSA's estimate, the Internet will carry 647 petabytes of data each day. "That's 647 followed by 15 zeros and by way of comparison, the holdings of the entire Library of Congress (130 million items, including 30 million books that occupy 530 miles of book shelves) represent only 0.02 petabytes."[37] Until 1978, such intelligence surveillance for foreign intelligence purposes within the United States was conducted pursuant to the president's constitutional authority, delegated as necessary within the executive branch.[38] However, historical and legal developments merged in 1978. Specifically, in the wake of the Church, Pike, and Rockefeller hearings and parallel evolution in Fourth Amendment doctrine, Congress passed the Foreign Intelligence Surveillance

Act of 1978 (FISA) to regulate electronic surveillance for foreign intelligence purposes within the United States.[39] *Keith* addressed domestic security and only by implication foreign intelligence, but the Court had noted the vagueness of the term "national security" and opened the door to the creation of "an appropriate prior warrant procedure" in domestic context.

At the time, the FISA represented a constitutional compromise between the political branches regarding the president's authority. As today, the executive argued the president's inherent constitutional authority as commander in chief, chief executive, and in foreign affairs, to engage in foreign intelligence gathering without congressional or judicial consent or encroachment. After all, the president had exercised such authority since the advent of the United States. Proponents of the legislation took the view that Congress was exercising *its* parallel national security authority as well as its authority to create inferior courts and oversee the executive branch. The fact that Congress had not previously chosen to exercise these authorities did not mean it did not possess the authority to do so, only that it had not found it necessary and proper to do so until revelation of the real and perceived abuses of the intelligence instrument by the president, FBI, NSA, CIA, Army, and other executive institutions in the 1960s and 1970s.

As enacted, the FISA accommodated, but did not fully satisfy both positions. The Congress defined a substantive standard for surveillance with a procedural safeguard in the form of an ad hoc judicial mechanism to approve executive requests for surveillance known as the Foreign Intelligence Court (FISC), with appellate review provided by an ad hoc surveillance court of review. In turn, some of the executive's core constitutional arguments were addressed in the statute's provision authorizing the attorney general to approve surveillance without a prior court order in emergency circumstances. Moreover, the executive branch rebuffed subsequent congressional efforts to oversee the actual conduct of surveillance, declining to report on all but the number of warrants approved and disapproved each year. In contrast to the War Powers Resolution, each political branch appeared to accept the FISA framework and compromise, while ultimately preserving their constitutional positions.

Foreshadowing later debate, the FISA was also understood at the time as not just an effort to accommodate competing constitutional claims, but also as an effort to balance security with civil liberties. This tension is identified in President Carter's signing statement, which bears quotation given its recognition of the relationships between law, culture, and personality in defining the process of government:

> One of the most difficult tasks in a free society like our own is the correlation between adequate intelligence to guarantee our Nation's security on the one hand, and the preservation of basic human rights on the other.

It is a difficult balance to strike, but the act I am signing today strikes it. It sacrifices neither our security nor our civil liberties. And it assures that those who serve this country in intelligence positions will have the affirmation of Congress that their activities are lawful.... In short the act helps to solidify the relationship of trust between the American people and their Government. It provides a basis for the trust of the American people in the fact that the activities of their intelligence agencies are both effective and lawful.[40]

Among other the things, the Act, as amended, establishes a predicate threshold for foreign intelligence surveillance: probable cause to believe that "the target of the electronic surveillance is a foreign power or agent of a foreign power."[41] Thus, the probable cause standard does not require a belief that the target has or will commit a crime, as in the case of Title III orders. However, the definition of agent of a foreign power includes some indication of predicate conduct. The standard is different for foreign and U.S. persons, lower in the case of "any person other than a United States person." For "any person," that is, including U.S. persons, the Act's definition includes predicate activities that may in fact amount to crimes. Thus, where U.S. persons are concerned, "Agent of a Foreign Power" includes "any person who –

(A) knowingly engages in clandestine intelligence gathering activities for or on behalf of a foreign power, which activities involve or may involve a violation of the criminal statutes of the United States;

(B) pursuant to the direction of an intelligence service or network of a foreign power, knowingly engages in any other clandestine intelligence activities for or on behalf of such foreign power, which activities involve a violation of the criminal statutes of the United States;

(C) knowingly engages in sabotage or international terrorism, or activities that are in preparation therefore, for on behalf of a foreign power;

(D) knowingly enters the United States under false or fraudulent identity for or on behalf of a foreign power or, while in the United States, knowingly assumes a false or fraudulent identity for or on behalf of a foreign power; or

(E) knowingly aids or abets any person in the conduct of activities described in subparagraph (A), (B), or (C) or knowingly conspires with any person to engage in activities described in subparagraph (A), (B), or (C).[42]

Electronic surveillance is defined as, among other things, "the acquisition by an electronic, mechanical, or other surveillance device of the contents of any wire communication to or from a person in the United States, without the consent of any party thereto, if such acquisition occurs in the United States."

Special requirements, known generally as "minimization procedures," pertain to the intended as well as inadvertent interception of the communications of "United States persons," which include a citizen, permanent resident alien, and "an unincorporated association a substantial number of members of which are citizens of the United States or [permanent resident] aliens." These procedures, which are implemented pursuant to classified directive, are designed to

> minimize the acquisition and retention, and prohibit the dissemination, of nonpublicly available information concerning unconsenting United States persons consistent with the need of the United States to obtain, produce, and disseminate foreign intelligence information. The names of U.S. persons shall not be disseminated in a manner that identifies any United States person, without such person's consent, unless such person's identity is necessary to understand foreign intelligence information or assess its importance.

Exceptions also permit retention and dissemination of information "that is evidence of a crime which has been, is being, or is about to be committed." As the Foreign Intelligence Surveillance Court of Review observed, many foreign intelligence inquiries are inherently criminal in nature, such as those pertaining to espionage and terrorism.[43]

As with law enforcement, use of pen registers and trap and trace devices does not require probable cause, but rather a showing of relevance:

> A certification by the applicant that the information likely to be obtained is foreign intelligence information not concerning a United States person or is relevant to an ongoing investigation to protect against international terrorism or clandestine intelligence activities, provided such investigation of a United States person is not conducted solely upon the basis of activities protected by the first amendment to the Constitution.[44]

The Act's definition of foreign power is broad as well, and includes groups engaged in or preparing for acts of international terrorism. In 2004, the Act was amended to explicitly address the so-called lone-wolf scenario, the individual actor with no discernible link to a foreign government or terrorist organization with which he is nonetheless allied in ideology or tactics. In short, although cast in terms of foreign powers and foreign intelligence, traditionally "nation state" oriented terms, the Act is not state-based or crime-based, but rather threat-based, offering a flexible, and realistic, perception of those actors that might threaten U.S. security.

Under the Act, surveillance requires an order from one of eleven district court judges appointed to seven-year terms by the chief justice. Three judges must reside within twenty miles of Washington, D.C. The other judges are geographically dispersed throughout the United States.[45] In exigent circumstances the attorney general may authorize surveillance in advance of FISA court approval, provided the court is notified and an application is made to a FISC judge as soon as practicable, but not more than seventy-two hours after the attorney general authorizes such surveillance.[46] In times of declared war, the president may authorize warrantless electronic surveillance to acquire foreign intelligence information for a period not to exceed fifteen days. However, this language does not appear to address the more frequent periods of armed conflict conducted pursuant to joint resolution or presidential authority, but not by declaration of war.

Violation of the Act carries criminal and civil sanctions.

A person is guilty of an offense if he intentionally – (1) Engages in electronic surveillance under color of law except as authorized by statute; or discloses or uses information obtained under color of law by electronic surveillance, knowing or having reason to know that the information was obtained through electronic surveillance not authorized by statute.[47]

In addition, as of September 2006, Title 18 provided that "procedures in this chapter or chapter 121 and the Foreign Intelligence Surveillance Act of 1978 shall be the exclusive means by which electronic surveillance, as defined in section 101 of such Act, and the interception of domestic wire, oral, and electronic communications may be conducted."[48]

Congressional oversight of FISA's implementation is provided largely in the form of annual reports from the attorney general providing the number of orders obtained during the previous year, but without specific detail as to the target, duration of surveillance, or the take.[49] The text of the 2005 FISA report states:

During calendar year 2005, the Government made 2,074 applications to the Foreign Intelligence Surveillance Court (hereinafter FISC) for authority to conduct electronic surveillance and physical search for foreign intelligence purposes. The 2,074 applications include applications made solely for electronic surveillance; applications made solely for physical search, and combined applications requesting authority for electronic surveillance and physical search simultaneously. Two of the 2,074 applications made during calendar year 2005 were withdrawn by the government prior to the FISC ruling on them. The Government later resubmitted one of the withdrawn applications as a new application, which was approved by the FISC.

During calendar year 2005, the FISC approved 2,072 applications for authority to conduct electronic surveillance and physical search. The FISC made substantive modifications to the government's proposed orders in 61 of those applications. The FISC did not deny, in whole or in part, any application filed by the government during calendar year 2005.[50]

As the report reflects, and the larger record indicates, the FISC has approved all but a handful of applications. It also reflects a progression in the number of requests from 199 (with 207 warrants approved) in 1979 to 2,074 in 2005. Note as well that the number of applications has increased steadily, rather than exponentially, including between calendar years 2000 (1,005 applications) and 2002 (1,228 applications). In fact, there was a drop in the number of applications to 932 in 2001. Overall, the number of applications has increased from a high of 635 in the 1980s, to a high of 886 in the 1990s, to 2,072 in 2005, with the number of applications doubling from 2000 to 2005.[51]

The 2005 report also reflects an iterative process, with judges appearing to withhold approval in two cases subject to amendment, as well as making modifications to the underlying orders in 61 cases. At least one former chief judge of the FISC has stated publicly that such iteration is an integral part of the process.[52] On the one hand, critics argue that the process is too secretive to reach informed judgments about the efficacy of the FISC and suggest that the batting percentage is simply too high to reflect rigorous review. In many cases, FISA surveillance does not result in criminal prosecution and therefore is not subject to the additional safeguard presented in the Title III context of having the surveillance tested through the adversarial adjudication of a suppression motion. On the other hand, the batting percentage is consistent with the number of applications and authorizations for Title III orders, a mainstay of the criminal justice system. In 2005, for example, there were 1,774 applications and 1,773 applications authorized. In 2004 there were 1,710 applications and 1,710 authorizations.[53] The FISA batting percentage might even be tested from the other side of the liberty/security coin. One might also ask: is the government pushing the national security envelope hard enough to obtain information if it is not having more orders denied?

By legislative design, the FISA results in a process of internal executive branch review as well. Indeed, as with many areas of national security, it is this internal process of appraisal that provides the primary opportunity for legal and factual review and subsequent appraisal. Following passage of the Act a specialized and compartmented bureaucracy emerged at Department of Justice, the FBI, and the CIA to handle the processing of FISA requests.[54] By requiring submission of applications by the attorney general, along with certification from designated senior officials "that the purpose of surveillance is to obtain foreign intelligence," the Act generates a process of layered executive review. That is because the attorney general does not generate his or her own paperwork, and senior attorneys within a bureaucracy are less likely to send documents to the attorney general, along with other certifying officials, without careful review. Indeed, some argue, the process is too layered and therefore cumbersome, resulting in delays while paperwork transits up the bureaucracy to the attorney general even in cases of emergency authorization.

At the same time, although layered, the process has always been a closed one, making it hard to appreciate the extent to which the views of a few lawyers, applied with little external reflection, or even knowledge, influence the interpretation and application of the law. National security process depends on secrecy and no area of intelligence practice more so than electronic surveillance. However, secrecy also limits opportunities for persons without an agenda or stake to test the why, when, what, and where of surveillance. Indeed, in the Act's history, only four persons had headed the Justice Department office responsible for its implementation before 9/11.[55]

With one notable exception, FISA law and process proceeded unabated and with little public scrutiny from 1978 until 2001. As originally drafted, the FISA did not address physical searches, but rather electronic surveillance, albeit a FISA warrant required specification as to "the means by which the electronic surveillance will be affected and whether physical entry will be used to affect the surveillance."[56] However, in the context of the Aldrich Ames espionage case in the early 1990s, the president authorized the physical search of Ames's residence pursuant to his constitutional authority. He did so outside the FISA framework. The executive subsequently sought amendment to the FISA to grant the FISC jurisdiction and authority to issue warrants for physical searches for foreign intelligence purposes. As in the case of President Ford, President Clinton did so without conceding the constitutional necessity of doing so. Rather, the president recognized the legal policy advantages of placing such conduct upon the sure footing of *Youngstown*'s first constitutional category. The president also judged that a FISA order would help insulate espionage prosecutions from the risk of having key evidence suppressed. It would also afford government agents authorizing and engaging in clandestine physical searches the certain protection of the law. The Act was subsequently passed as part of the Counterintelligence and Security Enhancements Act of 1994.

September 11, 2001, resulted in intensified intelligence collection against potential jihadist targets at home and abroad. September 11 also prompted reconsideration of the FISA process. Among other things, the process was criticized as slow to generate orders. The executive's interpretation of the law was also criticized for stifling risk taking.[57] Moreover, notwithstanding "reforms" undertaken in the wake of the Aldrich Ames case to improve information sharing between the CIA and FBI, there remained significant informational and coordination gaps between the law enforcement community and the intelligence community, as well as within each community. The problem was part technical (the FBI relying on an outdated computer system and in some cases pen and pencil files). The problem was part cultural (arising out of the jealousies of bureaucratic competition). But it was also a product of legal interpretation.

In particular, the Congress sought to address what came to be known as "the wall," restrictions on the direction and control of FISA surveillance by law enforcement personnel. "The wall" addressed the concern that law enforcement and prosecutorial personnel might use the FISA instrument, or information obtained from FISA surveillance, to either negate the necessity of a Title III order or to develop the probable cause to get one. This was a concern, because key actors perceived that probable cause for a FISA order was lower than that required for a Title III order. In addition, the Department of Justice, the FBI, and the Congress interpreted FISA's requirement that *"the* purpose for surveillance was intelligence" as a sole-purpose test, emphasis on the definite article "the." As a result, guidelines since the 1980s and across administrations had limited the extent to which the criminal division could direct and receive foreign intelligence surveillance.[58] The guidelines were ratified by the FISC, whose views had contributed to their adoption. "The wall" could be crossed with the attorney general's approval and FISC sanction, but real and perceived procedural, cultural, and substantive constraints remained.

Congress responded in the PATRIOT Act by changing the central FISA certification from "the purpose" to *"a significant* purpose."[59] Thus, those officials directing and using FISA surveillance could have both intelligence and law enforcement purposes for doing so. In addition, the Act addressed information sharing by expressly permitting disclosure of foreign intelligence information (including FISA information), Title III information, and grand jury information with national security, law enforcement, and immigration officials when matters involving foreign intelligence or counterintelligence were addressed.[60]

The PATRIOT Act was thought to have addressed the need for seamless intelligence collection and the sharing of FISA data between the intelligence and law enforcement communities. However, the FISC demurred. In 2002, the court found that certain of the procedures adopted by the attorney general to implement the PATRIOT Act were inconsistent with the FISA's statutory scheme in light of the different probable cause standards for intelligence and criminal surveillance. As a result, the Court modified the subject orders "to bring the minimization procedures into accord with the language used in the FISA, and reinstate the bright line used in the 1995 procedures, on which the Court has relied."[61] The executive appealed.

In the first ever opinion by the FISA Court of Review, the appellate court reversed. The court upheld the government's revised 2002 procedures, which, among other things, "eliminated the 'direction and control' test and allowed the exchange of advice among the FBI, the OIPR, and the Criminal Division regarding the 'initiation, operation, continuation, or expansion of FISA search or surveillances.'"[62] "So long as the government entertains a realistic option of dealing with an agent other than through criminal prosecution, it satisfies the significant purpose test."[63] In reaching this conclusion the court noted the seamless nature of intelligence and law enforcement inquiries – foreign intelligence information might necessarily evidence criminal conduct like espionage. In light of this nexus, the court wrote "a standard that punishes cooperation could well be thought dangerous to national security." Finally, the review court concluded that the balance struck in the amended FISA was consistent with *Keith*. Therefore "the FISA as amended is constitutional because the surveillances it authorizes are reasonable."[64]

In addition to addressing "the wall," the Congress authorized the use of roving wiretaps. As originally enacted, the FISA required the government to specify with particularity the location and carrier subject to surveillance. This requirement resulted in inflexible and often manpower-intensive methods of surveillance for targets seeking to evade detection, for example, by using multiple phones and carriers. Whatever merit this limitation possessed in 1978 when pay phones and landlines dominated the market, in a cellular age with technically sophisticated opponents, this limitation proved impractical. As a result, the executive sought roving intelligence authority in the 1990s, an authority it already possessed in law enforcement context. But the Congress did not respond until after 9/11.

Roving wiretap authority is now found in section 206 of the PATRIOT Act, which permits a FISA court judge to authorize surveillance of a subject without specifying the phone or carrier, where the judge finds the actions of the subject may thwart surveillance. As a result, the warrant authority travels with the individual across district boundaries as he switches telephones and locations, perhaps to evade detection. Gone are the days when FBI agents had to occupy every pay phone booth or picnic table at the surveillance site to ensure the correct phone was used by the target of surveillance.

These amendments to the FISA removed legal impediments to information sharing. However, as President Carter observed, operation and adaptation of the law is also dependent on culture and personality. The law enforcement or national security official must still identify information warranting national security treatment and transfer. That same official must then ensure the information traverses the intentional and unintentional bureaucratic obstacle course to the officials who are obliged to act (or choose not to act) in response to the information. Attorney General Guidelines in this area will help, but an ongoing process of appraisal is critical.

C. WARRANTLESS ELECTRONIC SURVEILLANCE

That brings us to the question of whether the president may lawfully authorize government agencies, notably the NSA, to engage in warrantless electronic surveillance. The issue was publicly raised on December 16, 2005, following the disclosure in *The New York Times* that

> under a presidential order signed in 2002, the [NSA] has monitored the international telephone calls and international e-mail messages of hundreds, perhaps thousands, of people inside the United States without warrants over the past three years in an effort to track possible 'dirty numbers' linked to Al Qaeda.[65]

The report was sourced to "nearly a dozen current and former officials, who were granted anonymity." The executive branch subsequently confirmed the existence of a program (or programs) conducted under the rubric "Terrorist Surveillance Program" (TSP).

A January 2006 Department of Justice press release indicates that the "program only applies to communications where one party is located outside the United States."[66] The release does not indicate whether the surveillance must originate with the number or device outside the United States. The statements further indicate that

> the NSA terrorist surveillance program described by the President is only focused on members of Al-Qaeda and affiliated groups. Communications are only intercepted if there is a reasonable basis to believe that one party to the communication is a member of Al-Qaeda, affiliated with Al-Qaeda, or a member of an organization affiliated with Al-Qaeda.

Thus, it is not clear whether the Justice analysis only applies to "the program described by the president" or parallel programs, if any, not described by the president.[67]

The statement indicates as well that the program applies a probable cause or "reasonable basis" standard for surveillance, but does not indicate by name or position who is accountable for this judgment. Further, the statements do not indicate whether the numbers or devices targeted are first generation, second generation, or third generation numbers (i.e., relating to numbers found in Al Qaeda documents, or the numbers called from the numbers found in Al Qaeda documents) or the extent to which the program is used for purposes of post-facto data-mining (e.g., applying algorithmic models to sets of numbers based on different criteria, like location in the United States or overseas). Therefore, it is not immediately clear to whom and to what "agent of a foreign power" might apply, if at all.

The Justice Department press release continues, "The NSA program is an 'early warning system' with only one purpose: to detect and prevent the next attack on the United States from foreign agents hiding in our midst. It is a program with a military nature that requires speed and agility." General Hayden, at the time he was director of the NSA, described the program as one designed for "hot pursuit," allowing intelligence personnel to immediately target numbers identified through the collection of intelligence in Iraq, Afghanistan, and other locales.[68] One can imagine that the value of the program(s) is in part contingent on speed, even instantaneous speed, as jihadist operatives continue to communicate unaware of the capture or disclosure of communications channels and documents.

The importance of speed is emphasized in government releases, which indicate that programmatic decision-making has been pushed down to the operational intelligence level and away from the hierarchy of approval required for FISA authorization. Thus the Department of Justice release states,

> To initiate surveillance under the FISA's emergency authorization, it is not enough to rely on the best judgment of our intelligence officers alone. Those intelligence officers would have to get the sign-off of lawyers at the NSA that all provisions of FISA have been satisfied, then lawyers in the Department of Justice would have to be similarly satisfied, and finally, the Attorney General would have to be satisfied that the search meets the requirements of FISA.

Thus, while the substantive standard is the same as that in FISA – reasonable basis – the process is not. It appears that the executive's concern with the FISA process is based on speed and efficiency, but also on concern that a FISA judge will not reach the same conclusions as an intelligence officer in applying the reasonable basis standard. In the words of General Hayden, this results in a "quicker trigger" and a "subtly softer trigger."[69] Note as well that the statement emphasizes those aspects of the program that play to the president's constitutional strength, including the military nature of the program and the necessity for speed and agility in defending the United States from attack.

Adopting a concept from the covert action provisions of the National Security Act, a limited number of congressional members were briefed on the program including the "Gang of Eight"; media accounts indicate that up to fourteen members were briefed on the program before the story broke.[70] However, media accounts reflect varying views among participants as to what was said and in what detail. Subsequently, in conjunction with General Hayden's confirmation hearings for director of the CIA, additional briefings of additional members were provided, an illustration of how members of Congress may accomplish through informal constitutional practice what they had not accomplished through the operation of law.[71] In addition, press reports at the time of disclosure indicated that the chief judge of the FISC was briefed on the program, but had not been asked to review or approve it. The judge is reported to have requested that the executive not rely on information garnered from the program as a basis for subsequent requests for FISA orders.

With this factual backdrop, and the constitutional framework presented in Chapter 4, consider now how one might frame the constitutional arguments in talking points a lawyer might use in briefing the president or national security advisor.[72] Consider how the arguments and accompanying prudential advice illustrate the constitutional principles previously identified in *Youngstown*. Regardless of which side of the issue one ultimately comes down on, note that both sides of the argument draw on the same constitutional ingredients: text, theory, history, statutory gloss, and case law.

ON THE ONE HAND
Arguments for Presidential Authority to Authorize Warrantless Surveillance

- *Constitutional Framework:* As a matter of constitutional text the president is the commander in chief and chief executive, and he possesses enumerated and derived authority over the foreign affairs function. The president is also responsible for "taking care that the laws be faithfully executed," including foremost the Constitution, which the president swears "to preserve, protect, and defend."
- *Court Recognition:* The Supreme Court has recognized the president's authority in *Curtiss-Wright*. Moreover, the Court has recognized that this authority is inherent, that is, it is not subject to legislative interference. Thus, the president is "the sole organ of the Nation in its external affairs."
- *Wartime Power and Responsibilities:* As presidents of both parties have recognized, and repeatedly stated, the president has no higher constitutional responsibility than to protect the United States from attack. Thus, as commander in chief the president is obliged to take those steps necessary to protect the United States. Further, as scholars of all stripes recognize, the president's war power is broadest where he is protecting the United States from attack. The Court has recognized the same in those few cases that address the president's war power. See *Totten*.
- With this authority comes the derived authority to take those steps necessary to effectively implement the express authority. Thus, the authority to defend the country includes the authority to engage the intelligence functions necessary to identify and respond to the threat, including electronic surveillance at home and abroad.
- *Longstanding Practice as Gloss on Power:* Presidents of both parties have long engaged in such intelligence gathering at home and abroad. As Justice Frankfurter noted, such longstanding practice, and congressional acquiescence in that practice (at least until 1978), represents a gloss on the president's powers.

- *Statutory Overlay – FISA Unconstitutional as Applied:* The question arises whether Congress, through operation of the FISA, can limit or regulate this presidential authority. Although the executive has not heretofore argued that FISA was unconstitutional on its face, certainly the FISA would be unconstitutional, as applied, if it prevented the president from undertaking his core functions. Therefore, the FISA would be unconstitutional if the president determined it prevented him from gathering essential terrorist intelligence in a timely and effective manner.
- *Statutory Overlay – The Authorization for Use of Military Force Resolution (AUMF):* Further, the AUMF authorizes the president to engage in activities incident to conflict. This was recognized in *Hamdi*, where the Court determined that the detention of enemy combatants was a necessary incident of force authorized by the AUMF. If detention is an incident of force, then surely so is intelligence collection wherever it may occur. Thus, the president is operating in a *Youngstown* category I or at worst a category II context. Moreover, even if the AUMF doesn't authorize the TSP, at minimum it recognizes that a wartime gloss on presidential power is in play, and if the president can be said to act at a low ebb, it is a high-low ebb at that.
- *Factual Arguments:* Finally, there may be an argument that the program(s) are factually outside the reach of FISA. However, for reasons of security, this line of argument is omitted, lest the reader (or classification reviewers) presume a classified knowledge on the author's part that does not exist. But the question is a fair one that should be asked by the reader as well as the lawyer testing arguments on both sides of the issue.

Note 1 (as part of the talking points): Independent of the president's power to authorize the program, the president will also have to determine whether the program as authorized must be reported to the Congress as a significant anticipated intelligence activity. Of course, the arguments used in support of the president's exercise of inherent authority also support the argument that the program is significant and reportable. To the extent the program is not reported, then the president should affirmatively make that decision based on the exercise of his constitutional authority over state secrets.

Note 2: Of course, as the authority is hinged to an exercise of the president's constitutional authority, the president alone can authorize such a program.

Note 3: If raised. There are some who argue that the president's inherent authority as commander in chief is per se beyond the reach of congressional regulation or limitation. However, this argument is not credible. It is not based on the commander-in-chief clause, but rather on a rejection of the fundamental structure of the Constitution, for it necessarily adopts the view that the president's actions as commander in chief, regardless of content, are beyond check or balance from the other branches.

This is clearly contrary to constitutional law and practice. First, such a theory would also posit that the president as commander in chief could raise armies and raise taxes to support those armies in the performance of his duties as commander in chief. However, these are clearly powers textually assigned to the Congress and not the president. Second, the *Youngstown* and *Hamdan* courts recognized that the commander-in-chief authority is subject to congressional check and balance. The legal question is not whether, but how. While broad in scope the president's authority as commander in chief is not unlimited, especially when exercised in a domestic setting, even during wartime. In short, adherence to this expansive reading of the commander-in-chief authority not only requires rejection of the separation of powers doctrine, but rejection of 200 years of precedent and practice that it is ultimately for the Supreme Court and not the president to decide what the law is, as Chief Justice Marshall concluded in *Marbury v. Madison* ("It is emphatically the province and duty of the judicial department to say what the law is." 5 U.S. 137 (1803)).

In summary: One might summarize the case for presidential authority as follows. Based on the president's broad constitutional authority in the area of national security, including his authority to collect the intelligence necessary to effectively execute those duties, the president may lawfully authorize the TSP. This argument is enhanced to the extent the president determines the FISA requirements are impractical in application and prevent the president from undertaking his core security functions.

ON THE OTHER HAND
Arguments Against the President's Authority in Light of the FISA

- *Constitutional Framework:* The Fourth Amendment states, "The right of the people to be secure in their persons, houses, papers, and effects, against unreasonable searches and seizures, shall not be violated, and no Warrants shall issue, but upon probable cause, supported by Oath or affirmation, and particularly describing the place to be searched, and the persons or things to be seized." In *Keith*, the Supreme Court determined that the warrant requirement applies to electronic surveillance for domestic security purposes. As the government has acknowledged, the TSP entails the search and seizure of communications where at least one party is located in the United States, without distinction as to whether these persons are U.S. citizens, permanent residents, or aliens. The purpose of the TSP is to prevent terrorist attacks in the United States. Therefore, it is manifest that the program is undertaken for purposes of domestic security as well as foreign intelligence collection.

- *Statutory Overlay:* Whether mandated by the Fourth Amendment or not, as a matter of statute, a judicial order is required to conduct electronic surveillance for foreign intelligence purposes within the United States. Indeed, the Congress has expressly provided that the FISA, along with Title III (not at issue here), "shall be the *exclusive means* by which electronic surveillance may be conducted."

- *Practice:* Heretofore, the FISA Act has not been challenged as unconstitutional by presidents of either party. Presidents have asserted an inherent authority, independent of the statute, to engage in intelligence collection, but not the correlated argument that the Congress is without power to regulate this authority.

- The fact that Congress did not legislate before 1978 does not mean that it could not do so in 1978. The law is full of examples where Congress has exercised its legislative power years after an executive practice was established. In the case of military justice, for example, the Congress did not assert its authority until 1951 with passage of the Uniform Code of Military Justice. Prior to that date military justice was dispensed within the framework of articles of war that were promulgated pursuant to the commander in chief's authority. Surely, the president and the courts, including the Supreme Court, have long accepted this exercise of Congress's authority over military justice notwithstanding the absence of such exercise for more than 150 years of the country's constitutional history.

- *Case Law:* While the president's authority is broad, both with intelligence and during wartime, we are not dealing here exclusively with conduct occurring in a war zone or overseas, but one with domestic nexus to U.S. persons. It is thus distinguishable from the case of detainees taken on the battlefield as discussed in *Hamdi*. The case is more analogous to *Youngstown* or *Hamdan*, not *Curtiss-Wright* or the *Prize* cases. And as the Supreme Court noted in *Youngstown*, the president is commander in chief of the armed forces, not the country.

- Of course, the Congress cannot alter a constitutional balance through passage of legislation. But this is a tautology. At best, the president would find himself in *Youngstown's* third category, at a low ebb of authority, for Congress has expressly legislated in this area. Moreover, depending on one's view of congressional authority over domestic intelligence, in light of the Court's footnote in *Hamdan*, it is not clear whether the president's authority is at a low ebb, or extinguished.

- *FISA Applied Constitutionally:* With respect to the "as applied" arguments, the Act provides constitutional outlets, allowing the president to authorize surveillance without warrants during periods of declared war and where emergency surveillance is necessary before a warrant can be obtained. Absent a showing of exigent circumstances, which has surely passed years after commencement of the program, the president has an obligation to apply the law in good faith and if necessary seek legislative amendment.

- *AUMF Not Relevant:* Finally, with respect to the statutory gloss provided by the AUMF.
  a. The law provides that FISA and Title III shall be the exclusive means by which the executive will conduct electronic surveillance.
  b. The AUMF is silent on this point, and silent repeal of a criminal statute is disfavored in the law.
  c. With respect to the "incident of war" arguments, the Court rejected a parallel argument in *Hamdan*, while accepting it in *Hamdi*. Thus, the question is whether the TSP is more analogous to the detention of enemy combatants taken on the battlefield or the prosecution of unlawful combatants.
  d. Finally, as a matter of statutory construction, where two statutes conflict, the specific statute (FISA) should be read to control the more general (the AUMF).

In summary: The argument against presidential authority might be summarized as follows. Absent a compelling demonstration that the surveillance falls outside the FISA's parameters, in which case it might yet run afoul of *Keith*, presidential authorization of warrantless surveillance at best places the president at a low ebb of his authority. The better view, in light of the specificity of the statute, and the longstanding acquiescence of the executive in the Act's constitutionality, is that FISA did not leave the president at a low ebb exercising residual inherent authority, but extinguished that authority.

As these draft talking points illustrate, not all legal issues invite clear yes and no responses. Even those questions that appear to be so may not be so upon careful factual and legal inspection. In short, for lawyers as for policymakers, there is no shortage of such 51–49 decisions – that is, close calls where arguments can be made on both sides with one argument ultimately presenting the better view, but only by a small margin. Such issues should leave the lawyer assessing not just whether the options presented are legally available but also whether there are legal policy or prudential reasons why one lawful argument might be preferred over another. In other words, if the decisionmaker is free to opt in either direction, are there reasons why he might favor one option over another?

Of course, if as counsel one concludes that the second argument is not only the stronger argument, but is the only legally available argument, one must then consider two additional questions. As chief executive, may the president nonetheless take an alternative legal view and authorize the program anyway? Does it matter whether the attorney general takes the same view? If the president authorizes the program over counsel's advice, what responsibility, if any, does counsel have to report or disclose the president's determination and to whom? Keep in mind the triad of privileges in play – state secrets, attorney-client, and deliberative, as well as the possible application of criminal sanctions for the unauthorized disclosure of classified information. Alternatively, should the attorney resign?[73]

Assuming for the sake of argument that counsel advises that both arguments are legally available. That is, counsel advises that the president acting in good faith might proceed to authorize the program(s) or as a matter of discretion might nonetheless seek judicial or legislative validation before or after doing so. Counsel should now address the prudential arguments. The president's lawyer(s) might identify one or all of the following prudential factors in the form of legal policy advice.

LEGAL POLICY ADVICE
Prudential Factors in Determining the President's Position

There are a number of legal policy reasons why the president (and his advisors) might favor one legal position over the other.

Legal policy arguments in favor of exercising inherent executive authority
- *Secrecy:* The program(s)' success as an intelligence tool depends on its secrecy. Authorization of the program pursuant to executive authority alone will minimize, but not remove the risk of unauthorized disclosure. As importantly, pursuit of additional authority, and in particular legislative authority, increases the risk of disclosure either through willful action or as an inadvertent byproduct of legislative drafting.
- *Efficiency:* The program(s)' success in pursuing potential terrorists from one phone connection to the next, or one computer connection to the next, depends on speed. The FISA process is too cumbersome to meet operational demands. Moreover, any alternative method of authorization is likely to also entail procedural delay and serve to distract from the mission.
- *Presidential Authority:* In this conflict, of uncertain threats from known and unknown enemies, the president should maximize his flexibility by relying on his inherent authority. External constraints may prove deadly if the president's authority is constrained today with unintended effect tomorrow. Further, reliance on presidential authority here will avoid expectations that the president will seek additional authority in any complex or new context arising in the future.
- *Legislative Tactics:* Be careful what you ask for. The Congress has reacted to the PATRIOT Act amendments in a mixed manner. The Congress may

time that it authorizes. Reliance on an argument of inherent authority eliminates this risk.

Legal policy arguments in favor of exercising executive authority contingent to the parallel pursuit of legislative or judicial ratification

- *Rule of Law and Public Diplomacy:* In a conflict over values, where the United States seeks to define an alternative to jihadism founded on the rule of law and principles of democracy, it matters that the United States and its president are perceived to follow the law. To the extent that the president relies exclusively on his authority and takes the program outside the FISA framework this perception may be undermined.
- *Sustained Public Support:* An endless conflict requires sustained and undivided public support. Adoption of potentially divisive legal arguments that may cut across constituencies may prove counterproductive and diminish support for national security programs in other areas.
- *Maximization of Presidential Authority:* Whatever can be said of the president's inherent authority, express authorization will maximize the president's authority, minimizing the potential impact or hesitation of intelligence actors to push the envelope.
- *Risk-Taking in the Field:* In light of the FISA's criminal sanctions, and as general matter of practice, officers are more likely to take risks if they know the law stands behind them and that a new president would not with the sweep of a pen determine that their conduct was unlawful? Public disclosures regarding CIA officers obtaining insurance to hire lawyers underscore this argument.[74] (With the benefit of hindsight it is also easy to add: lack of confidence in the legal underpinnings of the program, whether valid or not, may prompt disclosure by "whistleblowers.")
- *Private Sector Protection and Support:* As the executive argued at the time the FISA was adopted, whether legally required or not, a legislative framework will serve to protect companies from litigation challenging the program, should it be disclosed, and the subsequent risk of disclosure through litigation. Of course, to the extent carriers feel exposed on the TSP they may be less likely to assist in other known and unknown contexts that may arise tomorrow.

In either event, counsel should also address mitigation strategies to address the impact of the legal policy concerns identified above. These might include the following actions.

- *Executive Review:* There are at least two risks that warrant an internal process of review. First, as the Court recognized in *Keith*, security is an inherently vague term. The threat from Al Qaeda is not. Whether the individual actions or collective actions of specific persons or entities in the United States are reasonably linked to national security or Al Qaeda may vary depending on which watch officer is making the determination. A rigorous process of appraisal in the executive branch will help to ensure that consistent standards are applied and that intelligence decisionmakers do not stray from the president's authorization, either by limiting its intended reach (a security concern), or extending beyond his authorization (a liberty concern). Such a process of review will also mitigate, but not eliminate, blowback in the event the program is disclosed.

Further, if you do proceed unilaterally, there will be some who will argue the president is acting outside the law. To mitigate against this risk the president should consider: (1) establishing a process of intelligence review to ensure that the program is conducted in the manner intended – all the better if this review is conducted by an independent executive entity such as the Intelligence Oversight Board, which works directly for the president; (2) requesting the attorney general provide a memorandum in both classified and unclassified manner in advance of authorization providing the legal basis for the president's exercise of unilateral authority, with a view toward releasing the unclassified memorandum if the program is disclosed; and (3) give a limited briefing to the Congress.

- *Briefing the Congress – Legislative Context:* Whether the president has inherent authority or not, the FISA has served as the predicate for electronic surveillance for twenty-five years. Moreover, unlike the War Powers Resolution, the FISA has served as an effective constitutional rapprochement between the executive and the Congress. Whether or not the Act is constitutional in all contexts or not, the Act has defined legislative and judicial as well as executive expectations about the conduct of surveillance. Absent clear arguments that the Congress would not authorize the program, there may be unintended costs in comity in this and other areas where the separation of powers has worked well to this point.
- *Intelligence Risk Taking:* To encourage intelligence agency risk taking, the presidential authorization could be documented in a form available for watch officer display with reference to the program through a euphemism like "TSP." Such authorization could be reissued periodically to remove risk that officers may be concerned the authorization is stale.

D. EPILOGUE

The Congress considered a number of legislative responses following disclosure of the TSP. Senator Spector, the chairman of the Senate Judiciary Committee, for example, proposed (with executive branch support) legislation that would permit, but not require, the president to submit the program(s)s to the Foreign Intelligence Surveillance appellate review court for a determination as to the program(s)' constitutionality. Representative Wilson, a member of the House Intelligence Committee, proposed legislation that would authorize the program(s), but require additional congressional reporting as well as additional FISC review. However, apparently, there were insufficient votes to secure passage of a TSP–FISA bill. The program(s) proceeded pursuant to the president's constitutional authority.

Within the executive branch, the inspector general (IG) of the Department of Justice announced in November 2006 that his office was reviewing the department's connections to the program(s). However, the IG indicated that he would not review the constitutionality of the TSP, but rather address the manner in which TSP information was used by the department and whether the department's lawyers had complied with the program(s)' legal and administrative requirements. One can anticipate that additional IGs and oversight mechanisms within the executive branch have and will also appraise the TSP. Less certain is whether and to what extent executive conclusions will be shared with the Congress or the public.

In January 2007, the Attorney General notified the Congress that

> a Judge of the Foreign Intelligence Surveillance Court issued orders authorizing the Government to target for collection international communications into or out of the United States where there is probable cause to believe that one of the communicants is a member or agent of al Qaeda or an associated terrorist organization. As a result of these orders, any electronic surveillance that was occurring as part of the Terrorist Surveillance Program will now be conducted subject to the approval of the Foreign Intelligence Surveillance Court.

The Attorney General's letter continues,

> In the spring of 2005 – well before the first press account disclosing the existence of the Terrorist Surveillance Program – the Administration began exploring options for seeking such FISA Court approval. . . . These orders are innovative, they are complex, and it took considerable time and work for the Government to develop the approach that was proposed to the Court and for the Judge on the FISC to consider and approve these orders.[75]

The letter references "orders," but does not specify whether the TSP has been authorized on a programmatic basis or on a subject-by-subject basis or whether the "innovative approach" referenced in the letter is addressed to some other method of block or rolling authorization. This may not be evident until issuance of the annual FISA report, which may show a significant increase in the number of FISA orders, but may not. The letter states that the orders in question cover "any electronic surveillance that was occurring as part of the Terrorist Surveillance Program," but does not state whether any other surveillance is occurring outside the FISA framework for which comparable constitutional questions might arise.

Finally, the letter does not indicate the reasons for the president's change of view regarding FISA court review of the TSP. The letter states, without explanation, that "the orders the Government has obtained will allow the necessary speed and agility while providing substantial advantages." The advantages are not specified, nor the reasons why it took two years to obtain the orders once they were sought.

One can surmise, although the letter does not state, that informal constitutional factors influenced the executive decision to seek court approval. In November 2006, the majority party changed in the Congress, raising the prospect of more pressing legislative investigation of the program; the executive branch may have sought to preempt or defuse the energy behind such interest. Unidentified Justice Department sources also indicated that the FISA court orders might facilitate the potential prosecution of communicants who might otherwise challenge the basis for any surveillance used against them in court. Finally, department officials indicated a desire to moot pending court challenges to the president's authorization of the TSP outside the FISA framework.[76] A number of lawsuits are proceeding through the courts challenging the legality of common carrier support to the TSP. Issues of standing and state secrets have been resolved in diverse manner. This suggests that if FISA court approval does not moot these suits, in due course the issue may get to the Supreme Court. However, the Court might well address the issue on grounds of standing or state secrets and thus avoid at once a decision terminating a program the executive branch views as critical or that writes the president a blank check in a context in which the Court, the Congress, or the public will not ultimately know how it is spent.

Whatever one's view regarding the efficacy of the FISA court process and the TSP, electronic surveillance is an area that merits ongoing legal and cultural appraisal by each branch of government, to appraise result as well as legality. As a source of intelligence regarding, for example, the identification of terrorist sleepers in the United States, electronic surveillance is too important not to use and use to maximum effect. At the same time, history and practice have shown that this is an area susceptible to excess, particularly in a factual and bureaucratic environment that will default to a security preference.

Even where the general parameters of a program are known, as may be the case with the TSP, the underlying facts may remain secret. This increases the importance of the internal advice rendered by the handful of lawyers and policymakers "in the know." It also highlights the importance of moral integrity to any process of government dependent on secret legal and policy appraisal. These officials may be the only officials in a position to identify and weigh the enduring legal and security consequences of a program against its immediate benefits. Whether, and how, they do so is a matter of national security process.

6 National Security Process

This chapter is about national security process, with a focus on presidential decision-making. This emphasis reflects the central role of the executive branch and the president in national security policy and the day-to-day management of national security. This central role is a product of the constitutional and statutory responsibilities assigned to the president. It also reflects the executive's functional advantages in managing national security.

The president's central role also reflects the singular role of the commander in chief in time of conflict. Alexander Hamilton observed in *Federalist* Number 8: "It is the nature of war to increase the executive at the expense of the legislative authority."[1] The Cold War and now the conflict against jihadists have done nothing to dilute this observation. National security decision-making gravitates to the president in times of crisis and in times of perpetual alert. As the terrorist threat is henceforth perpetual, the president, and the executive branch, shall remain at the center of national security process. Perpetual conflict will place added strain on national security process as ad hoc and emergency processes adopted in the immediacy of conflict may become norms over time. The question is not whether the president will, or should, play the central national security role, but whether he will do so using an effective process subject to meaningful policy and legal appraisal.

Each of these factors places additional importance on understanding national security process within the executive branch. Indeed, most of the important counter-terrorism tools – electronic surveillance, rendition, detainee operations, and special military operations – are wielded with little or no external approval, consultation, or appraisal. However, these are not just among the most effective tools for countering terrorism; they are also potentially the most problematic from a legal and policy perspective. Thus, a failure to define a national security process that is both timely and meaningful for approving and then appraising the use of each instrument may result in Pyrrhic victories. We may gain the momentary advantage of tactical military and intelligence success, but at the long-term cost to America's image and our efforts to present an alternative to the jihadist movement based on the rule of law. We need not forego the one for the other if we use effective process. The national security process can be effective and rigorous, fast and thorough, as well as aggressive and lawful.

The chapter begins with brief consideration of some of the participants in the national security process and the legal underpinnings of their participation, including the president and the Congress, but also external actors like the media, and private non-governmental groups (NGOs). Next, the chapter describes some of the essential components of the president's national security process, including the National Security Council (NSC), the NSC staff, and the interagency process. Each president will define his own process; however, practice suggests that there are ingredients organic to good process, notwithstanding a tendency of successive administrations to cast themselves in contrast to their predecessors. Administrations ignore these core ingredients at their peril and the public's peril. The practice and texture of national security decision-making is considered with reference to four processes: the NSC, the office of the vice president, the Homeland Security Council (considered in Chapter 9), and the military chain of command (considered in Chapter 8). By understanding each process, the lawyer can better identify where he or she might most effectively guide and counsel. In turn, the observer might better identify those persons accountable for the success or failure of U.S. policy as well as the manner and means by which policy adheres to U.S. law and legal values.

The section closes by appraising those features of presidential process that are most effective and those elements that are potentially problematic. For example, the military chain of command is designed to maximize speed of decision and unity of command.[2] The principle of unity of command applies equally to policy operations as it does to military operations in support of policy objectives. Although it may be more apparent when military units are working at cross-purposes, the effect on policy implementation is also devastating when one arm of the government is pushing uphill while another is pushing down. However, where multidimensional or transcendent problems are presented, a narrow process does not invite external expertise in areas like diplomacy, refugee relief, and societal transition. Here the task force and NSC models may prove valuable as supplementary models to inform decision.

A. CONSTITUTIONAL FRAMEWORK AND OVERVIEW

1. Executive Decision

Within the executive branch, the majority of national security decisions are taken at the department and agency level, pursuant to statutory and delegated constitutional authority. This is true with respect to routine acts of national security, such as U.S. extradition practice implemented by the Department of State and Department of Justice, or border security undertaken by the Department of Homeland Security. It is also generally true of crisis decision-making. The majority of policy decisions taken in the context of the Iraq conflict, for example, are made in the field by combatant commanders and at the U.S. Embassy by the U.S. country team. These decisions are subject to policy guidance defined by Principals in Washington and where necessary, or appropriate, presidential direction. Moreover, the majority of military decisions are made within the uniformed chain of command, a process described in Chapter 8, and not within the president's NSC process. Similarly, agency officials implement the majority of presidential decisions. Even where the president is most visible in implementing policy, on or off stage during Middle East peace negotiation, for example, the majority of leg work and preparatory work is conducted by the secretary of state and her staff.

Nonetheless, there is no mistaking that, in terms of day-to-day impact, the president remains at the center of the national security process. This reflects the importance of the institution of the presidency not just in the United States, but on the world stage. The president alone can speak on behalf of the United States in a way that congressional and other national leaders cannot. As importantly, it is the president who holds authority over the tangible constitutional tools to shape policy and respond to crisis as chief executive, commander in chief, and pursuant to his foreign affairs powers. In addition, in time of crisis it is the president who often decides on whether and how to use the national security tools that are the product of legislative authorization and appropriation.

Finally, the modern presidency daily addresses modern modes of violence, which may offer little opportunity for deliberation or debate, both because of the consequences of their use and the rapidity necessary for the effective deployment to deter or respond to attack. This has been manifest with respect to nuclear weapons since the 1950s, but it is also true of homeland security where rapid, clear, and competent decisions can save thousands, if not hundreds of thousands, of lives. This may also mean that meaningful congressional participation in the national security process, as a practical reality, must occur prospectively before the crisis or predicate event, rather than during the crisis, when executive actors and energy will, and should, focus elsewhere.

As discussed in Chapter 4, the president's role is the product of law. The Constitution is the first source of the president's national security authority and process. But Congress has statutorily buttressed the president's place at the head of the national security table. The National Security Act of 1947, for example, envisions a policy process revolving around the president.

2. Congress

At the same time that the Constitution and statute empower the president, they also delimit that authority, most notably through the formal and informal exercise of national security powers that are separate and shared between the executive and the legislative branches. This constitutional structure alone dictates that national security process account for, and provide for, the meaningful interplay between branches. This includes mechanisms to implement enumerated authorities, and as importantly, to carry out the myriad informal contacts between the political branches that serve as the constitutional ball bearings between the political branches of government. Indeed, a national security lawyer at the national level will spend much of his or her time advising policymakers on just how these various powers interlock and where they are truly independent.

It is axiomatic that the process of national security includes the manner in which the Congress exercises its enumerated powers; for example, how it legislates in the area of national security, advises and consents on nominations and treaties, and engages in committee oversight. Within the Congress, national security helps to define which members and which committees will play informal as well as formal constitutional roles in shaping and funding national security policy, or perhaps as importantly, determining whether to give the executive a free hand.

Congress's most important procedural tool remains the power of the purse. While conditional funding authorizations and appropriations are subject to interpretation, funding prohibitions and limitations usually are not. The exercise of such authority can be a blunt instrument of policy, removing executive opportunities for nuanced policy. However, in terms of influence, it is the exercise of the appropriations power that can guarantee meaningful congressional participation in the national security process if it is used effectively. It is Congress's budget authority, which ultimately underpins Congress's ability to participate as an effective partner in the informal process of consulting, signaling, and validating, that oils the gears of constitutional process between the political branches. The senatorial authority to confirm appointments provides similar leverage, but such leverage is episodic and generally less reliable or effective, given the general sense that the president is entitled to select his senior advisors.

Congress also plays an important role in framing through statute the president's national security process. The National Security Act, for example, established the National Security Council, and in doing so reinforces the NSC model of decision-making. Similarly, the 1986 Goldwater-Nichols Act established a structure of military command within which the president exercises his constitutional authority as commander in chief.[3]

Other statutes create particular processes for addressing specific national security regimes. Thus, the Foreign Assistance Act establishes the basic framework and process for the administration of foreign aid. The Export Administration Act (which, though lapsed, has continued in effect through application of executive order) and the Arms Export Control Act do the same in the area of national security export controls. In each instance, executive regulations provide a further gloss and process upon the legislative frame. Finally, generalized grants of substantive authority like the International Emergency Economic Powers Act are implemented through specific executive branch applications, that is, a common law of actual practice.

In the day-to-day management of national security, Congress can play an essential informal role in validating, testing, and ultimately holding the executive branch accountable for its national security decisions. One might be inclined to describe this as an exercise in legislative oversight. But that is too formal a term, invoking images of committee hearings, subpoenas, and a certain amount of theater, which are part of the process but fail to convey the extent to which the separate and shared powers are exercised through informal process and communication. This is an essential unwritten ingredient in the national security process. This informal process of consultation, notification, and validation occurs in all substantive areas of government, but is nowhere more important than in the area of national security where much is intended to remain out of the public eye.

3. The Media

Discussion of national security process should also consider the role of the media. The media are a significant independent source of oversight and the primary conduit by which national security information and decisions are communicated to the public. While scholars, officials, and journalists debate particular applications of the First Amendment, there is no serious debate that these traditional roles associated with the media are part of the constitutional framework of national security process.

Policymakers and observers are less likely to identify the daily influence of the media as part of the national security process itself. Nevertheless, on a given day, principals and their staff will devote a significant segment of time to reading, digesting, responding, and using the media to amplify their own policy voices. Thus the national security day for many decision-makers will begin with a review of overnight intelligence product, and then move to the drafting and clearing of press guidance. Throughout the day, policymakers will seek to influence the policy process through authorized and unauthorized contacts with the press.

In addition, media inquiry often serves as a catalyst of decision by forcing policymakers to address issues on a timeline driven by the competition among media outlets for stories rather than timing considerations pegged to policy effect. For example, a policy proposal disclosed in advance of decision, or even the fact of discussion, may compel decisionmakers to truncate consideration of that proposal, lest domestic and international actors respond to the proposal as if it were a decision already taken. Of course, individual policymakers will incorporate the media wittingly and unwittingly into their process of decision-making with just this effect in mind.

Increasingly, national security process has recognized that the media play this same role worldwide, even if not pursuant to the same ground rules. This is manifest in executive decisions to form standing media "war rooms" first used during the Kosovo conflict to address worldwide news cycles. However, too often the media plan is relegated to the role of a planning annex, rather than an essential element of the decision process itself. However, the communication of a decision can be as important as the decision. A well-spoken, well-timed, or misspoken statement from the president may influence events more than a hundred Principals' meetings. More than one national security advisor has had to remind his or her staff that reviewing the president's standing press guidance first thing in the morning is a more important task, even if repetitive, than preparing for the next inter-agency meeting.

Finally, and most significantly for the purposes of this chapter, national security process is also driven by a desire of policymakers to control the flow of information to the press (offense) and to avoid unauthorized disclosures of information (defense). In this sense, the media may drive decisionmakers to dysfunctional processes. The legitimate thirst for secrecy may overwhelm the instinct for good government. Policymakers will insist on ever-smaller decision-making processes or, dangerously, move outside the established process itself. Key actors will be omitted. Where warranted, a good process is one that acknowledges and addresses these tensions. For example, where speed and secrecy are essential, rather than moving the decision outside the expected process and curtail the exchange of views, participation can move up the chain of command to limit the number of persons in the know and the number of layers that might delay decision.

4. Non-Governmental Organizations

There are many additional participants in the national security process. This book highlights those actors derivative of the constitutional framework and thus admittedly shortchanges critical additional actors that may play significant roles in context, like non-governmental organizations (NGOs), private citizens, and international organizations. Private actors, such as NGOs, are usually not formal participants in the national security process; however, they may play critical roles in influencing or implementing U.S. policy. Consider, for example, the role of Bill Gates and former President Clinton in raising awareness and funding for AIDS treatment and prevention, or the role of former presidents George H. W. Bush and Bill Clinton in raising money for tsunami relief in South Asia. Both efforts surpass in importance any governmental process addressed to the same ends.

Nowhere is the potential role of NGOs more evident than during relief operations, where NGOs often control a majority of the resources available for distribution and may have a monopoly on meaningful access to the affected area. They alone may possess the needed skills; think, for example, of Doctors Without Borders. They may also be the only foreign personnel who can safely enter the affected area as persons without governmental affiliation. NGOs have also played important roles in shaping the Ottawa Treaty on Land Mines and the Rome Treaty establishing an International Criminal Court. The governmental actor proceeds at his peril if he does not consider NGOs' views and capabilities as part of the process of policy development and implementation.

B. PRESIDENTIAL DECISION-MAKING

1. Formal Framework

The National Security Act of 1947, as amended, established the National Security Council (NSC).

> [The] function of the Council shall be to advise the president with respect to the integration of domestic, foreign, and military policies relating to the national security so as to enable the military services and the other departments and agencies of the government to cooperate more effectively in matters involving the national security.

The Council comprises four statutory members: the president, the vice president, the secretary of state, and the secretary of defense. The director of national intelligence and the chairman of the Joint Chiefs of Staff are statutorily designated as advisors to the NSC in their respective areas of expertise, "subject to the direction of the President."[4] This statutory distinction between membership and advisory status reflects practice as well as a tradition, founded in the culture of the armed forces and intelligence community, that the director of central intelligence (DCI), now the director of national intelligence (DNI), and chairman should limit their input to their areas of professional expertise and defer on questions of policy. Of course, that assumes that intelligence and policy are subject to bifurcation. Where, for example, a decision to use force is based on intelligence the two are inexorably bound.

The manner of application of this advisory tradition, of course, has varied depending on the personality of the participants and expectations of the president.[5] In intelligence practice, for example, DCI John McCone (1961–65) took a very different approach than DCI William Casey (1981–87). How the chairman defines his duties will also depend on his relationship with the secretary of defense he sits next to at Principals Committee meetings. However defined, a DNI or chairman who associates too closely with an administration's policy views, appearing as an advocate and not merely an advisor, may lose public or congressional credibility for calling it as he sees it on military and intelligence matters.

In practice, each president will define his own national security process within the constitutional and statutory framework of decision-making. This is usually accomplished at the outset of an administration by presidential directive. Foremost, such directives will include the president's concept for the National Security Council and corresponding NSC process. Through this practice, presidents have designated additional members of the National Security Council. President Clinton, for example, designated the secretary of the treasury, the U.S. ambassador to the United Nations (USUN), the assistant to the president for national security affairs (APNSA, a.k.a. national security advisor), the assistant to the president for economic policy, and the chief of staff to the president as members of his NSC and Principals Committee. President George W. Bush designated as his council the statutory members of the NSC as well as the secretary of the treasury and the APNSA, stipulating further that the chief of staff to the president and assistant to the president for economic policy "are invited to attend any NSC meeting." In both administrations, these additions theoretically signaled increased visibility and bureaucratic access for the incumbents of those offices. However, in practice, attendance at NSC and NSC Principals Committee meetings is dictated by the president's contextual preference, the issue presented, and the invitations meted out by the national security advisor. One will discern from inspecting photographs of NSC meetings that the ordinary membership of the NSC remains at its core the president, vice president, secretary of state, secretary of defense, DNI, chairman, and national security advisor.

Heretofore, national security has been defined broadly when defining the scope of the NSC process. For example, President George W. Bush's directive, "Organization of the National Security Council System," states:

> National security includes the defense of the United States of America, protection of our constitutional system of government, and the advancement of United States interests around the globe. National security also depends on America's opportunity to prosper in the world economy.[6]

The advancement of U.S. interests and the opportunity to prosper are, of course, broad statements of "national security." President Clinton's comparable directive, "Organization of the National Security Council," did not define "United States national security," but included equally expansive jurisdictional language drawn from the National Security Act of 1947:

> The NSC shall advise and assist me in integrating all aspects of national security policy as it affects the United States – domestic, foreign, military, intelligence and economic.[7]

With such a point of departure, national security process would encompass not only decisions on military force and intelligence, but also the use of the Exchange Stabilization Fund to shore up a foreign currency or the use of tariffs as an instrument of trade policy and domestic constituency. If national security is understood to mean the protection not only of our physical safety, but the security of our way of life, then there is little limit to what might be subject to national security process. While there are good arguments why trade, the economy, and the environment are, or in context may become, national security issues, the purpose of this chapter is to sketch a normative process by which core defense and foreign affairs issues are addressed within the executive branch, or should be. Understanding this framework, readers can decide for themselves those issues that should be subsumed within such a process according to their own definitions of national security. In doing so, they will have engaged in one of the first steps in the process – deciding which issues should be subject to national security review and decision. As important, readers can judge for themselves whether an incumbent president has adhered to a normative process of decision, and if not, consider the costs and benefits of deviation.

In addition to referring to *the* Council, "the NSC" has also come to refer to the process by which the president's national security team advises the president, and by which the president makes national security decisions. "The NSC" is also used to describe the president's immediate national security staff. Therefore, lawyers must caution precision when referencing *the* NSC. "The NSC," without more description, is the statutory four, including the president. Thus, a reference to the NSC invokes the constitutional authority of the president, as well as the statutory and delegated constitutional authority that the secretary of state and secretary of defense bring to bear. In contrast, the authority of the NSC *staff* is limited to advising and assisting the president in performing his duties.[8] Of course, "advice and assistance" is accompanied by all the force and persuasion one bears when communicating the decisions and policy intentions of the president.

In addition to presidential direction, the national security process is framed by the Principals Committee (PC) and Deputies Committee (DC).[9] As NSPD-1 states, the NSC Principals Committee serves as "the senior interagency forum for consideration of policy issues affecting national security, as it has since 1989."[10] The Deputies Committee is the senior sub-cabinet and interagency forum for doing the same. Among other things, the Principals Committee and Deputies Committee frame issues for presidential consideration or resolve issues that do not require presidential decision. The DC also serves as the principal mechanism for crisis management, at least where national security issues are handled out of the White House. One former APNSA has described the Deputies Committee as the "engine of decision-making."[11]

As their nomenclature suggests, these committees are constituted of the president's principal national security advisors; for example, the statutory members of the NSC such as the secretary of state, and designated members such as the APNSA. Through successive administrations, the APNSA has been designated the chair of the Principals Committee. The Deputies Committee in turn is constituted of the primary deputies to the principals (e.g., deputy secretary of defense); however, some flexibility is provided for Deputies' participation, given the range of issues considered and the necessity for Deputies to travel; thus, the undersecretaries of defense and state for policy are frequently designated members of the Deputies Committee as well. In contrast, it is unusual to substitute for principals; a principals meeting is effective, in part, because the participants can immediately and definitively advance their views as well as the views of their respective agencies.

The Principals and Deputies Committees typically meet on a regularly scheduled biweekly basis. However, by presidential direction and long-standing practice, a meeting of the Principals or Deputies Committee can be called from above, requested by a participant, or generated at the suggestion of subordinate staff.[12] In fact, typical is atypical. The best of organizational intentions invariably gives way to the reality of need, causing the principals and deputies to meet on a daily basis or even more frequently as events dictate.[13] In the case of the Kosovo conflict, for example, the Principals and Deputies Committees met every day, and sometimes more frequently. During the second Iraq conflict, media reports indicate that the Principals Committee has generally met at least three times a week at regularly scheduled intervals.

Typically, at the close of such a meeting the chair will summarize the conclusions of the meeting and the staff note taker (NSC action officer) will draft a Summary of Conclusions (SOC) for circulation to the participants. In my experience, SOCs are succinct, conveying the lowest common denominator essentials of decisions to trigger bureaucratic response, but without the policy nuance, which might prompt interagency debate and relitigation of disputes, undermining the value of the predicate meeting.

The work of the National Security Council and the Principals and the Deputies Committees is fueled by the briefing papers and issue papers generated by individual agencies and interagency working groups (IWGs),

IWGs ("eye-wigs" as they are known) are organized around geographic or functional disciplines and are chaired and staffed at the assistant secretary, deputy assistant secretary, or equivalent level. However, unlike assistant secretaries, NSC staff are not subject to Senate confirmation. Perhaps the best known of these working groups was the CSG, or Counterterrorism/Coordinating Sub-Group of the Principals Committee (or Deputies Committee, depending on who was asked). This IWG was chaired by Richard "Dick" Clarke and was responsible for coordinating the government's policy response to terrorism through multiple administrations prior to 9/11. IWG discussion papers are usually circulated in advance to Deputies and Principals Committees meetings through the NSC executive secretariat. In general, these papers frame the options and issues rather than serve as decision memos themselves.

In addition to defining his committee structure, the president will also promulgate a series of directives, which are used to review and establish presidential policies. These directives are given distinct titles by each administration; for example, Presidential Directive, National Security Decision Directive, National Security Directive, Presidential Decision Directive, and National Security Policy Directive, respectively, in the last five presidencies. This nomenclature distinguishes the directives of one administration from that of the next. In contrast to executive orders, the majority of presidential national security directives are classified, and therefore, remain unknown to the public.[14] However, these directives are no less binding on the executive branch than are executive orders, although they are often less formal and may offer more in policy framework than declaratory direction. Moreover, in the case of "closely held" directives, as a practical matter, they may in reality only direct those employees with knowledge of their existence, such as those pertaining to intelligence matters. In the case of publicly released directives, certain format detail is omitted to help deter and identify efforts at forgery, of which there have been a number of attempts.

Among other things, national security directives are used to establish policies and create decision-making frameworks in particular areas. For example, a directive may designate a lead agency responsible for a specific task, thus heading off in one presidential sentence thousands of hours of bureaucratic battle ... or at least hundreds of hours of effort at the headquarters level by lawyers to demonstrate the primacy of their policy officials. Battles may well continue in the field based on personality, practice, and culture, thus emphasizing that the moment of presidential decision marks the transition from deliberation to decision, but only the beginning of the process of implementation and appraisal.

Just as Executive Order 12333, issued in 1981, remains operable, certain presidential directives survive from administration to administration. For example, PD-27 "Procedures for Dealing with Non-Military Incidents," of January 19, 1978, remains the coordinating mechanism for certain non-military incidents like foreign flag boardings in the Caribbean; however, the majority of these directives are rescinded in favor of new directives more closely tracking the policies and bureaucratic structure of each new administration. For a lawyer, trying to determine which directives have been rescinded or, much more difficult, have been rescinded in part between successive administrations will make a tough title search seem routine.

2. National Security Council Staff

The central role of the president in national security decision-making necessitates the existence of a national security staff to advise and assist the president in the performance of his duties. For the post-world war presidency, at least until the creation of the Homeland Security Council, this has meant the National Security Council staff. The National Security Act provides that "The Council shall have a staff to be headed by a civilian executive secretary." As a matter of practice, the staff functions at the direction of the national security advisor and deputy national security advisors, with the executive secretary more akin to a chief of staff, staff secretary, and jack-of-all-trades bound in one.[15] The NSC staff is organized into functional (e.g., legislative, legal, nonproliferation, military affairs, administration) and geographic (e.g., Near East Asia, Europe, Africa) directorates (a.k.a. offices). Regardless of title, these directorates largely parallel the substantive structure at the Department of State and within the Office of the Secretary of Defense. With some exceptions, a special assistant to the president and senior director heads each office,[16] although, in the George W. Bush administration, the larger policy offices are headed by a deputy assistant to the president for national security affairs. But this is a matter of title inflation rather than bureaucratic change, for in reality, the national security advisor leads the NSC staff. Moreover, while there is usually more than one deputy national security advisor, one deputy is invariably the de facto principal deputy occupying the deputy's walk-in-closet-sized office in the APNSA's suite. Steven Hadley and Sandy Berger both served as the principal DAPNSAs before becoming national security advisor.

Subordinate policy staff are usually designated as directors, with the caveat that in offices now headed by deputy assistants to the president, subordinate staff may be designated as special assistants and senior directors. Directorates typically range in size from two to five persons. A directorate of ten is an empire. In addition, the NSC staff consists of a dedicated cadre of career NSC and detailed (assigned from other agencies) support staff, an executive secretariat staff, and the Situation Room staff. The Situation Room is in fact a complex of offices. In addition to providing the site for Principals and Deputies meetings, the Situation Room includes an intelligence analysis and support section and a communications hub capable of connecting the president by telephone or teleconference with heads of state, commanders, and officials worldwide. In addition, there is a telecommunications room, which, like the Situation Room itself, has the capacity to link agencies and personal by video camera on a global and secure basis.[17]

Traditionally about two-thirds of the NSC policy staff is drawn from the career diplomatic and military ranks with the remainder "true" political appointees drawn from think tanks, academia, and campaign staffs. Of course, regardless of origin, all NSC policy staff serve at the pleasure of the president (and national security advisor). The president is not bound as a matter of law to fill his immediate NSC staff using a particular profile so long as candidates meet the necessary requirements for government service, including, at the NSC, possession of Top Secret/Codeword clearance.

There are sound arguments in support of having a mix of career and political appointees on the staff. Career personnel might generally be said to offer expertise, knowledge, and continuity on matters of policy, as well as bureaucratic know-how, crisis management skills, and an understanding of the intelligence process. The NSC budget is also small, and the expense of detailees is assumed by the parent agencies. Political personnel might generally be said to offer policy loyalty and may have special bonds with the president and the national security advisor that facilitate communication and access on difficult policy issues. Political appointees may also bring fresh legs and fresh ideas to old problems. Of course, individual political and career personnel may offer a mix of all these attributes.

As a practical matter, the number of career detailees from any one agency may be limited by the views of the agency head regarding the relative role and influence of departmental officials and the NSC staff. As a matter of law, agencies represented on the NSC may lawfully use their appropriated funds to detail personnel to serve on the NSC staff, although in some cases there are statutory caps on the number of detailees that can serve on the NSC staff at one time. As a result, it should not surprise that for policy, legal, and financial reasons the majority of career staff at the NSC come from the State Department, Defense Department, the military, and the CIA. In addition, recent administrations have supplemented the NSC staff through secondment of Intergovernmental Personnel Act (IPA) interns, who are paid by their parent academic organizations and do not count against White House personnel ceilings. "IPAs" are "interns" in name only, as they are often accomplished experts in their fields rather than interns in the historic Washington sense of the word.

In 1962, when McGeorge Bundy served as APNSA, the NSC staff consisted of 12 persons.[18] Under President Clinton and President Bush, the policy staff has numbered approximately 80. The expansion in the number of NSC staff is arguably linked to the expansion in the president's national security responsibilities as well as the manner in which national security has been defined by successive administrations. By example, one would not have expected President Kennedy's staff to include a directorate dedicated to counter-terrorism. However, such a directorate has existed at the NSC since the 1980s. Similarly, in 1998, a Senior Director for Public Health was added to the NSC for the first time with an eye toward the threat of bioterrorism.

As *the* NSC's substantive responsibilities and correspondingly the NSC staff's responsibilities have grown, the functional requirements have grown as well, as reflected in the existence and size of the administrative, press, and legislative offices. Arguably, the size of the NSC staff also reflects the inherent tendency for those who seek to influence and implement policy to expand their responsibilities by expanding their capacity to attend meetings and generate work product, which means more staff.[19] However, one needs to exercise some caution in looking at numbers alone in assessing the influence of the NSC staff.[20] The critical test is not quantitative but qualitative. Is there sufficient staff to fulfill the president's responsibilities promptly, without creating a bureaucratic layer between cabinet agencies and the president?[21]

Whatever the differences in style and framework between presidents, recent manifestations of the NSC process have gravitated to certain common characteristics as well as shared tensions. The core duties are not defined in statute or by directive. They are derivative of the Constitution and the National Security Act. NSC staff advise and assist the president by serving as the president's eyes and ears within the policy-making bureaucracy. They write information and action memoranda to the APNSA and to the president, usually through or signed by the APNSA. As needed, they coordinate with other White House staff (e.g., speechwriters coordinate with the head of communications, the press office with the press secretary, etc.). They prepare and coordinate input for PC and DC briefing papers. Harder to quantify is the staff's critical role in serving as an engine of government, ensuring that disparate elements of the national security government come together in a coordinated fashion and on a timeline that meets the president's needs and objectives as well as real-world deadlines.

Fundamentally, the success or failure of the NSC staff hinges on its ability to rapidly coordinate the interagency process and in doing so serve as honest brokers of policy and legal input. Policy staff may prefer to become known as independent contributors to national security policy, but the success of the process depends on their willingness to subordinate their own perspectives and accurately communicate to the president not just their views, but those of cabinet officers and agencies. Where a principal has dissented from a policy option or disagrees with essential facts, the staff must honestly communicate this dissent to the president through the APNSA.[22] And, where the NSC staff have deviated from designated or accepted process, then the staff should advise the president as well. In the case of process that is the product of presidential direction, such notification and presidential assent are required as a matter of law. Of course, I am describing a normative but not necessarily uniform practice.

As a matter of longstanding practice based on the constitutional separation of powers, senior advisors to the president within the executive office of the president[23] do not testify before the Congress or legislative commissions. What constitutes a "senior" advisor as a matter of constitutional law or practice is subject to contextual analysis.[24] From an executive perspective, the concept covers senior advisors on the NSC staff who communicate on a regular basis and in a deliberative manner with the president. This legal policy is based on three related concerns. First, since the president cannot be called to testify in his status as chief executive of an independent branch his immediate staff, his alter egos, cannot be compelled to testify in his place. Otherwise, the Congress could accomplish through the president's immediate staff what it could not accomplish directly with the president.

Second, deliberative communications with the president are presumptively subject to an assertion of executive privilege. The president's immediate staff, who do not exercise authority independent of the president, would necessarily implicate that privilege if they were called upon to testify. In theory, there would be no basis to question a senior presidential advisor other than to inquire into the president's deliberations, for if the issue related to a policy decision or its implementation, then a department secretary or subordinate might appropriately provide testimony.

Third, there is a practical aspect to the policy. If the president's immediate advisors were subject to testifying before the Congress, they might do little else in light of the policy and political interests that members of Congress would have in fixing responsibility or credit at the White House. One can imagine the legislative desire to probe into Oval Office discussions, particularly across party lines. In Zbig Brezinski's view (President Carter's national security advisor), if the APNSA were subject to confirmation and subject to testifying on the Hill, it would burden an already complex schedule. It would also create ambiguity as to "who speaks for foreign policy in the government besides the president." In Brezinski's view, it should be the secretary of state.[25] To the extent these concerns are also grounded in concern that the president be able to perform his responsibilities in a timely manner by always having his staff on hand, the position is one of constitutional dimension.

Of course, like common-law privileges, this constitutional privilege is subject to waiver. Thus, exceptions have been made either on an institutional basis (e.g., the director of the Office of Management and Budget testifies regularly and is confirmed by the Senate) and on a specific basis. Administrations of both parties, for example, have "waived" applicable privileges when there have been credible questions of wrongdoing, as for example, when Sherman Adams, President Eisenhower's chief of staff, was authorized by the president to testify regarding the gift of a Vicuña coat from a lobbyist. However, the "credible allegation of wrongdoing" standard while well founded in concept is problematic in implementation. There are reasons a president might authorize his immediate staff to testify before the Congress without the necessity of conceding or appearing to concede the prospect of wrongdoing. Four circumstances come to mind. First, where the Congress (i.e., an applicable committee chair) has the votes to issue a subpoena, or to withhold funding on an important presidential initiative, a prospect more likely to occur across party lines, the president may choose to avoid a constitutional confrontation and accede to a testimonial appearance. Second, the president may do so to avoid an appearance that he is hiding something or covering up and where he is taking a public relations beating in the press for doing so. Third, there may be *sui generis* reasons for authorizing a waiver – for example, an extraordinary circumstance like the 9/11 Commission or the request of an aide to appear to clear his name. Fourth, the president may authorize an appearance where he perceives it in his best policy interests to communicate his message.

More likely, the president's representatives will seek to accommodate the competing legislative and executive interests by offering an alternative to testimony, such as a briefing. It is the national security lawyer's role to identify the enduring consequences of varying from the "no testimony" norm when it is in the president's policy interests to do so, and when it is not. As a matter of law the waiver of executive privilege in one instance does not waive the privilege in a distinct context. Nonetheless, such waivers serve as political precedents and may make it harder to hold the line in future cases.

In the case of the NSC staff, and the sorts of daily requests that occur for policy briefings on presidential decisions, administrations have sought to develop mechanisms of accommodation – constitutional rules of the road – to avoid endless separation of powers battles. Hence, as a general matter, NSC staff will not testify or appear before Congress in circumstances bearing "the indicia of testimony," such as hearings or briefings that include transcripts, oaths, and cameras. They do, however, informally brief members and staff.

Under the Hatch Act and Hatch Act Amendments Act of 1994, employees paid by the National Security Council, as well those employees paid by the State Department, Defense Department, Central Intelligence Agency, and the military services – which is to say a majority of personnel on the NSC staff – are prohibited from engaging in partisan political activities. Employees who violate the Act are subject to administrative sanctions, including removal from their positions. Partisan political activities are, among other things, activities intended to advance (or impede) the election of candidates for partisan political office.[26] Policy positions may be associated with a political party, but that does not inherently make a policy dispute subject to the in connection with a partisan political campaign. Consider the distinction between talking points drafted by NSC staff to articulate the president's policy on Iraq that are intended for use with foreign diplomats, members of Congress, or the press, and talking points that are drafted for the specific use of a campaign or candidate.

Although the law and corresponding regulations offer little black-letter clarity, during the 1990s, NSC staff were barred from writing or reviewing campaign materials and speeches, including those materials used by the president. Nor could staff speak at or attend political events. (NSC staff could attend in the capacity of NSC representatives on call to the president for the briefing of national security issues that might arise during his absence from the White House. In such cases, the NSC representative would sit in the holding room.) In addition, the Situation Room and facilities were not used to forward political materials to the president. What the staff could do was provide off-the-shelf policy materials to the president's staff engaged in political events applying a general rule of thumb: if it would not be provided to a public requester then it was not appropriately shared with campaign staff or used for a political event. It follows that NSC staff memoranda should not incorporate partisan political factors or considerations.

As a matter of process and legal policy, application of the Hatch Act ensures that the president and his senior staff have the benefit of national security advice, free from partisan political input. It also protects career nonpolitical staff, like military officers, from being directed or pressured to work on partisan political campaigns. In contrast, the president, who is accountable for his political and policy views through the electoral process, and employees paid by the White House Office (which would include the majority of the president's most senior staff including the APNSA) are "not Hatched," and thus, are permitted to engage in otherwise lawful partisan political activities. However, as a matter of tradition, but not law, national security advisors at least since Brent Scowcroft in the Ford Administration and their deputies (if they are White House Office payroll employees and not otherwise Hatched)[27] have refrained from taking visible political roles or visible participation in political events, including the mere attendance at political events. Readers can assess for themselves the degree to which they believe specific APNSAs have followed this policy.[28] Regardless, the APNSA is available (and should be available) as an interface between the policy components of the White House and the partisan political components of the White House to ensure that the president's political words both accurately track policy and/or do not unwittingly affect policy. Whether the APNSA's role should extend beyond this point is a question of personal judgment for the APNSA, subject, one hopes, to the prudential advice of counsel.[29] The APNSA's adherence to the policy will likely depend on, among other factors, his view on the importance of U.S. national security policy being viewed as nonpartisan and the degree to which he believes the APNSA should present objective national security advice to the president free of partisan political content.

3. Informal and Ad Hoc Process

Previous sections have considered the NSC and the NSC process, which along with the HSC process, serves as the president's principal mechanisms for national security decision-making. However, a president's national security process is as likely to be defined by the nature and tolerance for informal and ad hoc processes as it is by its formal arrangements. That is because the majority of contact between the president's advisors is not at Principals' meetings, but during the innumerable daily conversations on secure telephone lines or pull asides in the hall. National security process could not function otherwise. Issues do not wait for meetings. Neither do presidents. The national security lawyer cannot function effectively without identifying these informal mechanisms and figuring out how to provide meaningful and timely advice to these processes.

Considerations of time management and efficiency, as well as concerns of secrecy, leaks – and in some cases the desire to avoid debate and dissent – also result in establishment of ad hoc decisional mechanisms. Some of these mechanisms take on formality and structure. For example, the president and vice president typically have regular meetings scheduled around weekly meals. In addition, key principals might hold weekly meal meetings. During the Clinton Administration, for example, the secretaries of state, defense and the national security advisor held a weekly meeting known as "the ABC lunch" for Secretary Albright, Mr. Berger, and Secretary Cohen. President George W. Bush's second APNSA Steve Hadley favors a weekly breakfast meeting with the secretaries of state and defense. For his part, Frank Carlucci, who served as one of President Reagan's national security advisors, has stated that his NSC process was fraught with interagency tension and competition until he started holding one-on-one meals with his counterparts.

Additional bilateral meetings may occur as well between principals to address sensitive intelligence or bureaucratic problems. Vice President Cheney and Secretary Rumsfeld were known to hold regular bilateral meetings and conversations in Washington and at their Maryland vacation homes. APNSA Berger would meet on a weekly scheduled basis with the DCI, in addition to the many ad hoc meetings and principals meetings the two might otherwise attend together. The APNSA would also meet on a bimonthly basis with the attorney general and FBI director. These meetings were useful for discussing sensitive issues that might be avoided at larger group meetings. Such meetings also served to trigger bureaucracies to identify problems to resolve, as well as serving as regularly scheduled mechanisms to propel issues up and out, rather than allow them to linger in bureaucratic limbo between levels of decision. These bilateral meetings also gave the principal participants an opportunity to test whether differences in outlook at the staff level, in fact, reflected differences in agency views, or merely differences in personality, disputes over turf, or simply lack of confidence in the players at lower ranks.

More ad hoc were National Security Advisor Berger's meetings with the "Small Group." This small group of cabinet Principals and one to three NSC staff would meet as necessary to address sensitive issues relating to counter-terrorism, including operational proposals for taking military and intelligence actions against Al Qaeda and other terrorist targets. The Small Group would meet on short notice (by secure phone in the middle of the night if need be) and usually without a formal agenda or a formal record of decision. However, some Small Group meetings resulted in memoranda to or meetings with the president, proposing a particular action or indicating why a particular action was not recommended. The strength of the Small Group was its agility, secrecy, and the speed with which it could consider timely operational opportunities. The weakness in the process was that it could exclude critical actors, persons who might otherwise have a source of knowledge or policy view that could test the proposed action, but whom would not know that their knowledge was relevant or needed. Indeed, they may not have known the Small Group existed.

Such "small" processes are dependent on the knowledge and integrity of those who staff them, as they operate outside the ordinary staffing processes and patterns, which are designed to ensure key substantive and procedural elements of decision are not omitted. Thus, decisionmakers who employ or tolerate out-of-channel process, as all national security advisors ultimately do in one form or another, should ask: have they identified all the known information relevant to decision, and is there additional information that might bear on the decision within agencies not represented? Is there a devil's advocate or honest broker role-playing within the small group? Has the ad hoc process balanced the need for speed, decision, and secrecy against the parallel need for accuracy, efficacy, and in some cases law? Finally, is the process intended, or does it have the effect of, masking dissent?

As the majority of contact between national security Principals is informal, likewise, the majority of contact between the president and his senior cabinet and White House advisors occurs outside the context of formal NSC, HSC, or cabinet meetings. The APNSA meets on a daily basis with the president in the Oval Office in the context of formal meetings, informal meetings on specified topics, and during national security time. National security time is closely guarded time reserved for the APNSA to bring his or her list to the president and walk down the list. This is no different from any other staff context where the subordinate briefs the boss. Cabinet officers do not have the same degree of access, and depending on the APNSA and the extent of his prior relationship with the president, will rarely have opportunity to meet with the president one-on-one, which is to say without the APNSA present. More likely, time with the president will come in the context of formal but small meetings in the Oval Office or at formal NSC meetings.

Of course, these same officials may also communicate on a daily basis with the president on paper or by telephone. In the case of the APNSA, this may take the form of ten to thirty action and information memoranda a day, drafted by staff and edited and signed by the APNSA. One of the intentional Oz-like mysteries at the NSC and the White House is what happens to the paper when it leaves the APNSA's desk. In some cases, usually relatively routine, the staff secretary will summarize the memoranda with a short half note on the top. Where the matter is especially sensitive it will be delivered sealed to the president or by the hand of the APNSA or a deputy.

Cabinet officers regularly send the president updates, sometimes called "night notes." They visit one-on-one (or more likely with the APNSA present), and confer by telephone. In addition, they can request (or insist) upon attaching their specific views to memoranda going to the president. According to the 9/11 Commission, for example, Attorney General Reno attached a memorandum for the president raising policy concerns about a proposal to kill Osama Bin Laden, including the risk of reciprocal attacks.[30] The attorney general also stated her agreement, reflected in an NSC staff memorandum, that it was lawful under the law of armed conflict to resort to overt or covert lethal force against Osama Bin Laden in legitimate self-defense.[31] Of course, whether the president in fact reads such additional views will depend on the president's style and method for reviewing memoranda.[32]

It was my practice, in memoranda going to the president, to flag the dissenting or concurring views in the memorandum to ensure that the president was aware of the attachment and its intent. However, for the most part, Principals rely on the APNSA and the NSC staff to accurately portray and convey views to the president. Some Principals may insist on seeing the actual memorandum to the president. However, this practice is frowned upon by White House lawyers aware that documents circulated outside the NSC may become subject to external forms of discovery. The Freedom of Information Act, for example, does not apply to the NSC, but does apply to agencies. Moreover, agencies are more likely to produce such documents, including draft documents, to the Congress because agency personnel are generally less attuned to constitutional sensitivities about the president's deliberative process and more attuned to the costs of bucking their authorizing and appropriating committees. Of course, where precise wording is critical in characterizing a position, perhaps a constitutional nuance, a staff member might read portions of draft memoranda to a Principal over a secure line. Because these practices and processes are informal, they will vary from administration to administration and are heavily dependent on the views and personalities of the participants. As in other contexts, it is prudent not to create expectations that one cannot uphold or that do not reflect the president's or the APNSA's expectations.

Whether formal or informal, process can be dictated (or managed) by something as simple as the size of the room. A decisionmaker wanting a small meeting without staff might select a lunch venue. If the goal is to limit the number of staff to the "Principals plus one," a meeting in the Situation Room will do, given the room's small size. A meeting in the Roosevelt Room or the Cabinet Room, with their enormous tables and ample seating, will inevitably result in two or more staff showing up with each Principal. Similarly, an agency's ability to participate in the national security process, particularly an agency new to the process, may depend on something as mundane as the mechanical necessity of having a secure fax machine, or a cultural factor, such as the absence of staff with the necessary security clearances.

The success or failure of decision-making will depend on the success or failure of this informal process as much as it depends on the formal operation of working groups, Deputies Committee meetings, Principals Committee meetings, and presidential memoranda. Does it involve the same rigor of analysis and requirement for agreement and dissent as formal process or briefing papers, meetings, and summaries of conclusions will generate? Are the same relevant decisionmakers included in the discussion when the informal mechanism is employed as when the formal process is engaged? If not, is the president aware of who is missing and why? Does the APNSA insist on lawyers seeing all memos going to the president? Do the president and his senior advisors tolerate or encourage oral communications that may escape review, result in confusion regarding the scope of decision, and escape accountability? Does the APNSA include lawyers at the beginning of the policy process and not just at the end?

On the one hand, a president who insists on ad hoc meetings, or permits end-runs of the process, may not receive the same quality of briefing as one who adheres strictly to process. Critical views may be left out and Principals who were, or feel that they were, snubbed may implement the president's policy directives with less zeal, if at all. On the other hand, a president whose door is not figuratively open may miss frank input and exchange that may only emerge during the informal or casual moment, perhaps with the sort of look or words that cannot be, or will not be, conveyed in a presidential memo.

C. THE OFFICE OF THE VICE PRESIDENT

The vice president and his staff occupy an unusual position within the White House, straddling both the formal process of decision as well as embodying the most informal aspects of presidential decision. The Office of the Vice President's (OVP) formal national security role is a matter of public record, as reflected in NSPD-1. The vice president is a member of the council and "when the [president is] absent from a meeting of the NSC, at [the president's] direction may preside." In addition, "the Chief of Staff and the National Security Advisor to the Vice President shall attend all meetings of the NSC/PC." The directive also designates these officials as regular members of the Deputies Committee.

In contrast, President Clinton's comparable directive recognizes the vice president as a statutory member of the NSC, but does not contemplate his presiding over meetings in the president's place. The directive designates the assistant to the vice president for national security affairs a member of the Deputies Committee. However, there is continuity as well as distinction between administrations, particularly in practice.

In both administrations, the contemplated process affords the vice president multiple bites at the policy apple, with the vice president's national security advisor serving on the Deputies as well as the Principals Committees (by direction in the case of President Bush and by practice in the case of President Clinton). Although time consuming for the vice president's staff, this process comes with the added advantage that the vice president's national security advisor helps define how deputies shape and report issues to the principals, and then influences the manner in which the principals consider the issue. In contrast, however, the defined role of the vice president in NSPD-1 is more expansive than that in PDD-1. This is reflected in language designating both the vice president's national security advisor and chief of staff as members of the Principals and Deputies Committees.

At the same time, the vice president plays a significant informal national security role. While a statutory member of the NSC, the vice president also resides outside the NSC process and plays no formal decisional role. Unlike the president, who bears constitutional and statutory authority, and the secretaries of state and defense, who wield delegated constitutional and statutory authority, the vice president wields only the authority the president grants him and the stature and persuasion that come with the office. The vice president is effectively a minister without portfolio and without bureaucratic allegiance, or ultimate responsibility. Therefore, the vice president can wade in or out of issues depending on his interest and presidential expectations. In this way, the vice president and his staff are well positioned to "think outside the box," or play the role of devil's advocate.

In performing these functions, the vice president can call upon NSC staff as well as on his own national security staff for advice and assistance. Typically this staff is drawn from professional military officers, whereas the VP's national security advisor is typically a close confidant of the vice president's from political or policy life. However, the vice president is not subject to the same staffing requirements as the NSC staff, who for example, must submit memoranda to the president through the APNSA. Reworded, the vice president is subject only to the expectations and requirements imposed by the president, for it is the president alone who can direct the vice president to solicit the views of other principals before coming to the president. Alternatively, the president can accept the vice president's input as is.

Former Secretary of State Powell and others have asserted that many decisions involving Iraq were taken to the president outside the NSC process directly by the vice president and the secretary of defense. By implication, Colin Powell is suggesting that key voices and facts were omitted from discussion and critical decisions were not known to other policymakers. In the absence of formal memoranda or summaries of conclusion, the views of other principals were subject to intentional or unintentional mischaracterization by the handful of actors in the room with the president, if they were characterized at all.[33]

D. APPRAISAL

Observers have suggested that the president must select from two models of national security government. One model posits a cabinet government, comprised of principal agency officers like the secretaries of state and defense, who advise the president and implement policy using cabinet agencies and officers. The other model is an NSC model where decision-making authority and implementation is not only exercised by the president but is also ceded (or surrendered) by agencies to an ever expanding and powerful NSC staff. This NSC staff is viewed as moving beyond advising and assisting the president into actual policy control, direction, and implementation.

In theory, the president might be able to ignore his cabinet and rely exclusively on the NSC staff. In practice, there is no inherent clash of models. What varies is the difference in tone, emphasis, and balance between administrations. Individual staff will vie for policy impact and will seek to expand their reach by expanding their staff. Some NSC staff will seek to arrogate to themselves agency (and indeed presidential) authorities.

When evaluating the NSC staff and process, one needs to account for inductive reasoning. One's perspective on the process is often driven by one's reaction to a particular incident or a particular personality at the NSC and not the overall process. Oliver North is not indicative of the NSC process; he is indicative of a failure in process. But absent a conspiracy of evasion, a North can only operate with the concurrence, or acquiescence, of the APNSA and/or the cabinet principals who might later complain regarding their own loss of authority, for the president's principal cabinet officers and *the* NSC are one and the same.

The president must have a staff to advise, assist, and facilitate his execution of his responsibilities. An immediate staff is also essential to feed the Principals and Deputies Committees and the Oval Office inbox. Whether this staff goes further to exercise an independent policy voice and is allowed to challenge, and not just test, policy options proposed by agencies is a question of tone and leadership. As a matter of law, policy will continue to be implemented pursuant to presidential authority or agency authority, by agency officers (unless the president directs otherwise). The key to this national security process is finding the right balance between having enough staff to assist the president, without creating an additional layer of bureaucracy that impedes rather than facilitates decision and meaningful input. This balance cannot be dictated by directive alone. It must reflect the daily observation of the national security advisor, president, and principals on how the process is working . . . or not working. Each administration will make different adjustments in reaching for this balance.

Harder to define on paper are those issues that should come to the president for decision. Three factors should weigh in this determination. First, as a matter of constitutional and statutory law, some decisions *must* come to the president. For example, while lawyers may debate the scope of the president's authority as commander in chief, few lawyers seriously debate that it is the commander in chief and not the secretary of defense or a combatant commander who must, in the first instance, authorize the entry of U.S. forces into combat.[34] Whether additional decisions also require the commander in chief's authorization will depend on the scope of the president's initial authorization, the constitutional views of the president and his lawyers, and prudential factors.[35]

In more mundane fashion, the president alone can exercise certain statutory authority. At times this may seem ministerial and unduly burdensome on a chief executive who is already overextended. On the other hand, the process of generating a report for presidential signature should ensure a certain level of interagency review. This process will help to confirm that the policy proposed or reported on is in fact supported by the president's senior advisors and national security agencies and that the report itself is qualitatively appropriate for presidential signature.[36]

Second, there are matters of policy that *should* come to the president in light of their importance. For example, the secretary of state has ample legal authority to engage in diplomacy as the secretary of state, but it is not likely that the secretary would table a Middle East peace initiative without the president's concurrence. In contrast, the secretary might conclude a model extradition treaty or postal treaty, about which the president may not be constructively or actually aware until the treaty is transmitted under presidential signature for Senate advice and consent.

In addition, there are matters for which the president will be held accountable whether or not he in fact makes the decision. For example, the president may not be involved in a particular tactical deployment of U.S. armed forces; however, if there are U.S. casualties, the president may be asked to defend the policy that put the soldier in harm's way. Therefore, the president, or more likely his immediate staff, may insist on being kept informed of small details of policy implementation, which may be perceived in the field as micromanagement rather than information flow.

Finally, the president sits at the crossroads of executive branch decision-making. Where there are differences of view between agencies and/or cabinet officers, the president alone may have the legal, moral, or policy authority to resolve those differences. (Obviously not all differences between agencies warrant or are appropriate for presidential decision.) As important, where many national security issues were previously perceived as issues solely for the statutory members of the NSC to address, for example, arms control, most national security matters today cut across a wide array of functional and agency disciplines, like homeland security. Therefore, even where there is agreement among agencies on how to proceed, the president alone may carry the legal and policy weight to quickly integrate a decision into positive bureaucratic response.

There are inherent tensions in the president's national security process. In an age of modern communication there are few decisions, including tactical decisions, over which the president and White House might not exercise some control, should they choose to do so. This is not new. President Ford's White House communicated directly with an Air Force pilot regarding whether or not to disable the rudder of a fishing boat transporting the *Mayaguez* crew in the Gulf of Thailand.[37] What is new is the range of matters that the president and his immediate staff can directly control using secure communications reaching into almost every military rucksack or diplomatic briefcase. Moreover, the 24-hour news cycle tends to focus on the president and the White House, creating a sense that the White House must respond to every international event. The more the White House feels pressure to do so, the more pressure it will likely feel to control the outcome of these events, even if such control is dysfunctional at the tactical level and the issues not of a presidential character.

As a general rule, information flows faster uphill than down. A presidential request for information is (usually) quickly fulfilled. This is human nature. Managers expect subordinates to keep them informed; but not all managers feel the same sense of immediacy in reporting back to subordinates. Good process must also ensure that decisions and policy nuance are passed down the chain of command with the rapidity and clarity that the president intended.

Commentators sometimes paint White House control in broad strokes of approval or disdain. The right measure of presidential control is contextual. An essential component of national security process is finding the right balance between operational efficacy and presidential accountability for national security decisions that reflect the president's policy direction. In some cases, efficacy may mean more presidential control; for example, where a definitive change in policy is warranted or commanders do not agree on how to proceed. In other cases, presidential control can delay decision, or deprive a decision of the advantage in perception and immediacy afforded the actor on the ground. In addition to contextual factors specific to the issue addressed, the measure of White House control and participation will also depend on intangible and static factors like the personality and style of the president and his confidence in his subordinates.

Constitutional government is all about process, including who makes the decisions, how officials are elected or selected, and what process is due before the government acts. Process, like collegiality, is a value-neutral term. It describes the manner in which decisions are made, or are not made, not whether they are made in an efficient, thoughtful, or effective manner. Thus, process can facilitate national security or impede national security.

Whatever process a president ultimately adopts, decisionmakers and lawyers should recall the observations from Chapter 3. Bad process is bad. It may impede decision, dilute decision, and be used to bypass critical actors as well as the law. Good process is good. It leads to better national security decisions and it results in more meaningful application of the law and constitutional values. Good process ensures that the correct actors are in the room, with as much and as good information as is available at that time. It avoids oversights. In a constitutional democracy, good process also helps to ensure that decisions are made in accordance with law and by those actors the people elected to make those security decisions most important to our well-being. In turn, good process also establishes accountability, which in turn improves result.

Process need not be antithetical to timely decision, operational timelines, or to secrecy. Process must find the right balance between speed and strength, secrecy and input. But process can always meet deadlines. There is no excuse for shortcuts. Process can be made to work faster and smarter. By example, if legal review is warranted but time is short, the attorney general alone can review a matter. If need be, he or she can do so while sitting next to the president in the Oval Office. The problem some policymakers have with process is not "process," but the prospect of disagreement or legal objection and that can take time to resolve.

Process is substance when it determines or influences outcome. Where critical actors are excluded from the process of decision, for example, critical facts or insights may be omitted from policy consideration.

Finally, process is contextual. Will all presidents use the same process? No. Will all lawyers define their duties in like manner? No. Subject to law, these determinations are contextual, for process is also dependent on culture, personality, and style. Therefore, policymakers and lawyers must consciously evaluate the efficiency of their own process as well as to identify any seams between formal and informal mechanisms of decision. Whether formal or informal, the president will ultimately end up with the process he wants or the process that he tolerates. This is as true of intelligence as any of the national security tools.

7 *Intelligence*

This chapter considers the intelligence instrument, the means and methods of gathering, analyzing, and using information relevant to national security as well as covert action. The chapter starts by placing intelligence in historical, bureaucratic, and legal context. The chapter next considers the five intelligence functions: collection, analysis and dissemination, counterintelligence, covert action, and liaison. With each topic, the chapter identifies fundamental principles as well as current and coming legal policy issues. One of these issues is the practice of rendition. The text illustrates how, in a hypothetical context, the law might apply and how legal policy and process might pertain.

The chapter closes with three observations about the intelligence function. First, intelligence is the fuel of counter-terrorism. Second, the institution of the presidency is the engine of counter-terrorism. Third, national security lawyers are navigators that help guide the intelligence vessel away or through legal shoals. They also facilitate policy through the identification and appraisal of rigorous and timely process before, during, and after exercise of the function.

A. BUREAUCRATIC AND LEGAL FRAMEWORK

American intelligence gathering and counterintelligence pre-date the Republic. Nathan Hale's service and sacrifice as a revolutionary war spy is celebrated in statue at the Central Intelligence Agency, outside the Department of Justice, and at Yale University, from which he graduated in the class of 1773. Major Andre's trial as a British spy during the same war is depicted in lithograph in the offices of judge advocates throughout the U.S. Armed Forces with the regularity of a photograph of the commander in chief. But Hale and Andre were one-mission spies. As noted in Chapter 5, Benjamin Franklin, the colonial envoy to France, although less noted, was far more successful as an intelligence agent. Employing tradecraft such as secret writing and dead drops, Franklin organized an espionage ring, planted disinformation in the Paris press, and organized clandestine arms shipments to the colonies.[1]

Following independence, presidents made immediate use of intelligence agents to collect foreign intelligence and to influence events. This was done on the basis that intelligence was an instrument of executive authority and a necessary function of national defense.[2] More often than not, this was done without congressional authorization, input, or notification.[3] Presidents have asserted a parallel authority to engage in affirmative clandestine activities to influence events abroad that are characterized today as covert action.[4]

The president's intelligence powers are derived from his enumerated national security authorities described in Chapter 4. This authority is recognized in longstanding executive practice (Frankfurter's practice and gloss), as well as in those few Supreme Court decisions that address intelligence, such as *Totten*, *Doe*, *Curtiss-Wright*, *Snepp*, and *Nixon*, although generally, the intelligence references are oblique as in *Nixon* and *Curtiss-Wright*. This authority has also been recognized in statute at least since the National Security Act of 1947 recognized the president's central intelligence role.

Until World War II, the United States did not have a national and professional intelligence service, structure, or outlook. Intelligence remained the professional domain of the military services and the informal domain of ad hoc presidential agents and confidants.[5] The OSS, and subsequently the CIA, and more broadly a national intelligence framework emerged after Pearl Harbor, was shaped by World War II, and was subsequently transformed into a permanent national security tool with the advent of the Cold War. A corresponding bureaucracy and statutory intelligence framework followed.

1. Legal Framework

Although there are a number of statutes that address intelligence (if one includes those containing intelligence exceptions, there are numerous statutes), the National Security Act of 1947, as amended, remains the bedrock intelligence law. Over time there have been important amendments to the Act. The Intelligence Authorization Act of 1991, for example, included the first statutory definition of covert action. The Intelligence Reform and Terrorism Prevention Act of 2004 (Reform Act), among other things, established a new position of director of national intelligence (DNI), permitting the CIA director to focus on human intelligence collection.[6] Of course, intelligence law is also found in unclassified (e.g., E.O. 12333) and classified (e.g., the Attorney General Guidelines, intelligence community directives), and executive and presidential directives.[7]

The National Security Act creates and defines the national intelligence mission of the United States, recognizing both a strategic (geopolitical) need and a tactical military need. The Act established the Central Intelligence Agency and, along with the CIA Act of 1949, serves as the Agency's statutory foundation. In addition, the Act created the position of director of central intelligence, who until 2004 was designated "the principal adviser to the president for intelligence matters related to the national security," and served as head of the U.S. intelligence community, as well as head of the CIA.

However, in response to September 11, and recommendations by the 9/11 Commission, as well as intelligence shortcomings identified by the president's Weapons of Mass Destruction Commission,[8] the Congress amended the Act in 2004 to create the position of director of national intelligence. The DNI has three principal statutory responsibilities: (1) to "serve as head of the intelligence community"; (2) to "act as the principal advisor to the president, to the National Security Council, and the Homeland Security Council for intelligence matters related to national security"; and, (3) to "oversee and direct the implementation of the National Intelligence Program."[9] In addition, the DNI is responsible for providing national intelligence to the president, the heads of departments and agencies, the Chairman of the Joint Chiefs of Staff and senior military commanders, and the Congress.[10] The DNI is also charged with overseeing the National Intelligence Council, the Non-Proliferation Center, the Counterintelligence Center, and the Counter-Terrorism Center. Each "center" existed in some form prior to 9/11, but now functions under national (DNI) as opposed to agency (CIA) auspices. The DNI is also responsible for reporting to the president and the Congress each year on any legal impediments to his functions or legal requirements.[11] Although one might hope that this function would be performed in any event, this provision is noteworthy. It creates a requirement – a tripwire – for the DNI to appraise the state of the law each year and its impact on the intelligence function. It also places the DNI on record as to the results and then places the Congress on the hook for responding to the DNI's report. If intelligence officers are not satisfied with their authority to recruit, then here is a vehicle in which to communicate that concern internally, and if necessary, externally to the legislative branch. There is no excuse for identifying a legal obstacle after the fact.

In turn, the amended act assigns to the director of the CIA, who no longer serves concurrently as the DCI, four general responsibilities:

(1) collect intelligence through human sources and by other appropriate means [and repeating the language of the National Security Act] except that the Director of Central Intelligence Agency shall have no police, subpoena, or law enforcement powers or internal security functions;

(2) correlate and evaluate intelligence related to the national security and provide appropriate dissemination of such intelligence;

(3) provide overall direction for and coordination of the collection of national intelligence outside the United States through human sources by elements of the intelligence community authorized to undertake such collection and, in coordination . . . ; and,

(4) perform such other functions and duties related to intelligence affecting the national security as the president or the Director of National Intelligence may direct.[12]

Importantly, the Act confirms the special relationship between the president and the intelligence function. Thus, among other things, as originally enacted the Act charged the head of the Central Intelligence Agency to "perform such other functions and duties related to intelligence affecting national security as the president or the National Security Council may direct."[13] When originally used in the National Security Act of 1947, this description was understood to encompass the conduct of covert action. Such "special activities" were subsequently recognized in the 1974 Hughes-Ryan Amendment to the Foreign Assistance Act, the 1980 Intelligence Oversight Act, and most expressly, in the Intelligence Authorization Act of 1991, amending the National Security Act. The president's central role is also recognized in the Reform Act, which assigns to the president responsibility for implementing and overseeing what the Act refers to as an "information sharing environment" (ISE).[14] In plain English, the president is supposed to ensure that national security information is identified, shared, evaluated, and disseminated in a timely and effective manner between government agencies and within government agencies. The president has assigned this function to the DNI, but the responsibility remains with the president.

In short, the National Security Act recognizes that the president is not just a consumer of intelligence; he is an intelligence actor and decisionmaker. This observation should not be lost on intelligence officials who disagree with policy, or commentators who disagree with the acts of commission or omission placed at CIA's door, rather than at the door of the NSC Situation Room or the Oval Office.

This special relationship between president and intelligence is recognized in executive directives as well. E.O. 12333, for example, states as the first goal of the national intelligence effort:

Goals. The United States intelligence effort shall provide the president and the National Security Council with the necessary information on which to base decisions concerning the conduct and development of foreign, defense and economic policy, and the protection of United States national interests from foreign security threats. All departments and agencies shall cooperate fully to fulfill this goal. (Para. 1.1)

Further,

The NSC shall act as the highest Executive Branch entity that provides review of, guidance for and direction to the conduct of all national foreign intelligence, counterintelligence, and special activities, and attendant policies and programs. (Para. 1.2(a)).

Presidential direction of the intelligence function may take legal form in presidential directives (such as Presidential Decision Directive-35, "Intelligence Requirements," 2 March 1995, and its successor instruments, including National Security Presidential Decision-26 "Intelligence Priorities"[15]), covert action findings, or executive orders. Executive Order 12333 (1981), as amended, remains an enduring presidential directive addressing the structure of the intelligence community. Presidential direction will also take informal and persuasive form. This occurs, for example, when the president visits or responds to Principals meetings, during the president's intelligence briefings, or during the constant telephonic contact between principal actors or their staff during which the national security advisor or homeland security advisor will convey the president's views.

Of course, as the text cited in Executive Order 12333 above demonstrates, the success or failure of presidential oversight of the intelligence function is only partly based on formal presidential direction. While the president can order cooperation and coordination, only daily management and contact with the line officers can ensure its existence. Leadership and not law will ultimately determine whether the intelligence instrument is successfully employed.

2. Congressional Oversight

The National Security Act also provides the framework for congressional oversight of intelligence activities. Outside the framework statutes, the day-to-day function of intelligence remained an executive domain until the Watergate era, when Congress began to assert its authority over the intelligence function. In response to real, as well as perceived, abuses at home and abroad, in 1976 the Church Committee concluded that

Congress has failed to provide the necessary statutory guidelines to ensure that intelligence agencies carry out their necessary missions in accord with constitutional processes.[16]

Congress responded by passing, among other laws, the Intelligence Oversight Act and the Foreign Intelligence Surveillance Act (discussed earlier), as well as by establishing two permanent select committees to authorize intelligence budgets and oversee intelligence activities. Presidents have taken other enduring actions by executive order, in part, to forestall legislation that might later bind the president's hand. Notable in this category was President Ford's 1976 order prohibiting "assassination" presently documented in E.O. 12333.[17]

As with the war power, Congress's authority over the intelligence function is found in the funding power, the necessary and proper clause, its general legislative power, as well as the enumerated authorities the Congress possesses over national defense. But contrast Congress's portrayal of its constitutional authority over the military instrument in the War Powers Resolution with its authority over the intelligence instrument in the National Security Act. In the War Powers Resolution, the 93rd Congress imposed a requirement for prior consultation ("in every possible instance") before use of the military instrument. Further, the resolution purports to exercise Congress's war power on a contingent basis by limiting certain military deployments to sixty days or less absent subsequent congressional authorization. In contrast, with covert action the Congress receives "prior notification," and consistent with sources and methods is kept fully and currently informed of ongoing intelligence activities. Moreover, with covert action, the law acknowledges the possibility that the Congress may not receive even that.

For sure, each act captures a constitutional moment in time, representing the majority views of a particular Congress, and not necessarily settled constitutional law. But the differences are noteworthy as is the fact that both statutes were passed in the wake of presidential "scandal" where the constitutional perspective of the legislative branch was ascendant. Indeed, all three branches, as noted earlier, have recognized the president's special relationship to the intelligence function.

In an area where few outside the executive branch can assert policy insight based on access to intelligence information, members of the intelligence committees are better situated to test programs, audit funding, and validate clandestine executive actions, and where appropriate, inform the public that they have done so. Whether this role has been performed effectively is, and has been, a matter of debate, and sometimes distraction. What is certain is that Congress's role in intelligence is a permanent one. As discussed in Chapter 3, in a system of shared powers and separate branches the Congress can provide a source of legitimacy and constitutional safeguard to intelligence activities that are generally conducted outside the reach of public knowledge and review. At times, the committee members and staff may be the only persons outside the NSC process and the relevant intelligence agencies aware of an activity. Certainly, the witting members of the intelligence committees may be the only actors in the know without a direct policy stake in the success or funding of the activity other than the executive branch lawyers involved. Therefore, whether their views are desired or not, they may be the only source of "outside" perspective and validation, particularly with respect to whether an activity is worth the risk.

However, congressional oversight is also selective. Few members of Congress outside the committees possess the background or the standing to address intelligence issues. Moreover, by definition the intelligence committees operate with the inherently inductive and incomplete knowledge that comes from periodic briefings rather than daily contact with operators and policymakers. Members see only part of the picture, and then only that part of the picture contained in executive talking points that have survived layers of editing and that are designed to fend off policy or partisan attack. Moreover, where members do follow intelligence closely, the interest tends to flow toward the "sexy" areas, and not to areas like computer interoperability, where appraisal and funding may be needed most. Readers can judge for themselves the extent to which the committees have functioned in a nonpartisan, bipartisan, or partisan manner. In the past decade, both sides of the aisle have stated that the other side has acted with political motive. As a matter of voting record, neither committee has acted with bipartisan unity.

Both the 9/11 Commission and the WMD Commission included recommendations to reform the manner in which Congress conducts intelligence oversight. In particular, the commissions were critical of the episodic and reactive nature of oversight as well as the disparate sources of congressional input into the design and funding of the instrument.[18]

3. National–Military Bifurcation

From the beginning, intelligence in both qualitative and quantitative measure contained a significant, and some would argue, predominant military perspective, even as the public increasingly identified "intelligence" with the CIA, and then, disproportionately so with a subordinate fraction of the intelligence mission – covert action. The National Security Act recognizes the special role of the military in generating and using both tactical and strategic intelligence. Thus, Congress originally expressed its sense that either the director or the deputy director of central intelligence be a commissioned military officer, or have comparable experience, but that both positions could not be occupied by military officers at the same time.[19] Comparable language was included in the 2004 Reform Act. Thus, "not more than one of the individuals serving in the positions of DNI or principal deputy DNI may be a commissioned officer of the Armed Forces in active status." Further, the law expresses the sense of the Congress that, under ordinary circumstances, it is desirable that one of the individuals serving in these positions be an active duty officer, or "have by training or experience, an appreciation of military intelligence activities and requirements."[20]

The Reform Act recognizes the theoretical importance of fusing a military need for tactical and strategic intelligence with a policy need for political and strategic intelligence.[21] However, the law also incorporates a tense (rather than settled) compromise between proponents of a single centralized source of control over the nation's intelligence capabilities, and advocates of bifurcated military control over military intelligence. (Neither camp places much emphasis on the role of the president as the centralized source of control.) For example, the law adopts a bifurcation in responsibility over the day-to-day intelligence function between the secretary of defense and the director of national intelligence. Thus, the Act designates the DNI as the head of the intelligence community responsible for "establishing the requirements and priorities to govern national intelligence." At the same time it assigns the secretary of defense line and budget authority over a majority of intelligence agencies including the National Security Agency. This authority is generally exercised through the undersecretary of defense for intelligence. In fact, eight of the sixteen intelligence community components are subject to the direction of the secretary of defense, not the DNI. By another measure the secretary of defense, and not the DNI, controls 80–85 percent of the intelligence budget and most of its personnel.[22]

Not surprisingly, this bifurcation between the DNI and the secretary of defense mirrors a tradition in outlook between the four congressional committees whose policy and budget jurisdiction is most at stake – the intelligence committees and the armed services committees. Section 1018 of the Reform Act makes this tension explicit, stating:

> The President shall issue guidelines to ensure the effective implementation and execution within the executive branch of the authorities granted to the Director of National Intelligence by this title and the amendments made by this title, in a manner that respects and does not abrogate the statutory responsibilities of the heads of the departments of the United States Government concerning such departments, including, but not limited to: ... (2) the authority of the principal officers of the executive departments as heads of their respective departments. [Specific reference to the enabling statutes of the Departments of State, Energy, Homeland Security, and Defense follow in the text.]

In fairness, the Reform Act gives the DNI coordinating and concurring authority over certain personnel and budgetary matters throughout the intelligence community. That is bureaucratic code for a role that will have to be worked out based on the preferences and personalities of each DNI and secretary of defense. As a result, it is premature to conclude that the position of DNI (as opposed to the skills of a given incumbent) has or will result in improved control of the intelligence instrument and improved efficiency in the identification and sharing of intelligence information. What the law surely does is allow the head of the CIA to focus on the human intelligence function and the Agency's counter-terrorism efforts. And that is an improvement.

But the Reform Act, as the law always has, divides cabinet-level control over the intelligence instrument. That may not in itself prove dysfunctional. However, there is danger that in creating the position of DNI the Congress has created the impression, or worse yet convinced itself, that the intelligence puzzle is solved through bureaucratic shuffling and the position of DNI. We should have more concern if the president (and therefore also the national security advisor) believes this as well, and fails to realize the president's central role.[23]

In short, leadership and not law will determine whether information is shared and the intelligence instrument wielded effectively. Where the intelligence authority is bifurcated between the secretary of defense and the DNI, responsibility is bifurcated as well. Thus, the president and the NSC must play a central leadership role, as the commander in chief does in military context. Where intelligence is concerned the buck stops with the president . . . and not before, and that *is* a product of law, for only the president has the constitutional authority to perform this task. That is especially the case because the intelligence function is in fact performed throughout the government.

4. Intelligence Community

In addition to knowing the law, government lawyers must also understand the bureaucracy. This allows lawyers to guide policymakers more effectively. It also allows lawyers to garner the information necessary to apply fact to law and ask the right questions in doing so more effectively.

The intelligence community (IC) consists of more than the headline agencies within the Department of Defense and the CIA. To start, "community" is a misnomer. Community is a concept, not necessarily a condition. Membership in the community improves, but does not guarantee, informational connectivity, the opportunity for budget input, and potentially a place at the decision-making table.

Executive Order 12333, as amended, designates sixteen agencies or components of agencies as members of the "intelligence community." Subsequent to 9/11, the Coast Guard joined the IC in recognition of its homeland defense mission and the significance of maritime intelligence. Intelligence community components within larger agencies are often the point of entry for intelligence issues, where classification and cultural barriers are more easily addressed. Of course, the number of intelligence elements is less important than an understanding of their existence and their function.

(The number of community members will likely change again as the structure of the Homeland Security Department is modified and amended.)

Understanding this breadth and the range of bureaucratic cultures within the community, one will also understand the leadership and bureaucratic challenge for the DNI and the president. Whereas the military operates under a unified chain of command, with a clear start and finish that is known to lance corporals as well as lawyers, in the intelligence context there is sometimes only a top. The chain of command starts with the president and moves either to the secretary of defense, the DNI, or perhaps the attorney general. But from there, the lines of authority (and responsibility) disperse into a myriad of programs and compartments known only to those possessing access and a need to know.

Significantly, while the majority of intelligence assets reside within the Department of Defense, the majority of domestic intelligence capabilities are either within the Department of Justice (namely with the FBI or local law enforcement through the FBI) or are regulated or controlled by the attorney general. For a lawyer, that makes classified and unclassified Department of Defense Directives and Attorney General Guidelines as relevant as CIA regulations.[24]

B. THE FIVE INTELLIGENCE FUNCTIONS

The intelligence instrument has five functions: collection, analysis and dissemination, counterintelligence, covert action, and liaison.

1. Collection

However the IC is defined, if "intelligence" is information relevant to national security decision-making, then intelligence is generated and analyzed by virtually every component of national government as well as many components of state and local government as well as the private sector.[25] On the national level, the authority to collect is found in delegated presidential authority reflected in executive directives as well as in individual agency enabling legislation. Critical to this task is an understanding as to which information is indeed important to the national security. With homeland security, for example, the agricultural meat inspector or the private doctor may provide the first indication of a terrorist attack, not a radar station located in Thule, Greenland.

The existence of certain intelligence sources and methods is generally known and popularized. The basic methods of collection are described on the Office of the Director of National Intelligence (ODNI) website.[26] Among other things, agencies collect information through clandestine as well as open means and from technical as well as human sources (human intelligence or "humint"). In contrast to the general methods, specific capabilities and the targets of collection are preserved secrets.

Within the United States, and as described in Chapter 9, law enforcement agencies are the primary collectors and conduits of intelligence information. The National Security Act provides that the CIA "shall have no police, subpoena, or law enforcement powers or internal security functions."[27] But note that this language does not preclude a U.S. presence or foreign intelligence collection function within the United States, subject to the provisions of E.O. 12333 and applicable Attorney General Guidelines, as amended. With respect to the CIA, "the collection of foreign intelligence or counterintelligence within the United States shall be coordinated with the FBI as required by procedures agreed upon by the Directive of Central Intelligence and the Attorney General."[28] Further,

> Collection within the United States of foreign intelligence not otherwise obtainable shall be undertaken by the FBI or, or when significant foreign intelligence is sought, by other authorized agencies of the intelligence community, provided that no foreign intelligence collection by such agencies may be undertaken for the purpose of acquiring information concerning the domestic activities of United States persons.

Of course, limitations and permits contained within an executive order, which are not otherwise implementing law, may be amended and interpreted by the president, including in secret manner. Nonetheless, the provisions of 12333 create important baseline expectations. Moreover, the text offers the lawyer insight that the critical legal instruments in this area include the Attorney General Guidelines applicable in the context presented.

Within the United States and overseas distinct rules apply to intelligence collection that directly or incidentally target "U.S. persons." For example, as discussed in Chapter 5, electronic surveillance that captures the conversations of U.S. persons who are not themselves the target of collection is subject to "minimization" procedures. That is, information can only be retained, analyzed, and disseminated in delineated instances, such as when it relates to the purpose and target of lawful surveillance, where consent is given, where the surveillance evidences a crime, or where the U.S. person's name is necessary to understand the information collected.[29] Executive Order 12333 contains further limitations. As a threshold, "[a]gencies within the Intelligence Community are authorized to collect, retain or disseminate information concerning United States persons only in accordance with procedures established by the head of the agency concerned and approved by the Attorney General." (Para. 2.3). Internal directives, such as U.S. Signals Intelligence Directives, provide further detail regarding these limitations.

Rules pertaining to intelligence collection against U.S. persons may vary in nuance depending on the agency in question and the method of collection employed. For example, there may be variance in the default application of minimization procedures when the legal identity of a person in the United States is not known. As a result, some commentators have expressed concern that operators may inadvertently apply a more rigorous standard than necessary, raising the specter that critical intelligence may be missed. Alternatively, operators applying too narrow a definition may impinge on the protected privacy interests of U.S. persons. Some commentators also express concern that "U.S. person" rules that are well intentioned and are intended to exclude the names of U.S. persons, with exceptions, have in practice been inverted, with exceptions the norm, and gate-keeping officials having been too generous in responding to requests for U.S. person identification.[30]

When intelligence falls short, debate often follows as to whether the intelligence community was relying on the right mix of technical and human means of collection. Conventional wisdom assumes the United States relies too heavily on technical rather than human methods of collection. This may be true in context. Some targets lend themselves to technical collection, for example, the monitoring of a weapons test, although the human source may provide the critical indication that a test is imminent. It may also be true where technical means provide the only viable methods of gathering intelligence. In other words, the United States may rely on technical means not as a matter of choice, but for want of a horse.

Intelligence officers do not need to be told the value of recruiting more, or more importantly better human assets, in deeper locations, in more countries . . . if they can. I have never worked with a policymaker who would knowingly eschew the opportunity to collect more human intelligence. The problem is not a lack of vision or understanding as to the value of penetrating the terrorist or state target with human assets. Nor does it reflect a choice to rely on technology in lieu of humint. The reality is that some targets are difficult, if not impossible, to penetrate. This increases the importance of liaison – intelligence cooperation with other services – as well as the importance of constantly appraising the manner and method of human intelligence collection.[31]

The qualitative value of intelligence gathered against the jihadist target depends on finding the optimum degree of risk in three areas. First, intelligence decisionmakers will have to find the optimum balance between counterintelligence risk and collection need. Effective penetration of targets requires the employment or utilization of persons with necessary ethnic and cultural background. These persons may not be U.S. citizens, and if they are, the ordinary degree of background inquiry may not be available as a result of the applicant's place of birth or prior residences. If we assume too little risk of counterintelligence penetration, we may forgo important opportunity to recruit and train the sort of case officers or agents who can either penetrate the target themselves or achieve sufficient access to an agent base that is able to do so. If we assume too much counterintelligence risk, we may find our agents and officers dead and singular avenues of intelligence approach compromised.

Second, the humint mission requires modulation of the risk the United States is prepared to assume in introducing U.S. personnel into high-risk environments, with the encompassing risk they will be captured or killed. Intelligence collection on the battlefield, including the global terrorist battle-field, is exceptionally dangerous where the opponent does not "play" by the "rules of the road" that state intelligence services generally observed during the Cold War. In this conflict, exposed intelligence personnel are not declared *persona non grata* and expelled. But if one works back from the threat of a nuclear weapon detonated in a major U.S. city, then national security officials must continuously consider whether we have applied the necessary degree of policy (but not personal) tolerance for intelligence casualties. These same officials must consider whether such tolerance should exceed that tolerated during the Cold War, and if so, by how much.

Intelligence policy and law will also have to factor in the risk of moral or legal compromise. To penetrate criminal networks or solve violent crimes law enforcement agencies employ confidential informants that law enforce-ment personnel know engage in crime themselves. This is an integral part of the criminal investigative process. An informant's criminal conduct may pro-vide the basis for his access to the target, or at the very least serve as "cover." However, in context, there may be a thin line between informed tolerance and encouragement, or even government sanction of criminal conduct. As a result, the FBI and state and local police have guidelines on the handling of informants to address these moral and legal concerns.

The same issues arise in spades in the intelligence arena. But the moral tension is more severe in light of the subject matter and the timelines involved. Obviously an intelligence service cannot penetrate a terrorist net-work or illicit arms network through the front door. There is no front door. Moreover, such networks have their own mechanisms to test the bona fides of their members, assets, and contacts. Further, intelligence services are usu-ally in the business of collection rather than disruption or arrest. That means that the moral and legal issues associated with "the friends we keep" may per-sist over time. In a democracy, intelligence law and policy must account for these tensions and provide a meaningful mechanism for effectively, secretly, and rapidly assessing these risks and doing so on an ongoing basis.

The CIA sought to do just this in the mid-1990s with guidelines that necessitated headquarters approval before certain categories of assets were recruited. The DCI issued the guidelines following disclosure that CIA offi-cers recruited, retained, and paid a Guatemalan colonel at the same time that he was engaged in human rights abuses. The degree to which CIA offi-cers were aware of these abuses and the extent to which the abuses may have been perpetrated against U.S. nationals remain a matter of public dispute and were the subject of inquiry by the CIA Inspector General. In retrospect, there was no reasonable question that the policy cost of retaining the colonel outweighed the intelligence benefit. The colonel was not an Al Qaeda operative. He was of marginal intelligence value. In brief, the guidelines required headquarters (senior clandestine officers) to balance the costs and benefits of recruiting nefarious agents. Like the detached FISA judge, the idea was that senior officers might better evaluate the costs and benefits from a distance, without the case officer's incentives to recruit first and ask questions second. The guidelines did not prohibit recruitment; rather, they subjected exceptional cases of recruitment to a process of validation and approval. In theory as well, the guidelines were intended to increase risk-taking in the field by passing to headquarters the responsibility for recruiting the very bad agent.

These guidelines were subsequently attacked for chilling the recruitment process, particularly in the terrorist context where the potential agent pool is characterized by persons of dubious background who might themselves have engaged in terrorist acts. In context, one can see that such guidelines might chill. A case officer on the brink of recruitment, or engaged in a chance encounter, could not close the deal, or might be hesitant in closing the deal, without checking with headquarters first. He or she might also be hesitant to string the contact out for fear of operational exposure. The guidelines might also have been perceived in the field as a vehicle to second-guess the case officer, rather than a method to buttress risk-taking. In any event, in the wake of 9/11 some case officers argued that the guidelines had constrained the recruitment of agents, a complaint apparently not made before 9/11, or if so, in muted fashion. Of course, the fundamental problem was that the terrorist target was and is a hard target. Where the guidelines may have deterred the recruitment of borderline colonels with marginal information, they surely did not bar recruitment of Bin Laden's aides. Guidelines or not, the desire for more and better human intelligence was loud and clear and remains so.

Nonetheless, for lawyers there is a bureaucratic lesson. However well designed and logical, directives may have unintended impact. Case officers do not respond in the same manner as Marine infantry officers to the same instructions; neither do lawyers. To the Marine, "Take the hill" results in an immediate assault. The case officer might ask, "What's the catch?" and then look for an agent to create a diversionary ruse. The lawyer might litigate the necessity of taking the hill in the first instance. Of course, these are caricatures of bureaucratic stereotypes, which may or may not have roots in accuracy. The point is, different cultural audiences will respond to the same instruction differently. If there was a failure with the guidelines it was in not subsequently and constantly appraising the implementation and impact of the guidelines on field culture and doing so on the record (in intelligence channels).

The cadre of professional intelligence officers and potential (meaningful) agents is small, exceptionally small if one considers those officers and assets able to penetrate the zone of hard target recruitment and collection. For these reasons, leadership of the intelligence function will entail difficult choices between intelligence necessity and the three risks identified above. It will also require constant appraisal as to whether the United States has effectively calibrated the risk of penetration, the risk of casualties, the risk of values compromise, and the risk of attack.

No amount of law or structural reorganization can provide access to a human intelligence source or spark the intellect of an analyst. What bureaucratic and legal structure can do is improve the opportunity for success. In the area of analysis, for example, the law, or internal directives that can more readily be adjusted, can provide for efficient redundancy so that more than one person has a crack at the problem in a process that invites debate and records dissent. For humint collection, the law can incorporate incentives to increase the possibility of success. The law can authorize rewards, improve personnel practices, increase salaries and benefits to survivors, and offer incentives for particular skill sets, especially language skills. While the community has not lacked insight on the need for human intelligence, the function seems repeatedly to fall short in delivering a redundant capacity in critical language areas, including Arabic and Farsi. This is an area where the law can be used to set numeric thresholds and to create personnel incentives to master certain skill sets. Of course, for some assignments there will be no substitute for native capacity, which is part of the challenge.

The law can also require clear processes of authorization, and clear parameters for recruitment tailored to need so that risk takers in the field know that they will be protected from recrimination in the event of failure or compromise. In other words, standards for recruitment should not be uniform, any more than the potential value of each agent recruited is uniform. There is a difference between a Guatemalan colonel and Bin Laden's bodyguard. As military personnel operate with standing rules of engagement, case officers can do the same, without necessity of headquarters approval.

Ultimately, however, intelligence is not dependent on the law. It depends on what Graham Greene called "the human factor": a president who asks the right question; a national security advisor who pushes open every intelligence door (and then pushes some more); the analyst who finds the entrance to a clandestine arms facility from a pile of photos of valleys; and, with human intelligence, the source who turns the corner of betrayal for ego, for ideology, for family, for anger, or for money.

Nor is human intelligence a panacea, as those who evaluate hearsay will understand and as fans of the movie *Rashomon* will know. *Rashomon* tells the same story from the vantage points of different participants. Each participant accurately depicts what he saw from his perspective, but as the audience knows, each describes a different event. In the law, hearsay is the second-hand telling of what another person said. Double hearsay is a third-hand telling of what a second party reported a first party said.[32] (Of course, a document can also contain hearsay. This is obviously so when party A writes a letter to party B describing what C said.) Hearsay is disfavored as legal evidence because it interjects the perceptions, biases, and incomplete perspectives of the second or third party between a court and the "truth" of the spoken word – a Rashomon effect. Thus, in the absence of particular indicia of reliability and legal presumptions, hearsay is not admissible as evidence in federal court. But if hearsay is not evidence, it is intelligence. Second- and third-hand hearsay may be great intelligence. Imagine a second-hand account coming out of Kim Il Jong's palace. That intelligence is going straight to the president. Imagine third-hand hearsay about seeing Bin Laden in a cave in South Asia; that intelligence is going straight to the tip of a missile.

It is also useful to remember that much human intelligence is inductive. Definitive judgments are hard to draw from a single point of data, rather than deductively from empirical data or multiple points of reference. So too, facts are easier to fix than intent. Our most important Politburo spy, Oleg Penkovskiy, was a colonel, with a colonel's access and understanding of Politburo intent. However well placed, a staff member will have only so much access to and knowledge of the intentions of a state's or terrorist cell's leaders, especially when the state or the cell is structured to limit external exposure and penetration. Intelligence analysts speak in terms of mosaics, but in many intelligence scenarios these are ancient mosaics, broken, scattered, and buried, with few pieces in place.

Resources are also finite. Just as the United States cannot have military forces on station in every location, the intelligence agencies cannot treat every country with the priority of the Soviet Union. Unfortunately, a geographically fluid conflict with terrorists will find this out in ways a cold war against a geographically fixed opponent did not. Terrorists, like water, will seek the path of least resistance. That means that collection requires both an ability to surge to meet the need of the day and a deep base in the fundamentals, such as Arabic language, South Asian, and African dialects.

2. Analysis and Dissemination

Information is of little value if it is not sorted, prioritized, translated, and disseminated to the actionable level of decision. Some information cries out for action; other information only does so when fitted into a larger canvas. All of it must be gleaned from an enormous volume of intake,[33] much of it apparently alarming, and some of which is never translated or processed. In some cases these tasks can initially be performed by computer, as persons familiar with Internet search engines or the use of voice recognition technology will discern. However, intelligence assessment ultimately depends on human evaluation and judgment – the person who confirms that an image projects a military rather than a civilian aircraft, the person who links one report with another, or the person who links fact with a judgment about intent. Analysis is what makes most raw intelligence "actionable"; that is, information requiring an affirmative response or affirmative decision not to respond.

Once identified as national security information, intelligence is either disseminated in raw form or analyzed and disseminated as a product. Formal analysis intended for interagency distribution at the national level is produced by the National Intelligence Council (NIC), CIA's Directorate of Intelligence (DI), the Defense Intelligence Agency (DIA), and the State Department's Bureau of Intelligence and Research (INR), among other entities. (Informal analysis is, of course, provided by anyone who consumes the information.) In this way, policymakers are exposed to a range of views, and in theory, institutional or personal bias will be balanced by other analysts in parallel bureaucracies. However, this is only true if each analyst is exposed to the same information stream, as opposed to perceiving the same event differently because each is looking at different information. And it is only true if critical concurrences and dissents are included as information travels up the chain of command to the actionable level of decision.

National intelligence products include those prepared internally for the senior leadership of the executive branch, such as the Secretary's [of State's] Morning Brief (over time the names have changed; however, the product source and orientation tend to remain constant). In addition, the NSC Situation Room circulates intelligence updates to designated White House officials and the NSC staff. September 11 produced a new threat matrix, bringing to senior policymakers attention all-source reporting on potential threats against U.S. interests.[34]

The pinnacle of the analytic process is the National Intelligence Council. Operating under the bureaucratic direction of the DNI, the NIC is composed of government and academic analysts. The senior officer in each discipline is designated the National Intelligence Officer for that subject. The NIC is charged with producing, among other things, National Intelligence Estimates produced on an ad hoc or as-requested basis, addressing particularized policy issues or questions. National Intelligence Estimates (NIE), in theory, represent the best in the collective wisdom and views of the intelligence community, drawing on all relevant sources of information and viewpoints. In theory, as well, they have the strength of comprehension, but NIEs can also have the inherent pitfalls of committee drafting.[35]

In addition, the president receives a daily intelligence update known as the President's Daily Brief (PDB). In contrast to other national products, the PDB is more likely to include the source of the information and relate directly to the president's interests, inquiries, and matters pertaining to immediate crisis. Depending on the particular style of the president, this brief may be delivered in person by the DNI or a presidential briefer. In this way, the brief becomes iterative in nature as the president asks questions and influences the shape of the next day's brief. Both Presidents Bush are known to have preferred oral briefings. Some presidents, including Presidents Reagan and Clinton, limited their briefings to a written PDB product, with only occasional oral input. In such cases, presidential feedback is more likely to occur in the form of marginalia than direct comment, or through the national security advisor. Whether written or oral, presidents and their advisors must ensure that cryptic comments and asides are not received as commands and directives unless they are intended as such.

Regardless of presidential style, the national security advisor serves as the president's intelligence alter ego, a conduit to the intelligence community translating and tempering presidential input into the intelligence process. Significantly, given the divided nature of intelligence authority between agencies and principals, the national security advisor must ensure the president receives a comprehensive intelligence picture, which at minimum should include the facts and views of the DNI, the secretary of defense, the attorney general and the director of the FBI, and the secretary of homeland security. The president, operating through the national security advisor, alone has the capacity to fuse all sources of executive information and do so in a timely or urgent manner.

In practice, the written PDB is reviewed by a select group of senior policy officials as well as the president. This process can help to place the most senior decisionmakers on the same factual page. Such distribution of the PDB takes on legal importance where the distribution becomes sufficiently widespread that the product may lose its aura as a constitutionally privileged communication *between* the president and his senior intelligence advisor, the DNI. It is on this legal basis that administrations of both parties have resisted efforts by the Congress to receive distribution of the PDB or knowledge of its content. The president may hesitate to ask questions and the DNI respond if either official is concerned that their communications will be disclosed (and debated) by outside parties. Moreover, the DNI and CIA may hesitate to include the sources and methods of intelligence with the brief, making it harder for the president to assess the reliability of the intelligence provided.

In specific context, usually involving investigations, and as a matter of comity, accommodation has been made to identify the nature of information provided to the president. In the case of the 9/11 Commission, for example, select members of the commission were provided access to the PDB for review, and in only exceptional circumstances permitted to retain copies of it. One entry relating directly to the threat of Al Qaeda hijackings in the United States was considered sufficiently important and material to the investigation that the PDB entry was declassified and made public at the request of the commission, but only after extensive negotiation and media-generated political pressure.

In the case of a 1996 congressional inquiry involving Iranian arms shipments to Bosnia, the chairman and ranking members of the ad hoc committee of Congress conducting the inquiry were orally briefed on the contents of PDB entries pertaining to Bosnia. In that case, a NSC lawyer representing the president orally described for the members the substance of each PDB entry on Bosnia and in doing so demonstrated the absence of information relevant to the members' inquiry. Of course, this effort at balancing the constitutional interests of both branches of government depended on the members' accepting the integrity of the briefing process. Had material information been identified, the committee members might have pressed for additional access. The balance between the executive's need for an honest and direct deliberative process and the legislature's interest in specific fact would have changed, perhaps warranting additional executive accommodation of the legislative need.

Whether or not the PDB is itself shared with the Congress, presidents and their staff should consciously consider whether to share the underlying data with the Congress as a matter of constitutional process and as a product of the National Security Act's reporting provisions. For that matter, persons with access to the PDB and its data should consider whether additional members of the executive branch should be aware of portions of the brief or facts identified within. In the context of the PDB, it is not the intelligence information that is privileged (although it could be privileged as a state secret if it came from a source like a Penkovskiy), but rather the fact and manner of its communication to the president. As a result, it is often possible to accommodate the legitimate informational needs of the Congress while preserving the president's ability to run an intelligence process that allows senior advisors to give their best judgments to the president without risk of public recrimination or second-guessing. At the same time, it is important to realize that such cold data may not come with essential nuance or the background with which it is received in the executive branch.

As always there is a tension between informed decision-making and the protection of sources and methods. Policymakers should not assume that a critical piece of information has been, or will be, shared, with other necessary actors, including the Congress. Alternatively, policymakers may garner, and seek to garner, policy advantage through exclusive access to intelligence information. With national security, getting the information to the actionable level of decision can be as important as the information itself, distribution lists as important as the underlying information. This may mean dissemination to persons or entities outside the government, including the public, the United Nations, and allies. This can take the form of direct distribution, incorporation into talking points without attribution, or so-called tear line reporting, where the essential information is conveyed without indication of its source.

However, as a general rule, the government is more inclined toward risk in gathering information than in disseminating it. Nonetheless, in multilateral, United Nations, or unilateral contexts, effective dissemination of intelligence information may make the difference between public support or opposition. Therefore, the government should put as much effort into the external use of intelligence as into its generation, including its packaging, dissemination, and declassification, if appropriate. Intelligence producers and consumers should not only instinctively ask who should see this, in what form, and how soon, but also how, and in what form, can they then use this information? Are there ways of generating the same information from a sanitized or open source so that it can be publicly used? For example, in a homeland security context, the specific identification of threat information will have far more impact on public behavior than recantation of color codes to a public exposed to continuous exhortations of alert. In an international setting, such an observation may invoke images of Adlai Stevenson at the UN with pictures of Soviet missiles in Cuba. However, that is an easy scenario because it implicates a source of intelligence already known to the opposition (the Cubans shot down one of the U-2 planes over Cuba). More frequently, such scenarios will arise where the intelligence source is unknown to the target and could continue to supply information unless exposed, thereby raising more difficult issues of authority and balance.

For lawyers, these questions will implicate a range of legal authority. The DNI's and the director of the CIA's statutory authorities to protect intelligence sources and methods are found in section 102A(i) of the Intelligence Reform Act and section 103(c)(5) of the National Security Act.[36] The secretary of defense controls certain compartments of intelligence information. The attorney general has relevant authority as well found in the Privacy Act or enabling legislation or derived from rules pertaining to grand jury testimony contained in the Federal Rules of Criminal Procedure. However, complete legal analysis must also factor in the president's constitutional authority over state secrets (see Chapter 4).

The Congress has on occasion sought to limit the president's authority to disseminate intelligence outside the government; however, presidents have rebuffed such attempts, noting that authority over state secrets is derivative of their foreign affairs and commander-in-chief powers and therefore not subject to statutory constraint. Moreover, while courts as a general matter eschew an active role in resolving questions of constitutional balance between the political branches in the area of national security, the Court has spoken with uncommon direction in the area of state secrets. Thus, in *Department of the Navy v. Egan*, the Supreme Court concluded

> The President after all, is the "Commander in Chief of the Army and the Navy of the United States." U.S. Const., Art. II, 2. His authority to classify and control access to information bearing on national security and to determine whether an individual is sufficiently trustworthy to occupy a position in the Executive Branch that will give that person access to classified information flows primarily from this constitutional investment of power in the president and exists quite apart from any explicit congressional grant. *See Cafeteria Workers v. McElroy*, 367 U.S. 886, 890 (1961). This Court has recognized the government's 'compelling interest in withholding national security information from unauthorized persons in the course of executive business. *Snepp v. United States*, 444 U.S. 507, 509, n.3 (1980). *See also, United States v. Robel*, 389 U.S. 258, 267 (1967); *United States v. Reynolds*, 345 U.S. 1, 10 (1953); *Totten v. United States*, 92 U.S. 105, 106 (1876). The authority to protect such information falls on the president as head of the Executive Branch and as Commander in Chief.

Therefore, issues of dissemination and disclosure are not final until the president has decided or affirmatively deferred to a subordinate or decisionmakers have declined the opportunity to raise the matter to the president.

It is also worth noting how much of the intelligence process, like the national security process generally, is informal. For each NSC meeting or memo to the president, for example, there are ten times the number of discussions made in small meetings, hallway conversations, or over the secure phone. This is true with respect to the dissemination and use of intelligence as well. The delivery of a report may be followed by a discussion with the report's author. At the level of the NSC, much of the actionable intelligence is delivered in person; for example, at the outset of a Principals meeting, which might start with the DNI saying: "This is what we know . . . ," as well, one hopes, as "this is what we do not know."

Informal deliveries may not always bear the same careful bureaucratic manifestations of a written product, particularly if the policy side is testing and probing. This is evident in the remark by then DCI Tenet that the intelligence regarding Iraq's possession of WMD weapons was a "slam dunk," whereas the underlying National Intelligence Estimate reached more calculated conclusions regarding the state of the intelligence. Mr. Tenet's oral presentation surely included something more than those two words. However, intelligence officers like lawyers must remain vigilant lest policymakers hear only what they want to hear, focus on the bottom lines, forum shop, and skip the nuance when they get to "yes."

The most important intelligence exchanges may not be on the piece of paper the DNI delivers, but the question-and-answer session that follows. Such informal exchange may reveal what is not known and how reliable the information is that we do know, as well as include additional mosaic pieces drawn from other sources. In this informal process, the national security advisor plays a critical role in communicating and translating presidential views to the intelligence process. Thus, whether one is looking proactively at intelligence design or retroactively at intelligence performance, a complete picture can only follow from a review of the informal process as well as the formal intelligence mechanisms. Further, where the public and the Congress may ultimately see the finished intelligence product or the base conclusion found in a policy talking point, this informal measure of exchange, on which executive decisions so often depend, is rarely seen or disclosed.

3. Counterintelligence

A third intelligence function is counterintelligence. The classic counterintelligence function is "spy catching," the work of Le Carre's fictional George Smiley and the very real James Angleton, who ran CIA's counterintelligence arm at the height of the Cold War. Counterintelligence also includes the full range of defensive efforts to prevent technical or human penetration of the U.S. government, force protection in the field, and the protection of critical infrastructures from hostile penetration and misuse. It also encompasses the process of vetting employees before, during, and after employment, as well as the vetting and validation of field assets.

Four points merit note. First, unlike other areas of intelligence law, there is a considerable amount of unclassified black-letter law relevant to counterintelligence. This includes an array of personnel regulations pertaining to security clearances and vetting processes, such as Executive Order 12968, as amended, "Access to Classified Information" (August 2, 1995). There are also classified regulations pertaining to particular agencies and classified Attorney General Guidelines that may apply in context. In addition, statutory law includes ample investigative authorities for agency as well as law enforcement authorities to engage in counterintelligence, including and in particular the FBI's authority to obtain administrative records pertaining to financial, travel, and other records of employees.[37]

Second, although intuitive, bad security can cost lives, waste resources, and curtail or terminate singular sources of intelligence. The indirect consequences are harder to quantify, but no less real. Poor security or the perception of poor security can have an impact on liaison relationships – making others hesitant to share their secrets and their sources, which may be necessary to evaluate the veracity of their secrets. Agents, and potential agents, may be more hesitant or deterred from coming forward. At the same time, too aggressive a counterintelligence program can stifle creativity and risk taking and damage morale. In short, counterintelligence is more than a spy versus spy feature of the Cold War; it is a critical element in the conflict with jihadists as well as in the containment of rogue states and would-be nuclear states. The costs of failure ripple to distant intelligence liaison shores.

Nevertheless, counterintelligence has traditionally played second fiddle, or fifth fiddle, to other intelligence functions; that is, until a spy like Aldrich Ames or Robert Hansen comes along, at which point there is an external commission, an internal task force, and a search for new authority. Clearly, sustained commitment is central to this field, not just from the career professionals but also from the senior leadership who fund, lead, and appraise the function. For lawyers, sustained commitment means constant appraisal of the law and the impact of the law on the counterintelligence function to ensure the law is effective and fairly used.

Finally, there is a tension between counterintelligence and homeland security. Counterintelligence favors compartments and stovepipes; homeland security requires informational integration and the qualitative assessment of sources to know when in fact to "stand to" on alert. Counterintelligence is for secure phones; homeland security is about cell phones. Thus, as we improve homeland security we must ensure that counterintelligence adjusts to these changes, not by creating compartments, but by creating and funding review mechanisms that work in context. As in so many other areas, ongoing appraisal is critical.

4. Covert Action

As noted earlier, U.S. covert action pre-dates the Republic. Covert action has been one of America's national security tools ever since. However, covert action was not an integral policy tool until the Cold War. Resort to covert action also reflected the strategic view that the threat posed by communism warranted resort to all the instruments of national policy as embodied by the chilling words of the Doolittle Committee in 1954.

> It is now clear that we are facing an implacable enemy whose avowed objective is world domination by whatever means at whatever cost. There are no rules in such a game. Hitherto acceptable norms of human conduct do not apply.[38]

During the Cold War, the United States engaged in a number of "overt-covert actions," such as the landings at the Bay of Pigs, the supply of the so-called Contras, and provision of support to the Afghan mujahadeen. Such "covert" mechanisms allowed proxies to engage in hot war, while the great power conflict remained "cold." (However, most covert activities, then and now, are secret and remain so.)

Although covert action has historically claimed a small part of the overall intelligence budget and intelligence missions it has played a disproportionately large role in defining public perceptions of "intelligence,"[39] in shaping congressional oversight, and in policy impact. This reflects the reality that covert activities bear particular policy and legal risks as well as benefits. Consider, for example, the short- and long-term benefits and costs of U.S. Cold War actions in support of the coup against the elected Prime Minister of Iran in 1953, or the covert support for the mujahadeen against Soviet forces in Afghanistan. We live with the ramifications of both today. Of course, smaller scale actions like the placement of favorable press in the post-war Italian media had both fewer policy benefits and risks.

Covert action has historically included activities on a continuum between diplomacy and war[40] undertaken to hide the U.S. role. As a result, these activities are undertaken without the ordinary mechanisms of policy preview and external validation. Thus, while the law pertaining to covert action permits and prohibits, most of all it regulates its use by creating substantive thresholds that trigger statutory and executive processes for authorizing and then appraising covert activities. These processes are intended to ensure that the means to effect covert actions are lawful, but also to ensure that policy choices are sound and effective and that the gain from an action exceeds the pain, both in the short run and in the long run.

In a global conflict against nonstate actors intent on high-intensity attack, clandestine activities of the sort historically conducted as "covert action" will play an important role. Indeed, the instrument is well suited to address a nonstate opponent, acting outside the laws of armed conflict, and operating without necessity of a particular territory, base, or chain of command. In theory, and in law, and sometimes in practice, covert action is fast and flexible, allowing prompt response and proactive use against a mobile opponent within states either unwilling or unable to effect their capture. And, in theory and in law, and often in practice, covert action is nonattributable and secret. This allows "assisting states" to otherwise deny complicity in necessary, but locally unpopular actions. It also removes the "made in America" label, where for example, an audience might otherwise be receptive to the message, but not the messenger. For these reasons, the law related to the authorization and review of covert activity is on the front line of counterterrorism. For these same reasons, the law, process, and practice of covert action will surely evolve from Cold War understandings and applications. However, it is also wise to remember that covert action is no more a silver bullet than it was during the Cold War. It is an important but supplementary tool.

The means of covert action (the why, when, how, who) will also take on added importance in a conflict fought over values and with values, including legal values. The methods and means are also important because success in this conflict requires intelligence alliance. Covert action may tempt pursuit of policy options that would be eschewed if conducted overtly. But secrecy should be valued for its operational merit, not for its capacity to conceal bad ideas. The 1985 sinking of the *Rainbow Warrior* by French agents in New Zealand to disrupt nuclear protests was a bad idea before the agents unwittingly killed a photographer on the vessel. Contemporary law and executive directive provide a procedural framework for addressing these issues within a process of limited access that can also be fast. Findings can be drafted and reviewed by principals in an afternoon, faster if need be. And as with constitutional law, policymakers and lawyers alike should stay focused on the enduring consequences of their actions, not just the immediate gains. In an enduring conflict, the long-term consequence may prove as strategically important as the short-term gains.

a. Statutory Context

As with much else in national security law, the statutory point of departure for covert action is the National Security Act of 1947. Although, historically, covert action was conducted pursuant to the president's constitutional authority (considered in Chapters 4 and 5), the Act served as a statutory basis as well until passage of the Hughes-Ryan Amendment in 1974.[41] This Amendment to the Foreign Assistance Act, passed in the wake of revelations about CIA coup and assassination plots, sought to regulate covert activities by the CIA through exercise of the spending power.

> No funds appropriated under the authority of this or any other Act may be expended by or on behalf of the Central Intelligence Agency for operations in foreign countries, other than activities intended solely for obtaining necessary intelligence, unless and until the president finds that each such operation is important to the national security of the United States.[42]

It was not until 1990, following the Iran-Contra affair, that the Congress defined covert action in law. Covert action is defined by what it is,

> an activity or activities of the United States Government to influence political, economic, or military conditions abroad, where it is intended that the role of the United States Government will not be apparent or acknowledged publicly.[43]

And through negative definition, by what it is not.

> Covert action ... does not include – (1) activities the primary purpose of which is [sic] to acquire intelligence or traditional counterintelligence activities; (2) traditional diplomatic or military activities or routine support to such activities; (3) traditional law enforcement activities; or, (4) activities to provide routine support to overt U.S. activities abroad.[44]

The definition is intended to capture U.S. law and practice at the time of enactment. The legislative history states:

> It is not intended that the new definition exclude activities which were heretofore understood to be covert actions, nor to include activities not heretofore understood to be covert actions.[45]

As a result, historical practice is particularly relevant to legal interpretation, albeit hard to ascertain using ordinary methods of research. The legislative history also is particularly important in fleshing out the meaning of "traditional" activities exempt from the definition's reach.

Notably, the definition is act-based, not actor-based. Where the Hughes-Ryan Amendment addressed only activities conducted by the CIA, this definition potentially applies across the agency board. Thus, the activities of the Department of Defense and the Federal Bureau of Investigation, for example, might constitute covert action, *provided* a contemplated activity fits the positive definition of covert action and is not otherwise excluded by the negative definition because the activity is "traditional."

Notwithstanding the clarity in the law, misconceptions remain in practice that covert action process and law only apply to the CIA. Agency identity *is* relevant, however, in determining whether an activity is "traditional." For example, certain activities like raids might be "traditional" if undertaken by military actors in uniform; however, the same result may not follow if the raid were undertaken by U.S. surrogates in peacetime. Of course, activities that were "extraordinary" before 9/11 may have become ordinary and "traditional" since.

The Act also recognizes the president's policy responsibility for covert action. The president is required to find that "an action is necessary to support identifiable foreign policy objectives of the United States and is important to the national security of the United States."[46] Findings must be in writing, "unless immediate action by the United States is required," in which case a contemporaneous notation of the president's decision shall be made and a written finding produced within forty-eight hours. Reflecting some of the issues identified in the Iran-Contra context, findings must also specify the department or agencies authorized to fund or participate "in any significant way" in an action as well as specify whether the participation of third parties (e.g., third countries or persons) is contemplated.[47]

The Act also requires the president to ensure that findings are reported to the intelligence committees "as soon as possible after . . . approval and before initiation."[48] The ordinary process of notification is in writing to the full committees. In practice, this means not only to the members but also to designated staff with an oral briefing accompanying the underlying document. However, "[t]o meet extraordinary circumstances affecting vital interests of the United States"[49] the president may limit notification to the so-called

Gang of Eight (the chairmen and vice chairmen of the intelligence committees and the majority and minority leaders of each house of Congress) "and such other member or members of the congressional leadership as may be included by the President." Exercise of this option requires a statement from the president indicating why the action in question warrants limited notification. It follows that a limited notification is to members only and may be done orally. The president may authorize notification to additional members of Congress, or staff, something in between the full committee and the Gang of Eight. While there may be good tactical reasons to do so, as in the case of members serving on the appropriations committees, selective notification to preferred members of Congress or staff may erode the premise behind limited notification.

Finally, the Act implicitly authorizes the president to withhold notification altogether by stating that "whenever a finding is not reported [in one of the first two manners], the president shall fully inform the intelligence committees in a timely fashion and shall provide a statement of the reasons."[50] There is no public indication of whether this provision has ever been invoked. However, at the time the legislation was considered, President Carter's DCI, Stansfield Turner, described in *The Washington Post* certain covert activities undertaken by the CIA during preparation for the 1980 Iran hostage rescue mission. These activities included the infiltration into Tehran of officers to arrange for vehicles and safe houses, as well as flights undertaken by CIA officers to the Desert One transit site to determine its capacity to handle military aircraft. At the time, President Carter heeded Turner's advice and withheld notification of these activities from the Congress (under the Hughes-Ryan Amendment) until after the failed raid and safe extraction of clandestine U.S. personnel. Amendments to the law, Turner argued, should contemplate similar contexts warranting post facto notification. This view prevailed. The statute contemplates such a scenario, indicating, as noted above, that in situations in which the president does not provide prior notification to the committees or the Gang of Eight he should notify the committees as soon after initiation of an activity as possible and indicate the reasons. This provision was the subject of lengthy negotiation at the time.

The impasse was broken when, in a side letter to the chairmen of the intelligence committees, President George H.W. Bush undertook as a matter of practice not to withhold notification to the Congress "beyond a few days" after signing a finding. This was understood, or interpreted, on the Hill as meaning within forty-eight hours.[51] Of course, "the forty-eight-hour rule" is lore, not law neither is it binding on future presidents, but it is a good example of informal constitutional process in intelligence context. When President Bush signed the 1991 Intelligence Authorization Act into law, he stated his constitutional view that he was not required to report findings in advance or at all. But an informal constitutional mark was set.

In addition to reporting findings, "significant changes to" or "significant undertakings pursuant to a previously approved action" must be reported "in the same manner as findings are reported." This language is implemented through presidential Memoranda of Notification (MONs), which supplement, amend, or clarify previously approved findings. It follows that MONs are reported to the Congress using one of the three mechanisms specified for reporting findings. The triggering threshold for significant undertakings or changes has been the subject of internal executive debate as well as debate with the Congress. The legislative history gives two examples.

> This would occur when the president authorizes a change in the scope of a previously approved finding to authorize additional activities to occur. The second type of change specified in this subsection pertains to significant undertakings pursuant to a previously approved finding. This would occur when the president authorizes a significant activity under a previously-approved finding without changing the scope of the finding concerned.[52]

These are the same terms referenced in National Security Decision Directive 286, signed by President Reagan in the immediate wake of the Iran-Contra Affair, stating:

> In the event of any proposal to change substantially the means of implementation of, or the level of resources, assets, or activity under, a Finding; or in the event of any significant change in the operational condition, country or countries significantly engaged, or risks associated with a special activity, a written Memorandum of Notification (MON) shall be submitted to the president for his approval.[53]

Finally, the Act requires the president and the DNI to "ensure that the intelligence committees are kept fully and currently informed of the intelligence activities of the United States, including any significant anticipated intelligence activity as required by this Title."[54] Likewise, Section 503 of the Title pertaining to covert action requires the DNI and the heads of any other government entities involved in covert action

> [t]o the extent consistent with due regard for the protection from unauthorized disclosure of classified information relating to sensitive intelligence sources and methods or other exceptionally sensitive matters or other exceptionally sensitive matters . . . keep the intelligence committees fully and currently informed of all covert actions which are the responsibility of, are engaged in by, or are carried out for or on behalf of, any department, agency, or entity of the United States Government, including significant failures.[55]

These are important provisions. At the higher levels of the political branches, program initiation receives more attention and consideration than program administration. Moreover, policy-level oversight tends to focus on moments of crisis or failure, and less on ensuring that programs are on track and in fact accomplishing what they were intended to achieve and in the manner contemplated and represented to the president. Policymakers can mitigate this concern through effective executive appraisal.

b. Executive Process and Review

In addition to determining whether presidential approval is required, as a parallel matter, the definition of covert action triggers specific classified processes of executive review. As noted above, in the wake of the Iran-Contra scandal, President Reagan issued and released NSD-286, "Approval and Review of Special Activities." The document describes a process with covert action proposals reviewed at the working group level and then by the Deputies Committee and Principals Committee before submission to the president. The public record also reflects that in establishing his National Security Council system, President Clinton directed that "the Attorney General shall be invited to attend meetings pertaining to his jurisdiction, including covert actions."[56] Where the president has directed that a particular process of review occur, then the president must authorize deviation from that process, or otherwise delegate the authority to do so. Law or not, certainly the president should be informed when expected or important views are omitted from NSC consideration.

c. Legal Permits and Constraints

In addition to authorizing covert activities the law imposes certain constraints on the conduct of those activities. Relevant law is also found in classified presidential and executive directives. "A finding may not authorize any action that would violate the Constitution or any statute of the United States."[57] This means that an intelligence activity must comply with U.S. law unless the law exempts the government or intelligence actors from its reach or is otherwise inapplicable. This would include international law to the extent such law is incorporated into U.S. law.

For example, the law of armed conflict is found in the U.S. criminal code at Title 18 section 2441, as amended by the Military Commissions Act of 2006. Thus, when the United States changed the legal paradigm against Osama Bin Laden to one of armed conflict, as discussed in Chapter 6, before the embassy attacks in August 1998, this section of law was necessarily implicated. Indeed, lawyers advised the president that the United States might lawfully kill Bin Laden, but subject to U.S. law pertaining to the law of armed conflict. This is evident in the instructions conveyed to Afghan "tribals," which reference the staples of the law of armed of conflict that one would find on a lance corporal's rules of engagement card, like no killing prisoners and discrimination in attack. As a matter of policy, but not law, the instructions also expressed a preference for Bin Laden's capture.

> The United States preferred that Bin Laden and his lieutenants be captured, but if a successful capture operation was not feasible, the tribals were permitted to kill them. The instructions added that the tribals must avoid killing others unnecessarily and must not kill or abuse Bin Laden or his lieutenant if they surrendered.[58]

A prohibition on "assassination," originally promulgated by President Ford in 1976, is documented in E.O. 12333.

> 2.11 Prohibition on Assassination. No person employed by or acting on behalf of the United States Government shall engage in, or conspire to engage in, assassination.

This order continues in force, subject like other executive orders to classified presidential interpretation, amendment, or suspension. However, what is acknowledged publicly is that the targeting of legitimate military targets consistent with the law of armed conflict is not considered "assassination" under the executive order. As former National Security Advisor Samuel Berger testified before the Congress with respect to the (overt) August 1998 missile strikes in Afghanistan:

> We received rulings in the Department of Justice – [that the] executive order [did] not prohibit our ability – prohibit our effort to try to kill Bin Laden because it did not apply to situations in which you are acting in self-defense or you're acting against command and control targets against an enemy, which he certainly was.[59]

As evidenced by parallel executive statements, similar conclusions were reached at the time of the 1986 U.S. air strikes on Tripoli, which included a tent used at times by Colonel Qaddafi, and in spring 2003 when the United States targeted buildings where Saddam Hussein was thought to be located.

In addition, "[n]o covert action may be conducted which is intended to influence United States political processes, public opinion, policies, or media."[60] In the vernacular of intelligence law, the prospect of U.S. covert propaganda influencing the U.S. media and public is known as "blow-back," a realistic possibility in a global world with 24/7 news cycles. As criminal lawyers will recognize, the critical term in the prohibition is "intended," defining the restriction as one of specific intent.

Regardless of legal argument, as a matter of legal policy, decisionmakers must evaluate the consequences of U.S. covert activities "blowing back" into the United States even where such a result is not intended. The covert recruitment and insertion of a "rebel force," for example, may lead unwitting policy observers to make unfounded conclusions about the strength of the opposition to a regime if they are unaware of the force's pedigree. Likewise, were the United States to covertly place favorable news articles in the foreign press, a mechanism for disseminating propaganda during the Cold War, the potential for blow-back might hinge on whether the material was disseminated in English and/or in a forum likely to be covered by the U.S. media.

d. Legal Policy Issues

Three legal policy and process issues persist.

1. In what manner, if at all, will assertions regarding the president's wartime authority as commander in chief eclipse or marginalize the statutory framework for addressing covert action? What impact will such assertions have on executive processes for reviewing the efficacy and legality of covert action proposals and ongoing initiatives within previously authorized programs?

2. Does the statutory definition of covert action remain viable in light of the evolving use of "liaison" and "traditional activities" to combat terrorism?

3. Whatever legal determinations are made regarding an activity's status as "covert," is the measure of executive preview and review adequate to address the policy and legal risks inherent in activities once considered covert action, as well as those contemporary activities that bear comparable policy and legal risks?

Heretofore, the National Security Act has successfully served as an agreed mechanism between branches for addressing covert action. The Act incorporates the ultimate constitutional positions of both branches (prior reporting and no reporting), without either side having conceded ultimate authority. The Act leaves the political branches to work through the constitutional principles and tensions in an informal and contextual manner. In this way, the statute has played an overlooked, but important constitutional role by defining expectations and suggesting limits; that is, setting the constitutional "rules of the road" between the president and the Congress on the meaning and reporting requirements for covert action.

The questions presented today are (1) whether these same constitutional rules of the road still abide, given the president's constitutional position with respect to electronic surveillance; and (2) should they abide during conflict, but a conflict of indefinite duration? In the covert action context, there are arguments supporting a broad reading of presidential authority. However, the question is not just whether such a reading is lawful, but also whether it is a good idea. Such a claim of authority would be impenetrable, provided the action in question in fact remained covert. As noted in Chapter 3, the Congress may provide the only external mechanism for outside appraisal and validation for intelligence activities. Thus, while congressional oversight is imperfect it remains the only check on executive authority (read "check" here as in to "check something out" as opposed to putting something in check).

Concerns for security, speed, and flexibility may also drive activities that heretofore received internal and external appraisal as covert action into policy and legal pockets subject to less executive preview and review. The same result may occur as a product of the good faith application of law to fact. For example, activities historically considered covert actions may become commonplace in a global conflict with jihadists and thus legitimately constitute "traditional military, law enforcement, and diplomatic activities." These same activities may also properly fall within the construct of "liaison," discussed in the next section.

In the case of military operations, the effect may be significant, potentially removing some military activities from meaningful interagency review (including review by Principals) and eliminating a legal requirement to notify the Congress. As noted above the definition of covert action is act rather than actor based. However, uniformed military operations have historically not been considered or treated as covert activities. Thus, even if the definition is act based, the exception for "traditional military activities" may effectively remove clandestine military operations from its reach. This legal paradigm is reinforced by the military's longstanding cultural aversion to "covert action." This antipathy may reflect a desire to avoid the additional internal and external oversight that accrues to covert action, as well as a desire to avoid the tarnish that sometimes emerges from the retrospective consideration of certain covert activities. It may also emulate the traditional differences in military outlook and focus between Special Forces and regular units.

The military–covert action bifurcation is significant in light of the importance of special operations as an offensive weapon against jihadists. In the end, the critical question is not whether an activity is "covert," but whether those activities that raise the sorts of policy and legal risks that covert action historically has are subject to a process of rigorous policy and legal preview before they are undertaken. This is important not just if we value the rule of law, but also as a method to maximize the effect of a finite national security resource and to mitigate against value-based fallout. Certain special operations, renditions, and offensive uses of the predator drone arguably fit this description.

With respect to activities that are encompassed within the definition of covert action, two legal policy questions linger: How much executive process is appropriate before a finding or MON is signed or authorization for a specific operation given? How much detail should be specified in these documents beyond that necessary to satisfy the statutory requirements?

As noted in Chapter 3, there are arguments for and against "process." Process can be good or bad. Good process should be viewed as a source of policy strength in an area of historical risk like covert action, rather than an operational impediment. Good process alerts decisionmakers to the pros and cons of contemplated action, including the benefits and risks of accomplishing the task covertly rather than overtly. Process also helps to ensure that secret policies are consistent with overt policies and, where they are not, that there is good reason for any divergence. In an area where U.S. actions are intended to be kept secret, policymakers and those actors who may become aware of the underlying acts, if not their impetus, must also know of their existence to avoid blow-back, or inadvertent disclosure.

Streamlined executive decision has advantages of speed and secrecy. Speed comes in part from the absence of objection or dissent; conversely, delay with covert action is sometimes derivative of debate as opposed to process. But there are also benefits in the foreknowledge of objection and the improvements in policy or execution that dissent might influence. Because the conflict against jihadists is a conflict fought over values with words and not just territory with weapons, careful review also allows policymakers to balance the relative benefits and costs represented by both the means and ends of action.

This tension is surely found in the area of extraordinary rendition, where there are sometime difficult trade-offs between preventing attack and intelligence gathering on the one hand, and public diplomacy and human rights on the other. Where these decisions are taken solely within security agencies, the trade-offs will invariably balance in favor of action, just as company-grade infantry officers will instinctively lean toward protection when faced with questions balancing the needs of physical security and local support. Generally, process is more inclusive of views, and therefore more rigorous, when a decision is subject to interagency review and senior policy review than when it is subject alone to single agency review.

Additional checks do not necessarily eliminate mistakes; they diminish the potential for error. In the context of intelligence operations using military means, such as the use of the Predator to attack the enemy, whether covert or not, the value of rigorous process is obvious. As discussed in Chapter 8, the military, for example, uses multiple-tiered computer modeling to assess the potential for collateral damage. Targets are validated through a tested and recognized process. In short, rigorous but timely process can demonstrate confidence in policy choice, legal arguments, and a willingness to account for effect.

Where process proves "bureaucratic" the answer is not to remove internal mechanisms of appraisal, but to streamline them. For example, a legal question can go straight to the attorney general sitting in the Oval Office. As noted earlier, in the case of immediate needs, the Act provides for oral authorization of covert actions where "immediate action by the

United States is required," in which case a contemporaneous notation of the president's decision shall be made and a written finding produced within forty-eight hours.[61]

Policymakers and lawyers must also consider the measure of detail to include in a finding or MON. There exists a tension between the generic authorizing instrument that provides flexibility and the too specific instrument that may need amendment with every change in the field. From the standpoint of legal policy, such documents should be crafted with sufficient specificity so that it is clear to the president what he is approving and the policy implications and risks of doing so, including the risks of taking no action. Where flexibility is required, for example, where the geographic foci of activity may shift, there should also be sufficient authority to adjust in the field or a viable process to garner prompt policy consideration; for example, approval by the Principals or Deputies Committees or an appropriate subset of the committees.

Operators will almost always push for more flexibility as those familiar with headquarters-field relationships will appreciate. A worldwide threat from jihadists requires worldwide authority to respond and to do so on short or immediate time fuses. However, presidents should be careful they do not go too far, and surrender authority over the actual substance of decision. For you cannot have effective appraisal and accountability if there is no discernible standard against which to measure result. Moreover, presidential decision is an essential source of democratic legitimacy for actions taken in secret with limited or no external input or review. At the same time, field operatives should press for sufficient detail so that the policy intent is clear and operatives are protected from second-guessing in the event of failure, and therefore will take greater risks in accomplishing the intended objectives. Moreover, clear direction also helps to militate against the conscious and subconscious bias toward risk taking or risk aversion that individual field officers may possess.

5. Liaison

Liaison is a critical tool in any context dependent on human intelligence collection, such as a global contest against jihadist terrorists. Liaison involves the formal and informal ties among allied, like-minded, or contextually like-minded intelligence services. Liaison authority is expressly found in statute and unclassified executive directive. Section 104(e) of the National Security Act, for example, includes within the DNI's authorities "Coordination with Foreign Governments." Specifically,

> under the direction of the president and in a manner consistent with section 207 of the Foreign Service Act of 1980 (22 U.S.C. 3927),[62] (the Director shall oversee the coordination of the relationships between elements of the intelligence community and the intelligence or security

services of foreign governments or international organizations on all matters involving intelligence related to the national security or involving intelligence acquired through clandestine means.

The CIA director's responsibilities include the same charge with respect to coordination with foreign governments, "under the direction of the Director of National Intelligence."[63] How these responsibilities will mesh in practice will depend on personality and informal practice, as well as formal memoranda of understanding, and presidential directive. Clear lines of authority reduce opportunities for critical intelligence to fall between the metaphoric cracks. It also helps establish consistency in the application of U.S. legal policy on questions pertaining to rendition and the distinctions between liaison and covert action, for example. Good process also helps to address and mitigate the inconsistencies between overt U.S. foreign policies and clandestine intelligence relationships intended to foster liaison exchange.[64]

Liaison might also be conducted solely pursuant to the president's constitutional authority delegated by directive. (*See, Curtiss-Wright.*) Executive Order 12333, for example, includes language directing the (then) DCI to

> Formulate policies concerning foreign intelligence and counterintelligence arrangements with foreign governments, coordinate foreign intelligence and counterintelligence relationships between agencies of the Intelligence community and the intelligence and or internal security services of foreign governments, and establish procedures governing the conduct of liaison by any department or agency with such services on narcotics matters.

Significantly, the original definition of covert action passed after Iran-Contra included requests by the United States to a foreign government to conduct a covert action on behalf of the United States. The drafters had expressed concern in the Iran-Contra context about the use of third countries, in that case Brunei, to fund activities that were prohibited under U.S. law. The president vetoed this legislation on the ground that

> this provision purports to regulate diplomacy by the president and other members of the executive branch by forbidding the expression of certain views to foreign governments and private citizens absent compliance with specified procedures; this could require, in most instances, prior reporting to the Congress of the intent to express those views.... I am particularly concerned that the vagueness of this provision could seriously impair the effective conduct of our Nation's foreign relations . . . the very possibility of a broad construction of this term could have a chilling effect on the ability of our diplomats to conduct highly sensitive discussion concerning projects that are vital to our national security.[65]

In response to the president's veto, this element was dropped from the subsequent definition signed into law as part of the Intelligence Authorization Act of 1991. In signing the Act (and definition) into law, the president stated that he would interpret the Act's statutory definition of covert action including the exemption of traditional diplomatic activities in a manner consistent with the president's broad authority over the conduct of foreign affairs. This authority, the president indicated, extended to diplomatic communications where the president requested or urged third states to undertake clandestine actions. Such actions, without more, in the president's view, would not amount to U.S. covert action, but rather would fall within the president's constitutional exercise of the diplomatic instrument.

This view was echoed five years later during the dissolution of Yugoslavia and the civil war in Bosnia between Serbian, Croatian, and Muslim factions. The government of Croatia inquired of the U.S. ambassador in Zagreb how the United States would respond to Iranian arms shipments transiting Croatia to the Muslim forces in Bosnia. Following limited telephonic consultation with Washington, the ambassador was instructed to respond that "he had no instructions" (the "no instructions instruction"). The arms shipments proceeded without U.S. objection or acknowledgment. When the "no instructions" instruction was subsequently disclosed *within* the executive branch, the president's national security lawyers determined that, without more, the instruction did not amount to U.S. covert action. Thus, as a matter of law, it need not have been approved or reported to the intelligence committees as a covert activity. In addition, however, the President's Intelligence Oversight Board (IOB) was requested to determine whether as matter of fact, there was anything more involved that went beyond Washington's instructions and amounted to covert activity or otherwise violated U.S. law. To guard against what the *Katz* court recognized as the dangers of post-facto analysis and justification, the IOB was also encouraged to look at the legal issues with fresh eyes. The Board did so, concluding that without something more, a no instructions instruction was not a "covert action." The event and the IOB's conclusions were subsequently reported to the Congress as well.

There followed a congressional investigation into whether the "no instructions instruction" was "covert action." More importantly, the election-year inquiry examined the policy merits of looking the other way in the interest of preventing the slaughter of Bosnia's Muslims while Iran potentially gained access and influence in the Balkans. Policy merits aside, as a matter of law the instruction was not action, nor "U.S. covert action," but rather fell squarely within the construct of diplomatic conduct reflected in President George H. W. Bush's veto of the original covert action statute and his subsequent signing statement.

As an intelligence function, liaison lies somewhere between collection and covert action and between covert action and diplomacy. Liaison incorporates all that the United States brings to the collection table as well as all that foreign liaison services bring. This is particularly important in the area of human intelligence and counter-terrorism where foreign services may have greater access based on ethnicity, nationality, proximity, or security focus. Moreover, a global collection effort is too broad for any one service, however competent, to successfully cover the field.

However, liaison also entails action, although most liaison entails the routine passage of information that one might expect between allies. Closer to the edge of the liaison envelope there is a thin line between liaison and covert action. This line is in sight where, for example, U.S. information may not just inform a liaison partner, but predictably result in the partner taking action on the basis of the intelligence provided. The provision of satellite photographs, for example, or information pinpointing the location of a weapons lab might be used to inform defensive planning or it may provide the missing link in a decision to use military force. The legal question, in context, is how much is too much U.S. involvement such that the activities should be considered U.S. covert action? In other circumstances, where the United States is itself engaging in action, for example, an extraordinary rendition, with the participation of the host nation, the activity may fall outside the construct of covert action because the U.S. role is indeed apparent, at least to the assisting government.

Liaison can carry all the policy implications, benefits, and risks of a covert activity. (Our liaison counterparts would not be any good at intelligence if they were not getting something in return for their assistance other than goodwill.) This is noteworthy as U.S. liaison relationships may extend beyond a predictable ring of democracies. Moreover, there is additional policy risk with liaison, because, in general, liaison activities receive less formal executive review than covert action. Most intelligence liaison is considered an internal intelligence agency activity. The legal policy question is, are liaison activities subject to an adequate measure of preview and review to confirm that (1) we are accomplishing all that we can accomplish but (2) that we do so cognizant of the policy and legal risks involved and where appropriate that we mitigate, curtail, or eliminate those risks? The importance of finding the optimum process is illustrated with reference to rendition, regardless of whether rendition is conducted using law enforcement or intelligence authorities.

C. EXTRADITION, RENDITION, AND EXTRAORDINARY RENDITION: LAW APPLIED

Extradition is the ordinary treaty-based process by which one state surrenders a fugitive to another state for purposes of prosecution. The United States has more than 100 bilateral extradition treaties and is party to approximately

10 multilateral treaties that incorporate "extradite or prosecute" formulas for persons accused of certain acts of violence, without regard to motive.[66] (A list of operative agreements can be found a compendium called *Treaties in Force*, available on the Internet.)

U.S. extradition practice is subject to a number of legal constraints. As a general matter, for example, the United States will only extradite on the basis of a treaty, a statutory principle found in 18 U.S.C. 3183 and known in practice as "the Rule of Valentine."[67] The principle of dual criminality limits extradition to those offenses that are criminal in both the sending and receiving states. This is determined in older treaties by reference to lists of offenses (hence reference to these treaties as "list" treaties). Model and modern treaties incorporate the principle of dual criminality by reference to the conduct as defined by the elements of offense and not specific terminology or choice of title. This recognizes the varied manner in which similar offenses are treated in different national codes as well as the emergence in modern codes of offenses not recognized at the time of treaty negotiation.

The rule of specialty bars a receiving state from prosecuting an extraditee for an offense(s) other than the one(s) for which the sending state executed extradition. As with much of extradition law, the rule is intended to protect a state's treaty right, not provide the individual with a right of action. Thus, the rule may be waived by the sending state.

The political offense exception to extradition has historically been intended to prevent extradition in cases where the receiving state intended to prosecute a fugitive for what are considered political crimes, such as treason, desertion, and statements of opposition to the government. However, the modern trend, driven by concerns about terrorism, has been to limit the political offense exception, if not eliminate it altogether in the case of violent offenses. Thus, the multilateral terrorism conventions adopted in the 1970s and later[68] have adopted a "prosecute or extradite" obligation for certain acts of violence without consideration of motive or characterization of the acts as "terrorism." On a parallel bilateral basis, to address court rulings applying the political offense exception to British requests for IRA suspects, the United States and the United Kingdom amended their bilateral extradition treaty to exempt from the political offense exception a majority of violent crimes associated with terrorism.

Some bilateral treaties bar the extradition of nationals of the sending state; the terrorism conventions do not permit such exceptions. In some cases this reflects internal constitutional requirements, political sensitivities involving the extradition of persons to the United States, or both. In addition, European states, and some others, condition extradition to the United States on the receipt of assurances that the death penalty will not apply.

As a matter of process an extradition request is initiated by diplomatic note and may be preceded, where there is a risk of flight, by a request for provisional arrest. The requesting state then has a defined period of time (sixty days in U.S. model treaties) in which to obtain and submit the documentation necessary to meet treaty requirements for extradition. Typically, the requesting state need only show probable cause that the requested person is responsible for the offense.[69] There is a strong presumption against bail for extradition subjects.[70]

Extradition from the United States entails the exercise of authority found in all three branches of government. The treaty itself is negotiated by the executive branch and ratified by the Senate. In practice, the U.S. district court serving as the extradition court reviews the identity and treaty application and determines probable cause; it then certifies extraditability to the secretary of state. The secretary of state then decides if it is in the national interest to issue and execute an extradition warrant, a discretionary political act by the executive branch.[71]

The process of extradition is far more solicitous of state interests than individual interests. And, while marked by diplomatic notes with ribbons, the process itself can show both flexibility as well as rigidity. States that wish to extradite will work hard to do so. The United States, for example, in the absence of a bilateral treaty with Egypt, relied on a nineteenth-century treaty with the Ottoman Empire to obtain custody over a fugitive. Conversely, states that do not wish to extradite will find in the extradition process opportunities to erect legal obstacles or to delay a process sufficiently to dampen requesting state enthusiasm. Ultimately, like much of international law, extradition practice is based on reciprocity. If the United States does not honor its commitments to extradite, our partners may abstain from honoring their commitments, and vice versa. In short, the sanction for noncompliance is noncompliance.

These are the basic rules. However, terrorism is different. Since 1996, amendments to the code permit the transfer of fugitives from the United States in the absence of a treaty of persons other than U.S. citizens, nationals, or permanent resident aliens, who have committed crimes of violence against U.S. nationals. Such extra-treaty transfers require certification by the attorney general that, in effect, the principle of dual criminality and the political offense exception would not be applicable if the fugitive were transferred pursuant to treaty.[72] The amendment reflects and recognizes the treaty basis for extradition, the historical practice of states to differentiate between their own nationals and those of other states, and the importance of terrorism in driving changes to the practice of extradition as well as other means of transferring fugitives and suspects.

The United States transfers and receives suspects using other means as well. Where the fugitives are not legally in a country to begin with, deportation can be almost instantaneous with the requisite governmental will to act. Such transfers are not subject to extradition process or principles; however, as discussed below they are subject to the principle of nonrefoulement and, as considered below, U.S. criminal law pertaining to torture. Fugitives from U.S. justice are also "rendered" to the United States through other means.

Under the *Ker-Frisbie* doctrine, U.S. courts will not look to the manner in which a defendant came before the court so long as the court has personal jurisdiction and substantive jurisdiction over the charged offense.[73] However, where the manner of apprehension "shocks the conscience" and the U.S. government is complicit in such conduct, a court may divest itself of jurisdiction and order the accused returned to his or her status quo ante.[74] This exception to the *Ker-Frisbie* doctrine is known for the lead case in the area *Toscanino*. However, in practice *Toscanino* has not deterred U.S. practice in seizing fugitives abroad for national security purposes. Moreover, these doctrines recognize the availability of informal assistance, with or without a treaty, for obtaining custody of fugitives.

The *United States Attorney's Manual* also recognizes the practice of "extraordinary rendition" in unusually direct language. Section 9-15.630 addresses "lures," defined as a "subterfuge to entice a criminal defendant to leave a foreign country so that he or she can be arrested in the United States, in international waters or airspace, or in a third country for subsequent extradition, expulsion, or deportation to the United States."[75] Section 9-15.610 of the Manual is titled "deportations, expulsions, or other extraordinary renditions." It states,

> Due to the sensitivity of abducting defendants from a foreign country; prosecutors may not take steps to secure custody over persons outside the United States (by government agents or the use of private persons, like bounty hunters or private investigators) by means of Alvarez-Machain type renditions [abductions] without advance approval by the Department of Justice.

Of course, the Department of Justice is not the only agency involved in the rendering of fugitives to the United States or third countries.

In the national security area, extraordinary renditions are not extraordinary at all. Informal processes of transfer are the prevalent method for obtaining custody over fugitives abroad. This reflects the security risk inherent in initiating formal extradition requests. It also permits governments who are either unwilling or unable to transfer fugitives publicly via extradition to do so through quiet means. Rendition also affords governments with domestic constituencies who may disagree with a particular transfer or oppose the United States generally an opportunity to do so without notice as well as to transfer nationals outside legal frameworks that do not permit such extradition. Finally, rendition in any form is inherently faster than extradition, which can make all the difference where critical information may be forthcoming as part of the process of plea negotiation or threat of re-transfer to a third country.

Post 9/11, many renditions, certainly the majority in the national security area, are not undertaken for the purpose of prosecution, but rather to gather intelligence and to prevent persons from engaging in military or terrorist operations. These renditions are conducted using the same mechanisms described in the *United States Attorney's Manual*, as well as through direct capture on the battlefield, the use of proxies, and the provision of reward monies to persons rendering designated persons to U.S. custody. Rendition is also (usually) conducted in secret. From an intelligence and law enforcement perspective, this may allow operators the opportunity to identify and arrest additional cell members or conspirators before it is known that one of their number has been captured and/or the suspect's computer and documents exploited.

Rendition is not a new practice.[76] Public testimony of former DCI Tenet indicates that there were at least seventy such renditions before 9/11, and the Department of State has posted a list of renditions on its website. But there is also no question that after 9/11 the United States has increased the practice of so-called third-party renditions, where the United States facilitates the transfer of a fugitive from one state to a third state, in lieu of obtaining custody of the fugitive itself. If one includes transfers to and from the U.S. facilities at Guantanamo Bay, Cuba, and perhaps elsewhere, the number of U.S. third-party renditions is easily measured in the hundreds, perhaps more.

Third-party renditions may occur where the subject(s) is known to have committed acts of violence associated with terrorism, but over which the United States may not have jurisdiction or may not have adequate evidence to detain the individual. Such transfers may also occur where the sending state may not wish to be seen surrendering the subject to U.S. custody, but is prepared to send the subject to a third state, without U.S. fingerprints on the operation. Further, as occurs between concurrent jurisdictions in the United States (e.g., federal and local prosecutors), governments may themselves opt to send fugitives to "preferred" locations, where the rules of evidence may be relaxed or penalties more severe.

The United States also "renders" persons to third states to facilitate intelligence gathering, disrupt terrorism planning, as well as to facilitate the prosecution of terrorist suspects. In some cases, the threat of such transfer may itself induce cooperation. In less euphemistic terms, some states to which the United States renders persons are alleged to engage in torture, and are criticized in the State Department's Human Rights Reports. In short, as in other national security areas the practice of rendition, in context, can present difficult legal issues and trade-offs.

There is no question that rendition can generate valuable, perhaps essential intelligence. This is hard to demonstrate empirically without access to the intelligence information garnered. But the value of taking a terrorist out of action is intuitive, even without knowledge of the intelligence take. Immediate operations are disrupted. Moreover, there is a ripple effect as the enemy must operate on an assumption that cells and operations to which the subject was privy are compromised. In at least one case, there is public indication that a significant terrorist attack – in this case the July 2005 Underground bombings in London, which killed 52 persons – might have been disrupted had the government of the United Kingdom not been reluctant to render a UK citizen from South Africa to U.S. custody.[77]

There is also no question that the practice of rendition, especially after 9/11, raises legal and policy concerns not present in ordinary extradition practice. First, persons rendered to certain third countries may indeed be subjected to treatment considered abhorrent or unlawful in the United States or by the international community on whose assistance the United States depends. According to the government of Canada, this has occurred. The question is how often, not whether. Moreover, because terrorist renditions are usually accomplished in secret, ordinary safeguards that might exist through judicial or even media oversight are absent.

Second, in the absence of the procedural safeguards incumbent in ordinary extradition practice, subjects of rendition may be incorrectly identified and innocent persons transferred. Moreover, even where the correct person is rendered, the predicate information for doing so is unlikely to be subject to the same measure of validation as in the case of extradition. In contrast, extradition warrants are subject to independent judicial (as well as adversarial) review as well as executive review by Justice and State Department lawyers. Moreover, the warrants are ultimately signed by the secretary of state, who is unequivocally accountable for what happens.[78] Each of these factors elevates the importance of effective internal executive process in reviewing rendition practice.

Whatever moral judgments are made about the practice of rendition during a conflict with jihadist terrorism, lawyers must consider in context whether U.S. involvement is of a qualitative nature to implicate U.S. statutes and international legal norms that would bar such transfers, or alter the manner and conditions under which transfers occur. The legal template of review should include three areas of law: domestic, international, and foreign.

First, a rendition must comply with U.S. law. That means as a threshold, the operation must be properly authorized. Depending on the facts, an extraordinary rendition might constitute covert action, a liaison activity, or a traditional law enforcement activity. If the operation constitutes covert action, then the president must authorize the activity, or it must fall within the parameters of an existing authorization. If the rendition falls under existing authority, then lawyers would need to consider if the activity nonetheless constitutes a significant undertaking requiring additional authorization.

If not covert action, the operation must still be approved in a manner consistent with internal U.S. directives, unclassified in the case of the *United States Attorney's Manual*, but otherwise generally classified. An operation that involves special means or assets, special risks to U.S. persons or to bilateral relations, or includes the violation of the territory of an unwitting state, should be subject to special processes and mechanisms of review and decision. Depending on the circumstances of the rendition, congressional notification may also be warranted, or required (perhaps in the event an action is deemed a significant undertaking pursuant to existing covert action authority).

Rendition may also implicate U.S. criminal law, including Title 18, section 2340, which prohibits torture, and section 2441, which addresses certain war crimes, subject to the applicable provisions of the Military Commissions Act of 2006. In addition to these laws relating to torture and war crimes, other U.S. criminal laws may be implicated depending on the operational nature of the rendition contemplated. For example, if the subject is intended to be brought to the United States for prosecution then lawyers will need to consider whether and how Fifth Amendment rights and procedures might apply as a matter of law or legal policy. As an unclassified benchmark, a lawyer might consider the rendition of Fawaz Yunis from Beirut to the United States in 1987 recounted in numerous court opinions.[79] And, to take an extreme hypothetical, if the rendition is to be accomplished by storming a civilian aircraft on the tarmac at a civil airport, then lawyers would have to consider whether U.S. criminal statutes applicable to the safety of civil aircraft were implicated.

Where U.S. criminal law relating to torture is implicated the U.S. government has stated that it seeks assurances regarding the treatment of the subject from the receiving state, including regarding the manner of the subject's interrogation, prosecution, and U.S. access to the subject as well as the information obtained from interrogation. In context, assurances from the receiving state may be required as a matter of U.S. law, depending in part on the degree of U.S. involvement and direction during and after the rendition. It should also depend on the track record of the country in question, both with respect to its treatment of prisoners and its adherence to prior assurances.

Assurances may take different forms, such as oral assurances, diplomatic notes, and liaison channel agreements. The government of the United Kingdom and the government of Jordan, for example, have concluded a public "Memorandum of Understanding" on the subject of rendition, suggesting both a certain level of concern and a certain volume of traffic.[80] The qualitative nature of the assurance may also vary depending on the foreign governmental level at which it is given. The more authoritative the source or instrument of assurance, then in theory, the more reliable is the assurance.

The United States must also consider whether to impose sanctions in the event of noncompliance and/or to determine whether as a matter or law, or prudence, U.S. personnel should oversee the third-party compliance with any assurances provided. Of course, the more intrusive the U.S. requirements the less likely the third country will agree to the rendition and/or perhaps the less likely it will share the intelligence take from the operation.

In the context of detainees transferred from Guantanamo Bay to third countries, an assistant U.S. attorney representing the United States in litigation has stated in court:

> We have obtained assurances before they are released that it is more likely than not that they will not be tortured in a country that they go to. In fact it has happened where we have not been satisfied with the assurances that a foreign government has given the United States, and we have not transferred those detainees.[81]

This language is familiar to criminal and civil lawyers as a preponderance of the evidence standard, less than reasonable doubt and more than probable cause. Of course, one might test the measure of assurance by considering whether the United States would accept a similar standard on a reciprocal basis, that is, whether it is more likely than not that a captured U.S. soldier or citizen would not be subject to torture.

A number of subjects of rendition have alleged that they were rendered in cases of mistaken identity and tortured, notwithstanding U.S. policy on assurances and torture.[82] A Canadian Government Commission of Inquiry concluded that Maher Arar, a Canadian citizen who was not the subject or target of investigation in Canada, was rendered to Syria by the United States where he was tortured.[83] Other states, challenged by human rights groups for the treatment of prisoners, have cited the U.S. practice of rendition as justification for their conduct.[84]

Renditions also implicate international and foreign law. Under international law kidnapping (a.k.a., snatches without the consent of the host government) is viewed as a violation of the territorial integrity of the host state (and in all likelihood a violation of local foreign law as well). However, as a matter of international law, the violation of sovereignty implicates the rights of the host state and not necessarily the rights of the subject of rendition. Call this "the Eichmann rule," after Adolf Eichmann, a principal Nazi architect of the Holocaust, who was abducted by Israeli agents in Argentina in 1960. The government of Argentina protested the violation of its territorial integrity and requested a meeting of the Security Council to protest. The Security Council subsequently passed a resolution stating that "acts such as that under consideration . . . may, if repeated, endanger international peace and security." In addition, Israel was requested to "make appropriate reparation in accordance with the UN Charter and the rules of international law."

Then in a joint statement with the government of Argentina the government of Israel declared the matter closed and admitted that Israeli nationals had infringed the fundamental rights...of Argentina." Full diplomatic relations were restored. Eichmann was tried in Jerusalem and executed in 1962.[85]

Renditions may also implicate international law through operation of the Convention against Torture.[86] Article 2 of the Convention prohibits torture and requires parties to "take effective legislative, administrative, judicial or other measures to prevent acts of torture in any territory under its jurisdiction." "No exceptional circumstances whatsoever, whether a state of war or a threat of war, internal political instability or any other pubic emergency, may be invoked as justification for torture." Article 4, in turn requires each state party to "ensure that all acts of torture are offences under its criminal law." In addition, Article 3 contains a nonrefoulement clause. "No State Party shall expel, return ("refouler") or extradite a person to another State where there are substantial grounds for believing that he would be in danger of being subjected to torture." Thus, regardless of how the United States defines and interprets *its* criminal law implementing the Torture Convention, other states may define the term differently and seek to prosecute U.S. actors or their own officials involved in renditions that may be alleged to violate these norms. It should also be noted that the Rome Treaty, establishing the International Criminal Court, includes "torture" within its jurisdiction over crimes against humanity and "torture or inhuman treatment" within its jurisdiction over war crimes.[87]

Rendition can also implicate the local (foreign) law of the jurisdiction where the rendition takes place and along the route of ingress and egress (e.g., a refueling stop). Thus, even where an operation is conducted in a manner consistent with U.S. law, it may yet subject U.S. actors and others to criminal exposure in foreign states, for kidnapping, or for violating local law implementing international treaties or prescribing domestic rights. News accounts indicate that at least four states – Sweden, Switzerland, Spain, and Italy – are reported to have conducted criminal investigations into alleged U.S. activities in those countries to render terrorist suspects to third parties.[88] At minimum, such risks should be balanced against the importance of the seizure in question, and the risk to bilateral relations including the impact on future extradition cooperation, as well as to multilateral efforts to bring terrorists to justice. Recall as well that in *Ker*, the Supreme Court did not object to the manner in which the defendant was brought before the court. But, the Court noted as well, Peru was not without recourse, for the extradition treaty between the United States and Peru "provides for the extradition of persons charged with kidnapping, and, on demand...the party who is guilty of it, *could* be surrendered..." (emphasis supplied).[89]

In other words, the potential application of foreign law is not a new concern. In the case of the *Caroline*, discussed in the next chapter, British raiders sent a U.S. merchant vessel engaged in clandestine arms shipments to Canada over Niagara Falls. One of those agents was eventually apprehended in Buffalo, New York, and placed on trial for murder. In the case of the *Rainbow Warrior* incident in New Zealand, two French intelligence agents responsible for sinking the Greenpeace vessel in 1985, which killed a photographer on board, were arrested and subsequently pleaded guilty to manslaughter and damage to a ship by means of an explosive. The agents served abbreviated terms and were repatriated back to France by 1988.[90]

What is new is the multidimensional application of foreign law. In addition to local criminal laws, lawyers must consider the possible application of foreign laws implicating international conventions on torture, war crimes, and other offenses, as well as the multiple forums that might assert jurisdiction over such allegations. For example, the fact that U.S. lawyers or presidents take the view that an activity does not constitute torture, or that assurances are adequate as a matter of U.S. law, does not mean that a foreign state will have implemented the Torture Convention with the same interpretation in mind. Moreover, the U.S. view of the law may be predicated on principles of constitutional rather than international law, which would not apply in foreign context. In addition, good faith interpretations may vary depending on context, including the degree to which the foreign state's view of the law is informed by the same national security imperatives and pressures as the U.S. view.

As this review of U.S. law and legal policy indicates, the practice of rendition in context can present difficult trade-offs between security and liberty, or more precisely the democratic values associated with liberty. Bad choices can result in lost intelligence and the escape of terrorist operatives, but they can also undercut U.S. efforts to espouse the rule of law and in doing so present a value-based alternative to extremism. An erroneous rendition, or even a well-founded rendition poorly executed, may cost the U.S. more in public diplomacy than it gains in intelligence. It may also curtail future intelligence liaison cooperation.

These factors should prompt U.S. officials to apply rigorous process in approving "extraordinary renditions." Timely rigorous process allows the government to better measure the costs and benefits of such operations and the value of foreign assurances and assistance. However, "process" might also serve to drive rendition practice into deeper compartments of secrecy and further away from lawyers and persons who might test, but also mitigate, the risks and consequences of renditions raising heightened foreign policy and human rights concerns. As a result, national security lawyers might well consider whether decisionmakers are employing a process of decision that is likely to meet the speed and secrecy needs of national security, but at the same time meaningfully considers such questions as:

1. the factual predicate for rendition;
2. the range of alternatives for displacing the subject off the battlefield, including the U.S. experience with each;
3. the opportunities available to garner intelligence from the subject, based in part on projections of knowledge;
4. the relative merits of public prosecution in the United States or a third state; and
5. the actual and potential positive and negative repercussions of each rendition operation.

A process that includes only one agency, or only one outlook, will maximize speed and secrecy, but will diminish the opportunities for evaluating the relative positive and negative values associated with a particular rendition.

D. CONCLUSION

The threat of WMD terrorism, and in particular the use of a nuclear device, will place extreme pressure on the intelligence function and its ability to find facts and predict intent. Intelligence is the fuel of counter-terrorism. It is the predicate for anticipatory self-defense and it is at the root of rendition practice. The conflict with jihadist terrorism may not be won on the library shelves of America, but it may be lost there if we lack the contingent authority to find an essential connection in the intelligence mosaic. This means that a successful campaign against terrorism requires broad and flexible authority to gather and integrate information. However, the sine qua non for such authority should be a meaningful process of appraisal, meaning the considered application of constitutional structure, executive process, legal substance, and the review of decisions, both before and after they occur. The successful use of the intelligence instrument will require constant appraisal and reappraisal of risk, including the risk to our legal values and therefore our public image and capacity to deter the next generation of jihad.

If intelligence information is the fuel, the president (and his immediate staff) is the engine of intelligence. Lawyers will appreciate this statement as a legal paradigm. Exercise of the intelligence instrument is an exercise in presidential authority. For sure, the DNI, CIA, and Department of Defense hold extensive and sufficient statutory authority to employ the intelligence instrument without the president. However, the president alone possesses functional efficiencies that *should* place the president at the center of intelligence practice, either directly or through his immediate proxies, such as the national security advisor.

The national intelligence capacity is diffuse, as is responsibility over its function. There are numerous designated members of the intelligence community,[91] and that number does not account for the many other agencies that in context may collect and disseminate information relevant to national security. In reality, the only official with the necessary legal and policy authority to centrally control the entirety of America's intelligence function is the president. He is an engine like no other. His reach extends from agriculture to war. When he calls a meeting, people come. He alone (acting directly or through his advisors) has the legal and bureaucratic status to definitively resolve bureaucratic disputes between the DNI and the secretary of defense, or between the CIA and DOD and DHS.

Perhaps the president's most important efficiency is his ability, through the NSC, to fuse disparate sources of information. During the Millennium Threat (1999–2000), for example, the national security advisor found that the most efficient method to collate and consider warning information was through a daily meeting of the NSC principals. On the one hand, this process kick-started the search and identification within agencies of relevant information by pulling information up and out of the bureaucracy rather than relying on it to rise in the ordinary course of practice. The 9/11 Commission referred to this period as "the one period in which the government as a whole seemed to be acting in concert to deal with terrorism."[92] On the other hand, this methodology is not a normative model for the effective use of the Principals' time, absent extraordinary circumstances. In theory, the mousetrap has to work without the secretary of state, secretary of defense, attorney general, and secretary of homeland security personally triggering it.

The institution of the presidency is also capable of rapid intelligence decision. It is common knowledge that the president can communicate around the world; nonetheless, readers may be surprised to know just how quickly the president can indeed assess, decide, and communicate in tactical scenarios. General Franks made the same observation during the second Iraq war when he commented on the speed with which certain targeting decisions were forwarded to and decided by the president. The intelligence process is also capable of rapid decision. In the context of the early conflict with Al Qaeda one of the most important of the president's intelligence findings was drafted and signed in less than one day – on Christmas Eve.[93] If necessary, the president could have orally authorized the same activity in the course of a conversation, subject of course to the subsequent drafting of a finding. Thus, the question is not whether the secretary of defense, the DNI, or the secretary of homeland security should direct a central intelligence function, but how these officials might best assist the president in fulfilling his responsibility to do so.

If intelligence is the fuel of counter-terrorism, and the president is the engine, national security lawyers are part of the policy crew that helps to navigate the craft of state. Intelligence information marks the legal path. However, not all lawyers are immediately comfortable with intelligence. Some lawyers find it hard to transition to national security practice, particularly to questions involving the use of force, because they are looking for evidence and not indicators, facts and not judgments. They are looking for a crime scene or a trial transcript. What they find instead are random pages pulled from the record of trial mixed with random pages from other records. The crime scene itself is often inaccessible and the medical examiner is altering, disguising, or removing the evidence. As a result, intelligence rarely presents a complete picture.

It is also useful to remember that what makes information intelligence is not its quality but its source. A CIA analyst's judgment about Milosevic's intent, or a human report about such intent, is not necessarily more accurate than the observations of a diplomat engaged in face-to-face negotiation.

In considering intelligence, it is also useful for lawyers to consider how much they have in common with intelligence analysts. Lawyers, like intelligence analysts, distinguish carefully between words. They operate with nuance. They understand the difference between a holding and dicta, but also understand how both may be seized and spirited away to unanticipated locations. As a result, intelligence officials like lawyers can be cautious and conditional in their advice, when the facts or the law are uncertain or emerging. Lawyers will also understand that it is fair for policymakers to test intelligence personnel on their facts, judgments, and nuance, just as it is appropriate for clients to test the reach and certainty of legal advice. And, lawyers know what it is like to get pressed by a client who wants a particular answer, or who wants to push the envelope of the law. Intelligence officials know this pressure too. The reality is some lawyers and some analysts bend to policy pressure; others do not. And there is a lot of pressure in the national security arena. This means that, like so much else with secret government, personal integrity is as important as law.

Lawyers are also essential role players in sustaining the process of intelligence decision and subsequent mechanisms of appraisal. Appraisal tells you whether your policy is working. Is information in fact flowing freely from agency to agency? Are the necessary informational tripwires in place in U.S. Attorneys' offices? It also alerts you if an authority is being misread (think of the Foreign Intelligence Surveillance Court of Review's opinion) or misused, before the single event becomes the norm. External mechanisms of review are muted, if they exist at all. Lawyers, as masters and often keepers of process, help to ensure that national security decisions are subject to the process they are due. The critical question is not whether an activity is covert, but whether the proposal is subject to the proper level of preview and review consistent with the policy and legal risks involved. Where intelligence information is concerned the question is not just what it means, but also who should see it, and how quickly.

The intelligence and military targeting processes I observed demonstrate that you can have rigorous (not perfect) preview *and* act with speed and security. The strength of these processes came from two sources, peer review and role playing. Not only is the bureaucracy more likely to get it right when the product is going to the president, but in most cases that means running the gauntlet of Principals' review. As a result, other information and other views beyond that of the most interested agency are brought to bear. On a different scale, the same phenomenon occurs when decisions are run to the cabinet head, as opposed to the office director.

Role playing is also important because the pressure to "get it right" is so strong with national security and the defaults may all point in one direction. Therefore, good process should include a devil's advocate to test facts, apply law, and identify the enduring consequences, and not just the immediate benefits, of action or inaction. The lawyer is a good candidate to play this role because he or she may be the only participant not directly tied to the policy at stake, and may be well suited to test facts and arguments as a counselor and not just a lawyer.

These processes also demonstrate that lawyers can be meaningfully integrated into the life stream of intelligence activity and not just act as speed bumps on the road to decision or used to clean up after the fact. This is not a given. It depends on the right combination of leadership, personality, and integrity that allows admission to the secrets without being co-opted in the process. Nowhere are these tensions more evident than in decisions involving the use of force.

8 Use of Military Force

Cicero said laws are inoperative in war ("*silent enim leges inter arma*"). In fact, there is U.S. and international law that applies to the decision to use force and the manner and method in which it is used. In U.S. practice there are three contextual legal questions that should arise when the president or his advisors contemplate the use of military force. First, does the president have the constitutional authority to use force? This is a "war powers" question. Second, is the contemplated force lawful under international law? This is a question involving that portion of the law of armed conflict[1] known as the *jus ad bellum* (thresholds for resorting to force). Third, are the means selected lawful? This is a question involving the *jus in bello* (the law applying to the means and methods of war). It may also be a question of U.S. criminal law to the extent that U.S. law implements international law, or imposes obligations independent of international law.

Few areas of law are as important to national security as is this collective body of domestic and international law. This is intuitive in situations in which force is actually used; however, in other scenarios falling short of force the implied or express threat of military intervention is itself the catalyst for policy influence. For the national security lawyer, no area of law will have the same implications in defining a world of public order and individual security. So too, in few areas, if at all, will the lawyer feel the same measure of pressure from the policymaker. The importance of this law to the combatant and civilian noncombatant is even more evident.

This chapter identifies generally accepted – "black letter" – principles of domestic and international law involving military force with which every national security lawyer, policymaker, and informed citizen should be familiar. Section A returns to the war power in U.S. law, with focus on the Constitution and the War Powers Resolution. Section B addresses the resort to force in international law. Section C also addresses the conduct of war, in particular the overriding and interrelated principles of target selection: necessity, military objective, discrimination, and proportionality. It is the application of these principles, among other things, which distinguishes terrorism as a weapon from the lawful exercise of force. Section D introduces the reader to the military chain of command – national security process in military context. In understanding the military chain of command, the reader will better understand the process of constitutional command as well as better identify those points in the process where lawyers may meaningfully apply the law and legal policy.

A. THE WAR POWER

For the lawyer, policy consideration of resorting to force raises a threshold question – is it lawful under U.S. law? The answer requires application of constitutional text, theory, and practice. It may also require consideration of any applicable statutory overlay, including the War Powers Resolution and case-specific legislation, like Public Law 107–40, "Authorization for Use of Military Force,"[2] or Public Law 107–243, "Authorization for Use of Military Force Against Iraq Resolution of 2002."[3]

The power to resort to force is in some manner both separate and shared between the political branches. This is clear from the outset of the Constitution. The preamble states "the Constitution...is established by the people...to provide for the common defence." Of course, the preamble is not law, but it does suggest that the authority to defend the country derives from the people and not a singular branch of government or extra-constitutional theory of law. This is indicated as well by the enumerated text.

Congress's war power is found in Article I, Section 8, of the Constitution, which states *inter alia* that "Congress shall have power":

"To declare War, grant Letters of Marque and Reprisal, and make Rules concerning Captures on Land and Water,"

"To lay and collect Taxes...to...provide for the common Defence;"

"To define and punish...Offenses against the Law of Nations,"

"To raise and support Armies;"

"To provide and maintain a Navy;"

"To make Rules for the Government and Regulation of the land and naval Forces;"

"To provide for calling forth the Militia to execute the Laws of the Union, suppress Insurrection and repel Invasions"; and

"To provide for organizing, arming, and disciplining, the Militia, and for governing such Part of them as may be employed in the Service of the United States."

Congress also has the more general enumerated power of the purse and authority to pass such laws as are "necessary and proper" to effectuate its enumerated authorities.

The president's enumerated war powers include those as commander in chief, chief executive, and those authorities that collectively permit the president to conduct foreign relations. These are the authorities cited by successive presidents in more than 100 "War Powers" [Resolution] reports as the legal basis for military action. In a time of homeland security and terrorism it is also worth noting that the president is charged in Article II "to take care that the laws be faithfully executed." Indeed, many of the president's extraordinary statutory authorities to deploy armed forces within the United States are predicated on the breakdown of the rule of law, in particular the Insurrection Act, discussed in Chapter 9.

If law were math, we might add up the clauses and declare Congress the winner. However, the Constitution was designed to avoid winners, an intentional system of overlap and friction. The question is not whether the war power is shared. It is. The constitutional text demonstrates so. But the powers are separate as well. The question is, how do these interlocking powers relate? To what extent can the commander in chief exercise his authority absent Congress's exercise of its authority? If Congress acts, the question becomes one of *Youngstown* analysis. Is the president acting at the zenith of his authority, or at its ebb? Or perhaps, as suggested in *Hamdan's* Footnote 23, is the president's power extinguished?

Separate and shared powers were intended to serve as a check on the use of force and as a method to ensure popular, or at least representational, support when force is used by engaging both elected branches in the decision. That is black-letter principle, not necessarily black-letter law. The legal issue is whether, when, and for how long the president can resort to force solely pursuant to his authority, or in the face of congressional opposition. But no matter how hard (or repetitively) advocates work to extract the last ounce of authoritative weight from each word and phrase in the Constitution and each page in the *Federalist Papers*, text alone does not resolve these questions in a manner that lawyers and policymakers can agree is definitive and binding.

1. Theory and Law

Because the Constitution provides for shared and separate powers between the political branches, rather than exclusive responsibility, in the absence of controlling text, questions involving the president's authority to resort to military force often depend on constitutional perspective. Text alone, for example, does not resolve how much unilateral authority the president might properly derive from the commander-in-chief clause, or the extent to which the "declare war" clause checks this authority. As a result, war power questions are ultimately shaped by and depend on theory.

War power theory runs a continuum of view, from the narrow – Congress alone may authorize U.S. involvement in combat – to the broad: the military instrument is an extension of the president's foreign affairs power and it is subject only to the positive and specific exercise of Congress's authority over spending, if that. Indeed, moving further along the spectrum, Justice Sutherland's extra-constitutional sovereignty argument in *Curtiss-Wright* might suggest that the war power is an inherent executive authority independent of the Constitution. In the opposite direction, the War Powers Resolution reflects a constitutional perspective, that of the legislative branch in 1973, suggesting that prospective and inchoate exercise of the congressional war power can extinguish the president's later exercise of his authority after sixty days.

Six prominent themes are evident in war power theory, although admittedly a short summary does injustice to the proponents of each theme.

Declaration of War Theory. The congressional power over "war" is limited to the specific legal act of declaring war, as that concept was understood in international law at the time of constitutional ratification in 1789. In the view of Gene Rostow, for example,

> No provision of the Constitution is less ambiguous than the paragraphs of Article I Section 8.... The language of these paragraphs is peculiar to international law, and can only be understood in the setting of international law. The phrase "to declare war"... in the Constitution has a specific meaning in international law.... The president can use the national force under all the other circumstances in which international law acknowledges the right of states to use force in time of peace.[4]

In reality, nations then as well as now resort to uses of force short of, and sometimes parallel to, declared war. In accord with this theory, Congress alone may declare war. But the authority to use force falls within the president's power as commander in chief, subject only to exercise of the congressional funding power, and then only if that exercise does not impinge on a core presidential duty.[5]

Offense–Defense Distinction. The unilateral power of the president to resort to force unilaterally (without congressional authorization) hinges on whether the policy purpose is offensive or defensive in nature. This is the view of William Howard Taft, who, after serving as president, wrote,

> The president is the commander-in-chief of the army and navy... Under this he can order the army and navy anywhere he will. Under the Constitution Congress has the power to declare war, but with the army

and navy the president can take action such as to involve the country in war and to leave Congress no option but to declare it or to recognize its existence.... it was only in the case of a war of aggression that the power of Congress must be affirmatively asserted to establish its legal existence. Of course, what constitutes an act of war by the land or naval forces of the United States is sometimes a nice question of law and fact.[6]

Defining Constitutional "War." The Constitution provides for a shared authority over "war," but not necessarily lesser forms of force. Therefore, questions of authority hinge on defining the meaning of constitutional "war," which the Congress alone can authorize.[7] Under this theory, the analysis then shifts to consideration of those factors that turn "mere" combat missions into "wars," like the number of casualties, as well as the duration and intensity of combat.

Operational Common Law. Constitutional questions involving force are resolved through application of an operational common law of force based on practice. Presidents have resorted to force without congressional authorization on many occasions and will (and may) continue to do so absent an affirmative and limiting exercise of congressional authority. This practice defines the limits of presidential authority. Where there are overlapping areas of authority, each case will present a sufficiently different factual and legal mix making black-letter statements of law of limited use in deciding war power questions. As with the common law itself, lawyers must consider the Constitution in context.

Imminent Danger and Attack. The president's unilateral authority is limited to cases of imminent danger to U.S. lives or interests, or actual attack upon the United States.[8] The threads of this legislative perspective are woven into the War Powers Resolution, which identifies three circumstances where the president might "introduce armed forces into hostilities": (1) a declaration of war; (2) specific statutory authorization; or (3) a national emergency created by attack upon the United States, its territories or possessions, or its armed forces.[9]

Majoritarian Mix. Finally, in light of the indeterminate balance of constitutional powers, resort to force does not present a legal question as much as a political question. Such a view might find its roots in cynicism or in majoritarian principles and constitutional intent. Whether the president can unilaterally resort to the military instrument is a question of political will. Each branch is free to assert as broad an expression of its own authority, or as narrow, subject only to an assertion of countervailing authority by the other political branch. This is constitutional law, because the paradigm reflects the drafters' intent that the elected branches decide whether or not to use force, either by exercising authority or by abstaining from doing so.[10]

As this sketch of theory suggests, the *who* involved in constitutional analysis is often as important, if not more important, than the what, where, or the when of the question presented. Indeed, one can trace the rise and fall of different theories within the Office of Legal Counsel (OLC) war power opinions. Although published OLC opinions inevitably hold for the president, the tone and caution will reflect the legal personalities and views of the attorney general, senior OLC and White House attorneys, and sometimes the president.[11] Legal analysis also depends on how lawyers and policymakers read and apply history.

2. The Common Law of History

Presidents have resorted to military force on numerous occasions in the absence of implied or express congressional authorization. The congressional Research Service has documented more than 225 such instances.[12] Although these examples fall on a factual continuum, it is possible to detect four general trends.

In a majority of circumstances, the president authorized immediate military operations of limited duration, like the *Mayaguez* mission or an embassy evacuation (known in military doctrine as a noncombatant evacuation operation, or NEO). Lawyers of all stripes generally agree that the president may authorize the military to address an immediate physical threat to U.S. lives or property, absent congressional authorization, consultation, or, in some cases like the *Mayaguez*, in the face of congressional prohibitions.

A second category, which is more difficult to define and classify, or perhaps only more difficult to agree upon, involves the use of the military for sustained, but limited combat operations to accomplish limited (U.S.) policy objectives; for example, the use of air power in the Balkans to halt Serbian involvement in Bosnia's civil war (two weeks of air strikes in 1996) or to stymie Serbia's campaign of ethnic cleansing in Kosovo (seventy-eight days of air strikes in 1999). In the latter case, one might note that while the U.S. intent may have been narrow, the potential policy impact was not. In attempting to protect two million Kosovars from ethnic cleansing, NATO was also influencing the movement toward independence for Kosovo as well as the secession movement in Montenegro. The 1989 invasion of Panama might be viewed in the same manner, due to its limited duration and limited casualties, including forty U.S. dead; however, the U.S. objective was more expansive aimed as it was at the removal and arrest of the de facto head of government, Manuel Noriega.

Of course, in some cases it was only in implementation that operations proved limited in nature, and less like "war" than anticipated, or for that matter, prolonged in nature, and more like "war" than anticipated. For example, the 1994 U.S. intervention in Haiti started with troops boarding aircraft prepared to engage a hostile force but landing as peacekeepers. Clearly, the president believed he had the constitutional authority to go in "hot" in the absence of affirmative congressional authorization. In other cases, narrow "noncombat" operations have evolved into direct and sustained combat operations, such as in Lebanon in 1982–1984, and in Somalia in 1991–1994. The threshold constitutional determinations are made at the outset, before these ground truths are known; however, the constitutional precedent is set with the factual result in mind; that is, seventy-eight days of air strikes, not limited air strikes.

Typically, the Congress has expressed support for U.S. armed forces, but has not authorized, nor legislatively precluded, the president from engaging in military interventions on the scale and duration of a Panama, Haiti, Somalia, Bosnia, or Kosovo. Depending on one's perspective, this might be viewed as a product of political caution, a reflection of the political division between the branches at a given moment, or a reflection of institutional perspective. Most likely there are 535 different explanations, which draw on all three perspectives.

The Congress has declared war eleven times, in the context of five conflicts: the War of 1812, the Mexican War, the Spanish-American War, World War I, and World War II.[13] In other instances, the president has authorized the use of force for periods of significant duration or combat intensity without congressional authorization, and in some cases in the face of implied congressional opposition. For example, President McKinley ordered U.S. armed forces to put down a nationalist rebellion in the Philippines in 1900–1901 following U.S. acquisition of the former Spanish colony. This conflict, which was funded, but not expressly authorized by the Congress, was conducted at a cost of 6,000 U.S. lives, and many times that number in Filipino lives. In 1918–1919, President Wilson ordered 20,000 U.S. forces to occupy northern Russia to secure the ports of Murmansk and Archangel. This operation was conducted at a cost of 353 U.S. lives. The forces were withdrawn in 1919 without significant engagement or accomplishment.[14]

Post-Vietnam, and thus following passage of the War Powers Resolution, the United States has engaged in three sustained air-ground conflicts: the Persian Gulf War (1990–1991),[15] Afghanistan (2001–present), and Iraq (2003–present). In each case, significant casualties were anticipated in advance of combat, including up to 20,000 in the first Iraq conflict. In each case the Congress expressly authorized the use of force. And, in each case, the president asserted an inherent authority to act alone, but nonetheless sought and "welcomed" congressional authorization. Lawyers and commentators were left to sort out whether such authorization was required or merely prudential, signaling to an adversary that as a matter of law the president was acting at the zenith of his power and as a matter of policy the nation was acting with uniform political support (at least at the outset).

3. The War Powers Resolution

If not resolved by constitutional text, or theory, some argue the war powers framework is defined by statute, in particular, the War Powers Resolution of 1973. As recounted elsewhere,[16] at the close of the Vietnam conflict, the Congress sought to exercise its "war power" prospectively through creation of a statutory framework. The War Powers Resolution was "necessary and proper," proponents argued, in light of the American experience in Vietnam and Cambodia. Proponents perceived that the president had significantly expanded the presence of U.S. forces in Vietnam and secretly in Cambodia without express statutory authorization, and perhaps, without congressional knowledge. The resolution became law over President Nixon's veto,[17] and its constitutionality has been disputed ever since.

There are three elements of the Resolution directly relevant to the war power debate:

a. Consultation

Section 3 provides: "The president in every possible instance shall consult with Congress before introducing United States Armed Forces into hostilities or into situations where imminent hostilities are clearly indicated by the circumstances." In practice, presidents have authorized combat missions without consulting the Congress (e.g., the 1980 Iran hostage rescue mission); by notifying a limited number of members immediately prior to an action (e.g., the 1986 Libya raid, or 1998 Afghanistan and Sudan strikes); through extensive prior consultation (e.g., the 1999 Kosovo air war[18]); and following a request for and receipt of express congressional authorization (e.g., Desert Storm, Afghanistan, Iraq 2003). As noted in Chapter 4, this provision is generally viewed as constitutional, in part, because it contains its own constitutional trap door – "in every possible instance."

b. Reporting

The War Powers Resolution requires the president to report to the Congress within forty-eight hours *after* introducing U.S. armed forces into hostilities or into situations where hostilities are imminent; into the territory, airspace, or waters of a foreign nation while equipped for combat; or in numbers that substantially enlarge U.S. armed forces equipped for combat already located in a foreign nation.[19] As a matter of longstanding practice, the executive branch does not indicate under what section a report is filed. This reflects the factual difficulty and therefore legal difficulty that executive actors have in distinguishing among "imminent hostilities," "ongoing hostilities," and situations where forces are "equipped for combat," particularly where it is hoped that the latter will deter the former. As importantly, a report involving "hostilities" would in theory, trigger the sixty-day clock. Indeed, only one report, that pertaining to the *Mayaguez* incident, has expressly cited to Section 4(a)(1) of the Resolution, and there the predicate deployment was over by the time the report was filed.

Among other things, the president is required to report on the circumstances necessitating deployment, the legal authority for the deployment, and the estimated scope and duration of the hostilities or involvement. Where deployments are made into hostilities or situations where "imminent involvement in hostilities" is indicated, a periodic report is required no less than every six months.

Successive administrations have submitted war powers reports "consistent" with the Resolution, but not "pursuant" to it. In legal theory, this indicates that the reports are submitted as a matter of comity (as a matter of constitutional grace) and not out of a sense of legal obligation, which might appear to concede that all portions of the Resolution are constitutional. In practice, grudging and pedantic debates within the executive branch over whether a soldier was "equipped for combat"[20] have given way to general legal and bureaucratic acceptance that "war powers" reports are part of national security process. As a result, national security lawyers now put as much time into preparing the reports as they once did into thinking of legal reasons a report need not be submitted in a particular context.

The majority of such reports are inconsequential and ministerial, even pro forma. In the case of a noncombatant evacuation operation (NEO) the mission is often over before the forty-eight-hour report is filed. Nor should there be doubt that, if he felt it necessary, the president could construe the reporting requirement as permitting submission of a secret report if he determined that public disclosure might imperil U.S. lives or ongoing operations. In the case of deployments whose contexts are inherently short term, reporting elements like that requiring a statement as to the duration of a deployment seem absurd as do reports reflecting small, but "significant," changes to the number of U.S. armed forces personnel deployed. For example, the doubling of a handful of combat-equipped soldiers might be viewed by some as a "significant increase" in the overall number of deployed troops requiring a supplementary report. To avoid such "hair trigger" reports, the executive branch tends to submit reports of bland and flexible generalization, decreasing the value of the report as a source of information.

The reality is that the Congress, if not the public, will learn of most operations in advance, or immediately after commencement, through the informal process of consultation and communication that occurs between branches. And, if not advised informally by the executive, in likelihood the press will provide timely notification of significant combat deployments, certainly within forty-eight hours of their having occurred. In the case of military operations after 9/11, where press reports indicate the frequent global deployment of clandestine Special Forces teams, the president's war powers reports adopt broad generalizations that avoid secrecy concerns and afford the executive maximum flexibility. For example, in the president's first War Powers Report following 9/11, the president stated

> I ordered the deployment of various combat-equipped and combat support forces to a number of foreign nations in the Central and Pacific Command area of operations. In the future, as we act to prevent and deter terrorism, I may find it necessary to order additional forces into these and other areas of the world, including into foreign nations where U.S. Armed Forces are already located. . . . It is not possible to predict the scope and duration of these deployments, and the actions. . . . It is likely that the American campaign against terrorism will be a lengthy one.

The subsequent supplemental reports repeat these formulations.[21]

Although the reports may not in fact serve to notify the Congress of deployments, they can serve a useful bureaucratic purpose if executed in good faith. (Here it is helpful not just to think of the Iraq war or the conflict in Afghanistan but also of a Bosnia or hypothetical Darfur mission.) The reporting elements can serve as a vehicle within the executive branch to identify internal policy fissures at a time when policymakers may be focused on the predicate reasons for deployment. Further, because the report is sent under presidential signature the report can serve as a useful test of purpose. Forty-eight hours into the mission, do the national security agencies agree on how the mission is characterized for the president, its goals, and its anticipated length? Does the president agree with the bureaucracy's characterization in the draft report or cover memorandum? Have events played out as anticipated at the time the president approved the mission? For these same reasons the reports are usually diluted to the lowest common denominator of agreement so as to avoid placing the president on a policy limb. Nonetheless, in the process of drafting even the generic report the executive may identify policy issues that, while not ultimately reflected in a report, serve as touchstones for internal executive consideration. Reports may also serve as a useful method of creating a paper trail of congressional consultation for long-term deployments.

c. Sixty-Day Clock

The most controversial provision of the War Powers Resolution is the so-called sixty-day clock, which states

> Sec. 5 (b) Within sixty calendar days after a report is submitted or is required to submitted pursuant to section 4(a)(1)[hostilities or situations

where hostilities are imminent], whichever is earlier, the president shall terminate any use of United States Armed Forces with respect to which such report was submitted (or required to be submitted), unless the Congress (1) has declared war or has enacted a specific authorization for such use of United States Armed Forces, (2) has extended by law such sixty-day period, or (3) is physically unable to meet as a result of an armed attack upon the United States. Such sixty-day period shall be extended for not more than an additional thirty days if the president determines and certifies to the Congress in writing that unavoidable military necessity respecting the safety of United States Armed Forces requires the continued use of such armed forces in the course of bringing about a prompt removal of such forces.

This provision represents a prospective exercise of the congressional war power. It does not just require Congress to act in a truncated manner, as in fast-track trade legislation, but purports to require the president to withdraw U.S. armed forces sixty days after their introduction into hostilities, unless the Congress specifically authorizes their continued presence. Where necessary to effect a safe and orderly withdrawal, the president may take an additional thirty days to do so. The Resolution states that congressional authorization shall not be inferred "from any provision of law, including any provision contained in any appropriation Act, unless such provision specifically . . . states that it is intended to constitute specific statutory authorization within the meaning of this joint resolution."[22]

All administrations since the passage of the Resolution have objected to the sixty-day clock on policy grounds. Among other things, policy critics argue, the resolution may encourage opponents of U.S. intervention overseas to create "hostilities" so as to start the clock. As President Nixon's veto statement asserted, once running, U.S. enemies would have incentive to hang on and wait it out, in anticipation of eventual U.S. withdrawal. Whether this is a realistic argument is another matter. Since 1973, the Resolution has not served to trigger the withdrawal of U.S. armed forces. However, as President Nixon also asserted, "Until the Congress suspended the deadline, there would be at least a chance of United States withdrawal and an adversary would be tempted therefore to postpone serious negotiations until the 60 days were up." This potential impact is harder to assess.

The clock may also turn legitimate policy debates over the merits of a deployment into legal debates using arbitrary deadlines unrelated to military effect or world events. In his veto statement President Nixon stated,

The proper roles of the Congress and the Executive in the conduct of foreign affairs have been debated since the founding of our country. Only recently, however, has there been a serious challenge to the wisdom of the Founding Fathers in choosing not to draw a precise and detailed line of demarcation between the foreign policy powers of the two branches.

The Founding Fathers understood the impossibility of foreseeing every contingency that might arise in this complex area. They acknowledged the need for flexibility in responding to changing circumstances.

As one critic has stated, "The crucial question in any war powers situation should be how the political branches can best cooperate in the nation's interests, not which branch is right or wrong on particular legal issues."[23]

As a matter of law, opponents of the provision argue that Congress cannot limit through statute the president's broad constitutional authority as commander in chief, to conduct foreign relations, and as chief executive. Whatever the scope of presidential authority, the Constitution does not define it in temporal terms. Therefore, if the president may lawfully deploy U.S. forces in the first instance on his own authority then there is nothing in the Constitution that limits that authority to sixty days. This position is affirmed by longstanding executive branch practice, acquiesced to by Congress as a voting institution.

In addition, the Resolution identifies an inherent presidential authority to protect the United States from attack, but does not recognize the president's inherent authority to protect U.S. nationals, such as those seized on board the *Mayaguez*. At minimum, therefore, the Resolution would be unconstitutional as applied to such scenarios. Thus, the Resolution may reflect the relative power of the political branches at the height of Watergate, but it does not reflect constitutional law. In any event, the 93rd Congress cannot bind a future Congress in the manner of its own constitutional interpretation. The issue then is not whether Congress is free to act using *its* war power, but whether Congress can exercise that war power in prospective manner to *terminate the president's future* use of *his* war power.

Legal proponents of the war powers clock argue that the Resolution is a legitimate exercise of the "necessary and proper clause," creating a framework that history has shown is necessary if Congress is to meaningfully exercise its enumerated authorities over "war." The framework is necessary, because the president often presents the Congress with a policy fait accompli and because the Congress itself lacks the political will to play its constitutional role on a case-by-case basis. Much as the Congress cannot extinguish the president's constitutional authority through statute, presidential practice and congressional inaction cannot have extinguished Congress's own authority, later asserted, in this case by the 93rd Congress. Further, proponents argue that the intent behind a shared war power was to prevent a single person (a.k.a. the president) from entering the United States into "war." The sixty days, then, is a form of constitutional measure to distinguish short-term uses of force from "war."

All Republican administrations have argued that the clock is an unconstitutional infringement on the president's authority as commander in chief.[24]

Democratic administrations, which is to say Presidents Carter and Clinton, opposed the clock, but did not ultimately express a presidential view on the clock's constitutionality either on its face or as applied to a given scenario. Presidents Ford, Carter, George H. W. Bush, and Clinton have supported repeal of the War Powers Resolution.[25]

As a matter of practice, the clock has generated considerable debate, but has not in fact triggered the withdrawal of U.S. armed forces. Nor am I aware of evidence (anecdotal or evidentiary) that the clock has dictated the pace or nature of military strategy and tactics; for example, by changing the pace of a campaign against military judgment. The clock *has* served as a reminder to those in the executive branch of the need to meaningfully consult the Congress during ongoing military campaigns, in order to deter questions of authority or potentially distracting lawsuits by members challenging adherence to the Resolution in court. Executive branch actors also know that in the absence of express authorization, regardless of their constitutional positions, an administration will be required after sixty and ninety days to affirm and restate its legal authority for proceeding with unilateral force in light of congressional, press, and public inquiry. This "opportunity" to review the legal bidding is not such a bad thing in a constitutional democracy. If past is prologue, it requires Republican administrations to do more than assert blanket statements of constitutional authority, and Democratic administrations to face squarely the constitutional issue presented, or risk the adjudication of a court challenge on the basis of standing alone.

There have been two instances where the clock was arguably triggered. In the case of U.S. combat in Somalia (1993), recounted in the book and movie *Black Hawk Down*, the executive branch took the view that U.S. armed forces were not engaged in continuous hostilities, but rather were subject to intermittent hostilities, each falling short of sixty days in duration. Thus, the clock never tolled. Only in retrospect was it clear to executive actors (and their lawyers) in Washington that during the summer and into the fall of 1993, U.S. forces were in fact engaged in continuous combat in Somalia, most notably with the warlord Mohammad Aideed. Nonetheless, it appears that the executive's position was taken in good faith, mimicking the lack of policy recognition in both political branches that the United States was in fact engaged in daily combat and not simply a string of snatch operations to seize Aideed and his compatriots. On October 3, 1993, ground truth came to Washington. Whether one accepts this constructive "intermittent hostilities" argument or not, one detects with Somalia the beginning of an operational code reflective of longstanding executive assertion. Whether constitutional or not, the sixty-day clock is not in any event factually in play unless U.S. forces are engaged in significant and sustained combat, or as some lawyers might argue in a world "war."

This operational code was affirmed during the seventy-eight-day Kosovo air conflict where the president authorized, and executive lawyers ratified, more than sixty days of continuous air combat in and over the Former Republic of Yugoslavia. A subsequent lawsuit by thirty-one members of Congress challenging the conduct of the air campaign beyond sixty days was dismissed for lack of standing (*Campbell v. Clinton*). The executive branch argued that legislation passed expressly and solely to fund the campaign constituted authorization for the purpose of the War Powers Resolution. Acknowledging that the War Powers Resolution states that funding authorizations and appropriations shall not constitute authorization for the purposes of the Resolution, the executive branch argued that one Congress could not dictate the means by which a succeeding Congress exercised its war power.[26] In light of the Resolution's language one surmises that pivotal lawyers within the administration found this argument persuasive, were disingenuous in their application of the law, or held the view that the sixty-to-ninety-day clock was unconstitutional, at least as applied to the Kosovo conflict. In any event, the president never affirmatively expressed a public view on constitutionality. Neither did he certify to the Congress that an additional thirty days was necessary for a safe withdrawal. The air campaign ended twelve days short of the ninety days arguably permitted under the Resolution.[27]

d. Appraisal

In review, five observations about the sixty-day clock emerge. First, most debates about the war power start with the Constitution, pass through the statutory prism of the War Powers Resolution, and eventually circle back to constitutional theory. The war power debate is irresolvable. For each enumerated presidential authority there is as well a congressional authority. Moreover, each political branch has an inherent incentive to assert the broadest possible authority (in the case of the president to act unilaterally) and to eschew legal concessions, out of concern that policy "precedent" will in some manner serve as future concession in a different context. Further, presidents will do what they believe necessary in the interest of national security. Therefore, presidents and their lawyers unsure of what the future may bring will rarely, if ever, concede a limit to the president's authority to act in military defense of national security. This will surely remain so in the context of a threat of WMD attack by terrorists or irresponsible nuclear weapon states.

Nor is there controlling constitutional case law. For reasons discussed in Chapter 4 courts are hesitant to answer abstract constitutional questions, and where individual rights are concerned usually limit their rulings to narrow constructs. Neither political branch is likely to seek litigation that would result in a definitive statement of constitutional law. For each branch, lack of clarity is preferred to a definitive, but unfavorable ruling. As importantly, as a general matter, neither branch is prepared to defer to the courts on issues of war and peace, which are indeed in practical terms if not in law quintessentially political questions.

That being said, case law does instruct regarding the constitutional framework. *Youngstown* in particular offers two timeless lessons. As the paradigm states, where the president acts pursuant to congressional authority, he acts at the maximum of authority, combining his authority with that the Congress can expressly or implicitly delegate. Similarly, where the president acts in the face of congressional opposition he acts at the nadir of his authority. This is an intuitive truism, but it is a constitutional principle that can be lost in the heat of constitutional combat. Thus, even where the president may (rightly) argue that he does not need legislative authorization (as executive lawyers are invariably prepared to argue based on the theories presented above), he may nonetheless benefit from its existence. A president that acts pursuant to Justice Jackson's first category will have flexibility to act in unintended ways and is more likely to sustain public support in the face of setbacks and casualties. In the case of a sustained conflict, or a failed conflict, the assent of both political branches adds legitimacy to military action.

These policy benefits, of course, must be weighed against the risk of seeking, but not receiving, congressional authorization and thus confronting a situation where the president is operating at the ebb of his authority rather than in the twilight of a *Youngstown* category two where Congress is silent (or more likely votes to support the troops, but not the president's policy). Moreover, as a matter of policy, such a category three circumstance may have the same practical effect as a funding cut-off by making the use of military force politically untenable.

Second, in practice the congressional war power is not self-executing. In contrast, the president has an affirmative responsibility as commander in chief to defend the country and to conduct foreign affairs. Thus events will compel presidential response; Congress's authority must be affirmatively exercised. Again to Justice Jackson, "We may say that power to legislate for emergencies belongs in the hands of Congress, but only Congress itself can prevent power from slipping through its fingers."[28] That is what the 93rd Congress sought to accomplish with passage of the War Powers Resolution, and its theoretically self-executing clock.

Third, a broad reading of presidential authority is not a modern response to world war, cold war, the nuclear age, or potential WMD terrorism. Recent assertions of authority represent a continuum of precedent with the past. What has changed is the operational means of attack and defense, not the constitutional practice. In this sense, the naval wars of the eighteenth and early nineteenth centuries might parallel the use of air power in support of U.S. interests in later centuries. The WPR itself recognizes that the president has independent authority to use force for certain purposes, including in cases of armed attack. Moreover, whatever the president's authority is, even in the view of the 93rd Congress, this authority must exist for at least sixty days, for the Resolution states that it "shall not be construed as granting the president authority he would not have had in the absence of this joint resolution."

Fourth, the War Powers Resolution seeks to delimit what the Constitution has left unanswered, and do so in a quantitative manner, for which there is no textual support. Thus, while the Congress clearly possesses "war power," found for example, in the appropriations power, as well as the textually exclusive authority to "declare war," nowhere is there a temporal delimitation to these terms. Moreover, in the context of the founders' time, a sixty-day limitation on the president's exercise of a shared, or unilateral executive authority, would have been absurd, for any act of projecting U.S. military force beyond U.S. borders, that is, by sea, would necessarily have taken more than sixty days to accomplish.

Finally, even if the Resolution's clock is constitutional in some natural law sense, the Resolution will never control the constitutional outcome, unless the president applies it himself. But the executive branch has not felt bound by the sixty-day clock, either as a matter of law or policy. That will surely not change in the face of a WMD terrorist threat and the advent of new and unstable nuclear powers. As Justice Jackson observed, presidential advisors may not be able (or willing) to define the scope of the president's powers as commander in chief, but they certainly "would not waive or narrow it by nonassertion." Presidents, who bear the burden and singular responsibility to protect the United States, feel the same way.

In the absence of the president applying the Resolution's sixty-day limitation, members of Congress seeking to enforce the Resolution in court would have to obtain standing. That is unlikely to happen, as a matter of substance or process. Courts have consistently held that for members to achieve legislative standing to sue the executive they must demonstrate that their votes had been "completely nullified" and that they lacked political recourse.[29] Moreover, if Congress has the political will to obtain standing, it should also have the political capacity to effect its constitutional will directly, rather than through litigation. (Arguably a majority in one house might obtain standing; however, the same majority might then assert its will through exercise of the spending power.) In short, one can imagine that a political check on the president's use of his war power might apply before application of a judicially imposed War Powers Resolution timeline. The argument is succinctly summarized in the D.C. Circuit's opinion in *Campbell*.

Appellants fail because they continued, after the votes, to enjoy ample legislative power to have stopped prosecution of the 'war.' In this case, Congress certainly could have passed a law forbidding the use of U.S.

forces in the Yugoslav campaign; indeed, there was a measure...[but] it was defeated. Of course, Congress always retains appropriations author-ity and could have cut off funds for the American role in the conflict. Again there was an effort to do so but it failed; appropriations were authorized.[30]

Even were the clock to find its way substantively into court, it is doubt-ful a court would reach too far in its substantive analysis. The clock is a generalized and inchoate expression of one Congress's constitutional view that is intended to bind the constitutional view of a future Congress. More-over, the clock would apply in a context where the president will have acted in response to specific and articulated facts. In law, the rules of statutory interpretation generally favor reading seemingly competing statutes in a manner recognizing that specific language controls general language.[31] Sim-ilarly, in constitutional context, where competing constitutional claims are at issue, specific applications of particularized powers have controlled gen-eralized expressions of legislative or executive power. This was true, for example, in the case of the spending riders in place during the *Mayaguez* incident.

In those few cases where the Supreme Court has in fact balanced compet-ing constitutional claims it has applied the same principles. Thus, in *Nixon* the Court held that the Watergate grand jury's particularized investigative need outweighed the president's generalized concern about maintaining a deliberative process privilege. Likewise, the Resolution does not address the specific military and foreign affairs context in which the clock may actually toll. Thus, in constitutional balance, a Congress from the past will have spo-ken, but with a soft inchoate voice. In contrast, the president will have spo-ken with a current voice in a specific national security context, with specific foreign policy and military consequences.[32] The result is two expressions of constitutional view, the one inchoate and the other specific to circumstance and national security need.

B. INTERNATIONAL LAW

The law of armed conflict is based on textual instruments, most notably the Hague Conventions, the Geneva Conventions, and Protocol I, as well as cus-tomary law.[33] (Customary international law "consists of rules of law derived from the consistent conduct of States acting out of the belief that the law requires them to act that way."[34]) Protocol I, for example, reflects both treaty text and customary international law. Whereas the Parties view the Protocol as textually binding, the United States, which is not a Party, views many of the Protocol's statements as indicative of customary international law. In substance, the law of armed conflict addresses, among other topics, the resort to force, the use of force, the treatment of prisoners of war (POWs), the rights of belligerency, war crimes, the protection of civilians, and neutrality. The law does so by combining general principles (e.g., minimization of suffering) with specific tenets (e.g., a prohibition on "perfidy") and absolute prohibitions, such as that on the use of poison gas.

On a given basis, lawyers and policymakers must know and master specific provisions of the law. For example, the "war on terrorism" has generated numerous issues and debate regarding "detainees," "unlawful combatants," and "prisoners of war," and more generally, the applicability of the law of armed conflict to persons captured in a conflict involving nonstate actors. The descriptive nomenclature chosen to describe these issues may itself convey conclusions of law. These are essential questions, which have an impact directly on the success of U.S. offensive and defensive operations, as well as on perceptions about the values the United States projects overseas, and thus the success or failure of U.S. public diplomacy.

However, this section is not intended as a comprehensive survey of the law of armed conflict. Rather its goal is to convey essential principles that every national security lawyer and policymaker should know involving the use of force. As a matter of international law, when may a state resort to force? What principles apply to the application of military of force, and in particular to the selection of targets? How are general and specific principles of law sanctioned, if at all? References to additional general and specific sources are provided in the endnotes.

1. Resort to Force

Generally speaking, there are four widely recognized bases on which a state might lawfully use military force: (1) self-defense and collective self-defense; (2) anticipatory self-defense; (3) protection of nationals; and, (4) Security Council authorization. Qualification is necessary because in practice, governments, practitioners, and academics differ on their method of description and thus on the number of bases in law for using force. Protection of nationals, for example, might be subsumed within the concept of self-defense or represented as a distinct legal basis. This is true of regional authorization as well, which for reasons explained below, is included under the rubric of Security Council authorization. Further, the United States has asserted a right of preemption. However, there is insufficient clarity or continuity in U.S. practice to determine whether preemption warrants treatment distinct from anticipatory self-defense, as the 2003 invasion of Iraq would suggest, or whether preemption is anticipatory self-defense adapted to the WMD threat, as Al-Shifa might suggest. In any event, to the extent preemption differs from anticipatory self-defense, for example, in the predicate requirement of imminence, the doctrine does not (perhaps yet) reflect international law.

Qualification is also apt, because as explained below, other doctrines, like humanitarian intervention, are recognized by some governments and scholars, but are not yet generally recognized, nor, to this point, recognized by the U.S. government as a legal doctrine and not just a policy prescript. States also continue to resort to force without necessarily asserting a traditional legal basis for doing so. In some instances, the United States has in effect asserted a totality of the circumstances and adherence to the UN Charter principles as a basis for the use of force. Finally, even where lawyers agree on the law, they may not agree on the facts that underpin the assertion of that doctrine. In other cases, notably Israel's 1981 Osirik raid, legal assessments have evolved with the benefit of hindsight as seen through the lens of contemporary threat.

In addition to falling within a lawful construct, under international law the resort to force must also be necessary and proportional to the act giving rise to the right to use force. That is, peaceful mechanisms of resolution must be exhausted and the means, duration, and intensity of the force used cannot exceed that which is reasonably necessary to address the precipitating wrong.[35]

a. Self-Defense

Scholars, practitioners, and governments have long recognized a right of self-defense and of collective self-defense, in the case of requests for assistance where the requesting state has a lawful basis to act in self-defense. Classic U.S. illustrations of the exercise of the right after the UN Charter's adoption in 1947 include the invasion of Afghanistan in response to 9/11 and the 1986 U.S. air strikes on Libya following the La Belle bombing in Berlin, which targeted U.S. service members. However, scholars and governments have also long debated the threshold for resorting to force in self-defense in light of the UN Charter's limitation on the threat or use of force.[36] By extension the same is true of the right of collective self-defense where one state requests the assistance of another in defending itself. The scope of the right takes on heightened importance in light of the threat that jihadist terrorists may obtain and use weapons of mass destruction as well as the advent of additional and dangerous governments obtaining nuclear weapons.

Article Art 2(4) of the Charter states that

> All Members shall refrain in their international relations from the threat or use of force against the territorial integrity or political independence of any state, or in any other manner inconsistent with the Purposes of the United Nations.

Thus, as a baseline, the Charter is generally understood to prohibit the unilateral use of force, at least to the degree that force threatens "the territorial integrity or political independence of any state." Note as well that the Charter prohibits the threat of force and not just its actual use. As a result, the meaningful application of law requires national security lawyers to participate in the consideration of diplomatic options as well as military options. In theory, as well, the recipient of an overt or secret diplomatic threat of force should realize that if there are constraints on the subsequent use of force they derive from policy or diplomatic limitations and not the law.

However, Article 2(4) is also qualified by other Charter articles, such as those pertaining to the Security Council's Chapter VII powers (Action with Respect to Threats to the Peace, Breaches of the Peace, and Acts of Aggression) and regional organizations in Chapter VIII (Regional Arrangements). With respect to self-defense, Article 51 of the Charter recognizes that

> Nothing in the present Charter shall impair the inherent right of individual or collective self-defence if an armed attack occurs. Measures taken by Members in the exercise of this right of self-defence shall be immediately reported to the Security Council. . . .

Historical examples of such assertions by the U. S. government include Libya (1986), Iraq (1993), Afghanistan and Sudan (1998), and Afghanistan (2001) (although as discussed below the Sudan portion of this response might also be addressed in the construct of anticipatory self-defense). In each case the U.S. government filed an Article 51 report stating that the United States was exercising its right of self-defense.

The critical terms are "inherent" and "armed attack." For lawyers embedded in textual interpretation, this is critical text, for if there was an inherent right of self-defense before the Charter, the Charter arguably could not have extinguished that right even as the Charter seeks to limit that right to instances of armed attack. Two related issues arise. First, must an actual armed attack occur before a state may act in lawful self-defense, and if so, what constitutes "armed attack?"[37] Second, must a state wait for an attack to occur before defending itself, or does the inherent right of self-defense found in customary international law include a right to defend in anticipation of an armed attack?

For lawyers, debate over the meaning of "armed attack" centers on the International Court of Justice's decision in *Nicaragua v. United States* (1986). In the case, the government of Nicaragua sued the United States on the grounds that the United States had violated international law – including the territorial integrity of Nicaragua – by providing arms and training to the Contras and by mining Nicaraguan harbors in 1983.[38] The United States defended on the grounds that its actions were taken at the request of El Salvador and in the collective self-defense of El Salvador. Prior to any U.S. activities, El Salvador was the subject of cross-border incursions by Sandinista forces. Indeed, Nicaragua was supporting forces within El Salvador seeking to overthrow the elected government in San Salvador.

The ICJ ruled in favor of Nicaragua. Although there were multiple opinions, a majority of the court took issue with the clarity and transparency of El Salvador's request to the United States for collective assistance. Further, the court concluded that Nicaragua's incursions into El Salvador and its support for the Marxist insurgents in that country did not meet the threshold of "armed attack" under the Charter. Assistance to rebels in the form of weapons or logistical support "may be regarded as a threat of use of force, or amount to intervention in the internal or external affairs of other states," but it did not amount to armed attack. Thus, the U.S. use of force in response was not necessary or proportional. Nor did Nicaragua's actions give rise to a right to use military force in collective self-defense. The court did not seem to care that the objective of the insurgents was the overthrow of the elected government of El Salvador.

For those who seek clarity in law and find comfort in text, "armed attack" is a seemingly attractive threshold. "Armed attack" has evidentiary grain. It is, in theory, apparent to the world, and does not depend on subjective judgments about potential risk. For lawyers, it is also the nomenclature used in the Charter and in existing international "case law"; in other words, in those limited manifestations of international law found in text. But as *Nicaragua* illustrates, the threshold is not as clear as one might presume in practice. Moreover, it is not reflective of operational law, because it fails to account for customary law and state practice. In particular, the ICJ's 1986 characterization of the factual predicate for armed attack is inconsistent with state practice in responding to terrorism before *Nicaragua* and certainly afterward. States, including the United States, have asserted a right to respond in self-defense to singular acts of "terrorist" violence. Although total in reach and final for their victims, many of these incidents are clearly less significant threats to the territorial integrity and political independence of the attacked states than was an armed insurgency intended to overthrow an elected government. Second, the court's approach did not squarely address the evolving doctrine of anticipatory self-defense.

b. Anticipatory Self-Defense

Long before the Charter, let alone September 11, states recognized in military doctrine and law a need to preempt imminent attack, and in some cases the possibility of attack, rather than await the confirmation of armed attack. This is conceptually illustrated, for example, in the war plans of the European alliances prior to World War I. The German Schlieflen Plan, and those of other nations, was triggered not by actual attack, but by indications of the mobilization of national armies that might attack. The nature and necessity of reserve mobilization and the dependence on train transport to reach tactical and strategic positions meant that states felt compelled to respond to mobilization with countermobilization. The cascading effect resulted in armies anticipating the need to defend not necessarily based on concrete intelligence of hostile actions or intent, but based on mobilization necessities.[39] For without countermobilization there might be no opportunity to defend. Of course, the mobilization itself might in turn confirm hostile intent, leading to a circular march toward war.

For American lawyers the study of anticipatory self-defense usually starts with Secretary of State Daniel Webster's response to the *Caroline* incident of 1837. The *Caroline* was a private U.S. merchant ship used by U.S. sympathizers to run arms and supplies to Canadian rebels.[40] The supplies were shuttled to Navy Island located in the middle of the Niagara River where the rebels had retreated and were regrouping. During a lull while the ship was moored in New York, a British raiding party crossed the Niagara, set the *Caroline* on fire, and sent the vessel over Niagara Falls. Two Americans were killed in the process. The raiding party then withdrew to Canadian soil.

In the course of the next five years, the United States demanded redress. The British government defended the raid on the ground of anticipatory self-defense. Secretary of State Daniel Webster disagreed, arguing that the raid was neither in self-defense nor in anticipatory self-defense. He wrote his counterpart,

> It will be for that Government to show a necessity of self-defence instant, overwhelming, and leaving no choice of means, and no moment for deliberation. . . . It will be for it to show, also, that the local authorities of Canada, – even supposing the necessity of the moment authorized them to enter the territories of the United States at all, – did nothing unreasonable or excessive; since the act justified by the necessity of self-defence, must be limited by that necessity, and kept clearly within it.[41]

Here Webster identified the essential and related elements of anticipatory self-defense: imminence, necessity, and proportionality. Indeed, regardless of the predicate justification for resorting to force, under international law, the use of force must be necessary and proportional in relation to the conduct addressed. These terms are not authoritatively defined, and scholars and practitioners continue to debate their meaning as applied. Indeed, lawyers generally agree that Webster's formulation is too restrictive, placing too much emphasis on the immediate, near instantaneous, nature of the threat. This is certainly true with the advent of modern weapons like ICBMs and secret weapons like WMD, where lack of knowledge of the need to defend may well prevent any prospect of effective defense.

As stated at the outset, necessity requires the reasonable exhaustion of peaceful remedies with no reasonable possibility of peaceful means of resolution before a state resorts to force. Proportionality posits that states will not resort to a level of force beyond that which is reasonably necessary, in magnitude, scope, and duration, to deter or negate the predicate act. In general, countermeasures, of which force is the most extreme, should parallel the offending event; for example, the imposition of a trade restriction in response to an unlawful tariff. However, "an unrelated response is not unlawful so long as it is not excessive in relation to the violation."[42]

Illustrated in the context of the *Caroline*, the British response was arguably necessary and proportional. On the one hand, because peaceful remonstration to U.S. authorities regarding violations of Canadian territory went unheeded, military action was necessary. The response was also arguably proportional, because the use of force was limited to the destruction of the offending vessel; an invasion of New York, on the other hand, would have been disproportionate to the predicate offense. On the other hand, the U.S. actors had not directly attacked Canada nor manifested intent to do so. Forecasting the ICJ's later *Nicaragua* opinion, the crew of the *Caroline* had not crossed the threshold of "armed attack." They had supplied those who would do so in Canada; in doing so they may have had commercial as well as ideological reasons. As importantly, the British arguably could have accomplished their goal through lesser means by increasing the pressure on Washington to stop its citizens from interfering in Canadian affairs or by disabling the vessel and not by killing the Americans on board.

Today, the concept of anticipatory self-defense is generally accepted as black-letter law by most governments and scholars, notwithstanding *Nicaragua*. Moreover, the elements are generally agreed upon: an imminent threat of attack, a necessity of responding with military force to prevent the attack, and a resort to force that is proportional to the anticipated threat or to effectively deter the attack. The "classic" post-Charter example of anticipatory self-defense remains the 1967 Arab-Israeli Six-Day War. The government of Israel correctly assessed that the combined armies of Egypt, Syria, and Jordan were preparing to invade. Israel struck first, destroying much of the Egyptian Air Force on the ground as well as securing the Golan Heights and the Sinai.

The application of law to fact, however, is usually more controversial, especially in defining imminence. This is illustrated by the 1981 Israeli air strike that destroyed Iraq's nascent nuclear reactor at Osirik. At the time, this attack was uniformly condemned on legal grounds. The United States joined a unanimous Security Council (UNSCR 487, 19 June 1981) "Strongly condemn[ing] the military attack by Israel in clear violation of the Charter of the United Nations and the norms of international conduct." Legal criticism of Israel centered on the apparent absence of an imminent threat. The reactor was not yet operational. Indeed, the government of Israel acknowledged its judgment that the plant was eight months away from completion. Nor was there an apparent demonstration that Iraq would be capable of using the plant to produce weapons-grade fissile material, and there was no indication that Iraq possessed (at least at the time) a present intent to threaten or attack Israel.

Legal judgments depend on factual predicates. Determinations regarding the necessity and proportionality involving resort to force are contextual. They also entail judgments regarding the expected behavior of the recipient state. The United States has long held that such judgments must be made and evaluated in the context of historical practice. Where an equivalent measure of force may deter one actor, another actor may demonstrate over time that only a magnification of responsive force will terminate the unlawful action, a point demonstrated repeatedly by the actions of dictators like Hussein and Milosevic. Therefore, lawyers evaluating policy options resorting to force must understand and apply the policy and intelligence judgments influencing policy options and not just abstract law.

If policymakers believe a symbolic show of force (for instance, a fly-by) will accomplish the permitted goal, a lawyer will find it difficult, applying the principle of necessity, to concur in a significant use of force, such as the bombing of national-level military targets in a capital city. These judgments may be particularly hard to make in the context of anticipatory acts of self-defense, where the threat may be ill defined, inchoate, or unstated, but nonetheless instant and sudden if realized, as in the case of a WMD threat. These judgments are also difficult in an asymmetric terrorist context, where terrorists do not resort to ordinary military methods of command, mobilization, and attack, making it harder to discern the moment at which an attack is imminent and to discriminate between responsible actors and civilians in response. Thus, for lawyers, judgments about proportionality and necessity are hard to reach in the abstract without an appreciation for the policy context, policy views, and factual context. Sound national security process should therefore include a meaningful opportunity for the national security lawyer to engage policymakers and intelligence officials on the facts to inform judgments about the law.

The United States considered the prospect of catastrophic attack during the Cold War. However, the nature of the weaponry and the doctrine of Mutual Assured Destruction negated, in theory, any rational basis for launching a first strike, or defensive strike, in anticipation of attack. Assuming rational actors, the defense of the United States (and presumably of the Soviet Union) was not based on predicting the where and when of the opponent's attack and then preemptively striking first. Rather, defense was based on maintaining an arsenal with sufficient redundancy, mobility, and secrecy to guarantee the destruction of the opponent's government, cities, and military infrastructure in the event of an attack. Anticipatory self-defense ceded priority to Mutual Assured Destruction. But Mutual Assured Destruction means nothing to jihadists who affirmatively seek the assured destruction of their enemies, their populations, and their governments.

The ICJ's threshold for armed attack, to the extent it ever accurately reflected customary international law, is hopelessly outdated when a single vector might carry the smallpox contagion, or a suitcase-sized nuclear device could kill hundreds of thousands of people. The time to react and defend is not clear. There are no mobilization train schedules to watch and to warn. In this context as well, Secretary Webster's characterization of the predicate for exercising the right of anticipatory self-defense, "no moment for deliberation," seems firmly planted in the nineteenth rather than the twenty-first century. Neither the ICJ nor the Charter, and surely not Daniel Webster, anticipated the possession of weapons of mass destruction by non-state actors. This dynamic compels states to respond to indicators of intent and possibilities, as opposed to deeds of action. The risks of mass casualties preclude waiting for confirmation of armed attack. Where Webster had years to formulate his positions before transmitting them by letter across the Atlantic, lawyers and policymakers today may literally have minutes to do the same as they react to inchoate intelligence indicators.

c. From Anticipation to Preemption

The United States has sought to address this new threat in legal practice and doctrine. This evolution began in the mid-1990s when the U.S. government determined that it would apply not just the tools of law enforcement against the Al Qaeda threat but also the law of armed conflict, including the right of anticipatory self-defense. As noted earlier, this legal determination did not become public until after the 1998 Embassy bombings and the subsequent U.S. response. In August 1998, the United States conducted missile strikes against targets in Afghanistan intended to disrupt Al Qaeda by killing its command, including Osama Bin Laden. The strikes were described, and defended using the nomenclature of self-defense and anticipatory self-defense, not law enforcement.[43]

As important to the development of the law as this paradigm shift was the change in actual U.S. practice. Concurrent with the U.S. strikes against Al Qaeda in Afghanistan, the United States attacked and destroyed the Al-Shifa pharmaceutical plant in Khartoum, Sudan. From the Oval Office the president stated:

> We also struck a plant in Khartoum, Sudan, that was linked by intelligence information to chemical weapons and to the Bin Laden terror network. The strikes were a necessary and proportionate response to the imminent threat of further terrorist attacks against U.S. personnel and facilities, and demonstrated that no country can be a safe haven for terrorists.

Here one detects an effort by the United States to adapt the traditional doctrine of anticipatory self-defense to the untraditional threat of WMD attack by jihadist vectors. The United States also asserted a parallel right in the exercise of anticipatory self-defense to attack states that aided, or might aid and abet terrorists, at least those intent on WMD attack. In short, the United States argued with respect to Sudan that it could not wait for an armed attack, nor could it wait to determine whether an attack using chemical weapons developed in Sudan was imminent, as that term was previously understood.

Like Israel at Osirik, the United States could not hope to pinpoint the moment at which the plant would produce viable chemical weapons. Neither could the United States be confident it would detect the time and place where weapons or precursors might be transferred to third parties. Once in third hands, the United States could not track the weapons to determine in what manner they might be used. Thus, while the intelligence picture was incomplete, depending in part on information and in part on intelligence judgment, the security syllogism was complete. Al Qaeda had attacked the United States before and vowed to do so again. The United States had information that Al Qaeda was seeking chemical weapons. The United States possessed intelligence indicating, but not confirming, that Al-Shifa was the site of chemical weapons activity. The United States had information linking Osama Bin Laden to the Sudanese regime and which the DCI judged linked Bin Laden to the Al-Shifa plant. From the standpoint of national security decision-making the president's choice was evident, and more so today, than at the time; the intelligence judgment less so.

However, the U.S. legal message was lost in part because of variances in U.S. statements explaining the strikes as well as the corresponding skepticism regarding the quality of the intelligence linking the Al-Shifa plant to chemical weapons and to Bin Laden. As a result, it is hard to tell whether the absence of legal objection reflected a degree of state and scholarly acceptance of the U.S. legal argument, or whether it merely reflected that the focus of criticism was on the intelligence underpinnings behind the strike and lingering doubts that the United States had struck a civilian target.

September 11 would renew debate regarding the thresholds for anticipatory self-defense. This time the immediate catalyst was not practice, but the president's proclamation of a "preemption doctrine." The doctrine found textual manifestation in 2002 in the National Security Strategy of the United States of America, previously an unremarkable report to the Congress.[44] The Strategy stated:

For centuries, international law recognized that nations need not suffer an attack before they can lawfully take action to defend themselves against forces that present an imminent danger of attack. Legal scholars and international jurists often conditioned the legitimacy of preemption on the existence of an imminent threat – most often a visible mobilization of armies, navies, and air forces preparing to attack. We must adapt the concept of imminent threat to the capabilities and objectives of today's adversaries.

We make no distinction between terrorists and those who knowingly harbor or provide aid to them.[45]

The report left no doubt on the competence to determine necessity.

The United States has long maintained the option of preemptive actions to counter a sufficient threat to our national security. The greater the threat, the greater the risk of inaction – and the more compelling the case for taking anticipatory action to defend ourselves, even if uncertainty remains as to the time and place of the enemy's attack. To forestall or prevent such hostile acts by our adversaries, the United States will, if necessary, act preemptively.[46]

These same themes were presented in the National Security Strategy Report for 1999, before 9/11. Indeed, without citation it might be hard to distinguish the text in the documents.

America must be willing to act alone when our interests demand it, but we should also support the institutions and arrangements through which other countries help us bear the burdens of leadership.

But we must always be prepared to act alone when that is our most advantageous course, or when we have no alternative.

As long as terrorists continue to target American citizens, we reserve the right to act in self-defense by striking at their bases and those who sponsor, assist or actively support them.

The decision whether to use force is dictated first and foremost by our national interests. In those specific areas where our vital interests are at stake, our use of force will be decisive and, if necessary, unilateral. . . . We act in concert with the international community whenever possible, but do not hesitate to act unilaterally when necessary.[47]

If there are differences between the preemption doctrine and previous assertions of U.S. legal competence to act in anticipatory self-defense they are found in two areas. First, with preemption there is a presumption of uniform application, suggested by the elevation of this legal policy to "doctrine." Second, the threshold for resorting to preemptive force is apparently lower in practice than anticipatory self-defense, which is to say in the case of Iraq, described by some as a preventive war.

Where the government's lawyers described the 2003 invasion of Iraq using the nomenclature of UNSC resolutions and anticipatory self-defense, the president used the language of preemption.

> If the Iraqi regime is able to produce, buy, or steal an amount of highly enriched uranium a little larger than a single softball, it could have a nuclear weapon in less than a year. And if we allow that to happen.... He would be in a position to threaten America.... Knowing these realities, American must not ignore the threat gathering against us. Facing clear evidence of peril, we cannot wait for the final proof – the smoking gun – that could come in the form of a mushroom cloud.[48]

What do Al-Shifa and Iraq tell us about U.S. legal policy, if anything, at this time? First, there is continuity between Al-Shifa and Iraq. Both uses of force were directed (at least in part in the case of Iraq) at preventing terrorists from obtaining weapons of mass destruction. In both cases the U.S. action was predicated on intelligence judgments rather than factual certainties, and in both cases the intelligence predicates were subsequently put into question. However, there are differences as well in nomenclature and perhaps in the application of imminence. In the case of Al-Shifa, for example, the U.S. government held the view that the potential transfer of chemical weapons could be imminent in the traditional sense of the word. In the case of "preemption" the role of imminence is uncertain. The president's 2003 State of the Union Address seemed to suggest that imminence had been dropped from the legal equation altogether.

> Some have said we must not act until the threat is imminent. Since when have terrorists and tyrants announced their intentions, politely putting us on notice before they strike?

At minimum, the preemption doctrine appears to apply a lower threshold not only of imminence but also of factual judgment as to when force may be used. The vice president, for example, is reported to have said in 2001: "If there is a one percent chance that Pakistani scientists are helping Al Qaeda build or develop a nuclear weapon, we have to treat it as a certainty in terms of our response."[49]

After Iraq, the question is whether there is something more to preemption, or less (depending on how one looks at the equation) than anticipatory self-defense. Doubt arises because the doctrine has been described in different contexts in different ways. Lawyers tend to describe the preemption doctrine using the traditional vocabulary of imminence, necessity, and proportionality as in the National Security Strategy of 2002. Moreover, the 2006 National Security Strategy, in turn, seeks to place the concept within the framework of anticipatory self-defense:

> Yet the first duty of the United States Government remains what it always has been: to protect the American people and American interests. It is

an enduring American principle that this duty obligates the government to anticipate and counter threats, using all elements of national power, before the threats can do grave damage. The greater the threat, the greater is the risk of inaction – and the more compelling the case for taking anticipatory action to defend ourselves, even if uncertainty remains as to the time and place of the enemy's attack.

The 2006 Strategy also suggests a more contextual approach: "Though our principles are consistent, our tactics will vary."[50] The president's spokesperson has gone even further stating, "Preemption is not merely a military doctrine, it's also a diplomatic doctrine."[51] However, the president again stated in May 2006, "In this new war, we have set a clear doctrine. America will not wait to be attacked again. We will confront threats before they fully materialize."[52] There may be good reason for policymakers to obfuscate legal and policy doctrine, leaving potential enemies guessing as to U.S. intent.

Not surprisingly, after Iraq the preemption doctrine as a legal and policy prescript for force has been pronounced both dead and alive. Some argue, with hindsight, that the absence of WMD weapons in Iraq undermines the validity of a preemption doctrine. Certainly, the Iraq war has undermined public and international confidence in the U.S. capacity to accurately apply the doctrine, or perhaps alternatively, the capacity of the policy decisionmakers to effectively use intelligence in doing so. That is a matter of perspective.

Doctrine or not, legal concepts embedded in the concept of preemption are here to stay. First, as a synonym for anticipatory self-defense, preemption has always been part of the fabric of international law and U.S. legal policy. Second, whatever one calls the legal principle, after 9/11, no president will knowingly risk a WMD strike against America or an ally because they failed to act on incomplete intelligence that such an attack might occur. This trend was set in 1998, and it was repeated in 2003. It will continue. As Dean Acheson reminded, "The survival of states is not a matter of law."

Moreover, preemption and the threats that give it resonance are not solely a U.S. concern. One hears a policy, intelligence, and legal echo in the 2006 statement of the United Kingdom's Secretary of State for Defense, John Reid.

Another specific area of international law we need to think more about is whether the concept of imminence – i.e., the circumstances when a state can act in self-defense without waiting for an attack – is sufficiently well developed to take account of the new threats faced. In 2004, my colleague the attorney general explained the current position under international law when he said: "international law permits the use of force in self-defense against an imminent attack but does not authorize the use of force to mount a pre-emptive strike against a threat which is more remote...military action must only be used as a last resort...the force must be proportionate."

But what if another threat develops? Not Al Qaeda. Not Muslim extremism. Something none of us are thinking about at the moment. The proliferation of weapons of mass destruction has coincided with the growth of those prepared to use them. We know that terrorist groups continue to try and acquire such weapons and that they have described their willingness to use them. We also know that they continue to seek opportunities to launch attacks on a similar or greater scale as 9/11.

A debate would centre around 'imminence.' The very significant consequences of action or inaction these circumstances should give us all pause for thought....We all need to think about this problem. After all this is just as relevant – perhaps even more relevant – in the streets of Cairo and Karachi as it is in the streets of Cambridge and Cologne.[53]

The ongoing crisis on the Korean peninsula continues the debate. In June 2006, on the eve of North Korea's preparations for a long-range ballistic missile test, former Secretary of Defense William Perry called for a preemptive strike against North Korea.

The Bush administration has unwisely ballyhooed the doctrine of 'preemption,' which all previous presidents have sustained as an option rather than a dogma....But intervening before mortal threats to U.S. security can develop is surely a prudent policy. Therefore, if North Korea persists in its launch preparations, the United States should immediately make clear its intention to strike and destroy the North Korean Taepodong missile before it can be launched....South Koreans should understand that U.S. territory is now also being threatened, and we must respond.

Statements from the government of Japan made clear it was not only Secretary Perry who was thinking about military force. "If we accept that there is no other option to prevent an attack," Chief Cabinet Secretary Shinzo Abe said, "there is the view that attacking the launch base of the guided missiles is within the constitutional right of self-defense. We need to deepen discussion."[54] However, the U.S. government was not quick to endorse preemption as a universal norm. In the wake of North Korea's October 2006 test of a nuclear device Secretary Rice made clear to now-Prime Minister Abe that nuclear preemption should remain a U.S. option. "I reaffirmed the president's statement of October 9 that the United States has the will and the capability to meet the full range, and I underscore full range, of its deterrent and security commitments to Japan."[55]

States not subject themselves to a comparable threat of attack have eschewed endorsement of the doctrine out of concern for its misuse, and in response to events in Iraq. But there is also a geopolitical element to the legal debate. The Charter's "armed attack," in theory, provides an objective standard of international measure. Anticipatory self-defense, in turn is more subjective, relying on judgments of intent and indicators of preparation; preemption even more so. Preemption depends on intelligence and analytic judgments based on intelligence about future intent. This in turn means the United States on a global scale, and Israel on a regional scale, are better situated, if not singularly situated, to assert and exercise a preemptive right of self-defense because they alone have the intelligence capacity (incomplete as it is) to anticipate the requirement.

Moreover, because sources of intelligence information are usually sensitive the United States and Israel may be loath to make their full case in public, with specific data. As an illustration, contrast the reaction to the U.S. strikes on Libya in 1986 with the U.S. strike on Al-Shifa in 1998. In the former case, the United States identified a specific source of signals intelligence plainly demonstrating Libyan culpability in the predicate attack in Berlin. In the case of Al-Shifa, and U.S. concern regarding an ongoing WMD threat from Al Qaeda, the United States was not prepared to put its full case on the table of public opinion. The United States was left to express conclusions of fact and judgments, but without the underlying sources of information.

After Iraq it remains uncertain whether states will assert a right of "preemption" or return to the vernacular of anticipatory self-defense, while leaning forward in doing so. What is certain is that the real and potentially catastrophic WMD threat will continue to put new stress on old and theoretically settled constructs involving the right and scope of self-defense. The United States will continue to wrestle with the concept of imminence, with each president adopting and applying his view of the term in light of the intelligence presented and his perception of the threat.

In the end, different policymakers and lawyers may hold different views on what preemption means or should mean, and how it may vary from anticipatory self-defense. With preemption the three core elements of anticipatory self-defense (imminence, necessity, and proportionality) may receive different and competing emphasis, if they receive consideration at all.

What ultimately matters, however, is not what observers might make of the president's words, or how subordinate policymakers and lawyers might describe preemption. What counts is what the sitting president means by imminence or preemption and what that small handful of senior advisors who participate in threshold decisions involving the resort to force believe the concepts to mean. So long as a WMD threat remains, decision-makers who assume responsibility for protecting the United States from attack will wrestle with the intelligence and legal predicates for using force. Controversy over the potential and application of imminence will persist, whether the debate is described as preemption or anticipatory self-defense.

d. Protection of Nationals

In addition to self-defense, anticipatory self-defense, and perhaps preemption, the protection of nationals is an additional lawful basis on which states might resort to military force. The principle is accepted black-letter law. Thus, the Restatement of the Foreign Relations Law of the United States, concludes:

> It is generally accepted that Article 2(4) does not forbid limited use of force in the territory of another state incidental to attempts to rescue persons whose lives are endangered there, as in the rescue at Entebbe in 1976.[56]

Indeed, such a right has been recognized since the time of Hugo Grotius, the Dutch scholar whose seventeenth-century treatise is considered the baseline of modern international law.[57] Additional historical examples of the protection principle applied include Grenada (1983), the siege of the International Legation in Peking (1900), and the numerous instances recorded in War Powers reports involving noncombatant evacuations from U.S. Embassies overseas. In addition, the Israeli operations to rescue imperiled Jews in Ethiopia, Sudan, and Yemen during Operations Moses (1984), Joshua (1985), Solomon (1991), and Magic Carpet (1950) arguably fall within this rationale.

In theory, such interventions do not threaten the territorial integrity or political independence of the state in question because the goal is solely protective. In practice they need not do so. Significantly, the right is predicated, like other uses of force, on application of the principles of proportionality and necessity. Thus, the host state must be unwilling or unable to provide the necessary protection itself. The concept is also subject to false claim, as in the case of Nazi Germany's seizure of the Sudeten Land to "protect" the German population living there. The Serb interventions in Bosnia (1992) and Croatia (1991) further illustrate the capacity for false assertion. Thus, an observer might test the credibility of the protective claim by asking whether a state asserting such a right would accept a reciprocal application on its own territory.

e. Security Council Authorization

As a matter of Charter law, the Security Council has authority pursuant to Charter Chapters VI (Pacific Settlement of Disputes) and VII (Action with Respect to Threats to the Peace, Breaches of the Peace, and Acts of Aggression) to require member states to comply with its direction and to authorize member states to take actions that would be unlawful if engaged in unilaterally, including the use of force. Specifically, the Council's authority is found in Chapter VII, Articles 39, 41, and 42, which state:

Article 39

The Security Council shall determine the existence of any threat to the peace, breach of the peace, or act of aggression and shall make recommendations, or decide what measures shall be taken in accordance with Articles 41 and 42, to maintain or restore international peace and security.

Article 41

The Security Council may decide what measures not involving the use of armed force are to be employed to give effect to its decisions, and it may call upon the Members of the United Nations to apply such measures. These may include complete or partial interruption of economic relations and of rail, sea, air, postal, telegraphic, radio, and other means of communication, and the severance of diplomatic relations.

Article 42

Should the Security Council consider that measures provided for in Article 41 would be inadequate or have proved to be inadequate, it may take such action by air, sea, or land forces as may be necessary to maintain or restore international peace and security. Such action may include demonstrations, blockade, and other operations by air, sea, or land forces of Members of the United Nations.

As a result, so-called Chapter VII missions implicate the use of force and Chapter VI missions do not. This explains the cryptic focus in United Nations debates over whether a particular mission falls under Chapter VI or Chapter VII.

Resort to force pursuant to Article 42, in textual theory, requires a Security Council determination that the situation requires "all necessary means" "to maintain or restore international peace and security," "all necessary means" serving as the euphemistic trigger for authorizing member states to use military force.[58] United Nations Security Council Resolution 678, addressing the Iraqi invasion of Kuwait, for example, "authorize[d] Member States cooperating with the government of Kuwait, . . . to use all necessary means to uphold and implement Resolution 660 and all subsequent resolutions and to restore international peace and security in the area. . . ." Likewise, UNSCR 940, addressing the situation in Haiti in 1994, "authorize[d] states to use all necessary means to facilitate the departure from Haiti of the military leadership . . . and to effect the prompt return of the legitimately elected President."

In the Iraq context in 1998 and 2003, the issue was one of competence to revive "the all necessary means" language of UNSCR 678 (1990) following the 1991 Gulf War cease-fire (UNSCR 687). In the case of Operation Desert Fox (three days of air strikes against Iraq in December 1998), the United States argued that Iraq's material breach of the Gulf War cease-fire – the expulsion of UN weapons inspectors – reactivated the "all necessary means" language. Under the law of armed conflict a material breach of a cease-fire permits the party offended to resume the use of force. Thus, the critical questions were (1) whether Iraq's actions amounted to a material breach; and (2) whether such a judgment was subject to determination by an individual state (or a subgroup of those specifically offended, e.g., coalition members), or required the judgment of the Security Council, which authorized the use of force in the first instance. In the latter case, then the "reauthorization" of force would be subject to veto by a permanent member.

This same material breach argument was cited by the United States prior to the 2003 invasion of Iraq. The U.S. government also argued express authorization in the form of UNSCR 1441, which states that "serious consequences" would result from Iraq's continued breach of UNSCR 687. In context, the U.S. government argued, "serious consequences" had supplanted the normal nomenclature of "all necessary means" to reauthorize the use of force. Other states, notably France, took the view that "serious consequences" had been used in 1441 precisely because it did not trigger the use of force and in any event the United States undertook to return for express consideration of Security Council authorization to use force.[59] This was a technical argument among lawyers. On the world stage, as discussed earlier, the United States asserted the right to preempt based on the potential threat posed by Iraq's potential production of weapons of mass destruction and the possibility it would pass those weapons to terrorists.

There is insufficient state practice, and certainly insufficient recognition of that practice, to suggest that an operational code of tolerance presently exists to assert UN authority to use force outside the "necessary means" language, absent a Security Council understanding that in context other words carry the same meaning. However, Iraq resolutions subsequent to 9/11, in particular UNSCR 1441, have implicitly opened the door to an expanded vernacular of UN authorization to use force to include "serious consequences."

On the one hand, there is no legal reason the Security Council must authorize the use of force through the "all necessary means" language. In a diplomatic context there are advantages to alternative language that may enable critical parties to reach their own interpretive conclusions and assert their own preferred outcomes. Much like abstentions, some states may find it in their interest to adopt language affording a form of textual deniability if force is used. Likewise, there may be advantage in the element of surprise with the putative offending state not knowing whether or not force is authorized and will be used.

On the other hand, there are advantages to a confirmed vocabulary of force. Changes in vernacular from circumstance to circumstance will leave open the possibility for misunderstandings regarding Security Council intent and the intent of the relevant parties. At the extreme, if all words mean all things to all parties, then the value of Security Council authorization and responsibility will diminish. For the United States, such diplomatic sophistry cuts both ways. It may allow the United States to argue Security Council authorization in gray contexts, but it may also dilute the importance of the U.S. veto and result in dangerous reciprocal claims of authority. Moreover, members of the Security Council may be hesitant to ratchet up the pressure on recalcitrant states with increasingly robust resolutions if member states are concerned that states will use such language as authorization to use force. The Council might choose alternative language to authorize force. However, at this time, absent clear Council intent, it is hard to argue that authorization can be assumed or implied from alternative language.

As a distinct matter, states may assert UN "sanction" when they act consistent with Security Council resolutions calling for state parties to respond to a crisis or calling on states to take action in response to a threat to international peace and security. But this is not necessarily equivalent to language authorizing "all necessary means." In such cases, the United States has cited language in Security Council resolutions to justify use of military force as "consistent" with Security Council resolutions, and thus "the Purposes of the United Nations," while not necessarily asserting Council authority in doing so.[60]

Finally, Chapter VIII of the Charter also contemplates that force may be authorized through regional arrangements. Thus Article 52 states

> Nothing in the present charter precludes the existence of regional arrangements or agencies for dealing with such matters relating to the maintenance of international peace and security as are appropriate for regional action, provided that such arrangements or agencies and their activities are consistent with the Purposes and Principles of the United Nations.

However, the competence to use force under such Article 53 arrangements circles back to the Security Council. Thus, "no enforcement action shall be taken under regional arrangements or by regional agencies without the authorization of the Security Council . . . "

f. Humanitarian Intervention and Other Compelling Circumstances

States, including those most dedicated to the rule of law, have also asserted a right to use force outside traditional constructs, when in their view a totality of contextual circumstances justifies resort to military force. In the case of Panama, Grenada, and Kosovo, for example, the United States pointed to a series of factors, or totality of circumstances, justifying the use of military force. In each case the United States referenced principles of traditional doctrine, such as collective self-defense in the case of Kosovo and the protection of nationals in the case of Panama and Grenada. However, in arguing a totality of other circumstances, the United States was effectively acknowledging that the degree of force used exceeded that which was necessary and proportional to protect U.S. nationals alone. The U.S. military intervention in Somalia, of course, was also initially based on Council authorization on humanitarian grounds, but as in the case of Lebanon, the mission evolved into hostile combat operations as the initial legal basis drifted astern.

In the case of Lebanon, the invitation of the parties to the civil war to evacuate the PLO provided a lawful basis for the United States to enter Beirut, albeit as peacekeepers. However, after the initial successful withdrawal of the PLO, the American forces found themselves drawn into the conflict for a variety of reasons including the necessity of force protection. In Somalia, the United States intervened, consistent with Security Council resolutions authorizing member states to address the ongoing humanitarian catastrophe. Here too the mission evolved into hostile combat operations, and away from the original international legal basis. From these interventions emerged the concept of "mission creep": the transformation of a military mission (gradually and generally below the radar screen in Washington, hence "creep") from one of limited scale and duration to one of combat or "nation building" of indefinite duration. For lawyers the concept is important, because the mission may move away not only from the original military concept of operations but also from its legal underpinnings. This may have constitutional implications if the president has provided only limited authorization, or the Congress has delimited its funding of the operation in a relevant manner. It may also have international consequences if allied support is predicated on the application of particular legal doctrines. It may also undermine U.S. credibility if the U.S. basis for action under international law does not appear to comport with events on the ground.

In the case of the Kosovo conflict against Serbia, nineteen NATO allies found nineteen different paths to lawfully justify NATO air operations. The United States pointed to four factors as justifying NATO action: the unfolding humanitarian catastrophe; the threat of the Former Republic of Yugoslavia's actions to the security of neighboring states; the serious violation of international humanitarian law occurring in Kosovo; and resolutions of the Security Council, which did not authorize "all necessary means" (given Russia's veto), but did, pursuant to Chapter VII, declare the situation in Kosovo a threat to international peace and security, and "demand[ed] a halt to such actions."[61] However, while citing to the humanitarian situation for policy context, the United States did not assert a legal right to intervene on that basis. In effect, the United States argued a totality of circumstances, citing to concerns about regional security, collective self-defense, and humanitarian factors, but without asserting that any one factor expressly authorized U.S. military action against Serbia as a matter of international law.

In contrast, the British argued from the outset a lawful right of humanitarian intervention. The British position was motivated not only by events in Kosovo but also by a more general view that the law, and not just the policy decisions of state actors, had failed the hundreds of thousands of Rwandans massacred in 1994.

Under the legal doctrine of humanitarian intervention a state is presumed to have the lawful right to intervene in another state in response to violations of significant human rights violations. The right exists notwithstanding Article 2(4)'s principle of territorial integrity and even where the intervener does not have a direct connection to the persons affected. The doctrine, in theory, dates at least to the work of Grotius. In practice, humanitarian intervention dates at least to 1827 with the intervention by Britain, France, and Russia in Greece. This intervention ultimately helped to facilitate Greek independence from the Ottoman Empire in 1830. However, as Professor Sean Murphy argues the great power motives for intervening were far less beneficent than publicly presented at the time.[62]

After the Kosovo conflict, the British government, humanitarian NGOs, and some academic observers asserted that the conflict established as a matter of customary practice a lawful right of humanitarian intervention. Moreover, in reviewing the conduct of NATO's air strikes, the International Criminal Tribunal for the former Yugoslavia (ICTY) prosecutor concluded that NATO's resort to force was based on humanitarian intervention, but did not ultimately render an opinion on the resort to force, the prosecutor judging that her mandate extended only to the methods and means used.[63] This sentiment was also reflected by UN Secretary-General Annan, who espoused a "developing international norm in favour of intervention to protect civilians from wholesale slaughter."[64] With respect to Kosovo, the Secretary General said: "It is indeed tragic that diplomacy failed, but there are times when the use of force may be legitimate in the pursuit of peace." This statement can be viewed as supportive not just of humanitarian intervention, but also of alternative theories of legal authority outside the Charter context. A parallel debate occurred within the U.S. government behind not very closed doors as to whether the United States should, after the fact, recognize humanitarian intervention as operational customary international law, not just as a policy prescript.

Proponents of the doctrine argue that international law must be viewed in the context of the Charter's purposes and principles and not just its plain text, much as some argue in a constitutional context that rights are implied as well as express. Article 55 states that the United Nations shall promote human rights. Article 56 states that "All Members pledge themselves to take joint and separate action in co-operation with the Organization for the achievement of the purposes set forth in Article 55."[65] In this regard, Kosovo is indeed "precedent," whether or not states expressly asserted a legal right to intervene on that basis or not.

Opponents argue that this perspective should be balanced with the Charter's text and principles upholding the territorial integrity of states and limiting the prescripts for unilateral resort to force. Article 2(4) is after all an affirmation of the central role of the nation-state in the Charter. As importantly, as Professor Murphy concluded before Kosovo, there is little recognition in state practice that the doctrine is accepted as customary law, or indeed that those instances cited to validate practice were in fact truly motivated by humanitarian intent. Opponents of humanitarian intervention also note that the doctrine lacks objective criteria for application and is subject to malleable and reckless claims. The legal debate remains one of means, not ends. The question remains whether recognition of the doctrine is more likely to contribute to or undermine U.S. national security, human rights, and "international peace and security."

The Darfur crisis once seemed a likely catalyst to resume the debate. Indeed, in 2004 president Bush and Secretary of State Powell described events in Darfur as genocide, as did the Congress by concurrent resolution.[66] In the Genocide Convention the Parties "confirm that genocide, whether committed in time of peace or in time of war, is a crime under international law which they undertake to prevent and to punish" (Article 1). But the Convention is not self-executing nor does the treaty authorize unilateral resort to force. Rather, the Parties "undertake to enact" domestic law to "give effect to the provisions of the present convention" (Article 5) and "may call upon the United Nations to take such action under the Charter as they consider appropriate for the prevention and suppression of acts of genocide" (Article 8). Given the absence of Security Council authorization for member states to intervene in the Sudan with all necessary means, at one point it seemed that one or more states might assert a humanitarian basis for doing so.[67] But the slaughter and starvation persist years after the president of the United States first called it genocide. The absence of timely and meaningful state intervention appears to reflect a lack of political and policy will, not necessarily a sense of legal obstacle. There remains a recognized avenue of authorization at the Security Council. There remains as well the prospect that, in the face of a Security Council veto threat, one or more states may yet assert a lawful right to intervene on humanitarian grounds, as was done in the case of Kosovo.

2. Application of Force – Methods and Means of Warfare

If the president may lawfully resort to force under U.S. law,[68] policymakers and lawyers must also ensure the conduct of military operations is lawful because the law of armed conflict is disjunctive in application.[69] Lawful resort to force does not inherently make lawful the means and methods used in applying that force. For example, the principles of proportionality and necessity apply to the resort to force and as a distinct matter to the methods and means of force. Moreover, in contrast to some areas of international law that are soft in application (arguably including the law regarding the resort to force) the law regarding the methods and means of warfare is "hard," operational law. It is reflected in international treaty text, customary international law, and in U.S. domestic criminal statutes. It is also subject to U.S. punitive sanction, foreign state punitive sanction, and, on a more episodic basis, international punitive sanction.[70] As a result, the president as commander in chief not only has a duty to use force effectively in the interest of U.S. national security, but to do so in a manner that "take[s] Care that the Laws be faithfully executed."[71] Adherence to the law of armed conflict (LOAC) is also longstanding U.S. policy, regardless of military context. Indeed, the law is good national security policy and good military policy. However, U.S. perspectives on the scope of the law and its application in legal policy are evolving in the face of the enduring terrorist threat.[72]

a. Specific Rules and General Principles

The law of armed conflict seeks to minimize civilian casualties, collateral destruction, and human suffering for noncombatants and combatants. These critical legal policies are addressed in three ways: (1) through specific rules of conduct, (2) through absolute prohibitions, and (3) through the application of general principles.

The specific rules are generally found in treaty text, but are also the product of customary law. There are numerous generally applicable rules, as well as rules specifically applicable to ground, aerial, or naval (including submarine) combat. For example, the law generally prohibits the use of munitions intended to cause unnecessary human suffering, a principle often illustrated with reference to dumdum bullets. These were hollow-point cartridges used at the end of the nineteenth century that flattened and tumbled upon hitting flesh, therefore increasing the magnitude of physical destruction and suffering beyond that necessary to kill or incapacitate the opponent.[73] In modern context, scholars, governments, and soldiers debate whether other munitions like white phosphorous munitions, land mines, cluster bombs, and nuclear weapons should fall within this same category, especially when used in contexts where the weapons are unlikely to discriminate between combatants and civilians.[74]

By further example, the law prohibits perfidy, but permits ruses. A lawful ruse is an effort to fool the enemy, but that "does not invite the confidence of an adversary with respect to protection under the law."[75] The classic example of a ruse is the Trojan Horse. A classic modern ruse is the assignment of General Patton to command a fictional army in Scotland to deceive the Germans as to the true location of the D-Day landings. Patton's command came complete with radio transmissions to fictitious units, plywood tanks, and inflatable aircraft. Perfidy, which is usually equated with treachery, is unlawful, and involves a breach of faith with the enemy and is usually associated with the feigning of protected status like flying a false flag of truce or surrender, feigning civilian status, or feigning incapacitation. The Hague Convention and customary international law also forbid the use of a foreign flag or the uniforms of the enemy.[76] Thus, the wearing of the enemy's uniforms to reap confusion, as German soldiers did at the outset of the Battle of the Bulge, or the feigning of surrender under a false flag, are expressly cited as war crimes in the Rome Treaty.

The law of armed conflict also prohibits "treacherous killing," a more amorphous form of perfidy subject to interpretation. Treacherous killing is prohibited by Article 23(b) of the Hague Convention of 1907. The term is not defined; however, the prohibition is generally thought to prohibit the use of a civilian to poison a military leader. As this example illustrates, the law generates a number of potential ironies in the interest of higher principles and clarity. The law prohibits poisoning, but permits the use of more dramatic force, perhaps with significant collateral consequences, to attack the same military leader or a headquarters with the same objective – disrupting command and control. The intent, at least in theory, is to preserve the distinction between combatants and noncombatants (and thus generally protect civilians) as well as to regulate combat in a manner that promotes the use of regular units, wearing uniforms, carrying arms openly, and operating pursuant to recognized military chains of command. These principles, in turn, protect civilians (at least in theory) by making it easier to distinguish between combatants and noncombatants and giving combatants less reason to suspect civilians and shoot first and ask questions later.

Terms like treachery and perfidy are subject in context to interpretation. Other prohibitions are not. Thus, the law (including U.S. criminal law) contains absolute prohibitions on the manufacture, stockpiling, and use of chemical and biological weapons. That is not to say that some states do not harbor clandestine weapons or programs, only that there is no context in which their use might be lawful. The law also absolutely prohibits genocide, crimes against humanity, and war crimes, like the killing of prisoners. There may be legitimate debate on the elements of each war crime and application of fact to law, but not on the validity of the general prohibitions, which can be said to be *jus cogens*, or universally recognized peremptory norms subject to universal jurisdiction to sanction.

In addition, to the specific rules and absolute prohibitions, the methods and means of warfare are regulated through application of four related principles: (1) necessity, which requires that the military actions taken be militarily necessary; (2) military objective, which limits attacks to military objects that effectively contribute to the enemy's actions and whose partial or total destruction offers definite military advantage; (3) discrimination, also known as distinction, which requires combatants to distinguish between combatants and noncombatants in what they attack, but also how they fight; and (4) proportionality, which requires that loss of life and damage to property incidental to attacks must not be excessive in relation to the concrete and direct military advantage expected to be gained from the attack. In practice, states, NGOs, and academics may apply subtle (and not so subtle) differences in definition as well as in application of these agreed principles. I have sought only to describe the terms for the reader, rather than offer definitive definitions. (Some illustrative treaty and doctrinal definitions as well as the U.S. rules of engagement take from the Persian Gulf War are provided in the endnotes.)[77]

Whether you are a small unit leader applying rules of engagement on an index card, or a national actor in Washington reviewing the Geneva Convention commentaries before clearing strategic targets, these are the principles military decisionmakers apply. These principles are found in treaty text, customary international law, and US law through the application of the 18 U.S.C. 2441, the Military Commissions Act of 2006, and the Uniform Code of Military Justice. For the national security lawyer, understanding the source of law is important in determining the degree of legal and policy discretion, if any, available to the commander, as well as the potential ramifications of taking action that may be considered lawful in U.S. context, but controversial in international practice.

The source of law is also important in understanding where and at what level of command authoritative views on the meaning of the law may be rendered. For example, military lawyers cannot speak definitively to the meaning of the prohibition on assassination in E.O. 12333, unless they are certain their advice falls within the constructs of existing presidential views and any classified guidance the attorney general may have rendered on the subject.

However specifically defined, these four principles represent at once the strength of the law of armed conflict as well as some of its weakness. On the one hand, the principles account for the changing nature of the battlefield, because they are capable of being applied in context, whether that context is conventional warfare, counterinsurgency, or counter-terrorism. Where textual legal expression is, by its nature, frozen in time and requires interpretation the application of the law is consistently updated through customary and contextual application of these principles. Moreover, textual law is difficult to amend. As Protocol I, the Ottawa Treaty (on land mines), and the Rome Treaty (establishing the International Criminal Court) all illustrate, reaching agreement on critical text may be impossible, and where it is possible, may exclude critical actors, namely the United States. Customary application of principles in contrast has the advantage of deferring to specific context issues that cannot be resolved in the abstract with general rules. In the same way statutes like that pertaining to covert action defer critical constitutional differences to specific contexts, where particular circumstances may present clearer constitutional outcomes. As a result, the principles are adaptable to the operational environment as seen and felt by the combatant or civilian noncombatant in a way absolute rules are not. For example, Article 57 of Protocol I and customary international law require "all reasonable precautions" to avoid loss of civilian lives. What is reasonable will depend on the circumstances, including the nature of air suppression efforts or the past experience of military units in clearing houses and the means reasonably available to do so.

Even where a specific textual norm is implicated, decisionmakers, and lawyers often return to these principles to apply the law. The use of human shields illustrates the point. Consistent with the principle of discrimination, the law prohibits combatants from using civilians or civilian objects with protected status as shields to deter attack. Such use of human shields is considered a grave breach of the law of armed conflict and is included as an enumerated war crime in the Rome Statute (Article 8(b)(xxiii)). However, placement of human shields around a legitimate military target does not necessarily immunize the target from attack, not at least as a matter of law. Rather, in such situations, an opponent may attack the military object if such an attack is otherwise necessary, proportionate, and discriminate. In light of the heightened risk of civilian casualties, the use of human shields will likely change the application of proportionality to the putative target. If possible, for example, the method of attack would likely require adjustment to better discriminate and minimize collateral casualties. But the target does not obtain protected status on account of the hostages. In like manner and as a general rule, cultural landmarks, medical facilities, and places of worship are given protected status in the law and are prohibited from attack. However, a building or site with protected status may lose that status if it is used for military purposes and the principles described above are otherwise satisfied.

Such results may seem harsh. They are. But consider the alternative. If the law were otherwise, then human shields would be employed with regularity by military units, particularly those operating in occupied territory. Hospitals would become arms depots, and minarets snipers posts. Sometimes they do. Moreover, the necessity of such a principle is quickly seen if one imagines the enemy's critical communications node, or more dramatically, an Al Qaeda WMD cache surrounded by civilians, either as hostages (or volunteers) or unwittingly as inhabitants of a city surrounding a clandestine weapons laboratory. Lawyers might also note that concluding that an action is lawful is not the same thing as concluding that the action is prudent or that the direct military advantage garnered from attacking is not outweighed by the policy risks in doing so. Indeed, there are public instances where lawyers have "cleared" attacks, but commanders have nonetheless held fire out of policy concern for the impact of the action.[78]

At the same time, application of these core principles also reflects limitations in the law of armed conflict from both an operational and a humanitarian perspective. Professor Michael Reisman has noted that if customary international law "has the advantage of applying to everyone," it "has the disadvantage of often being hard to identify."[79] This is a source of frustration and sometime tension for commanders, policymakers, and lawyers, whether they are applying customary international law from an operational or human rights perspective. Likewise, the application of necessity, proportionality, and military objective at times is subject to imperfect definition and differing interpretation. Some prefer black-letter absolutes that make it clearer in combat what is permitted and what is not, rather than relying on a lance corporal faced with combat fatigue and fear to make morally complex split-second decisions. Not surprisingly, the cases that tend to drive debate with respect to U.S. actions often entail judgments involving the application of agreed principles to difficult facts, or that involve unintended errors in intelligence, equipment, munitions, or execution, but not necessarily in the legal framework applied or the result intended. There is also room for honest differences of view where the law is evolving based on practice.

Further, the law purports to establish, in the distinction between military objective and civilian object, a clarity that may not exist on the ground. Dual-use targets – for example, media relay towers or factories – largely fall on a continuum between objects that are distinctly civilian and those that are distinctly military in nature. Where they fit on this continuum may be a matter of intelligence judgment. The tension is also seen where a facility or enterprise financially sustains an adversary's regime – a perfume factory – and therefore ultimately the regime's military operations, but does not make a product that directly and effectively contributes to an adversary's military operations. This tension between choosing effective targets and traditional descriptions of military objectives will continue to shape customary international law. The policy frustration is that these may be exactly the targets that if attacked might not only persuade a dictatorial adversary of one's determination but also, more importantly, shorten the conflict and therefore limit the number of collateral casualties that would otherwise occur.

This tension is sometimes repeated in applying the principles of proportionality and necessity to the threshold for resorting to force. The commander and the lawyer might address the question from different ends of the force spectrum. The law of armed conflict seeks to limit the use of force to that which is necessary and not more, and by limiting the choice of acceptable targets to those whose destruction leads to a direct and concrete military advantage. As a result, the lawyer may look for that minimum increment of scope, duration, and intensity that will succeed, but at the same time, discriminate and minimize civilian suffering. The commander might work back from the top to ensure he employs sufficient force to accomplish the military mission. This is, of course, how decisionmakers approach policy. They define an objective and seek to identify instruments of policy that will achieve that objective, subject to law.

Asymmetric combat against terrorists and to counter insurgency presents particular problems in the application of the law. A mud hut is a lawful command-and-control target when occupied by a terrorist and his cell phone. Minutes later when the terrorist commander leaves, the hut may become another civilian home at risk of collateral damage. Both scenarios rely heavily on the quality of intelligence and the analysis that flows from that intelligence.

A further legal policy dilemma arises in military operations against terrorists, who do not care about the impact of combat on civilians or society at large. In these contexts, the destruction of traditional "military objectives" may be ineffective in influencing the enemy's behavior toward preferred policy outcomes. There may be a dearth of potential targets falling within the traditional "military objective" rubric; for example, training camps, laboratories, hideaways, arms caches. And, yet in the context of weapons of mass destruction, the most fundamental issues of national security are at stake. Therefore, in addition to striking the terrorist, there is pressure to find air and ground targets that will influence the behavior of the nonstate terrorist, or affect his base of financial and emotional support, and thus decisionmakers might hope his will or capacity to attack. Looking at the problem solely from the standpoint of policy effect rather than through a legal prism, this may mean a family compound or a home village. Similarly, and in specific factual context, the same tensions may arise in the case of protected sites used as barracks or to train jihadist terrorists.

b. Legal Policy and the Application of the Law

One function of the lawyer is to identify the critical legal policies at issue and to ensure that their objectives are likely to be realized in a new context by an appropriate and lawful application of force. This requires a process of meaningful and timely legal input to decision-making. It also requires not just an understanding of the law but an understanding of how the law often reflects good military policy.

Adherence to the law improves the prospects of, but of course does not guarantee, reciprocal application of the same principles by one's opponent. More broadly, as discussed in Chapter 3, the moral authority of the United States to espouse the rule of law is founded in part on its consistent and faithful adherence to the law. This is true in military operations as well. Adherence to the law helps to garner and then maintain international support (governmental, elite, and public) for US military operations. In the case of the 1999 NATO air campaign against Serbia application of the law was a *sine qua non* for the NATO political consensus necessary to authorize NATO military operations.[80]

Adherence to the law of armed conflict (LOAC) is also essential to sustaining U.S. public support for American conflict. This does not necessarily arise out of a societal sense of legal obligation, or commitment to the law, but out of a societal belief in the moral values embodied in concepts like discrimination and necessity. In corollary fashion, actual and perceived U.S. violations of the LOAC can erode public support for conflict and may overshadow or undermine the purpose and legitimacy of particular operations.[81] Commitment to the ideals embodied in the law in both rhetoric and reality also helps to sustain military morale, which is indelibly linked to the belief that the U.S. cause and means of warfare are honorable. Consider, for example, the words used by the Commanding General of the 1st Marine Expeditionary Force to exhort his Marines on the eve of the 2003 Iraq invasion: "While we will move swiftly and aggressively against those who resist, we will treat all others with decency, demonstrating chivalry and soldierly compassion for people who have endured a lifetime under Saddam's oppression."[82]

The LOAC is also generally consistent with military effectiveness. For example, the intentional use of ordnance against civilians is hardly economical and it is likely to reinforce an adversary's willingness to sacrifice and persist in the fight. Put more directly, indiscriminate or disproportionate use of force may have short-term military advantage, for example, in clearing a village or conducting an urban "reconnaissance by fire."[83] In the long run, excessive and indiscriminate force generally does not break the enemy's will to resist and ultimately can demean and degrade military discipline and professionalism. Indeed, indiscriminate bombing during World War II, for all sides, appears to have strengthened civilian resolve.[84] Moreover, unlawful force makes the transition to peace operations more difficult because of the civilian hostility that remains. Real and perceived violations of the law of armed conflict may also assist in the recruitment of soldiers to the insurgents' or jihadists' cause; conversely, there is evidence that the jihadists' indiscriminate use of force, at a Jordanian wedding in 2006, cost Abu Musab al-Zarqawi local support.[85]

In the counterinsurgency context, the law and sound military policy patrol hand in hand. To the extent military doctrine is predicated on winning and holding the support of the local population, the discriminate use of force is a prerequisite. At the same time discrimination in the use of force is particularly difficult in the counterinsurgency context where the enemy rarely is dressed in uniform, but rather seeks the cover and concealment of the civilian population. This is reflected in the revised U.S. counterinsurgency doctrine, which states,

> Any use of force generates a series of reactions. There may be times when an overwhelming effort is necessary to destroy or intimidate an opponent and reassure the populace. . . . In any case, however, counterinsurgents should calculate carefully the type and amount of force applied and who wields it for any operation. An operation that kills five insurgents is counterproductive if collateral damage leads to the recruitment of fifty more insurgents.

> It is vital for commanders to adopt appropriate and measured levels of force and apply that force precisely so that it accomplishes the mission without causing unnecessary loss of life or suffering. Normally, counterinsurgents can use escalation of force/force continuum procedures to minimize potential loss of life. These procedures are especially appropriate during convoy operations and at checkpoints and roadblocks. Escalation of force (Army)/force continuum (Marine Corps) refers to using lesser means of force when such use is likely to achieve the desired effects and Soldiers and Marines can do so without endangering themselves, others, or mission accomplishment. Escalation of force/force continuum procedures do not limit the right of self-defense, including the use of deadly force when such force is necessary to defend against a hostile act or demonstrated hostile intent. Commanders ensure that their Soldiers and Marines are properly trained in such procedures and, more importantly, in methods of shaping situations so that small-unit leaders have to make fewer split-second, life-or-death decisions.[86]

The fundamental principles of law – discrimination, proportionality, necessity, military objective – emerge from this text. But this doctrine was not written by lawyers. It appeared over the signature of General David Petraeus, arguably one of the Iraq war's most accomplished ground commanders.

The principles of precision embodied in necessity, discrimination, and proportionality are also important in the context of anticipatory self-defense and preemption. Where the United States exercises an anticipatory use of force, to the extent it is narrow and precise in its result, it is more likely to be accepted by observers and thus the norm of anticipatory self-defense recognized and sustained. Presidents may also be more likely to use force to protect against WMD attack when they can do so consistent with these principles, not just out of a sense of legal constraint, but because these principles also communicate policy constraint.

Finally, good faith adherence to the LOAC is the right thing to do. The protection of innocent civilian life remains the fundamental principle behind the Geneva Conventions and, more broadly, the LOAC.[87] The rule of law, and not just of men, remains one of the foundational distinctions between terrorism and tyranny on the one hand, and democracy on the other. In this context, the national security lawyer has a duty to provide not only legal advice but also legal policy advice, making clear to distinguish between the two.

Decisionmakers today often have an array of equally lawful and effective options that can accomplish the immediate and direct military objective, but that offer very different policy outcomes, repercussions, and risks depending on how they are employed. For example, where today's military commander may attack an electric grid to disable an air defense system, broader policy implications arise where technology enables the military to "turn off the lights" momentarily, permanently, or something in between. In contrast, the aerial destruction of a city's power supply during World War II presumptively entailed an exercise in area bombing. In short, precision targeting options today introduce a new array of legal and policy considerations that extend beyond the immediate military objective of the strike. Questions of proportionality and necessity in turn may depend on analytic judgments about the impact of such actions on the enemy and long-term effect on civilian populations. Likewise, for example, "dual-use" targets in a city should entail a further degree of policy and legal review than military targets in the desert, not just because they often present more complex legal questions of proportionality, discrimination, and military objective, but because the policy consequences of U.S. decisions are compounded.

Where controversial targets are struck, or will be struck, including targets where the direct and concrete military advantage may not be apparent, lawyers have a special role to play in testing the intelligence and subsequently articulating how the target is consistent with law and the principles behind the law. Consider, for example, the Israeli air strikes on Beirut International Airport during the conflict between Israel and Hezbollah during July–August 2006. The overt incapacitation of the runways was immediately questioned in the media. Among other things, the civilian airport was being used by civilian aircraft and by civilians seeking to evacuate Beirut. Opinion shifted, and in some cases changed, however, when the government of Israel revealed that the airport was also used by the government of Iran to resupply Hezbollah with rockets to attack Israel. Further, Israel indicated that Iran's resupply was undertaken by an Iranian civil 747 aircraft and Beirut airport was the only airport within Hezbollah-controlled or accessed territory in Lebanon that could accommodate such an aircraft.[88]

Aerial and land warfare generally offer distinct contexts and opportunities for civilian policy and legal review of targets. In many cases, air power is more susceptible to legal and policy adjustment than ground combat. Pre-planned and fixed targets, like runways, permit more time for legal policy review than mobile targets and targets of opportunity. For example, the commander, and in some cases the pilot, has multiple means and methods to vary an attack that can modulate the opportunity for mission success as well as vary the degree of associated risk to civilians, pilots, and ground combatants. Among other things, the commander can adjust:

Munitions – varying the size and type of the munitions delivered. For example, depending on the military target and its location a commander may choose to deploy a 500- or 2,000-pound bomb. A cluster munition will obviously bear greater collateral risk to civilians than a smart weapon; however, a smart weapon will not effectively block or channel an infantry advance. The United States has introduced a 37-pound smart bomb into its munitions inventory, the smallest in the arsenal, which permits additional precision in target acquisition.

Delivery azimuth and aim point – whether using smart or dumb weapons, the delivery azimuth will affect the nature and extent of collateral damage. For example, if there is a school located within the collateral glass ring 200 meters to the north of the target, the weapon might be delivered on an east-west azimuth on the southern rim of the target.

Angle of attack – the circle of collateral damage is also shaped by the angle at which the weapon strikes a target.

Fuse – the impact of a munition may also vary depending on the fuse used. For example, a delay fuse designed to carry the munition through fortification before exploding will have a very different collateral (and military) impact than a proximity fuse designed to explode the munition 200 feet above the ground.

Warning – in the case of a static target that cannot be disassembled or moved, commanders can also consider generic or specific warnings to local populations without jeopardizing pilots or military effect. For example, policy or military leaders may warn that all the bridges or rail heads will be severed across the Danube in Belgrade or across the Tigris in Baghdad, alerting civilians to stay clear.

Time of attack – on the same basis, the commander can modulate the time of attack so as to minimize civilian exposure to collateral effect. In general, city streets are less likely to be crowded at night or during certain days of the week. President Clinton, for example, noted the fact that the Al-Shifa plant had been attacked at night, which minimized civilian casualties as the plant did not employ a night shift.

The U.S. military has also developed the capacity to provide an extra set of eyes and additional data in the manned cockpit allowing air and ground support units to assist pilots in making target calls. Combined with detailed and rapid computer models, which can project blast effects, and a professional cadre of "targeteers," the U.S. capability to maximize discrimination and minimize civilian casualties is remarkable, and easily unmatched in history. But a few words of caution are needed.

The advent and increasing prevalence of precision weapons in the U.S. arsenal has led to unrealistic expectations that armed conflict, at least U.S. air-to-ground warfare, can be conducted with fewer or even no collateral casualties.[89] This is a worthy objective not just because it reflects the intent of the LOAC and is morally sound but also because it is good military practice. But precision weapons do not lift the fog of war, and lawyers should not confuse "precision weapon" with "precision decision." They do not address questions of perfidy and ruse, human and technical errors, or limitations in intelligence. And they do not address technical or logistical capabilities. Precision weapons are simply not the right choice for every strategic or tactical scenario and may not be "on station" in every tactical situation.

Further, because many precision weapons are either unmanned or incapable of effective launch from afar, or both, some may perceive that the United States is not taking "all reasonable measures"[90] to prevent collateral casualties when its pilots do not break a certain ceiling or even enter the airspace of the country affected in order to launch the weapon. Caution is warranted here as well. "Eyes on" can make the difference in distinguishing between a column of buses with refugees and one with combatants. But pilot "eyes on" will not necessarily change the quality of intelligence, if for example the target is a building or the target coordinates are simply incorrect.

Moreover, discrimination is not measured by the equivalence between civilian and military casualties, but by the avoidance and minimization of civilian casualties. Precision aerial weapons accomplish that end. Moreover, precision weapons can allow risk taking in verification that might be unacceptable, or in the words of the law "unreasonable," in manned vehicles. Further, increased pilot risk often means an increase in civilian risk as well. This might be the case where helicopters are employed in lieu of precision weapons and area suppression munitions are used to prep the area for helicopter operations. Further, regardless of platform, if pilots are shot down, ground troops will follow. And, ground combat is often more destructive and indiscriminate to civilians than aerial attack.

In contrast to aerial attack, ground combatants have less opportunity to modulate the methods and means of their attack. Company-grade infantry officers, for example, do not speak in terms of attack azimuths and aim points; their attack azimuths are envelopments from the left, right, up the middle, and over the top (airlift). The nature of indirect fire support weapons also limits options for variance. Such weapons are imprecise in relation to most aerial weapons. Fire, for example, is generally adjusted onto the target. Moreover, as in the case of naval gunfire, the trajectory of the weapon minimizes opportunities for adjustment. Naval gunfire, for example has a flat trajectory; therefore, if the target is missed, the munition will tend to go long as opposed to landing in the vicinity of the target. In context, this can make near misses appear like indiscriminate large misses and amplify the negative impact of any collateral casualties.

Ground operations also tend to be more fluid than aerial operations against pre-planned or fixed targets, at least where the United States maintains air supremacy or superiority. Even when aerial targets are emergent, there is often some time for command consideration as aircraft or weapons platforms move into position. In ground combat there are fewer fixed targets, and emerging targets usually require immediate response. Thus, there is rarely opportunity for senior commanders, including in context the president, to apply policy and law to targets other than through the provision of generalized guidance.

C. CONSTITUTIONAL CHAIN OF COMMAND

As a matter of U.S. law, military decisions must not only be made in accordance with the proper substantive law but they must also be made by the appropriate person or persons. Moreover, the appropriate person or persons must authorize not just the use of force but also the manner and method in which force is used. These decisions are made by, and then implemented through, the military chain of command. As a result, the national security lawyer must understand the military chain of command to understand where to provide meaningful advice and how to better appraise the operation of law and consider if the process or practice warrants adjustment.

The military chain of command originates with the president. The plain text of the Constitution states so:

> The president shall be Commander in Chief of the Army and the Navy of the United States, and of the Militia of the several States, when called into the actual Service of the United States.

That means the military authority to conduct operations originates with the commander in chief. This authority is transmitted to the war fighter through the chain of command. This can be accomplished by the president delegating authority and responsibility to the secretary of defense or to subordinate commanders. The president might also provide authorization in contingency form, or through case-specific direction.

As a matter of constitutional discretion and statutory design the operational military chain of command runs from the commander in chief to the secretary of defense and from the secretary of defense to the unified or specified combatant commanders, "unless otherwise directed by the president."[91] This latter language represents congressional recognition of the president's discretion as commander in chief to shape the structure of his own command (or at least a constitutional accommodation between the political branches, where the executive position is adopted). In other words, the language is permissive rather than obligatory. But it creates the norm, which has generally held. That means that the president and secretary of defense are the only two civilians in the chain of command. Therefore, they are also the only two civilians with direct responsibility for upholding and interpreting the law of armed conflict in U.S. practice. As a result, as a matter of practice the civilian lawyers that will engage on operational questions involving the means and methods of conflict (as opposed to the development of doctrine) are the lawyers the president, the secretary of defense, and their immediate advisors designate.[92]

As a matter of constitutional principle, presidents have reserved the right to exercise their responsibilities as commander in chief as they see fit, rather than as legislated by the Congress. Where reasonable persons might disagree on how much "war power" the president might derive from the commander-in-chief clause, there is no reasonable debate that the president is the commander in chief, and the essence of military command is the conveyance of lawful orders from commander to combatant soldier. In theory, and sometimes in practice, the president can exercise command by directing individual pilots,[93] or destroyer commanders,[94] or in a less tactical manner by providing his commander's intent to the secretary of defense and delegating the responsibility for implementation to the secretary, who may himself delegate further, so long as the president has not directed otherwise.[95]

However, as a matter of presidential practice and statutory intent, command is generally exercised "through" the chairman of the Joint Chiefs of Staff (C/JCS), who is statutorily designated the president's "senior military advisor"[96] as well as a "statutory advisor" to the National Security Council. In practice, "through" has meant different things to different presidents, secretaries, and chairmen. Not every unified commander has appreciated receiving his orders "through" the chairman rather than directly from the president or secretary of defense as indicated in the chain of command. It is as often the chairman who briefs the president on military operations and target sets as it is the combatant commander, there being an obvious trade-off between the commander spending his time in Washington briefing the president and in the field commanding. Of course, practice has varied depending on the president and the military context.

Under the Goldwater-Nichols Act, the Joint Chiefs of Staff serve as military advisors to the president regarding the operational use of the armed forces. The service chiefs are also the senior administrative officers of their services, responsible for training, funding, and equipping forces for subsequent operational use by the combatant commands.[97] In the case of "advice or an opinion in disagreement with" the chairman, the chairman "shall present the advice or opinion of such member at the time he presents his own advice to the president, the National Security Council, the Homeland Security Council, or the Secretary of Defense."[98] But there is no question either in law or in practice that it is ultimately the chairman's view that is authoritative. It is the chairman and the vice chairman that alone attend National Security Council meetings as Principals and Deputies. Thus, unless the chairman makes a point of noting dissent before the president or the Principals, informal dissent in the "JCS tank" (a secure conference room where the chiefs meet) will only indirectly influence national security policy or national command, if at all.

To assist the chairman, vice chairman, and the chiefs, there is a Joint Staff composed of military personnel from all the services on rotation to the staff. As a matter of theory, this staffing mechanism avoids creation of a permanent general staff of the pre-World War II German model, which staff was thought too powerful and too much a state within a state with emphasis on internal loyalties. As a matter of practice, the rotation ensures that personnel serve outside their immediate service environments and are qualified to plan national-scale military missions. Such rotation also helps bring "ground truth" to the Washington planning cycle.

The staff is organized along traditional functional military lines. The J-1, like the G-1 at division level and the S-1 at battalion level, for example, is the senior officer responsible to the chairman for administrative matters, formally "Manpower and Personnel." The J-2 is the chairman's senior intelligence officer, as are the G-2 and the S-2. The J-3 is the operations officer; ditto the G-3 and S-3. The J-4 handles logistics, as do the G-4 and S-4. In addition, the Joint Staff has four additional senior staff billets directed toward the Joint Chiefs' force management and planning functions.

At the national level, military input is generated in a myriad of formal and informal ways. Through the inter-agency process the Joint Staff will represent the chairman and JCS at inter-agency working groups or through the endless process of clearing cables, talking points, and speeches in the context of operational commitments, crisis management, and policy development. The Joint Staff also prepare and update contingency plans covering a full spectrum of potential scenarios. As a practical matter, much of the chairman's advice comes informally at Principals Committee meetings, in NSC meetings, and in parallel phone calls on secure lines that mimic the more formal process of principals and deputies meetings. In addition, the chairman's advice is often rendered through the secretary of defense to the president or the NSC principals.

Prior to enactment and implementation of the Goldwater-Nichols Act, the Joint Chiefs served collectively as the president's senior military advisors. Proponents of the Act argued that this resulted in a dilution of advice, that is, consensus-based advice, rather than clear and sometimes sharp guidance accountable to one officer. One author has described the Joint Chiefs' sub-par performance in providing honest and accurate military advice during the Vietnam War, for example, as a dereliction of duty.[99] Although the Act's roots were in Vietnam, the immediate catalyst was the 1983 Beirut barracks bombing. The Long Commission subsequently concluded that command responsibility for the forces in Beirut was so fragmented and layered (eleven separate links) that accountability and mission clarity were undermined, with the battalion commander receiving multiple perspectives on his mission and his posture. Nor did the Grenada operation inspire confidence in the efficacy and unity of the operational chain of command. Communications broke down and field units famously used public telephones to communicate commands and to call for supporting arms fire across service lines.

Proponents also argued that a panel of equal chiefs sometimes resulted in equal assignment of mission responsibility to each service, as opposed to task-organized forces based on the specific needs of the mission and specific unit capabilities. The failed Iran hostage rescue mission of 1980 served as Exhibit One in this regard. Among other things, the operational force was cobbled together from off-the-shelf units from each service eager to participate in the mission, rather than from a single unified command integrated by training, equipment, and personnel. Moreover, a combination of necessary secrecy and command relationships apparently kept critical operational dissent from reaching the attention of the president. As a result, the Act also sought to address the perception and reality that, on the Joint Staff service, loyalty colored staff work and that officers who lost sight of their service identity were penalized when they returned to the parent service's arms. Thus, the Act requires military officers to serve joint tours to remain competitive for promotion.

Within a system where the chairman is subordinate to the secretary of defense, but is independently charged with providing military advice to the commander in chief, there remains an inherent tension. Does the C/JCS retain an independent view or must the chairman defer to the secretary of defense? If so when? Should it make a difference whether the issue presented is purely military in nature, (e.g., the force structure necessary to accomplish a tactical mission) or a question of mixed politico-military advice (e.g., what position would the United States take regarding the International Criminal Court or on land mines)? Should the chairman offer policy advice at NSC meetings or stick to "pure" military input?

Critics of the Act and its implementation argue that it places too much authority in the hands of the secretary of defense. The secretary is free to overrule the military chain of command on operational as well as policy questions and to do so in a manner that may not be evident to the president, or for that matter outside observers. By extension, critics argue

Goldwater-Nichols leaves too little authority in the hands of the professional military, represented by the chairman and the joint staff. This observation has been made of both strong and weak secretaries of defense and in time of war as well as relative peace. In particular critics cite perceptions and realities related to two events. The first involves Secretary Les Aspin's 1993 decision delaying the transfer of armor to U.S. forces in Somalia prior to the incidents portrayed in *Black Hawk Down*. The second involves Secretary Donald Rumsfeld's direction of the second Iraq war, and particularly, decisions taken regarding the number of troops necessary to seize Baghdad and then restore and hold order in Iraq. In both cases, as a matter of perception and perhaps fact, the secretaries in question overrode professional military advice, or as appears more likely in the second scenario, chose to select between competing advice. The competing duties of the chiefs under the Act has also prompted criticism that the chiefs spend too much time on administrative command, and not enough on advising with respect to the operational matters.

How the chairman (and each service chief) executes his role depends on his sense of his role as a statutory military advisor to the president and his view of military tradition in policy and political context. As a matter of law, the chairman is subordinate to and subject to the direction of the secretary of defense. This is a matter of statute, but more importantly, of constitutional law, founded in the principle of civilian control of the military instrument. At the same time, decisionmakers should not overlook that the chairman serves as the senior military advisor to the president, and thus has a responsibility to provide military advice independent of the secretary of defense's views. This responsibility is specified in the National Security Act and in Goldwater-Nichols. It is also grounded in common sense. Presidents who do not probe for gaps between the civilian leadership of the Department of Defense and the military leadership may learn after that fact that critical points of disagreement subsequently play out on the battlefield and in the pressroom and not just in the JCS tank. As with intelligence, too much focus on the law rather than on leadership can detract from the real issues in command relationship. Whether the command relationship between the secretary and the chairman and the chiefs is a successful one has more to do with personality, leadership, and style than the law.

There is no question that chairmen find themselves in difficult positions. On the one hand, the chairman may want to be a team player, exhibit a can-do approach, and respect the constitutional chain of command. On the other hand, the chairman may disagree with the secretary's policy and military advice, or think it important to convey qualifications in certitude. But such a tension is not resolved through law. If the president is concerned about getting frank military advice, without policy gloss, he need only ask. Moreover, if the chairman disagrees with the tone or substance of the advice the president is rendered, or the absence of advice, it is not a question of law as to whether the chairman does something about it; it is a question of moral integrity.

From a lawyer's perspective and, for that matter, a policymaking perspective, it is important to know whose voice is being heard when military advice is rendered and whether the other relevant military actors agree with the advice. In particular, the president should know whether the chairman agrees with the secretary on military options, even if ultimately, the secretary alone asserts a policy voice. Of course, as a matter of constitutional law, the president as commander in chief remains free to adjust the chain of command as he sees fit and to receive military advice as he determines.

In the final analysis, whether proponents or detractors of the Goldwater-Nichols framework, those who advise the president on how to structure the chain of command must not lose sight of the issues the Act was intended to address: unity of command, speed in decision, and accountability in result.

1. Combatant Commands

There are currently nine combatant commands, the military's term of art for operational war fighting commands.[100] More precisely, according to the *JCS Dictionary of Terms*, a combatant command is

> a unified or specified command with a broad continuing mission under a single commander established and so designated by the president, through the Secretary of Defense and with the advice and assistance of the Chairman of the Joint Chiefs of Staff. Combatant commands typically have geographic or functional responsibilities.

A unified command is made up of joint forces; that is, its units are drawn from different services. In contrast, a specified command is a single service command performing a distinct mission. For example, the military airlift command is a specified Air Force command, which comprises the Air Force airlift element of the Transportation Command, the unified combatant command responsible for providing the air, ground, and sealift capacity for war fighting forces. The current combatant commands, as described by the Department of Defense, are:

United States Central Command: The U.S. Central Command is the unified command responsible for U.S. security interests in 25 nations that stretch from the horn of Africa through the Arabian Gulf into Central Asia.

United States European Command: The mission of the European Command is to support and advance U.S. interests and policies throughout the assigned area of responsibility; provide combat-ready land, maritime, and air forces to Allied Command Europe or U.S. unified commands; and conduct operations unilaterally or in concert with coalition partners.

United States Joint Forces Command: U.S. Joint Forces Command has a unique mission. While unified commands may be categorized as geographic or functional, the Joint Forces Command forms a hybrid. Its main effort goes to the functional role as the chief advocate for jointness and leaders of U.S. military transformation. It also applies a powerful effort supporting other commanders in chief, our own Atlantic Theater, and emerging domestic U.S. requirements.

United States Northern Command: The U.S. Northern Command debuted in October 2002. The new command is responsible for homeland defense and also serves as head of the North American Aerospace Defense Command, a U.S.-Canada command. The command takes the homeland defense role from the U.S. Joint Forces Command. JFCOM's Joint Task Force–Civil Support and related activities now report to NORTHCOM.

United States Pacific Command: The U.S. Pacific Command enhances security and promotes peaceful development in the Asia-Pacific region by deterring aggression, responding to crises, and fighting to win.

United States Southern Command: The mission of U.S. Southern Command is to shape the environment within our area of responsibility by conducting military-to-military engagement and counterdrug activities throughout the theater to promote democracy, stability, and collective approaches to threats to regional security. The command will, when required, respond unilaterally or multilaterally to crises that threaten regional stability or national interests, and prepare to meet future hemispheric challenges.

United States Special Operations Command: In April 1987, the Defense Department established the U.S. Special Operations Command. The Special Operations Command is primarily responsible for providing combat-ready special operations forces to the geographic combatant commands in support of U.S. national security interests. It is not limited to a specific geographic area of responsibility but must respond wherever the president or the secretary of defense directs in peacetime and across the complete spectrum of conflict.

United States Strategic Command: The mission of United States Strategic Command is to establish and provide full-spectrum global strike, coordinated space, and information operations capabilities to meet both deterrent and decisive national security objectives. U.S. Strategic Command provides operational space support, integrated missile defense, global C4ISR, and specialized planning expertise to the joint war fighter.

United States Transportation Command: The U.S. Transportation Command is the single manager of America's global defense transportation system. USTRANSCOM is tasked with the coordination of people and transportation assets to allow our country to project and sustain forces, whenever, wherever, and for as long as they are needed.[101]

Each combatant command is headed by a four-star general officer, nominated by the president and confirmed by the Senate for that command. (Commissioned officers in the armed forces are confirmed by the Senate pursuant to Article II, section 2 of the Constitution: the president "shall nominate, and by and with the Advice and Consent of the Senate, shall appoint Ambassadors . . . and all other officers of the United States"; however, for military officers selected for promotion, this function is usually accomplished on a list basis e.g., all majors rather than through individual consideration of officers for specific promotions and assignments.)

From the combatant commander the chain of command generally flows to subordinate operational commanders, task organized for each particular mission. Such task forces typically have a ground element commander, an air element commander, and a logistics element commander operating under the overall command of the task force commander. A typical infantry chain of command for a unit deployed in combat might run like this: commander in chief, secretary of defense, combatant commander, theater commander, ground element commander, division commander, regimental commander, battalion commander, company commander, platoon commander, squad leader, fire team leader, and rifleman. However, it is important to emphasize, once the chain of command proceeds from the president to the secretary of defense to the combatant commander, there is no legally required or normative operational chain. Commanders are free to task organize for particular missions and seek to employ lines of command that optimize speed, efficiency, and accountability, while avoiding redundancy and delay. Thus, a combatant commander may truncate the chain of command in the case of a hostage rescue mission by personally communicating with the ground force element under the command of a colonel, for example.

The administrative and garrison chains of command are different. By example, the service chain of command runs from the president, to the secretary of defense, to the service secretaries, and to the service chiefs. In the case of the Marine Corps Recruit Depot at Parris Island, for example, the chain runs from the Commandant of the Marine Corps to the Deputy Chief of Staff for Manpower at Headquarters, Marine Corps, to the Commanding General of the Marine Corps Recruit Depot, a one-star general.

It is intuitive that for lawyers the identity of the commander and the level of command will govern the type and substance of practice, as will the military mission. For example, lawyers operating below the level of the commander in chief or secretary of defense are unlikely to address questions regarding the resort to war, either as a matter of constitutional law or international law. Nonetheless, it may be useful for them to be able to explain the legal basis for U.S. action to their commanders. Conversely, it is rare for national-level lawyers to draft tactical rules of engagement, although they might review such rules if, for example, they are implementing specific guidance from the president or secretary of defense. This might be the case during a naval quarantine of Cuba, or in execution of No Fly Zones over pre-war Iraq.

The senior lawyer in a combatant command is usually the commander's judge advocate, who generally serves at the grade of 0–6; that is, he or she is a colonel or a Navy captain.[102] Within operational units the type of legal questions that arise will depend on the component and the mission. At present, the Marine Corps assigns judge advocates down to the battalion level in Iraq. But this is not the general practice. The Army is more likely to deploy judge advocates down to the regimental level. Among other things, these lawyers provide commanders with operational guidance on war fighting, such as the methods and means of combat and the handling of civilian and military personnel encountered by the unit. In addition, these lawyers handle matters of military justice, financial claims from civilians affected by military operations, and the myriad of issues that will arise for personnel deployed for extended periods of time in the field – advice regarding dependents, divorce, wills, and debt collection.[103]

Is all this important to the national security lawyer in Washington? Yes. If guidance is issued at the national level on the law of armed conflict, for example regarding the treatment of detainees, national lawyers need to anticipate by whom and at what level of command those decisions will be implemented and overseen. In turn, they can more effectively convey advice and appraise the legal and practical effect of its subsequent implementation. Such knowledge will also allow the president and his immediate policy and legal advisors to determine whether legal and policy guidance is best implemented by presidential directive, DOD directive, subordinate military order, the rules of engagement, or other manner. Moreover, if the commander in chief has particular views on the law, his lawyers need to understand who will implement those views and then whom to hold accountable for doing so.

2. Opcon, TacCon, AdCon, and Foreign Command

Within an operational unit, command and control can be shifted from one headquarters to another on a tactical (taccon), operational (opcon), or administrative basis (adcon). For example, if two divisions are advancing on parallel tracks, but one unit is anticipating armored resistance, the Corps commander with command over both units might shift a regiment of tanks usually assigned to one division to the other for the purpose of the pending maneuver. This is a shift in tactical control. If the unit is going to generally fall under the direction of the new division commander, then operational control will be transferred. However, if the shift is temporary in nature, then the senior commander will make clear to both units that administrative control has not shifted, thus alerting the parent division that it is still responsible for resupplying the tank regiment in question.

In addition, the president as commander in chief can authorize placement of U.S. armed forces under foreign operational control, as in the case of UN peacekeeping missions or coalition operations. In October 2006, for example, certain U.S. forces in Afghanistan were placed under the tactical control of a British NATO commander.[104]

The Congress has sought on occasion to delimit the exercise of this authority. However, the executive branch has definitively and consistently taken the view that, while the president cannot delegate constitutional command of U.S. armed forces to a foreign commander, he can delegate operational command, which is to say operational control.[105] U.S. forces have, of course, fought and operated under foreign command for more than 200 years. The distinction is important as a matter of constitutional law and theory and should not be misperceived.

As a legal truism, the president cannot relinquish a constitutional responsibility or function any more than the Congress can delegate to the judiciary the authority to raise taxes. The distinction is found in the difference between assigning the overall mission, for example, the invasion of France, to the force and delegating individual tactical choices to the commander on the spot (e.g., decisions over which units would land at Omaha Beach, which strike for Caen, and the date of landing).

3. Appraisal

In contrast to other national security processes, the military chain of command is clear and often crisp. It runs distinctly from the president, as commander in chief, to the pilot in the cockpit or the soldier in the field. There is but one stop at each level of command. The chain is transparent, with each member (generally) able to identify the lawful links. Nonetheless, like other national security processes, the application of the military chain of command warrants consistent contextual appraisal to ensure that in operation it is effective and that it is accountable as a matter of policy and law. National security lawyers should consider five factors in particular when assessing the operation of the chain of command.

First, is the chain of command configured in a manner that provides for meaningful *and* timely legal advice? For example, are lawyers embedded at the critical points where legal issues are first raised? And, are they embedded at a level and are they vested with sufficient authority where they can effectively advise the commander? At the national level, are lawyers participating in the policy consideration of military options? In the field, are lawyers trained in the necessary areas of operational law and in the military skills necessary to provide for their personal safety and to establish credibility with their commanders?

Second, is the chain of command educated on the law? Have soldiers, airmen, and Marines been briefed on the law of armed conflict as is in fact required by the law of armed conflict and the Uniform Code of Military Justice (UCMJ), and have they received up-to-date briefing relevant to their area of responsibility? In homeland security, are the rules applicable to the enforcement of civil law understood? Do soldiers and aviators understand where orders originate and understand the procedures to follow if they do not understand orders? Do soldiers understand that orders originating through the chain of command are presumed lawful?

A soldier disobeys an order at his peril.[106] Thus, in the U.S. military justice system,

> It is a defense to any offense that the accused was acting pursuant to order unless the accused knew the order to be unlawful or a person of ordinary sense and understanding would have known the orders to be unlawful.

Likewise, in international law, Article 33 of the Rome Treaty provides that the superior orders defense shall not apply unless (1) the person was under a legal obligation to follow the orders, (2) the person did not know the order was unlawful, and (3) the order was not manifestly unlawful. Orders to commit genocide or crimes against humanity are considered manifestly unlawful. Are these principles understood at each level of command?

Third, is the chain of command configured in a manner that clarifies or obfuscates decisions? Are the rules of engagement not just lawful, but clear in the context offered? These questions pertain to the commander in chief as well. Are the president's directives clear and operationally functional as opposed to laden with policy nuance more appropriate for Washington than a military concept of operations or a rules of engagement card?

Fourth, does the chain of command integrate the correct measure of civilian authority? In a constitutional democracy, presidential decision and accountability should not be eschewed, but embraced as a tenet of civilian command and control of the military instrument, first embedded in American practice when General Washington surrendered his commission to the Congress at Annapolis. This is also a question of law. Where Congress has not expressly authorized military action, the democratic legitimacy of U.S. military operations arises from the president's constitutional authority and ultimately his electoral accountability to the people. Moreover, it is with the civilian chain of command – the president and the secretary of defense – that constitutional responsibility over military command and adherence to the law rest. In the homeland security context, presidential command may take on additional legal importance. To start, where U.S. troops operate in a domestic context in which the statutory basis for doing so is a close call, presidential command may provide the essential constitutional gloss or "plus" comprising the difference between lawful command and a violation of the Posse Comitatus Act. This may occur because the facts are uncertain or it may occur because the level of assistance does not fit squarely within a statutory term.

The balance between civilian and military command is also a matter of legal policy and presidential preference. Whether one agrees with Clemenceau[107] or not, in modern conflict, many military decisions are integrated with policy questions. As the British military historian Max Hastings observes,

> The great progressive change since 1945 is that the conduct of limited wars has become intensely political. The interventions of civilian leaders are ever more detailed and explicit in matters that were once deemed military turf. Gen. Douglas MacArthur was sacked in Korea in 1951 for conduct no more imperious than his World War II norm in the Pacific. The general failed to understand that the principle on which he had always justified his own mandate – when wars start, politicians must leave soldiers to run them – was a dead letter in the nuclear age.[108]

As others note, we are now in a second nuclear age where second-tier states and perhaps private actors may obtain nuclear weapons; perilous times indeed. Rephrased, in modern context the pilot should decide if he can hit the rudder, but in the context of enforcing a Cuban quarantine, rescuing hostages in the Gulf of Cambodia, or while enforcing an embargo against North Korea or Iran, the president may well want to decide whether he takes the shot.

Similarly, some targets that may appear on the ground as raising purely tactical military considerations will nonetheless warrant policy consideration when viewed with a wider perspective. For example, a decision whether to pursue an Al Qaeda fighter across the border into Pakistan or Syria perhaps presents a question of force protection and capacity at the company or battalion level weighed with the value of the target. However, such a scenario also raises broader considerations of foreign policy, intelligence liaison, and regional stability that should be addressed by policymakers and not just soldiers, preferably in advance of the scenario presented.

There are advantages and disadvantages to civilian command. Civilian decision can enhance public support for military operations. From a military perspective, the participation of the commander in chief can buffer the field commander from the spotlight of 24/7 media inspection by assuming or sharing the responsibility of decision in the same manner that athletic coaches may try to deflect unwanted attention from players. In a democracy, the buck *should* stop with the president and not with the lance corporal or even the secretary of defense when the hardest legal and policy questions are presented. It is also at the level of the president and the secretary of defense, rather than at the level of the combatant commander, that the process of congressional consultation and briefing occurs. This in turn, is an important element of constitutional process, democratic legitimacy, as well as a necessary step in building and sustaining public support for conflict.

However, the corollary is also true. With presidential decision comes direct responsibility for result. Civilian participation may also increase the political content of decision, prompting officials to delay decisions or eschew tough field choices on other than military grounds.

The reality is that presidents and secretaries are briefed on military operations so that command decision at the level of the commander in chief can be taken, in the words of General Tommy Franks, on an "amazing timeline."[109] With global communication, presidential decision need not cause undue delay where decisions flow directly from the president to the secretary of defense and are communicated to the combatant command (often by the chairman of the Joint Chiefs). Moreover, where it is not practicable to brief targets on a case-by-case basis, the president can, and should, exercise his constitutional command function through the review of theater ROE and concepts of operation. But if not exercised with contextual forethought, civilian command can negate significant U.S. military advantages in professionalism, including a U.S. leadership corps unmatched in training, ability, and independent thought, from combatant commander to small unit leader. And it emphasizes ground truth, with decisions taken on the basis of the observations by those with "eyes-on-target."

Make no mistake; the *majority* of tactical and targeting decisions are purely military decisions. In an ongoing conflict like those in Iraq and Afghanistan the chain of command should be pushed horizontally to the field. This is especially true in a counterinsurgency context where rapid and immediate small unit actions and decisions will determine the tactical military outcome. In such a contest, policy and strategy should be set from above, but command should be exercised in the field. However, there is also an obvious smaller set of decisions defined by the factors identified above that are presidential in scope, and some that are contextually in between, including of course the policy context in which small unit actions are conducted.

Fifth, and in a related manner, the lawyer and in particular the military lawyer should consider whether the chain of command adopted in context provides the optimum balance between what is colloquially referred to as vertical and horizontal command. As with other processes, this question presents an apparent tension between security and speed, on the one hand,

and decision processes requiring referral up the chain of command, on the other. Where a vertical structure is adopted, decisionmakers must also specify those decisions capable of and intended for civilian command, which means the secretary of defense or the president. Where horizontal command is utilized, commanders must decide how far down the chain of command decisional capacity should extend.

From a legal policy perspective, vertical command adds consistency in the application of the LOAC in targeting and in the manner that detainees are treated, for example. It also helps to fix accountability for both. Where, for example, difficult targeting decisions are taken at the combatant command or national level, the influence of service culture and a combat arms perspective in determining legal results are less important. Personality (other than the president's) will also play less of a role in how the LOAC is interpreted and applied. The cautious military lawyer or aggressive commander (and sometimes the other way around) becomes less determinative when legal policy is set at the top.

Vertical command also enhances the institutional capacity to fuse disparate interagency and command information and views into an analytic package for decision. This is particularly important in a conflict to deter terrorist WMD attack where pop-up targets will emerge for moments and strike decisions must be taken in difficult geopolitical contexts with imperfect information. Vertical command and fusion can also serve as a fail-safe where such process helps to channel target review into a routine and specialized process of review at the national level and combatant command level.

There are also risks to vertical command, or better said, too much vertical command, either because of layering or micromanagement. Vertical civilian command is less important, indeed potentially disruptive, where the military objective is set and the concept of operations calls for traditional and rapid maneuver warfare. First, as the Long Commission demonstrated in the context of the Beirut bombing, vertical command – in that case involving eleven layers between the president and the Battalion Landing Team commander – can diffuse responsibility and accountability in dangerous ways.[110] Vertical command can take time and delay critical decision.

Second, where combat operations are fluid, vertical target decisionmaking is inherently dysfunctional unless it is exercised through a commander's intent or ROE. This might be illustrated with reference to weaponized unmanned aerial vehicle (UAV) platforms that can be deployed both as point-to-point weapons (that is, launched with a specific coordinate in mind) or used to patrol for targets of opportunity. In the initial mode, vertical commanders can appropriately participate in a target decision where the target is pre-planned or fixed. In the latter case, the tactical setting will dictate that command discretion and the LOAC be applied through rules of engagement or target-class approval, rather than an assessment of specific target circumstances at the time of attack.

In summary, the constitutional chain of command should be exercised in a contextual manner that accounts for a range of legal, policy, and military factors in deciding when and how presidents, secretaries, and military commanders exercise command and, in doing so, apply the law.

9 *Homeland Security*

A successful strategy to combat terrorism should incorporate at least four elements: offense (efforts to capture and kill terrorists and disrupt their networks); defense (the physical protection of the United States and the global protection of WMD materials); preventive diplomacy (efforts to address the root causes of terrorism, and thus mitigate both the duration of conflict as well as the potential number of persons willing to attack the United States)[1]; and, a response and recovery capacity to respond to homeland incidents regardless of cause. Such a strategy should employ the full array of national security tools and, through employment of these tools, offer geographically and functionally concentric opportunities to prevent and deter attack.

This chapter considers legal aspects relating to the element of defense, that aspect of national security known after 9/11 as homeland security.[2] The chapter starts by reviewing the nature of the homeland threat. However, part of the difficulty in reaching agreement on the elements, costs, and benefits of a homeland security plan derives from disagreements on the nature of the threat. In some cases, disagreements on implementation, in fact, reflect underlying disagreements on the risk presented. Therefore, the threat is defined up front, from which the homeland security regime should follow.

Included in the discussion of the threat are facts and figures that should give the reader a sense of the scope of the defensive problem. However, the facts are evolving as the United States improves its security. Moreover, even where the facts should be fixed – for example, the length of the shoreline – different figures are used in the literature (see footnote 31). I offer the figures to give the reader a sense of scale, knowing that the number of containers entering the country will vary, as I hope, will the number of containers searched.

The chapter then addresses the structure for homeland decision-making. In particular, the text considers the strengths and weaknesses of a Homeland Security Council process that is parallel to, but distinct from the NSC process. Next, the vertical arrangements between federal and state authorities for responding to emergencies are considered. As in other contexts, special emphasis is placed on intelligence. Without intelligence, the United States cannot effectively allocate finite resources against infinite risks.

The chapter then considers two structural issues that permeate homeland security: the distribution of authority and responsibility among federal, state, and local governments, examined under the rubric of federalism; and, second, the legal and policy concerns associated with the domestic use of the military. These issues are addressed throughout the chapter and in the conclusion.

The chapter next turns to three topical homeland security regimes addressed to different aspects of homeland security strategy. The first is the nonproliferation regime, because WMD attack represents the gravest threat to U.S. national security and will remain so for the foreseeable future. Nonetheless, the regime has not received commensurate attention. Next, I consider maritime security, because the regime is well developed, but nonetheless illustrates that even where the risk and law are finite, and the need agreed, there remain significant gaps in regime implementation. The maritime regime also illustrates the relationship between U.S. and international law in the homeland security context. Third, the chapter considers public health, because it serves as a necessary base capacity whether the threat is avian flu or a weapon of mass destruction. Some experts forecast that avian flu is the most likely homeland "catastrophe," although not without rebuttal.[3] What is clear is that if a "pandemic" does occur, the physical and economic consequences will be extreme, with potential for as many as 1.9 million deaths according to the government's "worst-case" estimates.[4] Of course, a comprehensive treatment of homeland security should consider additional regimes including those addressed to critical infrastructures, like chemical plants and nuclear plants, as well as food security and rail transport. That is one of the dilemmas with homeland security: when box-cutters can be turned into weapons of mass terrorism there is no end to the potential number of threats, targets, or legal regimes in play.

That puts additional pressure on maintaining and creating a flexible policy and decision-making framework. The decisional framework and law in each of these areas are evolving. Therefore, this chapter offers a sketch, not a comprehensive review. For this same reason, the chapter concludes with a series of lessons learned from Hurricanes Katrina and Rita in 2005 along with principles that should apply when shaping the legal framework for homeland security.

PART I
HOMELAND SECURITY DECISION-MAKING, RESOURCES, AND LEGAL FRAMEWORK

A. THE THREAT REVISITED

As stated at the outset of this book, the prospect of a WMD attack in the United States is real, relentless, and potentially catastrophic. The vice chairman of the 9/11 Commission has stated that the greatest threat to the United States in the foreseeable future is the threat that a terrorist, or terrorist group, will obtain a nuclear weapon and detonate it in Washington, New York, or another U.S. city.[5] Reasonable persons might disagree on the probability of such an attack. One's sense of the immediacy and likelihood of the threat may vary depending on where you live, including whether you live in Washington or New York, whether you fly, and how you interpret the relative frequency or absence of attack in particular regions of the globe.

A 2006 poll of 116 terrorism specialists representing a cross-section of political perspectives placed the likelihood of "a terrorist attack on the scale of 9/11 occurring in the United States" in the next five years (by the end of 2011) at 79 percent. Of this percentage, 9 percent said an attack was certain, 29 percent said it was very likely, and 41 percent said somewhat likely. When asked to project the likelihood of an attack occurring in the next ten years, the same respondents placed the likelihood at 84 percent, with 26 percent in the certain camp and 34 percent choosing the very likely category.[6]

We should have no illusions about whether Al Qaeda, and other jihadists, or perhaps homegrown terrorists like Timothy McVeigh or Eric Rudolph, are trying to get weapons of mass destruction and no illusions about whether they will use them, or try to use them, if they get them. The jihadist enemy is impatient to kill, but patient in waiting for an opportunity to do so. Recall that Al Qaeda waited eight years between its 1993 and 2001 attacks on the World Trade Center. Therefore, we face for the foreseeable future what Harold Lasswell called the "socialization of danger," a sense of threat throughout society and not isolated to the political elites and the security infrastructure.[7] That makes society's members potential participants in, and not just observers of, national security policy and process.

The problem is magnified because this threat comes without prospect of rational deterrence. The enemy does not bear the necessity of defending a territory, a people, or an elite. Moreover, although we call this enemy Al Qaeda, the enemy consists of many different groups and individuals that are even less recognizable than Al Qaeda. The enemy may be unknown until he acts. Thus, unlike the Cold War, we do not face a fixed and known enemy with known weapons. We face, in part, an unknown enemy, with unknown weapons and tactics. To use Donald Rumsfeld's sometime maligned phrase, in this conflict there are "known unknowns" and "unknown unknowns."[8] What seems to unify the opponent is the tactic selected – terrorism – and the foci of hatred, including hatred of the United States, not necessarily bonds of ethnicity, nationality, or religion.

In the face of this threat, it is possible to become obsessed, or hysterical, like the man in Connecticut who encased his house with duct tape after the federal government suggested keeping a supply of tape on hand to ward off the atmospheric effects of a dirty bomb.[9] Alternatively, one might adopt a position of "optimism bias," placing the risk out of mind, or simply damning the torpedoes and moving full speed ahead. Why not something between extremes? The homeland security paradigm requires a realistic assessment of the threat as one that is perpetual and potentially catastrophic. The threat is also intermittent, and perhaps, subject to containment. But containment will require sustained investment and a steady policy commitment designed to garner a century of dividends, not the short-term return of four-year political certificates of deposit.

Homeland security will also require adoption of a legal framework and, as importantly, implementation of that framework through bureaucratic process and cultural adhesion. As Professor Kellman has observed, law is an antidote to panic.[10] In time of crisis law provides structure, predictability, and therefore a source of calm. Observers and participants in the national security process must therefore consider and reconsider whether as a society, and as a government, the United States has responded on a steady course, with the necessary and correlative sense of urgency, resources, and continuity. We should ask as well whether our process of decision and our legal framework is sufficient to deter, defend and respond to these threats and to do so in a manner that mitigates and manages the impact any future attack may have on our way of government and our way of life.

B. HOMELAND SECURITY STRATEGY

With this backdrop, policymakers and lawyers must define homeland security and, in light of that definition, design a corresponding strategy and decision-making architecture. As discussed in Chapter 2, national security has an objective physical element and a subjective "values" element. The two may come in tension. However, we need not concede that this tension is inherent or that it presents a zero-sum equation. But that depends on whether you view liberty and security as absolute values or contextual values. For example, your view of security checkpoints or data-mining may vary depending on whether you view due process or "privacy" as contextual or absolute measures.

Consider, for example, the difference in the criminal law's treatment of Fourth Amendment searches with the law's treatment of the Sixth Amendment right to jury trial. In applying the Fourth Amendment, for example, courts balance society's interest in law enforcement with the search subject's expectation of privacy; where a person possesses a subjective expectation of privacy that is objectively reasonable under the circumstances, then government intrusion amounts to a search and requires a warrant or the application of an exception to the warrant requirement. What is reasonable therefore will depend on the circumstances, including the nature of the place to be searched and the predicate for the government's interest. In contrast, the right to a jury trial in federal civilian criminal law is absolute and in state law absolute for serious offenses.[11]

In national security context, one might consider whether presidential authority, "data-mining," or "profiling" should be subject to absolute measures presenting zero-sum equations with liberty, or whether they warrant contextual measure, requiring assessment as to whether a particular exercise of power is "reasonable." In this latter approach, what is reasonable may depend on necessity, as well as on the application of contextual checks and balances through operation of law. For example, the Fourth Amendment warrant requirement is a procedural check on the power of the police to search. In data-mining, similar procedural and substantive mechanisms might apply. The government might data-mine for pattern-based information using internal safeguards, but require a substantive and procedural external trigger before resorting to subject identification or subject-based searches. In this example, data-mining and privacy do not present absolute values, but rather contextual values.

In August 2006 UK authorities disrupted a plot to use liquid explosives to bring down ten U.S.-bound aircraft over the Atlantic. The plot focused attention on differences between U.S. and UK law, including real and perceived differences in the length of time police could detain a terrorist suspect without charges. U.S. officials and reporters focused on the temporal distinction between UK law, under which a terrorist suspect may be held for twenty-eight days without charges, and U.S. law, which has a comparable seven-day limitation, but without identification of the procedural distinction.

Under UK law, detention of the suspect is subject to court order and review no less than once every twelve hours, whereas a U.S. suspect may be detained incommunicado on the authority of the attorney general alone for renewable seven-day periods.[12] Moreover, as one judge has noted, there are other options under U.S. law for addressing the problem presented.[13] Thus, the UK model offers an enhanced timeline, but with enhanced oversight by an independent and detached judge. Moreover, the debate bypasses an additional critical distinction in U.S. practice regarding the treatment of "enemy combatants" who may be subject to indefinite detention without recourse to federal courts, depending of course on how the government and the courts interpret and apply the Military Commissions Act.

With homeland security, the paradigmatic challenge is apparent and difficult because it entails value *and* security judgments applied to known unknowns and unknown unknowns. Further, unlike the Fourth Amendment example, which is reactive in application, the homeland security model must be proactive if it is to be effective. To prevent, the government must necessarily act with inchoate information or risk acting too late. If you adopt a contextual as opposed to an absolute "rights" model, this argues for emphasis on procedural checks and balances rather than substantive checks and balances.

Paradigm shifts are also difficult because public perceptions, and therefore public tolerances, are substantively and temporally inconsistent. They vary as perceptions of the threat ebb and wane. They also seemingly vary between disciplines. The public, for example, tolerates a high degree of physical intrusion and inspection prior to boarding an aircraft, but also apparently possesses a disproportionate willingness to assume the risk that the aircraft's cargo has gone unscreened or lightly surveyed. An endless conflict requires long-term, consistent, and continuous policy.

The homeland security paradigm is also complex because the scope of the defensive problem is so large. A quick and necessarily static review suggests the enormity of the physical challenge of stopping a terrorist attack within the United States or at the border. The United States has 95,000 miles of shoreline, 361 separate land and water ports of entry, and an exclusive economic zone of roughly 3.4 million square miles. The U.S. land border with Canada is 5,225 miles in length and the border with Mexico 1,989 miles. Across these borders approximately 11 million trucks and more than 2 million rail cars enter the country each year. In the maritime sphere, there are more than 50,000 maritime port calls in the United States each year, involving, among other vessels, 7,500 foreign flag vessels. Each year, approximately16 million containers are transported into the United States. Depending on which year's statistics and which DHS materials are cited, 5–10 million of these are transported by sea, of which 95 percent enter twenty "megaports." Indeed, 90 percent of the world's cargo moves by container. In a given year there are 500 million legal entries into the United States, including 330 million by noncitizen foreign nationals. The number of illegal entries into the United States is more difficult to estimate. Estimates place the number of illegal immigrants in the United States at approximately 7–10 million persons.[14] Of course, all of these statistics will change over time, perhaps in reaction to U.S. security measures. For the purposes of this chapter, the specific statistics are less important than conveying a sense of scale and thus an appreciation for the legal and bureaucratic challenge.

Moreover, a state or nonstate actor's "soldiers" need not enter the United States to cause havoc. A remote computer attack might bring down an energy grid or shut down an air traffic control system. Government officials have reported that government computers face "relentless" attack from governmental and nongovernmental sources overseas.[15] Moreover, the opponent may obtain the capability to launch a physical attack from locations adjacent to the border. Consider, for example, that the Northern Command's area of responsibility extends 500 miles off the coast into the maritime approaches to the United States, extending the opportunity to interdict incoming vessels beyond the effective range of most sea-launched missiles.

As many ways as there are to access the United States there are an equal number of potential targets. At any given time there are upward of 60,000 persons airborne over the United States in commercial aircraft. There are more than 100 licensed nuclear power reactors in the United States according to the Nuclear Regulatory Commission website, which also provides their locations. In New York City, the Metropolitan Transit Authority carries 7 million riders per day. Every power grid is a target of opportunity and every mall a symbolic target.

This returns us to the paradigm problem. If we do too little we will fail to stop the next attack, and may even encourage it. If we do too much, we may undermine our present way of life even in the absence of attack, and diminish our physical and values-based resources in the process.

C. DECISION-MAKING STRUCTURE

Given the functional and geographic breadth of potential targets in the United States and the myriad potential avenues of attack, homeland security requires a decision-making process that can, if necessary, effectively fuse information and exercise command across vertical and horizontal lines of responsibility at the federal, state, and local level. As is immediately apparent, unlike most other national security issues, the chain of command and chain of responsibility may take an uncertain path from first responder to the president, if it runs to the president at all.

Yet, speed and unity of command are essential. The law can assist by creating processes that emphasize unity of command and clarity in decision and that offer mechanisms that rapidly identify and process jurisdictional or policy disputes. The Joint Terrorism Task Forces serve as a vehicle for accomplishing this end with respect to intelligence. The Homeland Security Operations Center, in theory, can connect federal, state, and local decision-makers with the same speed. This might also be accomplished bureaucratically through the use of template command structures, with the advance designation of lead agencies, task groups, or master plans, like the National Response Plan (NRP). It might also be accomplished through the conduct of joint exercises, which help to identify policy, legal, and personality issues and solutions (!) in advance of crisis.

At the same time, as much as any other area of security, homeland security depends on informal process. Whereas the president can dictate an executive branch framework for sharing intelligence or coordinating port security, the relationships across federal, state, and local jurisdictions while subject to law are rarely governed by law. Rather, they are a product of personal connection and friendship, what some call "donut diplomacy," as opposed to directive. Where the intelligence coordination or emergency response has worked best between federal and state officials, the participants invariably cite friendship and community bonding as reasons. The national security lawyer therefore must master not only the formal process but also the informal process and methods of decision and response used in the field. In other words, in building the legal sidewalk, lawyers should observe where the bureaucratic pedestrians in fact walk the trodden path, and see if they can facilitate these connections.

1. Presidential Process and Decision

On October 8, 2001, one month after the Al-Qaeda attacks on New York and Washington, president Bush established the Homeland Security Council (HSC).[16] The president charged the Council with responsibility for "advising and assisting the president with respect to all aspects of homeland security" including "coordinat[ing] the executive branch's efforts to detect, prepare for, prevent, protect against, respond to, and recover from terrorist attacks within the United States." The president has designated twelve officials as members of the Council[17] and ten additional officials to "attend meetings pertaining to their responsibilities."[18] Five members of the president's immediate staff were also "invited to attend any Council meeting."[19]

Significantly, the president established the HSC process distinct from and parallel to the NSC process, rather than incorporating the function within the NSC process. To advise and assist the president and the HSC, the president created the Office of Homeland Security (OHS) under the direction of an assistant to the president for homeland security. Of course, the NSC staff already had a directorate dedicated to counter-terrorism and in the prior administration a directorate for bioterrorism and public health. However, Executive Order 13228 represented the first effort to create a distinct and unified presidential staff dedicated to homeland security and thus to addressing the array of disciplines now associated with homeland security.

The OHS was not immediately embraced by the national security community. This is reflected in the president's directive. The word "coordinate" appears forty times in the six-page document, making it "redundantly clear" that the office would not exercise line authority over government agencies. Moreover, the phrase "as appropriate" appears twenty times in relation to the Office's duties, deferring for future debate whether an exercise of an OHS function was in fact appropriate. Homeland Security Policy Directive 5 is even more direct. Paragraph 13 states: "Nothing in this directive shall be construed to grant any Assistant to the president any authority to issue orders to Federal departments and agencies, their officers, or their employees."

These terms also reflect legal truisms involving the president's immediate staff: they do not possess authority independent of the president, but rather advise and assist the president. At the same time, the repetitive emphasis on coordination illustrates the frequent tension that occurs when new governmental mechanisms cut or alter existing lines of bureaucratic authority, even in times of national emergency. Thus, the order presaged later resistance to the establishment of the Department of Homeland Security and to intelligence "reform." These words of qualification also reflect ambiguity as to responsibility. Such ambiguity increases the importance and effect of practice and personality in defining an operational and functional chain of command and control.

Congress provided statutory standing to the Homeland Security Council in the Homeland Security Act of 2002.[20] The statute is similar in design, but not necessarily in effect, to the National Security Act's enabling language regarding the NSC. The Act follows the president's lead. Thus, the law establishes a Homeland Security Council within the Executive Office of the president to be headed by a civilian executive secretary. The function of the council is succinctly stated in expansive manner: "to advise the president on Homeland Security matters." Toward this end, the Council is legislatively charged with assessing the objectives, commitments, and risks of the United States involving homeland security; overseeing and reviewing policies; and, "perform[ing] such other functions as the president directs . . . for the purpose of more effectively coordinating the policies and functions of the United States Government relating to homeland security."[21]

The statutory members of the HSC "shall be" the president, the vice president, the secretary of Homeland Security, the attorney general, the secretary of defense and "such other individuals as may be designated by the president."[22] As with the NSC, the chairman and DNI are designated statutory advisors to the HSC in their respective areas of responsibility. In addition, the Act expressly recognizes the overlap and potential tension with NSC process while also acknowledging the constitutionally obvious: "The president may convene joint meetings of the Homeland Security Council and the National Security Council with participation by members of either Council or as the president otherwise directs."[23]

As in the case of the National Security Act, the statute finesses the constitutional tension between the president's inherent authority as chief executive to organize his immediate staff within the Executive Office of the President as he sees fit and Congress's legislative power to make those laws necessary and proper to effect a functioning government. Thus, the membership of the Council is designated, but also qualified to include "such other members as the president designates." In like fashion the functions of the Council are specified in broad stroke and include "such other functions as the president may direct."

The full membership of the HSC is too numerous for it or its Principals Committee to serve as a mechanism for crisis management or day-to-day decision-making. That means there must be an alternative process of decision. As in other contexts, attendance at HSC, principals, or deputies meetings is dictated by the assistant to the president for homeland security, who chairs the Principals Committee, and not ultimately by presidential directive or statute.

Of course, HSPD-1 describes a normative process of presidential decision-making. Changes in administration will result in subtle and not so subtle changes to this structure. Moreover, the directive does not address or account for the navigational drift caused by incumbent personalities and the tendency of work to gravitate to the persons the president trusts most or who get the job done. Finally, as with national security generally, the majority of homeland security process is informal, taking place in countless telephone calls, meetings, and e-mail.

The importance of these formal directives, and the Homeland Security Act, lies in creating expectations and responsibilities as well as in specifying a normative process of decision. In turn, bureaucracies will create mechanisms to address those expectations and responsibilities. This is essential in the case of agencies new to the national security process, like the Departments of Commerce, Health and Human Services, and Agriculture. These agencies do not have the prior experience of the NSC or military process to draw from in defining a disciplined process for fusing intelligence, staffing issues, and meeting deadlines.

A statutory base is also important in providing legislative authority for diverse agencies to dedicate agency personnel and resources to the homeland security mission. Where Congress has designated a cabinet officer to serve on the Homeland Security Council, for example, the department's resources are appropriately expended for homeland security as directed by the president.[24] Further, keeping the *Youngstown* paradigm in mind, where the HSC acts, it does so with the procedural authority of both the president and the Congress.

As with the NSC, the HSC process is organized in tripartite manner. The Homeland Security Council Principals Committee (HSC/PC) serves as the "senior inter-agency forum under the HSC for homeland security issues." Significantly, the APNSA and deputy national security advisor shall "be invited to attend all meetings of the HSC/PC."[25] As a matter of practice, this means that the APNSA and, through the APNSA, the NSC staff have access to the agenda and papers associated with HSC and HSC/PC meetings. The HSC Deputies Committee serves in turn as the senior sub-cabinet and inter-agency forum for homeland security policy. The Principals and Deputies Committees are bureaucratically fed by inter-agency working groups designated in the Bush administration as Policy Coordinating Committees (PCCs). HSPD-1 established eleven such committees covering such topics as "Detection, Surveillance, and Intelligence," "Medical and Public Health Preparedness," and "Weapons of Mass Destruction Consequence Management." However, the titles have changed (and will change) as bureaucracies evolve and administrations change.

As with the NSC staff, the HSC staff are responsible for advising and assisting the president, under the direction of the assistant to the president and deputy assistant to the president for Homeland Security. The staff consists of approximately fifty policy personnel, which is roughly half the size of the NSC policy staff (see Attachment 6). Once again, the directorate titles will change over time, but the functions will persist so long as homeland security remains a core security function. Among other things, the staff is responsible for developing federal homeland security policy. As with national security generally, presidential policy is usually disseminated on a formal basis via presidential directives. President Bush has designated these documents Homeland Security Policy Directives (HSPDs). As with NSC directives the designation will change from administration to administration. Lawyers should not lose sight of the fact that such directives are presidential orders with the same legal standing, if not stature, as executive orders. A separate series of directives for homeland security is logical, for it allows wider dissemination of the policy product to a tailored and larger homeland security audience.

The OHS is also responsible for overseeing the implementation of the president's policy directives. This is done formally through operation of inter-agency working groups and informally through a myriad of daily informal contacts with federal, state, local, and private actors. This is a critical role, as these directives tend to be goal oriented and hortatory, rather than concrete in direction. Special focus on implementation and appraisal is warranted.

The OHS staff also takes the lead in coordination between the HSC and the Department of Homeland Security, overseeing on behalf of the president the inter-agency and intra-agency operations. This is a daunting task. Consider that prior to 2003 this would have entailed the coordination of twenty-two separate and diverse agencies and departments. The staff of the OHS also serves as the president's interlocutors with DHS and the attorney general with regard to the Homeland Security Advisory System (HSPD-3, March 11, 2002). Most importantly, OHS serves as a principal conduit for information flowing to and from the president regarding homeland security, which information serves as the predicate for the exercise of the legal authorities identified in this chapter. In each context, the OHS manages the paper flow to and from the president, principals, and deputies through an executive secretariat. Like the NSC staff, the OHS is also responsible for the daily grind of government: the drafting and review of press guidance, responding to legislative inquiries, keeping the chain of command informed, and overseeing policy implementation.

Two related procedural questions arise. Is the Homeland Security Council process the most effective mechanism for addressing homeland security? And, would the president be better served by a singular national security process or, perhaps, a process distinct from both the National Security Council and the Homeland Security Council?

On the one hand, parallel processes in the area of national security bear inherent peril. As September 11 revealed, the United States must address the terrorist threat as a seamless national security problem, rather than one with a domestic and international façade. For example, having parallel officials handling domestic and international intelligence creates the possibility that information will fall between the seams of two separate processes advising and assisting the president, or that one entity will not make the essential mosaic link in the absence of being privy to a discussion occurring in a separate channel. The various centers established to fuse intelligence since 9/11, in particular, the National Counter-Terrorism Center (NCTC), are intended to address this concern; but, on a cautionary note, we have had intelligence centers since the 1980s with comparable missions. Moreover, the issue here is not fusion within the intelligence community, but the fusion of intelligence with policy at the presidential and Principals level. Information garnered at an HSC meeting could be relevant to a NSC meeting, and vice versa.

Certainly, as a matter of logic, information will ultimately "fuse" in any process that culminates with a singular actor – the president. But it is the NSC and HSC staff, on behalf of their Principals, who are best situated to pull relevant information from within the bureaucracy – and to transcend issues of personality and bureaucratic conflict. These same officials are also more likely to know the context in which a seemingly innocuous piece of information may bear actionable policy intelligence. The concern is that critical information will go missing if it is known only to a staff member in the NSC pipeline, but not to the staff member in the HSC pipeline and vice versa.

Dual processes also result in potential procedural inefficiencies as well as potential rivalries for time, access, and authority. Thus, principals and deputies, who may be asked to attend multiple NSC meetings, may decline to attend HSC meetings, or pick and choose between NSC or HSC meetings as a matter of topical choice, thus negating the value of having principals or deputies meetings as opposed to inter-agency meetings.

Dual processes can also result in mixed external messages and means. By design, or chance, the NSC and HSC may adopt different policies, and different procedures, for example in dealing with the Congress. This can undermine policy, cause confusion, and increase the necessity for, and time committed to, internal as well as external coordination. This concern magnifies where the Congress is controlled in whole or in part by a party distinct from the president's and legislative "oversight" plays a more prominent policy, legal, and political role.

As importantly, dual processes may be inefficient for managing the president's time, requiring two meetings instead of one, for example, in the case of daily national security time. More assistants vying for time with the president may also result in bureaucratic gamesmanship. Within the White House, the national security advisor is typically "more equal than other" assistants to the president, on account of his or her role and the size of his or her immediate supporting policy and functional staff. Whereas the president will always make time for the national security advisor, if there is more than one assistant vying for the president's "national security time" the president may spend less time than necessary with one or the other official. That is not to say that any current or past incumbents have exhibited such conduct. It is to say that personality as much as legal directives will determine whether a dual-track process works.

Further, there is risk that if the homeland security process is too closely aligned with the White House, at the NSC or HSC, the mission may take on perceived and real partisan political dimensions. This is more likely to happen, in any event, where the subject matter is domestic in nature and there are grants at stake. Further, where the coordinating mechanism is at the White House, the success or failure of a homeland security task will necessarily carry political baggage or benefit, which would not otherwise accrue if handled at arms length at the agency level. This may prove a distraction as well as a temptation at precisely the moment when national unity is warranted and all energy should focus on the prevention or mitigation of a threat. Moreover, terrorism warnings and predictions may be discounted or dismissed if they are viewed as bearing political as well as security motivation, thus undermining rather than maximizing use of the bully pulpit to exhort the nation to the sort of paradigm shifts and choices discussed at the outset of this chapter.

On the other hand, the homeland security mission may be too complex and too diverse for a singular presidential mechanism to handle at the same time that it handles the traditional and daily NSC issues. Inverse to the concern that dual processes may impede information and policy fusion is the concern that a singular process may breed bureaucratic chokepoints. Policy issues, for example, may linger as they wait in queue for Principals Committee attention, or perhaps sit in the national security advisor's inbox during moments of crisis. Further, a single process would, in theory, require a staff with the combined strength of the NSC and OHS staff. This would invite bureaucratic layering and potentially undermine the efficiencies behind the president having a small but energetic security staff. So too, the principal officers in such a process might spend undue time handling the sort of personnel and administrative issues that inevitably arise within a bureaucracy, involving titles, clearances, hiring, and firing.

The reality is that the disciplines necessary to manage homeland security are varied and distinct from those traditionally handled at the NSC. Public health or food security, for example, require specialized knowledge and do not lend themselves to dual-hatting even within the OHS. Equally important, the nature and scope of the coordination mission is different. Presidential coordination of homeland security merits special attention. Where the NSC is engaged in the horizontal coordination among traditional federal agencies, homeland security entails vertical coordination with state and local governments as well as coordination with numerous private actors. Restated, a functioning homeland security process should spend as much time coordinating as it does on policy development. This requires an investment in time – phone calls, meetings, and visits – that would overwhelm a staff and process already responsible for Iraq, Iran, and North Korea.

Finally, multiple deputy teams allow tracking of multiple crises at the sub-cabinet level simultaneously, maximizing the opportunity for inter-agency expertise and coordination just below the level of the principals and the president. Having multiple assistants and staffing teams also mitigates, but does not eliminate, the risk that exhaustion or crisis fatigue will slow reflexes or dampen the instinct to dig deeper and push harder at what might become the moment of peril. Presidents may vacation in August, but the NSC and HSC processes cannot.

In the final analysis, the homeland security problem is too substantively diffuse and the coordination task too complex to accomplish without drawing on the moral, persuasive, and legal wherewithal of the president. That requires a staff dedicated solely to this mission to frame, and tee up the critical issues and then ride herd on recalcitrant agencies, as well as exhort, persuade, and, if necessary, direct, state and local authorities. Without such a staff to prompt, the president's intervention issues like communications and computer interoperability will lack the necessary muscle and urgency to survive the budget competition or receive the Principals' attention.

In the intermediate as well as the long run the success or failure of the HSC process will depend on three factors. First, the process will depend on the personality of the players. This is particularly so with a process that is not yet embedded in the bureaucratic culture, as the NSC process is, and therefore is susceptible to being undermined by the resistance of one or more actors or agencies. If the critical players, in which category the president is central, back the process with the weight of their participation and their adherence to its parameters, then the process will succeed. If the president permits end runs or ad hoc decision-making mechanisms, then the process will fail.

Second, whatever process is ultimately sustained or adopted, it must consciously account for and, when necessary, mitigate the concerns identified above involving the fusion of intelligence, unity of command, and speed. In the case of the president's daily intelligence brief, for example, representatives from the CIA, State, DHS, and Defense attend with the DNI, a process that helps to fuse information and streamline the uniform conveyance of presidential views.[26]

Third, and closely related to the first factor, whether the latent homeland security bureaucracy obtains a foothold will depend in part on whether the HSC process embeds itself in agency culture and expectations. Have the HSC and OHS established an identity and authority parallel to that of NSC? Or is this authority dependent alone on the personality of an incumbent or the relationship of the incumbent to the president? Will the staff at DHS or JCS, for example, presume a continuation of the function, or will they look for opportunities to undermine or eliminate the function? A critical point will come in the next presidential transition when the HSC and OHS transition from one administration to the next and are either gone with the wind or hold their transitional positions, becoming, like the NSC, a permanent fixture of the national security presidency.

2. Sub-Cabinet Coordination

The number of federal departments and agencies with a potential hand in homeland security is staggering. The president's executive order establishing the HSC designates thirteen principal agency officials to serve on the Principals Committee. Nine additional officials are designated to attend meetings on a contingent basis. In context, numerous other subordinate agencies have a role to play as well, such as the Centers for Disease Control and Prevention, the Federal Aviation Administration, the Maritime Administration, the Food Safety Inspection Service, the Animal and Plant Health Inspection Service, and the list continues.[27] The Northern Command, with responsibility for the military defense of the United States and certain civil support functions, includes within its planning process a template for coordinating with more than sixty different federal, state, and local entities.[28]

The scope of the bureaucratic challenge at the federal level alone is immediately evident if one considers the DHS. At its inception in March 2003 the department consolidated twenty-two "legacy" agencies, involving

180,000 employees, utilizing fifteen different pay systems, ten hiring systems, nineteen different performance systems, and seven different benefit systems. This bureaucratic tangle is not reconciled by a clear or concise mission statement. To the contrary, the department is statutorily assigned eight "primary" and seemingly competitive missions. The first three address the terrorist threat.

The primary mission of the department is to

(A) prevent terrorist attacks within the United States;

(B) reduce the vulnerability of the United States to terrorism;

(C) minimize the damage, and assist in the recovery, from terrorist attacks that do occur within the United States.

The remaining mission statements pull in other directions.

(D) carry out all functions of entities transferred to the department, including by acting as a focal point regarding natural and manmade crises and emergency planning;

(E) ensure that the functions of the agencies and subdivisions within the department that are not related directly to securing the homeland are not diminished or neglected except by specific explicit Act of Congress;

(F) ensure that the overall economic security of the United States is not diminished by efforts, activities, and programs aimed at securing the homeland;

(G) ensure that the civil rights and civil liberties of persons are not diminished by efforts, activities, and programs aimed at securing the homeland; and

(H) monitor connections between illegal drug trafficking and terrorism, coordinate efforts to sever such connections, and otherwise contribute to efforts to interdict illegal drug trafficking. (6 U.S.C. 111(b))

Moreover, the subordinate agencies are diverse in mission and structure. The Secret Service, for example, has as its focus presidential protection, protection of designated senior officials, and a narrow band of criminal jurisdiction over offenses relating to U.S. currency. The Federal Emergency Management Agency's (FEMA) mission is "to lead the effort to prepare the nation for all hazards and effectively manage federal response and recovery efforts following any national incident."[29] The Coast Guard, in turn, is both a military service and law enforcement agency, as well as a life-saving and environmental agency. Long relegated in budgetary status as the fifth military service, the Coast Guard now finds itself on the front line of homeland security, but with secondary resources. The Coast Guard has approximately 160 "cutters"[30] to patrol a shoreline of approximately 90,000 miles (55,000 of which are along the continental United States) and 3.4 million square miles of ocean contained within the Exclusive Economic Zone (EEZ), the largest EEZ in the world.[31]

The law has not helped the department's leadership nurture a departmental esprit de corps, of the sort one might associate with the Marine Corps or the CIA, which is especially hard to do in a large and disparate organization. But grow it must. Nor has the department's enabling statute helped to address the essential paradigm shifts or resource choices the United States must make to adequately secure the homeland. Rather, the statute asks DHS to protect the homeland, preserve liberties, and leave the resources devoted to pre-9/11 tasks untouched.

But one need not focus on (or pick on) DHS to appreciate the complexity of the procedural and leadership challenge. Twelve separate agencies, for example, share responsibility for food health and security. A separate agency is responsible for the safety of eggs depending on whether or not the egg is shelled or broken in the course of production and processing.[32] Thus, if one considers the difficulty in fusing intelligence within the sixteen components of the intelligence community, one might better appreciate the challenge of coordinating homeland security at just the federal level where HSPD-1 identifies at least twenty-five agencies with responsibility. That is counting just the primary agencies, and not the subordinate elements within DHS, Agriculture, or HHS that are also involved.

One of the missions of the Homeland Security Council, Office of Homeland Security, and DHS is to bring coherence to these constituent parts both on an intra- and inter-agency basis. Toward this end, presidents have sought to define overall policy parameters and lead agency responsibilities through use of presidential directives. For example, President Clinton first designated lead agency responsibilities for domestic terrorism response in Presidential Decision Directive 39, "U.S. Policy on Counter-terrorism," (1995). The directive was intended to head off or dampen the inevitable bureaucratic turf battles over responsibilities (read: credit, blame, and resources) in advance of a crisis.

President Bush provided comparable designation in HSPD-5 "Management of Domestic Incidents." In particular, the directive designates the Secretary of Homeland Security as "the principal federal official for domestic incident management." However, the directive glosses over many of the difficult points of decision and command. In particular, the division of federal, state, and local responsibilities is amorphous. Vague triggers for federal action abound. Paragraph 6 illustrates.

> The Federal Government recognizes the role and responsibilities of State and local authorities in domestic incident management. Initial responsibility for managing domestic incidents generally falls on State and local authorities. The Federal Government will assist State and local

authorities when their resources are overwhelmed, or when Federal interests are involved. The Secretary will coordinate with State and local governments to ensure adequate planning, equipment, training, and exercise activities.

Subordinate plans seek to take the planning cycle to the next level of detail. The National Response Plan (NRP), for example, establishes a federal framework for responding to specific incidents, just as NSC directives do in the context of national security incidents.[33] A Federal Response Plan drafted by FEMA in 1999 was used as an organizational basis for the federal response to 9/11. Much like military operations orders, the 2004 NRP includes specific annexes directed toward specific functions, like public affairs and worker safety and health, as well as specific incidents, like a biological incident or cyber incident. The NRP is an "all hazards" plan. It is initiated as needed, in a rolling manner, rather than all at once. In short, the NRP serves as the mechanism for national-level policy and operational coordination.

Under the plan, unity of command on the ground is established through designation of a Principal Federal Officer (PFO). The PFO is responsible for establishing a joint field office to manage federal agency response and federal, state, and local coordination at the scene of an incident. The PFO reports up the chain of command through the DHS Homeland Security Operations Center. The Operations Center in turn is a 24/7 operation with forty-five federal, state, and local agencies represented with a strength of about 300 staff. The Center "is the primary, national-level nerve center and conduit for information flowing into and out of these [homeland security] events." In turn, the inter-agency incident management group at the Washington level serves as the DHS secretary's crisis working group and strategic planning cell. The Incident Management Division of DHS, which serves in the group, is then responsible for coordinating the specific federal response to the incident.[34]

3. State and Local Coordination

Unlike traditional national security issues associated with the Cold War or foreign relations, which are predominantly if not exclusively national in character, homeland security is also characterized by its local and regional focus. This is evident from the nature of the threat, which in the case of terrorism and disease is oriented toward civilian casualties. It is also evident because the majority of assets that are available to respond to homeland security events are local. Moreover, whatever the authority of the federal government, as a matter of law, state and local governments retain a shared constitutional responsibility for the public safety and welfare of their citizens.

Present statistics illustrate the point, and the corresponding coordination problem. There are approximately 800,000 law enforcement officers in the United States serving in approximately 18,000 separate state and local law enforcement agencies.[35] The New York City Police Department alone consists of 39,000 police officers, more personnel than serve in the Australian Army. In contrast, there are approximately 130,000 law enforcement officers in England and Wales serving within forty-three agencies.[36] There are one million full-time and 750,000 volunteer firefighters in the United States serving in approximately 30,400 federal, state, and local fire departments. Likewise, there are approximately 155,000 emergency medical technicians (EMTs). These are the first responders, or as some prefer, the "first preventers."[37]

However, most specialized expertise and funding capacity remains at the national level. The federal government initiated its first programs to train local responders in terrorism incident response and in particular chemical, biological, radiological, and nuclear (CBRN) response in the 1990s. In addition, in 1999 the Department of Defense formed its first Weapons of Mass Destruction-Civil Support Teams (WMD-CST Teams). Forty teams have now been authorized and certified, of the fifty-five authorized by Congress.[38] Department of Homeland Security grants remain a principal source of funding for additional first responder training and equipment.

Moreover, where incidents, or the repercussions from such incidents, are transboundary in implication, then the federal government is specially situated to lead and direct the response. That makes uniform standards in equipment and training across jurisdictional lines essential. The federal government alone has the legal and funding wherewithal to effect that result. Most importantly, with respect to intelligence fusion, the federal government retains sole custody of the national intelligence capacity and the sole capacity to serve as the hub for interstate intelligence analysis and dissemination. This makes vertical process and decision-making across state and local boundaries as important as horizontal federal organization.

At the federal level, responsibility for state and local coordination reside with the secretary of homeland security. In particular, the department includes an Office of State and Local Government Coordination, responsible for coordinating the activities of the department with state and local governments and advocating for the resources needed by state and local governments to implement national strategy for combating terrorism.[39] Of course, federal, state, and local coordination occurs throughout the bureaucracy. Many of the department's functions are inherently local in nature and are exercised through local or regional federal actors, such as the ten regional FEMA offices that coordinate training and implementation of the National Incident Management System (NIMS).

Whereas the National Response Plan is directed toward the federal response to homeland security incidents, the NIMS is a more detailed effort to implement the concepts contained in the NRP at the federal, state, and local levels. Thus, "NIMS establishes standardized incident management processes, protocols, and procedures that all responders – Federal, state, tribal, and local – will use to coordinate and conduct response actions."[40] In theory, the NIMS adopts "best practices" and creates a uniform methodology for responding to events wherever they occur. In addition, these plans are generally predicated on a process of graduated response, with local authorities providing management and control in the immediate aftermath of an incident. Then, if necessary, regional authorities would assume management and control within hours after an incident. All fifty states now have homeland security agencies, or comparable institutions. Then, if necessary, the federal government would respond, typically assuming a sixteen- to twenty-four-hour window following the incident, with deployment of the National Emergency Support Team and any necessary push packages (discussed below).[41]

Intelligence integration is accomplished in five basic ways. First, the FBI has established Joint Terrorism Task Forces (JTTFs) throughout the country in association with its fifty-six field offices and at other locations. As of 2006, there were 101 such task forces with responsibility for serving as clearing committees for identifying and sharing information among federal agencies as well as with state and local agencies.[42] With the JTTF mechanism, the local law enforcement officer who is unsure whether information he has heard or obtained is relevant to national security has a readily available forum to test the information. Second, as part of the Terrorist Alert Network, the DHS provides generalized and specific threat information to state and local law enforcement agencies. As with allies or international organizations, intelligence can be shared on a tear-line basis; that is, without identifying the source of the information. Third, local law enforcement is connected with federal law enforcement through normal mechanisms of police work, including the National Crime Information Center (NCIC) system, the computer network an officer will check when someone is pulled over for speeding to see if there are any outstanding warrants for the person and to verify registration and license.[43] Fourth, a number of states have established regional fusion centers for the sharing of homeland security information. As of 2006, forty-six such centers were operational. Finally, information is shared "the old-fashioned way"; one officer knows another officer and picks up the phone or walks over and tells him something. Interestingly, some local police forces have taken the concept one step further and now conduct their own foreign intelligence liaison.[44]

Intelligence issues abound. First, there is the difficulty of volume. Where a national UK terrorist alert requires coordination with forty-three regional police forces, a national alert in the United States might theoretically require notification of 18,000 separate agencies. In San Diego County alone there are twenty-eight local police and fire departments, eighteen city governments, and the harbor police, a figure that does not account for state and federal agencies.[45] If the notification is considered law enforcement sensitive, or classified, the logistics arrangements and costs are compounded. Clearly, intelligence is more effective where it lends itself to geographic or functional refinement.[46]

Second, an effective intelligence function requires two-way dissemination. At the national level, federal officials have access to intelligence community data and assets. They also have access to the nation's analysts and laboratory capacity. But as many have noted, counter-terrorism is human intelligence intensive. As the 2006 London airport plot demonstrates, against decentralized terrorist cells local intelligence collection is as likely as national intelligence to detect the threat. In plain English, the police officer on the beat who pressures an informant to report on a colleague at the local mosque is as likely to find the intelligence needle in the haystack as the National Security Agency analyst relying on state-of-the-art signals intelligence. That means it is as important for information to flow up the local, state, and federal ladder as it is that it flow down.

This two-way street leads to a third problem: training law enforcement officers to identify and disseminate national security information derived from criminal context. Here the focus is on training 800,000 law enforcement officers to identify the piece of information, which may appear innocuous, but nonetheless informs the larger intelligence mosaic. In the past, the cultural default was for law enforcement officers to retain all but the most obvious national security information within the confidential confines of the investigative file. The JTTFs and Fusion Centers are intended to serve as outlets to test information for mosaic value at the local level before pushing intelligence up the chain of command. On the international level information may be shared through intelligence liaison channels, diplomatic channels, or through the more than fifty legal attaches (or Legats) the Department of Justice and the FBI have stationed throughout the world.[47] A critical question for ongoing appraisal is whether the default instinct is now one of identification and flow.

Fourth, in homeland security context, intelligence fusion requires the integration not just of law enforcement information with intelligence information but also the seamless integration of information collected overseas and at home. This function also requires the effective integration of intelligence from a plurality of agencies, including many outside the national security community. For public health specialists, for example, intelligence integration means a capacity to identify emerging patterns before they blossom from local to regional to national events.

As intelligence fusion illustrates, there is no shortage of issues incumbent in homeland security coordination. It is in this nexus between federal and local authority that three critical structural issues are found.

D. THREE WHOS: WHO DECIDES? WHO PAYS? WHO ACTS?

In the area of federal, state, and local coordination three legal considerations are endemic: Who decides? Who pays? Who acts? The answers will depend on the specific facts and law applicable to each circumstance. However, invariably, whether one is addressing a breaking incident or the structure of a topical regime, like maritime security, two legal shoals lurk beneath the governmental sea: federalism as well as the limits and permits applicable to the domestic use of the U.S. military.

1. Federalism

As discussed in Chapter 4, the Constitution contains a number of structural checks on the exercise of governmental power, including the separation of powers between the federal branches of government; the shared powers between the branches, creating the opportunity for checks and balances between branches; the Bill of Rights, the first ten amendments to the Constitution; and federalism, the division of power between the federal government and the states. In constitutional theory, the powers of the federal government are necessarily enumerated in the Constitution, or derived from enumerated authorities found in the text. The states, in voluntarily establishing the United States and ratifying the Constitution, surrendered to the federal government only that portion of their authority specified in the Constitution. As a result, those powers that are not enumerated or implied from the text are retained by the states. This constitutional principle is found in the text of the Tenth Amendment:

> The powers not delegated to the United States by the Constitution, nor prohibited by it to the States, are reserved to the States respectively, or to the people.[48]

Among the powers reserved to the states is what is known as the police power, the residual authority of each state to provide for the public safety and welfare of its citizens. Toward this end, the states retain, among other authority, the power to maintain and call forth state militias.[49]

Traditional uses of the state police power include the enforcement of civil and criminal law, and the enactment and enforcement of regulations to protect public health. Thus, in the lead case on the subject, the Supreme Court in 1905 upheld the authority of the state of Massachusetts, through the Board of Public Health of the City of Cambridge, to require vaccination and revaccination of all inhabitants for smallpox. The plaintiff, Henning Jacobson, argued among other things that the requirement violated his constitutional liberty interest.[50]

Conflicts between federal and state law are addressed in the Constitution by the Supremacy Clause.

> This Constitution, and the Laws of the United States which shall be made in Pursuance thereof; and all Treaties made, or which shall be made, under the Authority of the United States, shall be the supreme Law of the Land; and the Judges in every State shall be bound thereby, any Thing in the Constitution or Laws of any State to the Contrary notwithstanding.[51]

However, it is not always clear whether federal or state law applies in the context presented. And, where both apply, it is not always clear whether federal and state laws are actually in conflict. This might be the case at the outset of a homeland security incident when timely federal intervention in support of the state's police power might prevent the later necessity of using the president's national security power. Imagine, for example, a scenario involving the arrival of a traveler infected with SARS (or other contagious disease) at a regional airport. Imagine as well that the individual is not identified until after he departs the airport and has entered the commerce stream. As a matter of law, both the state and local authorities would likely have authority to quarantine the individual and persons who have come into contact with him. But the state, fearing panic, or anticipating that it can manage the incident without quarantine, does not act, or acts only with respect to the infected individual.

- Should the Secretary of HHS act, using his federal authority to quarantine the individual or those who have come into contact with the subject?
- Does it matter if the subject has crossed multiple state borders?
- What if the traveler might have smallpox or hemorrhagic fever?
- Does it matter that the individual is suspected of having the disease, but tests have yet to confirm so?

As this scenario illustrates, homeland security presents a new array of questions of law for national security specialists involving principles of federalism and the related police power of the states identified in the Tenth Amendment. One can see as well the potential for conflict between federal law designed to protect the national security and those Tenth Amendment concepts embodied in the state police power intended to preserve the autonomy and choice of local government.

The supremacy clause is applied contextually through application of the doctrine of preemption. As a general matter, there are three categories of preemption.[52] Express preemption, as the term implies, occurs where the Congress in statute explicitly states that a federal law is intended to trump any alternative state law. This might be the case where the Congress creates an exclusive federal cause of action for a type of tort. Such a law might be addressed to the inequities between the uneven application of state laws as well as to limit the risk and impact of liability. The federal government has done so with respect to airline liability for international air accidents through operation of the Warsaw Treaty. It says so in the small print on the back of your ticket.[53] Likewise, the contracts National Guard soldiers sign expressly provide that those portions of the contract addressing federal service "preempt" those addressed to state service, when the soldier is serving in a federal capacity.[54]

Preemption also occurs "[w]hen Congress intends federal law to 'occupy the field'" even if the Congress has not expressly preempted state law. Two relevant examples illustrate. The Arms Export Control Act (AECA) regulates the sale and transfer of designated arms and munitions to foreign purchasers through a federal licensing regime administered by the Department of State. Although the AECA does not expressly state so, Congress could not have intended individual states to authorize the transfer of weapons overseas when it so closely regulates such transfers through State Department licensing. In other words, Congress intended the AECA to occupy this field of foreign commerce and related to foreign affairs. Of course, this same result might be reached through alternative constitutional analysis. The Tenth Amendment recognizes that states might not exercise powers otherwise prohibited to them by the Constitution.[55]

Third, "even if Congress has not occupied the field, state law is naturally preempted to the extent of any conflict with a federal statute." This form of preemption is alternatively referred to as actual, implied, or natural preemption. The Supreme Court has identified at least two situations where this might occur: (1) "where it is impossible for a private party to comply with both state and federal law" or (2) where state law "stands as an obstacle to the accomplishment and execution of the full purposes and objectives of Congress."[56] Such a conflict might occur in a homeland security context where both the federal government and the state have concurrent authority, for example, in the area of public health and quarantine; however, the purpose of the federal quarantine might be undermined by the countervailing direction, or absence of direction, of the state regulation or quarantine.[57]

Here is the legal policy dilemma. Although federal law will clearly prevail over conflicting state law through application of the supremacy clause and preemption doctrine, when dealing with homeland security scenarios, it is not always clear at what factual point, and therefore at what legal point, a police issue should become or has become a national security issue. Therefore, it will not always be clear at what point a federal statute and scheme intended to address national security might conflict with state law. As the

Supreme Court has stated, "We recognize, of course, that the categories of preemption are not 'rigidly distinct.'"

Moreover, court cases addressing preemption occur in the context of legislation or treaties, where there is text to compare. Yet, the supremacy clause clearly applies to constitutional assertions of federal authority, and not just statutory or treaty-based assertions. The text states so. Where the president is exercising his national security authority in domestic context and asserting a constitutionally based right of preemption, the application of the doctrine will be less certain, at least in the close case.

Consider the earlier SARS-smallpox-hemorrhagic fever scenario. On the one hand, if the federal government asserts its federal interest and preempts state law too soon or too readily, the federal government may be challenged, on legal and policy grounds, as acting with too heavy a hand and without constitutional authority. In doing so, the president may take on political, economic, moral, and legal responsibilities (and costs) for the state and local impact of actions that may prove unwarranted as facts play out. In this manner, the exercise of homeland security prevention may come to be exercises not only in crisis management but also in litigation management.

On the other hand, with many homeland security scenarios the better result is often obtained by acting at an incipient stage of concern, when the facts may be unknown, and the proper characterization of the event as natural or manmade, security or police, is uncertain. In the communicable disease scenario, if the federal government waits too long to assert its national security interest and preempt the hesitant or incomplete application of state law, the moment of containment may be lost. Crisis becomes tragedy. Military medics speak of the golden hour after a combat wound in which to stabilize and transport the casualty to sustained medical care. Might there be a similar golden hour, day, or week during which rapid and overwhelming federal intervention will prevent widespread catastrophe?

This moment may be evident in the case of a nuclear attack, but it may be less evident in the case of a biological attack using a contagious disease. It may also be less evident in the case of a naturally occurring event, like avian flu, that may morph or migrate from private health emergency, to public health emergency, to national security crisis depending on how many people catch the disease, how contagious it is, and thus how quickly it spreads. Put directly: if local authorities do not impose quarantine because they perceive the threat as a matter of individual health, manageable, or in good faith balance the health and economic interests in favor of quiet and private treatment, a minor outbreak of disease may become contagion.

Consider as well a cyber attack on a critical infrastructure that appears at the outset to originate from an individual hacker. As a result, the private company or the government entity does not alert federal authorities or the national security side of the federal bureaucracy. The matter is treated as a law enforcement concern, or perhaps, just a firewall concern. But what if this is just one in a pattern of probes by a foreign entity using the cover and concealment of a hacker's identity and this pattern is known only to intelligence specialists in Washington? Further, what if this hacker is the one who is leading the attack or is the hacker who ultimately breaks the firewall? The operation of law and principles of federalism will depend in part on whether the advent events are viewed through a local, police power, or national security lens.

The legal policy dilemma is enhanced because there are strong disincentives for federal and state officials to resolve such critical issues of preemption in advance and in the abstract. First, there is the concept of federalism itself. The states have reserved to themselves the police power, and as a matter of constitutional design the federal government is not supposed to turn every local event or crisis into a federal emergency. This would not be efficient and it would not represent good law. As a result, most but not all statutory authorities authorizing federal security assistance to local authorities are predicated on receiving a state request.

Second, the federal government does not want to take political or financial ownership of every state and local crisis.[58] This is bad policy, bad resource management, and in all likelihood bad politics. Conversely, local officials may not want to concede an inability or failure to address their own problems. State officials may also, with good cause, want to avoid undue alarm or undue economic impact.

Third, the federal government's most potent and effective homeland security instrument is the military instrument, and here there are significant legal, policy, and cultural obstacles to deployment in domestic civil context.

2. The Military Instrument

The 2005 Department of Defense "Strategy for Homeland Defense and Civil Support" states: "Protecting the United States homeland from attack is the highest priority of the Department of Defense." The Homeland Security Strategy of 2002[59] identified three specific domestic military missions. First, in extraordinary circumstances the military will undertake specific military missions, like the flying of combat air patrols over U.S. cities. Second, the military will provide capabilities in support of emergency response efforts by other federal agencies and for ongoing homeland security activities, like drug interdiction. Third, the military will perform limited scope special security missions, like the provision of security support to the Olympics, the Super Bowl, and political conventions.[60]

The Northern Command, established in 2002, is the primary combatant command responsible for undertaking these missions. In defense policy terms, Northern Command is "responsible for planning, organizing, and executing homeland defense and civil support missions within the continental United States, Alaska and territorial waters." Specifically, the command's area of responsibility extends 500 miles off the coast, covering the maritime approaches to the United States as well as potential seaborne threats, ship-to-shore missiles. The command is also responsible for coordinating security cooperation with Canada and Mexico. As part of both efforts, Northern Command conducts national and binational exercises each year, which serve as realistic training for the homeland mission, in the absence of actual events.

The Pacific Command has comparable responsibility in its area of responsibility, which includes the Hawaiian Islands and the Pacific territories. Strategic Command is responsible for "planning, integrating, and coordinating global missile defense operations...including providing warning of missile attack, across all combatant commands."[61] Strategic Command is also responsible for integrating and "synchronizing" the U.S. military's information operations and WMD efforts throughout the world. The command is also responsible for coordinating global intelligence collection to address DOD's worldwide operations and national intelligence requirements.[62]

However, the homeland security mission is centered on the Northern Command with headquarters at Peterson Air Force Base, Colorado Springs, Colorado. Northern Command's mission statement distinguishes between a direct defense mission and an indirect support mission.

> Conduct operations to deter, prevent and defeat threats and aggression aimed at the Untied States, its territories, and interests within assigned area of responsibility.
>
> As directed by the president or secretary of defense, provide military assistance to civil authorities, including consequence management operations.[63]

The command identifies seven elements to these missions: ballistic missile defense; support for natural disaster relief; airport security; maritime security; chemical, biological, radiological, and nuclear (CBRN) event consequence management; the provision of mobile redundant command centers; and aviation support to the Secret Service for continuity of government operations. The Northern Command is also charged with coordinating the National Guard response to domestic events and, where Guard units are serving in a federal homeland capacity, commanding those units.

As its mission statement indicates, Northern Command is an operational combatant command. Thus, the chain of command runs from the president to the secretary of defense to the four-star commander. (The assistant secretary of defense for homeland defense provides policy direction and oversight of the Defense Department's homeland defense activities.)

The Commander of Northern Command is dual-hatted as the U.S. commander of the North American Air Defense Command (NORAD). This binational (U.S.–Canadian) command is responsible for the air defense of the North American continent and, as of 2006, of the maritime approaches as well.[64] The commander of Northern Command has stated that the president has delegated to the secretary of defense and, when necessary, the combatant commander, authority to shoot down civil aircraft that in the commander's judgment pose a national security threat within the United States.[65]

The command has dedicated forces to undertake certain of its missions, in particular those necessary for air defense, command and control, and CBRNE response; however, generally the command task organizes for specific missions with the military chain of command assigning specific forces to the Northern Command as needed. This methodology has the strength of being substantively and geographically flexible. It has the weakness in the potential for delay as forces are assembled and in the prospect that critical elements will already be assigned to another combatant command at the moment of need. In October 2006, Army North stood up in San Antonio, Texas, with the purpose of providing dedicated Army resources for undertaking certain Northern Command missions including deploying in crisis and training U.S. forces for the homeland defense and civil support missions.[66]

Given its mission, Northern Command has one of, if not the largest, command legal offices in the military. In 2006, the Staff Judge Advocates Office consisted of fifteen military and civil attorneys, tangible recognition that the military appreciates the range of legal issues involved in civil deployment.[67]

a. Legal Framework

Use of the armed forces in domestic circumstances is governed by constitutional law, statute, and Department of Defense directives, among other law. As in other national security areas legal analysis starts with the Constitution. In homeland context, the commander-in-chief clause and take care clause are particularly relevant in defining the president's responsibilities and authorities. The authority of the president and, pursuant to the president's direction, the Northern Command to defend the United States from attack represents an exercise in core constitutional authority. Even the most legislative-oriented or cautious legal views of the "war power" would recognize this authority. The constitutional basis for presidential decision is also important in implementation. As noted in Chapter 2, where the president is exercising his constitutional authority as commander in chief, in addition to or distinct from legislative grants of authority, he may lawfully direct the use of Defense Department resources. Fiscal lawyers may fuss, or their policy bosses may ask them to fuss. But this is black-letter law for which there is ample precedent.

With respect to military support to civil authorities as well as the direct military involvement in civil law enforcement, Congress's Article I powers are also in play, in particular its authority to "make such rules and regulations for the Army and the Navy" along with its legislative power to define the criminal law. Using these authorities the Congress enacted the first of three relevant framework statutes in 1878, the Posse Comitatus Act.

(1) Posse Comitatus

The immediate catalysis behind the Posse Comitatus Act was the disputed election between Rutherford B. Hayes and Samuel J. Tilden in 1876, which Hayes won by one electoral vote. In the broader context of Reconstruction, the law's sponsors argued that federal troops had advanced the interest of Hayes over Tilden while serving as security at Southern polling locations. Congress responded with the Posse Comitatus Act[68] imposing a criminal prohibition on certain uses of the military to enforce the "power of the county" ("posse comitatus"), which is to say, assist local authorities uphold civil law.

> Whoever, except in cases and under circumstances expressly authorized by the Constitution or Act of Congress, willfully uses any part of the Army or the Air Force as a posse comitatus or otherwise to execute the laws shall be fined under this title or imprisoned not more than two years, or both.[69]

The Air Force was added to the statute in 1956. Congress subsequently enacted legislation requiring the secretary of defense to extend comparable restrictions to military personnel generally.

> The Secretary of Defense shall prescribe such regulations as may be necessary to ensure that any activity (including the provision of any equipment or facility or the assignment or detail of any personnel) under this chapter does not include or prompt direct participation by a member of the Army, Navy, Air force, or Marine Corps in a search, seizure, arrest or other similar activity unless participation in such activity by such member is otherwise authorized by law.[70]

The secretary of defense has done so by directive, first setting out the policy and then the restrictions involved.

Policy

It is DOD policy to cooperate with civilian law enforcement officials to the extent practical. The implementation of this policy shall be consistent with the needs of national security and military preparedness, the historic tradition of limiting direct military involvement in civilian law enforcement activities, and the requirements of applicable law, as developed in enclosures 2 through 7.

Enclosure 4 addresses "Restrictions on Participation of DoD Personnel in civilian Law Enforcement Activities."

> **Restrictions on direct Assistance.** Except as otherwise provided in this enclosure, the prohibition on the use of military personnel 'as a posse comitatus or otherwise to execute the laws' prohibits the following forms of direct assistance:
>
> Interdiction of a vehicle, vessel, aircraft, or other similar activity.
>
> A search or seizure.
>
> An arrest, apprehension, stop and frisk, or similar activity.
>
> Use of military personnel for surveillance or pursuit of individuals, or as undercover agents, informants, investigators, or interrogators.[71]

The Act and directives apply to the National Guard when operating in federal service, but not when they are operating under state command. In contrast, the Coast Guard has express law enforcement jurisdiction over certain offenses in the territorial and inland waterways found in Title 14.

On its face, the Posse Comitatus Act would appear to impose significant restrictions on the use of the armed forces in homeland security context. However, the Act has been interpreted as applying only to "'the direct active use of federal troops by civil law enforcement officers' to enforce the laws of this nation."[72] Thus, courts have rejected posse comitatus challenges to the admission of evidence derived from "aerial photographic reconnaissance flights and other activities [that] do not reflect direct military involvement," as well as the use of military training missions. Moreover, "even where a violation of the Posse Comitatus Act is found or suspected, courts have generally found that creation or application of an exclusionary rule is not warranted."[73]

In addition, there are numerous legislative exceptions to the Act, and inapplicable defense directives. Considered collectively, these exceptions provide a comprehensive framework and, as a matter of law, adequate latitude for use of the military in homeland context. Defense Department directives reference more than twenty-five such exceptions, including one for protecting the rights of a discoverer of a guano island, as well as matters arising under the Uniform Code of Military Justice.[74] The most important exceptions for homeland security purposes are those pertaining to the provision of intelligence gathered in military operations (10 U.S.C. 371), supplying military equipment and facilities (10 U.S.C. 372), and providing training and advising on the use of equipment (10 U.S.C. 373) to state and local law enforcement authorities.[75]

In addition, in 1996 and 1997 the secretary of defense was authorized to provide military assistance "in support of Department of Justice activities relating to the enforcement of [the law] during an emergency situation involving a biological or chemical weapon of mass destruction." The authorization is predicated on a request from the Attorney General and a joint determination by the Attorney General and Secretary of Defense that an emergency situation exists and "the Secretary determines the provision of such assistance will not adversely affect the military preparedness of the United States."[76] Comparable authorities and conditions apply to emergencies involving nuclear materials.[77]

Two exceptions are particularly important given their general applicability to homeland security and disaster assistance and the frequency in which they are invoked: the Insurrection Act and the Stafford Act.

(2) The Insurrection Act

The Insurrection Act, 10 U.S.C. 331–334, permits the president to use federal forces to enforce the law in three related circumstances. Each section of the law was passed at a different time to address a different factual scenario. Specifically, section 331, "Federal Aid for State Governments," addresses requests from a state governor for assistance "whenever there is an insurrection in any state against its government." The provision dates to 1794 and the Whiskey Rebellion, a popular movement in western Pennsylvania to prevent enforcement of an excise tax on whiskey. After local authorities proved unable to enforce the tax, President Washington called on federal troops to enforce the tax and uphold the law. This authority was used in 1992 following a request from the governor of California for federal troops to help restore order after rioting in Los Angeles.[78]

Section 332, "Use of Militia and Armed Forces to Enforce Federal Authority," is intended to address scenarios involving domestic disturbance and the breakdown of civil authority, "whenever the president considers that unlawful obstructions, combinations, or assemblages, or rebellion against the authority of the United States, make it impracticable to enforce the laws of the United States in any State or Territory by the ordinary course of judicial proceedings." Not surprisingly, this provision was passed at the outbreak of the Civil War. It was relied upon by presidents to address public school desegregation in Arkansas and Alabama.[79]

Section 333, "Interference with State and Federal Law," authorizes the president using the military or armed forces, or by any other means, "as he considers necessary to suppress, in a State, any insurrection, domestic violence, unlawful combination, or conspiracy, if it – (1) so hinders the execution of the laws of that state and of the United States within that State, that any part or class of its people is deprived of a right, privilege, immunity, or protection named in the Constitution and secured by law . . . or (2) opposes or obstructs the execution of the law of the United States or impedes the course of justice under those laws." This provision as originally drafted was directed at state governments that were not enforcing the Constitution and was passed during Reconstruction. It was cited as authority for use of federal troops during civil rights protests in Birmingham in 1963.[80] As in the case of Section 332, this section may be invoked by the president in his sole discretion and is not predicated on a request from a state legislature or its governor.

Significantly, this section of the Act was amended in October 2006 to expand the president's authority to use the armed forces to respond to Major Public Emergencies. The amendments accomplish three ends.[81] First, where the original Act required that the loss of order results from an insurrection or domestic violence, the amended Act establishes a second predicate: "To – (A) restore public order and enforce the laws of the United States when, as a result of a natural disaster, epidemic, or other serious public health emergency, terrorist attack or incident, or other condition in any State or possession of the United States, the president determines that" state authorities are incapable of upholding the law and the resulting circumstance that deprives any part of the population of a right (as provided in the original Act). Second, the amendments authorize the president to use the National Guard in such federal service as well as the armed forces.

Third, the president is authorized to direct the secretary of defense to supply services and equipment "and other assistance necessary for the immediate preservation of life and property." Unlike the Stafford Act, this authority is without time limitation; however, the DOD role is limited to that period of time during which state authorities are unable to provide the necessary assistance and "only until such state authorities or other departments of the United States charged" with this mission (e.g., DHS and FEMA) are able to do so.

In summary, the president on his initiative can jump in heavy with military assistance if need be in response to a wide array of events including a natural disaster, public health emergencies, and terrorist attacks. Moreover, he can federalize the National Guard to facilitate command and control on the ground and minimize the pull on federal forces. Moreover, there is no time limit. The principal constraint on the use of the authority is the inability of the state to effectively assert its own police power. The catalyst for these amendments was Hurricane Katrina; however, the text reflects that federal officials and the amendment's sponsors were looking ahead to other potential scenarios.

Finally, section 334 of the Act, "Proclamation to Disperse," requires the president to issue a proclamation to disperse.

> Whenever the president considers it necessary to use the militia of the armed forces under this chapter, he shall, by proclamation, immediately

order the insurgents to disperse and retire peaceably to their abodes within a limited time.

This section reflects the theory that in democratic society those acting outside the law should receive notice to cease and desist before the president takes the extraordinary step of using federal forces to enforce the law.

This latter section is appropriately viewed as upholding the constitutional and democratic principles that domestic law enforcement belongs in civil hands as well as reflecting Congress's judgment that the use of federal troops or "calling forth" of state militia for federal service are extraordinary events warranting a form of fair notice and an exhaustion of remedies. In the case of the amended "Katrina" authority, the president must notify Congress of his intention to use the specific authority "as soon as practicable after the determination." In other words, the use is not subject to consultation or prior notification. However, the president must notify the Congress of his continued determination to use the authority every fourteen days thereafter, inviting but not guaranteeing congressional review and check on how this authority is used.

(3) The Stafford Act

The Robert Stafford Disaster Relief and Emergency Assistance Act[82] (the Stafford Act) authorizes the president to provide federal, including military, assistance in response to domestic incidents. There are three mechanisms for invoking the authority of the Stafford Act: in cases of declared disaster or emergency in response to a state request, or on the president's initiative in response to an emergency for which the federal government has primary responsibility.

In most cases, Stafford assistance will originate with a request from the governor of a state for assistance in the case of a natural disaster. "Such a request shall be based on a finding that the disaster is of such severity and magnitude that effective response is beyond the capabilities of the State and the affected local governments and that Federal assistance is necessary." In addition, the governor is required to first take appropriate responsive action under state law and direct execution of the state's emergency plan. The governor is also required to furnish information on state and local expenditures as well as to commit to comply with applicable cost-sharing requirements.[83]

Where the president declares that a major disaster exists, he may direct any federal agency, with or without reimbursement, to utilize its authorities and resources in support of state and local assistance efforts.[84] The federal share of assistance shall be not less than 75 percent. A wide array of assistance is available under this section of the Act, including medical, food, debris removal, search and rescue, and technical assistance.[85]

Historically the Stafford Act was used to respond to disasters like hurricanes; however, it was also used as authority during the first World Trade Center attack in 1993. In 1994, language was added to the Act to clarify that the military could be used for disasters "regardless of cause." Thus, the Act provides authority for the president to provide military assistance in the domestic context in response to manmade disasters like attacks, as well as natural disasters. This legal mechanism was used to provide military assistance to civil authorities in the context of the 1995 Oklahoma City bombing and on 9/11.

Significantly, the president may also initiate the provision of essential emergency assistance to meet immediate threats to life and property resulting from an incident without the state first meeting the prerequisites for declaring a disaster. This can occur in two instances. First, upon the request of the governor of the affected state, the president may direct the secretary of defense to authorize "any emergency work that is made necessary by the incident." "If the president determines that such work is essential for the preservation of life and property, the president shall grant such a request to the extent the president determines is practicable. Such emergency work may only be carried out for a period not to exceed 10 days."[86]

Most importantly in the homeland security context, the law also provides that in the case of "certain emergencies involving Federal primary responsibility,"

> The president may exercise any authority vested in him by section 5192 of this title or section 5193 of this title with respect to an emergency when he determines that an emergency exists for which the primary responsibility for response rests with the United States because the emergency involves a subject area for which, under the Constitution or laws of the United States, the United States exercises exclusive or preeminent responsibility and authority. In determining whether or not such an emergency exists the president shall consult the Governor of the affected State, if practicable. The president's determination may be made without regard to subsection (a) of this section.[87]

Primary responsibility is not defined in the law. In context, difficult questions of federalism involving the application of central preemption might arise, particularly if a state governor does not agree with the president's emergency determination or the federal government's primary role. However, it is not a reach to conclude that the prevention of a terrorist attack using a WMD is a primary federal responsibility as would efforts to respond to the attack.

Under this emergency presidential authority, assistance is delimited in a manner not done during disasters: there is a financial cap on the amount of assistance that can be provided for a single emergency and Defense Department assistance is limited to ten days. Thus, one can see that the limitations found in the Stafford Act may well drive the president and his homeland security advisors to use of the Insurrection Act, as amended.

PART II
SPECIFIC REGIMES AND APPRAISAL

The homeland security legal regime also includes (or should include) framework statutes covering critical interest areas. These areas include nonproliferation, maritime security, aviation security, public health, cyber security, and infrastructure security, such as the protection of critical industries (power) and plants (chemical). However, these legal regimes are evolving and in some cases are nascent (food and water security) or nonexistent at this time (chemical plants). As importantly, where frameworks do exist there remain significant gaps between legal prescripts and the resources necessary to fulfill those prescripts.

This section identifies a few of the essential elements of the homeland security legal architecture. My goal is to sketch the framework so that the reader obtains a sense of where the United States resides on a continuum of preparedness; the specifics of these regimes are detailed elsewhere.[88] The section starts with the nonproliferation regime, because this regime should reside at the heart of U.S. national security law and policy. The greatest threat the United States faces in the immediate future is the prospect of a nonstate actor obtaining a weapon of mass destruction and trying to use it in the United States or against an ally. This threat is tied to the certain prospect that "rogue" state actors, like Iran and North Korea, will obtain or have obtained nuclear weapons or capacities. The nonproliferation regime is at the core of U.S. efforts to walk the dog back, or if that is not possible, contain the repercussion of such acquisitions.

Next, the section considers maritime security. The regime shows the evolution in law and practice in an area that is generally accepted as critical to the homeland security mission. It also illustrates in clear geographic manner the concept of concentric defense. However, if that defense fails, then the United States will have to rely on its capacity to respond and recover from attack. This will depend in part on the resilience of the public health sector, which is the third regime discussed. Public health has emerged as a core national security issue in the past ten years. It is implicated in almost every homeland security scenario, natural or manmade. However, the regime illustrates how significant gaps remain between legal prescript and policy implementation.

The chapter concludes with an appraisal of the homeland security regime in law, and in practice. In light of these lessons, I identify five principles that should apply to homeland security generally. Some of these principles are already embodied in law, process, and practice. For example, the concept of concentric defense is embedded in maritime policy (e.g., HSPD-13 and the Department of Defense 2005 Strategy for Homeland Defense and Civil Support), military doctrine (e.g., Northern Command AOR), and law (the Maritime Transportation Security Act). Other principles, such as those pertaining to risk management and appraisal, have proven more difficult to isolate and implement.

A. NONPROLIFERATION

Nonproliferation in concept is simple. There is defense; and, there is offense. If the precursor, technology, or weapon is not on the open, gray, or black market, don't let it get there. If the material is on the open or black market, or may become so, get it off the street before the bad guys do. The nonproliferation legal regime offers tools to accomplish both offense and defense that supplement those already provided by the intelligence and military instruments.

In application, however, nonproliferation policy is anything but simple. The gray and black markets are hard to discern and hard to penetrate.[89] Moreover, when state and nonstate actors obtain WMD, or obtain the apparent capacity to do so, the correct course of action is not always evident. Decisionmakers are often faced with a choice between bad options, or what Henry Kissinger called 51–49 decisions. These decisions are made harder because intelligence is usually incomplete.

The post Cold War years have been marked by serial confrontations with states attempting to obtain weapons of mass destruction: Iraq, North Korea, Iran, and Libya. These are also states that have sponsored or continue to sponsor terrorism either directly or through proxies. In these conflicts, the United States has brought to bear the full range of national security instruments. The nonproliferation regime resides on the continuum of national security tools between overt force and diplomacy. The policy question is whether and when to employ each instrument and within what strategic framework. Compare for example the approach and construct taken with Libya as opposed to Iraq, Iran, or North Korea.[90] The legal questions tend to coalesce around the predicate for using military force, the factual and legal thresholds for imposing sanctions as well as the availability of incentives in a legal landscape already inundated with domestic and international sanctions. Think of the consequences if we do not merge law and policy to maximum effect in this area, not only from the risk of terrorism but also the risk from failed states and rogue states acting within pockets of regional instability.

According to the congressional Research Service, more than eighty countries possess some form of cruise missile. Eighteen countries manufacture cruise missiles, including Iran and North Korea.[91] Significantly, the 2006

Israeli conflict with Hezbollah saw the first apparent use of a "cruise missile" by a nonstate terrorist organization.[92] The nonproliferation regime is the body of domestic, international, and foreign law that, in theory, will prevent states, and nonstate actors, from acquiring similar capacity or missiles of greater range with greater warheads. Where states and nonstate actors already have such capacity, this is the body of law that is intended to contain that threat and deter the transfer of such weapons capability to additional parties.

In the homeland security context, the nonproliferation regime is intended to provide a measure of concentric defense around the geographic boundaries of the United States. Hence, U.S. domestic law provides threshold mechanisms intended to deny certain actors access to militarily useful equipment or know-how through export controls and foreign export agreements, even as the United States remains one of the world's leading arms merchants. The basic U.S. mechanisms for doing so are the Arms Export Control Act (AECA), the Export Administration Act (EAA), and the International Emergency Economic Powers Act (IEEPA).[93]

The AECA regulates the sale of military materials designated on the Munitions List from the United States to third parties. The EAA, implemented since 1994 through executive order,[94] requires a Commerce Department license prior to transfer from the United States to third parties of "dual-use" equipment; that is, equipment that has both civil and military purpose. This might be the case with scuba equipment, for example, or a centrifuge with capacity for laboratory work or use in a cascade to produce enriched uranium. Under both the AECA and the EAA, transfer of an item requires a State Department or Commerce Department license and in some cases assurances against subsequent third-party transfers. Toward this end, there is an inter-agency process for each licensing regime intended to verify the veracity of the use as well as the end-user identified in the license application.

Each of these export laws is supplemented by specific regimes intended to tighten controls on particular states for nonproliferation as well as other policy purposes. In particular, using the International Emergency Economic Powers Act (IEEPA) the president may impose sanctions on financial and commercial transactions with states or parties, where the president declares that "there is an unusual and extraordinary threat to the national security, foreign policy, or economy of the United States."[95] Using this authority, for example, the president has prohibited transactions for national security reasons with designated state sponsors of terrorism and with companies and persons identified as aiding or abetting terrorism.[96]

Congress has also enacted specific laws intended to restrict transactions with states of nonproliferation, or other policy concern, as well as to remove the president's discretion in the imposition of IEEPA-type sanctions. Significantly, many of these statutes are addressed not only to U.S. trade but also to foreign trade by penalizing foreign corporations or states for engaging in transactions that are otherwise prohibited to U.S. companies.[97]

In addition, a series of nonbinding political agreements between like-minded states are intended to address the problem presented by commercial fungibility. That is, a U.S. sanction is only effective if other states adhere to the same sanctions. Otherwise, the United States not only loses the prospect of receiving the commercial benefit of the transaction but may also lose the informational value of knowing that the transaction has occurred in the first instance, and thus any follow-on capacity for monitoring the end use and end-user. As a result, application of the nonproliferation law requires not only knowledge as to whether a widget belongs on the Dual-Use, or Munitions List, or is prohibited by IEEPA sanctions or a specific nonproliferation law, but also knowledge as to whether it is covered by one of a number of voluntary political agreements designed to prevent or regulate the transfer of certain weapons, weapons know-how, and other proliferation materials. These regimes include

- The Wassenaar Arrangement, regulating conventional and dual use materials;[98]
- The Australia Group, regulating the transfer and licensing of chemical and biological agents that could be used to make biological or chemical weapons;[99]
- The Missile Technology Control Regime (MTCR), regulating technology relevant to missiles of particular range and capability;[100] and
- The Nuclear Suppliers Group, regulating nuclear and nuclear-related exports in an effort to avoid the proliferation of nuclear weapons.[101]

In addition, the international nonproliferation regime is based in part on three foundational treaties addressed to the proliferation of weapons of mass destruction. The Nuclear Nonproliferation Treaty (NPT)[102] prohibits parties from acquiring nuclear technology for weapons purposes. In theory, the benefit or trade for nonweapon states is found in the treaty's recognition of a "right" to acquire nuclear technology and knowledge for peaceful purposes. Further, Article VI requires weapon states to "undertake[s] to pursue negotiations in good faith on effective measures relating to cessation of the nuclear arms race at an early date and to nuclear disarmament...." Of course, there is room for debate as to the degree to which declared weapon states have fulfilled Article VI.

The treaty's benefit derives from its textual recognition of the essential nonproliferation goal – a prohibition on the receipt, transfer, or acquisition of nuclear weapons. In addition, the treaty serves as the legal mechanism through which the IAEA monitors compliance with the NPT's nonproliferation objectives. Article III requires each party to accept safeguards for the purpose of verification as established in agreements negotiated and concluded with the IAEA. On the other hand, verification of the NPT has proven difficult, and in any event, its provisions are binding only on state parties. There are 189 parties; the treaty has more members than any other arms control treaty. But as North Korea demonstrated, the treaty may not ultimately constrain and it is subject to withdrawal with three months notice. Further, the NPT's recognition of a nonweapon state's right to engage in peaceful nuclear programs offers legal and physical cover and conceal-ment to states like Iran, which are intent on developing a nuclear weapons capacity.

As noted in Chapter 7, the Chemical Weapons Convention (CWC) pro-hibits parties from acquiring, transferring, or possessing chemical weapons for any purpose.[103] It further requires parties to implement these prohibi-tions through domestic criminal sanctions. The Biological Weapons Con-vention (BWC) contains comparable prohibitions with respect to biological weapons.[104] The strength of these regimes is found in the clarity of their prohibitions. Their weakness is found in the verification of compliance. The treaties exempt substances held "for peaceful purposes." Of course, many chemicals and biological agents have dual uses. Moreover, unlike efforts to manufacture nuclear weapons, the manufacture of biological and chemical weapons is more readily hidden.

In the case of the CWC, the parties have sought to address this compliance gap through inclusion of extensive provisions addressing verification proce-dures. However, to date, this effort has been marked by disagreements on implementation based on, among other things, conflicts between the treaty's verification mechanisms and the domestic law of the parties addressing pri-vate rights and trade protections. In the case of the BWC, efforts to negotiate a verification protocol have faltered. Verification is also marked by the per-sistent concern that these mechanisms, in any event, only have an impact on compliant states; those states in violation, or that intend to violate the treaties, will keep their illicit facilities undeclared and under wraps.

Where weapons or weapons-grade materials are on the market or at risk, U.S. law provides a number of mechanisms to secure or destroy them. Two of the most visible programs are the Megatons to Megawatts program,[105] which provides a legal and funding structure to recycle weapons-grade uranium from Russia, and what is colloquially known as "Nunn-Lugar," or the Coop-erative Threat Reduction Program (CTR). "Nunn-Lugar" provides authority and funding for equipment, services, and support to secure and dismantle weapons of mass destruction in the states of the former Soviet Union.[106] The program's managers list among its accomplishments the return to Russia of more than 1,000 warheads from Belarus, Kazakhstan, and Ukraine, the removal and secure storage of more than 2,500 warheads from mis-sile and bomber bases, the removal of 750 missiles from their launchers, and the elimination of approximately 630 strategic launchers and bombers throughout the former Soviet Union. In addition, "over 5,000 former Soviet weapon scientists and engineers once engaged in nuclear weapons research are now or soon will be employed on peaceful, civilian research projects."[107] However, proponents argue that the program has suffered from chronic lack of funding and a foundering Russian commitment. Critics declaim a lack of accountability over money spent in the former Soviet Union and suggest that the program creates its own market incentives encouraging the sale of nuclear material. Legislative debates about whether to make the Nunn-Lugar authorities global in reach linger.

On the bilateral and multilateral plane, the principal post-9/11 nonproliferation effort is the Proliferation Security Initiative (PSI).[108] This initiative is intended to harness existing international, domestic, and foreign law to create nonbinding policy mechanisms, and corresponding expectations, to seize and control WMD materials on the high seas, on land, and transported through the air. As of 2006, the PSI included seventy countries within its umbrella. Fifteen of these countries are core members, with the others apparently agreeing to cooperate on an ad hoc basis. Members of the PSI, in theory, agree to principles of interdiction and agree to adopt pre-set coordinating mechanisms for facilitating interdiction. The PSI has served as a mechanism for the negotiation and conclusion of bilateral ship boarding agreements, including agreements with Panama and Liberia. Although legally nonbinding, the PSI creates the political expectation, and therefore corollary political costs, that states will consent to the search and seizure of their flagged vessels suspected of transporting illicit WMD shipments. Further, as PD-27 offers a U.S. domestic process for maritime interdiction, the PSI serves as a mechanism for coordinating intelligence and maritime interdiction on a global scale.

Whether addressed to centrifuges or enriched uranium, the importance of the nonproliferation regime is self-evident. Nonproliferation encompasses those efforts of the United States and its international partners to control, eliminate, and otherwise prevent rogue states and nonstate actors from obtaining those weapons that pose the greatest risk to U.S. national security. The regime represents a series of concentric nets backed up by the harpoon of military force. But these nets have holes.

The legal problem is that the international framework is porous and incomplete and lacks enforcement mechanisms. If the PATRIOT Act represents the apex of public attention to national security law, our nonproliferation framework resides near the other extreme. We could use more librarians expressing concern about proliferation; which is to say, this area of the law merits the same level of scrutiny and appraisal as the PATRIOT Act has received.

The policy dilemma is that the same tensions that exist in domestic law exist globally – economic and security interests may not align. Moreover, commercial and political interests create an international "prisoner's dilemma," an incentive for each state to cut its own deal. These tensions are evident in the uneven, one might say schizophrenic, treatment nonproliferation receives in domestic and international practice.[109] The threat of a WMD attack is our greatest national security threat. And yet, discussion of nonproliferation does not appear until page 95 of the 2006 National Security Strategy of the United States.

More important than rhetorical treatment is practice. Here the commitment is lukewarm rather than overriding. In December 2005, the 9/11 Public Discourse Project gave the United States a grade of D in its efforts to contain and secure WMD. In the words of the Discourse Project, "countering the greatest threat to U.S. national security is still not the top national security priority of the president and the Congress."[110] This should be our central bilateral and multilateral legal and policy concern linked as it is to the gravest threat the United States faces, the risk of nuclear attack by a nonstate actor. Nonetheless, there are indications the regime receives rhetorical emphasis, but has not risen near or to the top of the bilateral and multilateral agenda. The PSI, for example, remains nonbinding and continues to include only like-minded states, as opposed to those most likely to engage on the margin of proliferation. Moreover, allied states like Australia wrestle with the relative commercial benefits of enriching and transporting uranium at the same time that they are committed to preventing other states from doing so.[111]

With homeland security, one should not underestimate the complexity of the bureaucratic and legal challenges, even where the policy choice is obvious. In a pluralistic society that seeks to balance liberty and security as well as economic security with physical security, the policy choices are not always obvious, especially when the issue is framed in terms of margins of return and increments of risk. However, here there is one obvious policy choice.

United States law and policy should treat the prospect of a nuclear attack as the most immediate national security threat to the homeland and therefore place nonproliferation at the top of the security agenda. This requires a degree of policy, legal, and public mobilization heretofore absent from U.S. policy. The National Security Strategy for 2006 states that "the proliferation of nuclear weapons poses the greatest threat to our national security." However, this statement is not found until page 19 of the report. Nonproliferation belongs on page 1 of national security. American diplomacy must mobilize to address this threat. Committed membership in the PSI should be viewed as the quid pro quo for effective bilateral relations with the United States. We should put as much energy and focus into CTR, ship boarding agreements and air interdiction agreements as the United States put into concluding Article 98 agreements regarding the International Criminal Court.[112] To obtain Article 98 agreements, for example, the United States was willing to terminate military assistance and aid even after 9/11.

If the nonproliferation regime fails in preventing rogue states and non-state actors from obtaining and trying to use WMD, then the security of the United States will depend in part on the strength and weakness of the next level of defense in the homeland security regime.

B. MARITIME SECURITY

During the 1980s, U.S. Ambassador to Japan Mike Mansfield predicted that the twenty-first century would be a Pacific century. Mansfield did not mean a peaceful century. He meant a century oriented toward the trade and security interests of the Pacific Rim countries and the vast maritime environment that defined their geographic place in the world.[113]

More recently, Henry Kissinger described the importance of the Pacific to nation-state relations in the twenty-first century. Like Mansfield, Kissinger was thinking of nations like Russia, China, Japan, India, and Korea when he wrote:

> The rise of China – and of Asia – will, over the next decades, bring about substantial reordering of the international system. The center of gravity of world affairs is shifting from the Atlantic, where it was lodged for the past three centuries, to the Pacific. The most rapidly developing countries are in Asia, with a growing means to vindicate their perception of national interest.[114]

After 9/11 the importance of maritime security to U.S. national security became even more evident. It is evident in terms of our commercial and economic security. Ninety-five percent of non-North American trade with the United States is conducted by ship.[115] The impact of interrupting this commercial stream is illustrated by the 2001 dockworkers strike in Long Beach, California. The direct and indirect losses from the strike were estimated at from $1 billion to $2 billion a day.[116]

The importance of maritime security to U.S. physical security is also evident. The maritime domain is one of the triad of border control areas of responsibility. Using present statistics for reference, in any given year, 21,000 commercial vessels make port calls in the United States. Another 110,000 fishing vessels and 58,000 recreational boats use U.S. ports each year.[117] The Coast Guard designates approximately two vessels a day as "high interest." Each high-interest vessel is boarded and searched before it is allowed into a U.S. port of entry, a process that can take from forty-five minutes to one week.[118] In addition, in fiscal year 2005 (October 1, 2004–September 30, 2005) the Coast Guard reported detecting 174 foreign vessel incursions into the Exclusive Economic Zone (EEZ).[119]

As for containers, over 200 million containers are transported among seaports around the world each year. Approximately 16 million containers are transported across U.S. borders each year, up to 10 million through maritime traffic. That is roughly 26,000 per day. In this context, "the nuke in the harbor," or purported nuke in the harbor, is on most experts' short list of homeland security nightmares.[120] Although the oceans do not afford the United States the sense of protection they once did, they do provide an opportunity to apply a concentric strategy of defense, based on the time and distance of sea passage.

There is a considerable body of domestic, international, and foreign law relevant to U.S. maritime security. The Law of the Sea, in text,[121] and through operation of customary international law, addresses issues of jurisdiction to enforce domestic, international, and foreign law on the high seas; in the territorial sea, which generally extends 12 miles out from the coast, and in the contiguous zone, which extends 200 miles from the coastline.[122] The Proliferation Security Initiative (PSI), for example, is among other things, an effort to agree in advance on the application of the Law of the Sea and principles of self-defense in advance of crisis so that fleeting operational opportunity is not lost to legal or political wrangling.

Closer to the continental United States, the Northern Command's Area of Responsibility (AOR) extends out 500 miles into the Atlantic and Pacific ocean and air approaches to the United States, well beyond the twelve-mile territorial sea. The AOR thus recognizes the nature of the potential threat as well as the importance of maximizing the amount of time to identify and respond to potential threats, while maintaining the equivalent of a maritime explosive setback. Title 14 of the United States Code, in turn, provides the Coast Guard with broad law enforcement and regulatory enforcement authorities. As described in Section 89 of Title 14, "The Coast Guard may make inquiries, examinations, inspections, searches, seizures, and arrests upon the high seas and waters over which the United States has jurisdiction, for the prevention, detection, and suppression of violations of law of the United States."

To date, Congress has provided one framework statute in this area. The Maritime Transportation Security Act of 2002 implements amendments to the 1974 Safety of Life at Sea Convention (SOLAS). The amendments were adopted at U.S. urging by the International Maritime Organization (IMO) to address post-9/11 security concerns. In accordance with the 2002 IMO amendments the Act's requirements entered into force on July 1, 2004. The Act requires U.S. flagged vessels as well as foreign flagged[123] vessels entering U.S. ports to have ship security plans, ship security officers, and company security officers, as well as on onboard security equipment like silent alarms. Vessels are certified by the flag state as having satisfied these requirements. In accordance with the IMO regulations, the Act also requires that each port of a certain capacity have a port facility security plan, a port security officer, and port security equipment. Further, the Act requires monitoring and access control at U.S. ports for personnel and cargo. The IMO regulations also require a capacity for secure shipboard communications and installation of automated information systems (AIS). These systems are in essence beacons identifying vessels at sea in much the same manner as IFF transmitters identify commercial aircraft. Under the IMO regulations AIS must have a ship-to-shore range of 2,000 miles. In the case of the United States, the IMO regulations and the Act implicate 9,500 U.S. flagged vessels, 3,500 port facilities, and 55 sea ports.[124]

The Act demonstrates, at least in the sphere of maritime security, a link between international law and U.S. law and security. The SOLAS Convention and the IMO provided the legal vehicle and multilateral mechanism to address U.S. security concerns on a global basis. The Act, like the IMO regulations, also illustrates the adoption in law of a concentric theory of defense, by providing an opportunity for security in foreign ports and on the high seas before vessels reach U.S. shores.

However, the IMO regulations and subsequently the Act also reveal the shortcomings in implementing an agreed international framework. The IMO has no organic enforcement mechanism. Like much of international law, the IMO regulations are based on reciprocity: the principle that parties will adhere to the norm, because it is in their self-interest that other states adhere to the norm and thus assume comparable benefits and burdens on maritime commerce. Moreover, implementation of the Act is costly. In the case of the United States full implementation is estimated to cost up to $7 billion over ten years.[125] In light of the cost, other maritime states, including flag states of convenience, may not perceive the necessity for improved maritime controls with the same cost-benefit perspective as the United States does after 9/11.

Not surprisingly, as of 2006, the IMO projected 50 percent compliance by member states. There remain significant incentives for flag states of convenience not to assume the cost of compliance. Moreover, rogue actors will likely not comply with the requirements, unless they do so as camouflage.[126] Nonetheless, as implementation increases, these mechanisms should help U.S. authorities better identify vessels warranting seaborne challenge and inspection. Moreover, in intelligence vernacular, increased "maritime domain awareness" will limit the number of vessels necessitating challenge.

Maritime security falls within the bureaucratic jurisdiction of the Department of Homeland Security and the Department of Defense. Thus, the bureaucratic stew includes the Coast Guard, Customs and Border Protection (CBP), Immigration and Customs Enforcement (ICE), and the Northern Command. Bureaucratic coordination is addressed through inter-agency mechanisms like the Aviation Management Council and the Commodity Boat Council. Operational coordination is addressed in fusion centers on the East and West coasts and in harbor control facilities.

Foreign vessels intending to enter U.S. ports must provide ninety-six hours' prior notice and documentation of the last ten ports visited. In addition, the DHS runs a Sea Marshals program to assume positive control of vessels entering U.S. ports.

These mechanisms and process are well along. However, a number of problems remain. First, the intelligence challenge is considerable. Unlike smugglers, persons intent on attacking the United States are less defined by the patterns of conduct and therefore of detection associated with regular smugglers. Second, the scale of the challenge is enormous, both in terms of geographic reach and complexity. Consider the ability of the United States to stop drug shipments into the United States. Third, there is an inherent tension between security and commerce. Too heavy a security blanket may have an impact on commerce in unintended ways. Finally, the task at hand is not matched by comparable resources. The Coast Guard is an able service, which demonstrated its institutional leadership and responsive capacity during Hurricane Katrina, but it is retooling and has finite resources. In 2004, for example, funding was provided for just fifty-three sea marshals.

Given these contextual elements, maritime security necessarily employs the principle of risk management as well as concentric defense. This is illustrated with reference to the Container Security Initiative. Depending on which statistics are cited, up to sixteen million containers enter the United States each year by rail, truck, and boat. Customs and Border Protection has stated that as of 2006 approximately 12 percent of these containers are searched for contraband, migrants, and national security threats. In the case of maritime containers, approximately 5 percent are physically searched. However, this figure varies widely depending on how the term "search" is defined. As this is an evolving practice, the numbers are less important than obtaining a sense of scale. Which containers are searched and what are the questions? To reduce the number of containers warranting search in U.S. ports, CBP has stationed inspectors in eighteen countries at thirty-five seaports to inspect and certify containers at the point of shipment.[127] Employing methodology developed to address drug smuggling, the remaining containers are evaluated by an automated target modeling system (computer model) at the National Targeting Center, which is intended to identify containers and shipments warranting targeted as well as random inspection. The modeling to address the terrorist threat is evolving.

Finally, with respect to the risk of nuclear infiltration, the Department of Energy Megaports Initiative has since 2003 provided radiation detection equipment and training to personnel at foreign and U.S. ports to screen cargo. According to its statistics, CBP operates more than 825 radiation portal monitors at U.S. ports of entry, including 181 at seaports, and has issued 14,000 handheld radiation detection devices.[128] According to the

GAO, however, the "Megaports Initiative has had limited success in initiating work at seaports identified as high priority by DOE's "Maritime Prioritization Model." As of March 31, 2005 DOE had completed work at two foreign ports and signed agreements to initiate work at five other ports.[129] Moreover, these developments notwithstanding, stories about infiltrating materials proliferate.[130]

If the nonproliferation regime is geared toward preventing the WMD threat, and maritime security is geared toward casting a net to detect and deter, the public health regime is oriented toward detection, response, and recovery.

C. PUBLIC HEALTH

Perhaps no area of homeland security law is as complex for the national security lawyer as that pertaining to public health preparedness and emergency response. First, this area of law is new, as is much of the law directed toward emergency preparedness. Until the 1990s, the public health profession soldiered along in relative national security anonymity. This is evident in the growth of informational websites that in five years have ballooned from slim pickings to encyclopedic in scope.

Second, the law is complex because the applicable bureaucratic and legal frameworks lack precise boundaries, in part because health emergencies themselves lack precise boundaries. Thus, the bureaucratic interplay between, for example, the National Response Plan, directed to the federal response, and the National Incident Management System, directed to state and local response, and State Emergency Response Plans is not immediately clear. This already complex federalism model is made more complex by the addition of a third leg, the private doctors, nurses, and hospitals essential to responding to health emergencies.

This area of law is a maze to begin with, but it is also untried and therefore unproven in the homeland security context. Moreover, if one looks behind the legal curtain one often finds that good intentions are unfunded or unfulfilled. The lawyer is left to explain how a legal mechanism will function in the absence of resources. These factors increase the importance of field exercises, not just to appreciate how the various plans and authorities might merge in crisis but also to establish the personal ties and friendships that will oil bureaucratic gears that catch or stick in crisis.

The 1990s witnessed an initial, then growing, recognition of the necessity for a revitalized public health system to address national security threats, closely but not exclusively linked to terrorism. In Presidential Decision Directive 39, "U.S. Policy on Counter-terrorism" (June 21, 1995), for example, President Clinton returned public health to the national security agenda, including bioterrorism response as a federal planning requirement.

In addition, the directive designated lead agencies to respond to foreign and domestic terrorist incidents and established dedicated modules (equipment, personnel, and airlift) to address specific WMD scenarios.

An executive framework for responding to bioterrorist events began to emerge. In 1999, the National Pharmaceutical Stockpile (now the Strategic National Stockpile) was created with a focus on threats from nonstate actors. Included in the stockpile were "push-packages" containing medicines, vaccines, and medical equipment. These packages are placed at strategic locations with air support designated to move the packages to affected areas within twelve hours of an identified need or less. The stockpile also includes vendor-managed inventories maintained in the private sector of vaccines that are on call for delivery within thirty-six hours of identified need.

A bureaucratic framework developed on a parallel track. In 1998, a special assistant to the president and senior director was added to the NSC staff to advise the president on public health, and in particular bioterrorism. The Office of Emergency Preparedness was created within the Department of Health and Human Services, and a National Health Alert Network and Laboratory Response Network (LRN) established. The LRN coordinates, through the CDC, private, state, and federal laboratories with the capacity to test for pathogens and identify possible patterns indicative of terrorist attack. During the anthrax attacks in October–December 2001, for example, the LRN processed 125,000 samples for anthrax involving 1 million separate tests at 100 different labs.

The 1990s also saw the beginning of efforts to bridge the gap between the federal government's national security responsibilities and the states' police power. In 1999, for example, the Bioterrorism Initiative resulted in $40 million in funding through HHS for state programs to address bioterrorism. This was a start; however, funding remained constant until 2002, when after 9/11, it increased to almost $1 billion. In addition, the first federal, state, and local exercises were conducted with bioterrorism as the centerpiece, such as the 1999 Top-Off Exercise (for "top officials" exercise) and the 2000 Dark Winter Exercise, with former officials playing the lead roles, including former state officials giving added realism to the intergovernmental debates that ensued. The Top-Off Exercise remains the government's lead homeland security exercise.

These efforts received statutory impetus in the Public Health Threats and Emergencies Act, PL 106–505, November 13, 2000, which included $180 million in grant funding for programs to train, plan, and coordinate between state and local authorities. The Act also established an interdepartmental working group on preparedness to coordinate bioterrorism research and develop shared standards between federal and state agencies.

After 9/11 a more comprehensive statutory framework addressing public health as a national security concern emerged. A number of framework laws are particularly important and warrant review. The first is the Public Health Service Act, 42 U.S.C. 201, et seq. This is the basic enabling statute for the federal public health system dating to 1944. Among other things, the Act as amended provides authority for federal funding of public health activities at the state and local level. It also includes two essential emergency authorities for the Secretary of HHS. First, the surgeon general, with the approval of the secretary

> Is authorized to make and enforce such regulations as in his judgment are necessary to prevent the introduction, transmission or spread of communicable diseases from foreign countries into the States or possessions, or from one State or possession into any other State or possession. For the purposes of carrying out and enforcing such regulations, the Surgeon General may provide for such inspection, fumigation, disinfection, sanitation, pest extermination, destruction of animals or articles found to be so infected or contaminated as to be sources of dangerous infection to human beings, as in his judgment may be necessary.

> Regulations prescribed under this section shall not provide for the apprehension, detention, or conditional release of individuals except for the purpose of preventing the introduction, transmission, or spread of such communicable diseases as may be specified from time to time in Executive orders of the president upon the recommendation of the Secretary in consultation with the Surgeon General. 42 U.S.C. Section 264.

The law and regulations elaborate on the exercise of this quarantine authority. But note that the trigger designation originates with an executive order from the president. On April 1, 2005, the president added avian flu to the list of diseases subject to federal quarantine authority in Executive Order 13375. The federal quarantine authority is based on Congress's interstate commerce power; however, in today's context it might arguably be based on the president's national security authority as well. State and local authorities also have quarantine authority based on the state police power; indeed, this quarantine authority is considered a primary vehicle in addressing the outbreak of communicable disease.

Second, the Act authorizes the secretary of HHS to declare a public health emergency, including, in cases of significant outbreaks of infectious disease or bioterrorist attack, allowing the secretary to provide certain technical assistance to state and local authorities such as lab, workforce, and medicinal assistance. But note that this law assumes that state and local authorities will take the lead. The secretary has declared three such emergencies since 2000, in response to 9/11 and in response to Hurricanes Katrina and Rita. In addition, the Act serves as the enabling legislation for the Public Health Service, defining among other things its organizational structure and mission.

The Public Health Security and Bioterrorism Preparedness and Response Act of 2002 (June 12, 2002)[131] addresses the framework, funding, and authority for responding to national security health events. The law required the secretary of health and human services (HHS) to develop a biopreparedness plan, with benchmarks, addressed to surveillance, laboratories, training, protection of workers, and communications. A legal mandate benefits from having a bureaucratic champion. The Act established a position at the level of assistant secretary responsible for public health emergency preparedness, with lead responsibility for matters related to bioterrorism and other public health emergencies as well as federal, state, and local coordination for emergency preparedness. Further, the Act assigned to the secretary of HHS responsibility for the Strategic National Stockpile (Sec. 121) including its security, placement, and the review and revision of its contents.

The Act also reflects congressional efforts to address specific and perceived homeland threats. In particular, HHS was required to stockpile a smallpox vaccine, either by actually stockpiling the vaccine, or securing vendor agreements to provide vaccine if needed. In addition, HHS was required to make potassium iodide tablets available for stockpiling and distribution to public facilities in quantities to cover populations within twenty miles of a nuclear power plant.

In the area of funding, the Act provides authorization and funding for grant programs now administered by DHS, which provide links in the federal-state coordination process, including grants for community and hospital preparedness. Significantly, the Act establishes "risk-based" and "pass through" principles for allocating federal funds, principles further developed by DHS. Thus, under the Bioterrorism Preparedness program all fifty states initially received base amounts of funding increased on a pro rata population basis. Four cities – New York, Washington, Los Angeles, and Chicago – received additional risk-based funding. In addition, to qualify for funding a certain percentage of each grant must "pass through" to the first responder level. In some cases up to 80 percent of the grant must pass through. In addition, the Act's hospital preparedness programs adopted formulas to increase amounts going to entities with regional as opposed to local responsibilities. According to the DHS, the Department is now largely administering grants on a risk-formula basis.[132] Nonetheless, as the 2006 uproar over DHS designation of potential terrorist targets reveals, where there is funding and safety involved the principle of risk management will remain controversial in implementation and subject to the influence of legislative pressure.

Finally, the Act supplemented existing legal authorities to respond to emergencies. For example, the Act streamlined the process for declaring public health emergencies by executive order. Previously, such declarations were based on the recommendation of a Federal Health Advisory Council and the Surgeon General. However, Section 142 of the Act permits presidential specification of communicable diseases subject to quarantine based on the recommendation of the secretary of HHS in consultation with the surgeon general. At the same time, the law preempts state law in the event of a conflict between the secretary's federal quarantine authority and a state's exercise of authority.[133] In addition, the Act authorized the secretary of HHS to modify or waive Medicare, Medicaid, and State Children's Health Insurance Program requirements by time, geography, or provider. The Act also authorizes and requires the Department of Veterans Affairs (VA) to provide decontamination equipment and training for emergency preparedness and expands controls on biologic agents and toxins by adding to the list of such agents requiring registration and providing criminal penalties for violation of the control requirements.

The Project Bioshield Act of 2004, P.L. 108-276, transferred the Strategic Stockpile back to HHS from DHS and provided budgetary and legal authority for HHS and DHS to deploy the stockpile in emergencies within twelve hours of direction. The Act also reauthorized the National Disaster Medical System (NDMS), the federal mechanism for providing federal medical assistance and capabilities to state and local authorities in the event of emergencies and disasters, while providing authority for HHS to conclude participation agreements with state, local, and private hospitals. The Act was also intended to serve as a framework for generating bioterrorism countermeasures, including through identification of market incentives to encourage private sector development and production of countermeasures like vaccines and antidotes. Thus, the Act streamlined processes and exceptions for introducing products on an emergency basis that have not been approved as products or for the countermeasures use intended. But the Act did not resolve the market dilemma presented when companies develop vaccines that have no remunerative use other than in response to an attack that may not come.

The Pandemic and All-Hazards Preparedness Act, P.L. 109-417, of December 2006, attempts to fill this gap. The Act is an effort to consolidate in legislative form the practical and bureaucratic lessons drawn from the successes and failures in implementing previous law. To start, the Act acknowledges that public health planning and preparedness have not evolved in the manner anticipated. Thus, among other things, the Act addresses concerns about unity of command and responsibility by plainly designating the secretary of health and human services as the official (other than the president) responsible for leading the federal response to public health emergencies and responses. Toward this end, HHS in lieu of DHS, is placed in charge of the National Disaster Medical System (NDMS). The secretary is further charged with concluding an agreement with relevant agencies defining specific operational responsibilities and, starting in 2009, producing an annual National Health Security Strategy.

The Act also acknowledges that public health preparedness at the state and local levels has not met essential benchmarks. The Act seeks to vitalize this process by conditioning federal funding on assurances that certain benchmarks are met. In addition, the secretary is tasked with providing pandemic flu guidance to states, developing capacities to surge medical assets, and developing "telehealth" programs to provide for remote health care in the event of contagion. If the public has lost sight of the potential for a flu pandemic, HHS and its congressional committees have not.

Finally, the Act recognizes the failure to date of market mechanisms to provide for vaccines and other bioterror countermeasures. The Act establishes a new federal authority to bird-dog the effort. Loosely based on the Defense Advance Research and Projects Agency (DARPA) model, the Biomedical Advanced Research and Development Authority (BARDA) is given authority to consolidate federal efforts to promote the development and procurement of bioterror countermeasures. Toward this end, BARDA is given a range of incentive authorities and over $1 billion in funding.

D. APPRAISAL

1. Katrina and the GAO Reality Gap

As stated earlier, homeland security necessitates four related strategies: offense, defense, diplomacy, and response. Defense, in turn, requires a multidisciplinary approach that recognizes and integrates law, culture, process, leadership, personality, and resources. Each factor, or combination of factors, will distinguish success from failure in responding to manmade as well as naturally occurring threats to U.S. national security.

The 9/11 Public Discourse Project gave the U.S. government an overall grade of D for homeland security preparedness.[134] Hurricane Katrina arguably demonstrated that the grade was no fluke. There is room for improvement, and not just at the margins of security. Consider the cautionary comments of Assistant Secretary of Defense for Homeland Defense Paul McHale, a leading homeland security proponent and expert:

> As tragic and painful as Katrina was, Katrina by comparison to foreseeable terrorist attacks must be viewed as a catastrophic event at the low-end of the spectrum. Many terrorist scenarios would involve a loss of life and destruction of property far exceeding that which was inflicted on the Gulf Coast by Katrina.[135]

When it comes to homeland security, there remain significant gaps between legal and policy prescription on the one hand, and implementation and practice, on the other hand. Moreover, these gaps extend beyond the responsibilities and capabilities of any one agency, actor, or political administration.

On paper, in the form of the National Response Plan (NRP), and the National Incident Management System (NIMS) among other planning documents, the U.S. government is organized to respond in a timely and meaningful manner to homeland security incidents. Significant steps have been taken since the mid-1990s to upgrade the U.S. capacity to deter and respond to terrorism. At the outset of the federal response to Hurricane Katrina, the secretary of homeland security stated that Katrina was "an incident of National Significance, the first ever use of the designation under the new National Response Plan." The secretary explained the designation "gives the Department of Homeland Security the lead responsibility to coordinate the federal response and recovery efforts. The plan is designed to bring together all federal resources to increase our ability to quickly get relief to those who need it most."[136] An earlier federal response plan had been used successfully in response to the World Trade Center attack. With four years of additional work and the new NRP, officials spoke with confidence about the impending federal response in New Orleans.

Line diagrams and operations plans, however well designed, do not always account for personality; bureaucratic culture; or, the "fog of war." Each factor played a defining role during Katrina. In execution, there was confusion and disagreement regarding the roles and integration of federal, state, and local authorities. Moreover, the National Response Plan was hinged to local first responders leading the response and recovery effort. However, for a variety of reasons, these officials were themselves either taken out of play by the hurricane or overwhelmed by the breadth of its impact, after the levees broke.

In addition, personality issues and conflicts involving the director of FEMA, designated the "Principal Federal Officer" responsible for all federal coordination, exacerbated the already difficult task of getting accurate information from the streets of New Orleans to decisionmakers in Washington. The Principal Federal Officer did not operate within the operational chain of command, or at least a functional chain of command. As a result, information did not make its way to Washington. Critical decisions were delayed.

On a tactical level, an absence of coordination resulted in multiple helicopters being sent on the same missions, at a time when life-saving airlift capacity was at a premium. Katrina also demonstrated that the capabilities of National Guard units vary from state to state, and therefore, military contingency plans must incorporate sufficient flexibility to respond to local variants in personnel, equipment, and skill. The military lessons from Katrina included as well an appreciation of the importance of integrating National Guard plans and operations with Northern Command's plans and operations.

There were positive lessons as well. Foremost, once dispatched, military leadership and organization, exemplified by the performance of Coast Guard Admiral Allen, rapidly stabilized the federal, state, and local response. The Coast Guard, along with the military generally, demonstrated considerable capacity at search and rescue (a Coast Guard staple) as well as response and recovery. Moreover, the military restored order in New Orleans with proportionate and discriminate grace.

The legal lessons from Katrina range from the specific, such as the necessity of safeguarding court records, to the fundamental, the necessity of defining in a federal system of government when the federal government should intervene and when it should do so with military personnel. In my view, the abiding legal lesson from Katrina is that the legal and policy issues associated with federalism and the domestic use of the military persist. Left unaddressed in a clear and transparent manner, these legal issues will impede the U.S. response to future homeland security incidents. The problem is all the more challenging because there is no template for the relationship. Each context will be different and therefore should dictate a different scale of response. But clear expectations and tripwires will minimize confusion, delay, and bureaucratic gamesmanship, and thus save lives.

Katrina also demonstrated the gap between prescription and plan on the one hand, and capacity and practice on the other. This gap exists even in areas where the United States appears closest to agreeing on the nature of the threat and the response, and where there is a legal framework to execute that response. This is evident, for example, with respect to the screening of aviation cargo, the provision of sea marshals to board and observe vessels entering U.S. ports, and the percentage of incoming containers and cargo that are presently screened for radiological or nuclear material. I call this the Government Accountability Office or "GAO reality gap," because the GAO has documented with specificity circumstances where a law intended to address a problem has faltered on the rocks and shoals of implementation.

This concern is illustrated with respect to public health. Return to the earlier scenario involving the passenger arriving at an airport with SARS, smallpox, or hemorrhagic fever. Imagine as well that the passenger is a witting human vector with instructions to communicate the disease as far as he can before succumbing. At what factual, legal, or policy point should the federal government intervene? As a general matter, public health is a local issue, which is to say generally an area subject to the state police power. The structure of the public health system reflects this outlook. The majority of public health activities are conducted locally by 3,000 county and city public health departments and state boards and departments of health.[137] However, with the prospect of epidemic disease or a WMD attack, public health is also a national security concern falling on a legal continuum between the state police power and the federal government's national security powers.

As a matter of law, there seems little question that, in context, the federal government could preempt the exercise (or lack of exercise) of state law relying on the commerce power, the take care clause, as well as the broad executive and legislative authority over national security. The secretary of health and human services could declare a national health emergency and impose a quarantine without state or local consent.[138] Moreover, under the Stafford Act and amended Insurrection Act, the president could declare an emergency and assert primary responsibility to intervene with federal resources. In context, the president's constitutional authority to protect and defend the United States might extend well beyond the authority Congress is prepared to recognize in legislation on a prospective or abstract basis.

Notwithstanding this array of authority, real and potential, the present legal framework for public health has largely defined the federal role as one of setting standards, coordinating information, and providing financial assistance to state and local authorities.[139] Some excellent work has occurred. In 1998, the Department of HHS had limited secure phone and secure fax capability. This reflected an absence of national security urgency or participation. It also made it difficult to integrate HHS into the national security process. Today, HHS has an operations center and a bureaucratic framework to address public health issues with national security impact. This evolution is also reflected on the Centers for Disease Control and Prevention's (CDC's) website, which is teeming with information on bioterrorism.

Public health as a national security mission is also now embedded in the department's and CDC's institutional outlook. CDC, for example, funded efforts by scholars such as Larry Gostin at Georgetown to draft a model state health law, which is now widely adopted. (It is also an excellent place to start for anyone seeking an understanding of state law and needs in this area.[140]) Mechanisms have also evolved to better allocate funding on a risk management basis and that dictate pass-through mechanisms to ensure that grant funding finds its way to local first responders and laboratories and not just state agencies. This is no small feat given the political incentives in Congress to spread the wealth.

However, two related elements are missing. First, public health as a national security issue lacks a definitive legal or institutional framework. The law does not ultimately fix responsibility, and therefore accountability, between federal, state, or local health officials. Moreover, there is no apparent factual or legal understanding in the law or in policy as to when a local event should or shall become a national security event warranting a national response.

This concern is compounded by a second shortcoming: capacity and resources at the state and local level are inadequate to handle homeland security incidents. As in other areas of homeland security, even where the necessity is agreed and clear, there remain significant gaps in capacity. The Pandemic and All-Hazards Preparedness Act recognizes this fact.

For example, GAO's 2004 findings regarding implementation of the CDC's Benchmarks for Public Health Preparedness show substantial distance between prescript and practice.[141] The GAO found uneven compliance. As of 2004, no state had completed all the program requirements. Most states had established bioterrorism advisory committees and covered 90 percent of the state's population with the Health Alert Network. Few states had developed statewide response or regional response plans. The remaining benchmarks were met by about half the states. Here is the most troubling part. These benchmarks call for plans and designations, not actual capabilities. The response to Project Bioshield has fallen short of legislative and policy intent as well,[142] and as noted earlier, so has the Megaports program. Moreover, these are not areas where there remains dispute over policy necessity; these are resource and implementation issues.

The gap between mandate and effect was also evident in the response to the federal government's call to inoculate first responders against small-pox in 2003. The purpose was to vaccinate the vaccinators, approximately 500,000 state and local first responders. However, by year's end only 39,000 state and local health care workers accepted the voluntary vaccine in light of lingering concerns about the nature of the terrorist threat as well as concerns about liability and possible side effects from the vaccine. Moreover, the program drained state and local health departments of financial and personnel resources available for other needs. It also demonstrated the incapacity of local authorities to administer a large-scale inoculation campaign.[143] In the absence of alternative mechanisms, designated in advance and possessed of adequate capacity, public health authorities will by necessity turn to the military to accomplish the mission.

2. Toward a Homeland Security Legal Strategy

This brief review of the law, practice, and the "GAO reality gap" suggests three observations that should guide the substance of homeland security law and its application. First, speed is essential. This is intuitive in circumstances involving the necessity for search and rescue, where lives are at risk. But it is also imperative with respect to the collection of homeland security intelligence and then the decision whether and when to deploy federal authorities and assets. As a matter of law, that means legal issues need to be addressed in advance and in a realistic manner. Clear constitutional and statutory lines of authority are essential so that critical actors are prepared to act and feel responsible for doing so. If done in a transparent manner, public observers will better distinguish between the expected response and the alarming response. Essential bureaucratic actors, in turn, can adjust their cultural framework to match the legal framework.

Second, intelligence is as important to homeland security as it is to national security generally. Katrina demonstrated the necessity of accurate and timely intelligence. In the case of Katrina, the DHS operations center (HSOC) was, or perceived that it was, receiving conflicting reports about the gravity of the situation, that is, whether and which levees had been breached.[144] Certainly, CNN was showing horrific pictures of destruction and human suffering. However, spot news reports tend to offer inductive images focusing on dramatic circumstance.

Just as policymakers might reasonably hesitate to make decisions involving the use of military force abroad based on media reports, they might be equally hesitant to send the Marines to New York based on media reports alone. In the words of the HSOC director during Katrina,

> We were desperately pursuing all avenues in an effort to obtain confirmed reports from knowledgeable, objective sources. It is our job at the HSCO to distill and confirm reports. Based upon my years of experience, we should not help spread rumors or innuendo, nor should we rely on speculation of hype, and we should not react to initial or unconfirmed reports which are almost invariably lacking or incomplete.[145]

To his credit, the director took responsibility for the performance of the Center (although surely he was not helped by the performance of the FEMA director in the field). The director and DHS then applied the lessons learned. Among other things, DHS has established a six-person national reconnaissance team that can be deployed in the immediate aftermath of an incident to help collect and transmit ground intelligence to decisionmakers. Customs and Border Protection has also designated twenty-six two-person teams throughout the country that can provide immediate situational awareness before the national team arrives. In addition, DHS intends to designate potential "Principal Federal Officials in waiting" in advance of incidents. This will permit these officials to work with state and local officials, developing personal connections that might later serve to ease bureaucratic friction and confusion during moments of stress and crisis. It will also allow headquarters to identify in advance leadership strengths and weaknesses.

In addition, the Department of Homeland Security and the Department of Defense are developing the capability to deploy unmanned aerial vehicles (UAVs) to gather intelligence in the domestic disaster context where human access may be limited.[146] One can imagine that this resource would be especially critical in surveying contaminated areas before sending in first responders. Each push package and intelligence team should have the means to access this capacity. "Capacity" also means that any bureaucratic and legal issues over the control and funding of UAV platforms are resolved in advance, for example, through the execution of agreements between the Defense Department and DHS. If the secretaries concerned cannot reach agreement, the president can resolve these matters now and use his constitutional authority to do so, in writing and in a form accessible to those responsible for homeland incident intelligence and response.

Sound intelligence is all the more important in light of the legal, policy, and political implications of using the national security power to preempt the police power. For different reasons, federal and state authorities are undoubtedly hesitant to authorize or acquiesce in an overwhelming federal response without their own "eyes on the target," yet in the realm of infectious disease and certain WMD weapons, speed is essential in containing the scope of the attack and the fallout. However, as Katrina illustrated, intelligence is not yet fully integrated into the U.S. homeland security function. Neither are the redundant, reliable, and interoperable means of communication required to communicate intelligence up and down the chain of command.[147]

Third, unity of command is essential, but inherently complex where events and responses cut across federal, state, and local jurisdictions, which is to say in virtually all homeland security contexts. Where responsibility is divided (or unclear) decisions may be delayed, as officials acting in good faith wait for someone else to act, or officials acting with bureaucratic motive wait for someone else to assume the cost or the responsibility of doing so. Conversely, more than one agency may react to a problem, undermining a finite resource base.

Unity of command arises in part from familiarity with process and personality. Rather than debating whether FEMA should be part of DHS or an independent agency, the Congress and the president should consider making the agency's leadership permanent, including its ten regional directors. Each might be drawn from the ranks of professional first responders and serve terms of office like the director of the FBI. This will enhance unity of command within DHS, focusing authority on its secretary. It will also allow FEMA officials to develop the bonds of professional friendship and continuity that are essential at the local level and avoid situations where the critical regional positions are unfilled or in constant flux. The federal government can designate lead agencies and officials, but the relationship among federal, state, and local authorities will ultimately vary depending on circumstance and personality. Continued exercises in turn will help to identify areas of policy, personality, or legal fissure.

a. Herding the Legal Elephants

Recognizing the generic importance of speed, intelligence, and command, three areas of law will continue to delay and divide the U.S. homeland security response unless they are clarified: use of the military; private responsibility for public security; and federal, state, and local coordination.

(1) Use of the Military

By design, by necessity, or by default, most large homeland security incidents will become federal events, and that means military events. As Katrina demonstrated, only the military has the quantitative capacity and skills to address many homeland security scenarios. For example, Katrina demonstrated that "the military plans better than anybody."[148] The military also understands worst-case planning better than any other bureaucracy. Like General George Marshall, many military officers have seen worse cases. Worst-case planning includes within its parameters, redundancy, cross-training, flexibility, and the deployment of overwhelming resources. It also involves a measure of controlled urgency.

The U.S. military is, and will remain, the essential homeland security tool in responding to both manmade and natural disasters. However, policymakers, lawyers, and most importantly the public and the military may not be culturally prepared for this result. If not, we may miss the golden hour or day in which to respond and contain a public health emergency with national implications. We may also fail to develop adequate tripwires and policies to ensure that the military hand is sufficient in strength, but not so heavy or permanent as to transform our sense of liberty or the military's sense of purpose.

We know from 9/11, and daily service as well, that local first responders are as courageous and selfless as military personnel. However, the reality remains that the military alone has the capacity and expertise to respond to many homeland scenarios, such as those involving WMD fallout, operation of a quarantine, or establishment of mass casualty field hospitals. In the case of Hurricane Katrina the military contribution included the deployment of 75,000 personnel, 293 helicopters, 68 aircraft, and 21 vessels.[149] This is a quantum of response not available to state and local entities, even if their first responders are not knocked out of commission.

This makes military assistance to civil authorities, in a lead or supporting role, one of the two critical homeland security legal issues. The law is permissive. The Insurrection Act and the Stafford Act and, in context, the president's constitutional authority, provide sufficient authority for the federal government to respond to state requests for assistance *and*, as importantly, for the president to intervene without such requests. Nonetheless, two problems persist.

First, while generalizations are dangerous, the military remains hesitant if not apprehensive about its deployment in domestic contexts. Such concerns are reflected in applicable Defense Department directives, such as the directive titled "DOD Cooperation with Civilian Law Enforcement Officials," which states,

> It is DoD policy to cooperate with civilian law enforcement officials to the extent practical. The implementation of this policy shall be consistent with the needs of national security and military preparedness, the historic tradition of limiting direct military involvement in civilian law enforcement activities, and the requirements of applicable law, as developed in enclosures 2 through 7.[150]

Reflected in this policy is a traditional and well-founded concern that domestic civil missions may distract and drain the military's capacity to confront the nation's overseas threats.

Hesitation also derives from well-founded democratic principles. Consider the statement of former Deputy Secretary of Defense, John Hamre, at a conference on catastrophic terrorism (before 9/11): "the most frightening event for me in the years I was at DOD was when the four Marines shot that young man on the Southwest border. You don't ever want to be in a situation where an American kills another American."[151] Democratic societies do not use their armed forces to enforce the law, and if they do so, it should only be as a last resort. If used in domestic context the military may lose its standing as America's most respected institution, with a corresponding impact on recruiting and morale.

Military doctrine does not expressly adopt this perspective. The Department of Defense's 2005 Strategy for Homeland Defense and Civil Support states: "Protecting the United States from direct attack is the highest priority of the Department of Defense."[152] Northern Command's mission statement reflects this commitment. The Command's leadership, willingness, or capacity to enforce combat air patrols over United States cities is not in doubt.

But the question remains. When the call is a close one, or the facts are not yet developed, will civilian authorities resort to the military instrument? Which part of the Strategy for Homeland Defense and Civil Support will be stressed and cited – that occurring on page 10, which states

> To safeguard the American way of life and to secure our freedom we cannot depend on passive or reactive defenses;

or that occurring on page 26, which states

> The employment of military forces to conduct missions on US territory is constrained by law and historic public policy. It is the primary mission of the Department of Homeland Security to prevent terrorist attacks within the United States … Domestic security is primarily a civilian law enforcement function.

Ironically, where the post 9/11 presidency has asserted broad authority to deploy the national security instruments overseas, and electronic surveillance somewhere in between, with respect to homeland security the president has walked with comparatively uncertain and light constitutional steps. And yet, the potential threat to U.S. national security – to our physical security at home and to our way of life and values – could not be greater than in the context of a pandemic or WMD attack in the United States.

Reasonable people might disagree on how best to balance security and liberty when allocating responsibility to the federal government and in particular to the military. However, I do not believe that reasonable people can differ on the importance of identifying the distribution of responsibility in advance of crisis and demarking with equal clarity the thresholds that will trigger execution of these responsibilities. Otherwise we cannot be confident that the entities involved – military, federal, state, or local – will have institutionally accepted the responsibilities and provided the assets necessary to do so. Nor can we be confident that necessary debate over the scope of the president's authority (and responsibility) and the military's authority (and responsibility) will not occur at the moment of crisis, as opposed to the calm before.

(2) Private Sector Responsibilities

Homeland security will have to rely on the military as well because the United States, either on a case-by-case basis, or as an overall paradigm, has yet to adequately address the relationship between national security necessity and private sector cost. Homeland security specialists, for example, are virtually uniform in agreeing that the United States lacks the necessary hospital capacity to address a large-scale WMD attack or pandemic. Hospitals, like hotels, are run on business models not worst-case security models. They want to function at or near full capacity. In addition, according to a 2006 CDC study, between 40 percent and 50 percent of the nation's emergency departments experienced crowding during the sample years 2003 and 2004, with two-thirds of the hospitals in urban areas experiencing crowding. "The problem is exacerbated by a shortage of nurses. More than 5 percent of nursing staff positions were vacant at half of all emergency departments in metropolitan areas."[153]

A successful homeland security framework will have to come to grips with the role of the private sector. Eight-five percent of America's infrastructure is privately owned,[154] including chemical plants and nuclear power reactors. Providing a capacity to surge to meet public health needs or to provide protection at critical infrastructure sites will require more than exhortation, coordination, and calls for the adoption of best business practices. To date this has occurred on a limited basis.[155] The need for federal involvement in areas like contingent vaccine manufacture, where (one hopes) there will be no opportunity to transmit the cost to the consumer and the need for national standards and applications, clearly require a federal solution. The Pandemic and All-Hazards Preparedness Act is a step in the right direction. But it is only a step, for law and capacity are not one and the same.

(3) Federalism

Federalism concerns also linger. In fairness, the principles embedded in federalism raise difficult issues implicating both the security and the values components of "national security." The tension is acute because where the law if not the will is ultimately clear with respect to use of the military instrument, the relationship between the federal national security power and state and local police power remains in the twilight.

At the extremes of a continuum lawyers will agree on the appropriate level of jurisdictional and federal response, if any. But the difficulty in most homeland security contexts is in determining the factual moment when a federal and a military response is necessary. This was evident during Katrina; and we have practice with hurricanes. Drawing on an earlier scenario, imagine the difficulty in determining when the nation is under biological attack. Consider as well the commercial consequences of responding too quickly, and restricting travel, or responding too late as local tragedy turns to national emergency. Most scenarios will reside in the middle, at least until they break in one direction or another.

The dilemma is compounded by differences in expectation between state and federal authorities, who share the same sense of duty to protect the security and welfare of their constituents but not the same sense of how to accomplish that end. In the context of Katrina, these expectations appeared to evolve as the circumstances on the ground evolved. In abstract terms, the expectation of state authorities is clear. While state governors may want federal assistance, they do not want federal management of events in their states ... until really needed. This view is reflected in the Stafford Act's general predicate for a state request, and it is reflected in the opposition of many state governors to the 2006 Insurrection Act amendments permitting the president to federalize National Guard units in response to certain emergencies.[156] It is also captured in the statement of Governor Perry of Texas addressing the lessons learned from Hurricane Katrina.

> I'm greatly concerned that others would place too much authority in the hands of the federal bureaucrats and force state and local officials to stand idly by while the lives of their citizens hang in the balance. Let me be clear: if the federal government assumes control of first response to catastrophes, I believe it will add needless layers of bureaucracy, create indecisiveness, lead to rampant miscommunications and ultimately cost lives.[157]

This statement illustrates the importance of clarity in the law or, at least, clarity in how the law will be applied.

Here, homeland security again finds itself at the crossroads of security and liberty, as well as at a societal junction where economic security and physical security intersect. Would that we could let the facts develop. The problem is that any hesitation to allow the facts to develop could result in loss of the golden moment that allows responders to prevent a bad incident from becoming a catastrophic incident. Thus, although the law is ultimately clear that the federal government may act, the facts may not offer the same clarity as to when the government should act.

Policy consensus should not be expected. Where policymakers disagree on the nature of the threat, they will also disagree on the remedy. A comprehensive homeland security strategy may remain elusive. Even where there is agreement on the threat and the response, there will remain issues of funding and decisional capacity. Nonetheless, even in such a policy environment it should be possible to agree on the principles that should inform a homeland security legal regime, including the following five principles starting with legal transparency.

b. Principles to Inform Homeland Security Law
(1) Transparency

Transparency is an essential homeland security value. Transparency helps to fix accountability, making it clear to the public who is responsible and for what. Transparency helps mitigate concerns involving the use of the military in civil context. Clear policy statements about the predicate for using the military will improve efficacy, because state, local, and federal civilian authorities will better understand their substantive responsibilities and their temporal duration.

Transparency is also a building block of expectation. Transparency regarding the threat at the local level allows state and local authorities to better allocate resources, and it avoids public alarm fatigue. Tabletop and field exercises add a further dimension to transparency, permitting state and local actors (and their constituents) to see first hand what to expect in the event of a crisis.

Legal transparency means that the attorney general or Office of Legal Counsel should publish opinions stating unequivocally the federal government's view as to the reach of the president's constitutional authority to use the military in homeland context. If there is disagreement, then the disagreement should be aired, with governors holding a full seat at the discussion table. The president should declare as well whether he will lean forward or back in responding to homeland incidents and what criteria or factors will trigger the federal response. In this regard, the Homeland Security Operations Center must maintain a standing capacity to reach state governors instantly and securely so that the president or his designee can quickly resolve disputes.

At the national level, transparency regarding the nature of the threat will help solidify support for the societal paradigm shifts necessary to address the threat. Security specialists, for example, treat the threat of a WMD attack in the United States as a realistic possibility, even a likely one. Recall the poll indicating that 80 percent of the specialists polled thought it certain or very likely that the United States would be attacked on the scale of 9/11 within the next ten years. General Barry McCaffrey[158] places the risk of attack at 100 percent.

However, national leaders tend to speak of the terrorist threat in general terms, and in the format of political talking points and color-coded generalities. policymakers at the national level – meaning the president – should be clear about the stakes and how they define the threat. Where possible, intelligence should be declassified and shared with the public. Transparency will help to clarify whether differences regarding policy response reflect different assessments of the threat, the risk the threat poses, the nature of the remedy, or the allocation of financial and political responsibility for implementing the remedy.

(2) Dual-Use Capacity/Dual Benefit Policy

We cannot be certain where, in what form, or whether, the next attack will occur. However, we can be sure that we will face the continuing prospect of natural disasters, like hurricanes, as well as a century that threatens outbreaks of pathogenic disease, like SARS and avian flu. At some point (I hope sooner rather than later), we will also have to realistically address the ramifications of climate change and environmental degradation before they become matters of national security crisis. Therefore, we can be certain that the public health capacity of the United States will be tested regardless of one's views about the probability of WMD attack. Thus, the law should favor the funding of dual-use capacities, like public health, whose benefits will be reaped in more than one context and regardless of whether our gravest security concerns come true.

Communications interoperability is another example. Decision-making speed, intelligence, and command all depend on communication, as does the coordination of local response. While essential for responding to a bioterror event, it is also essential for responding to any event crossing jurisdictional lines. Indeed, communications interoperability was on every short list of lessons learned from the first World Trade Center attack and the Oklahoma City Murrah Building bombing. There it remains after 9/11 and Katrina. But the concept never seems to reach the point of implementation. The 9/11 Public Discourse Project gave the government an "F" for its effort to provide adequate radio spectrum for first responders.[159]

Similarly, policy initiatives like the PSI – that should be pushed for WMD reasons alone – will reap additional policy benefits by providing intelligence and enforcement mechanisms to uphold public order on the high seas by preventing piracy, deterring dangerous migration patterns, enforcing environmental laws, and interdicting drugs.[160]

The same is true of an energy policy that would curtail U.S. dependence on foreign oil. A significant change in the fuel efficiency standards for U.S. vehicles, for example, would not only diminish the influence of foreign cartels but also generate a public diplomacy bonanza in the long-term conflict against jihadism. The United States might also address today the impending security crises of tomorrow associated with global warming.

Finally consider the case of food security. We know that domestic and international terrorists have plotted to contaminate food supplies.[161] That makes food security a homeland security issue. But it is also a health issue. Food-borne illnesses result in 5,000 deaths per year and 76 million illnesses. The reaction to the *E. coli* contamination of spinach in fall 2006 indicates that incidents of food poisoning and contamination can have commercial and consumer impact disproportionate to the actual threat. In short, food security is an area where energy and money invested in inspections and warning methodologies will be well spent whether policymakers agree on the nature and risk of terrorist attack or not. A dual-use/dual policy approach means that if we have one dollar to spend, we should spend it in an area where it will have multiple policy and effects.

(3) Risk Management, Not Risk Acceptance

Given the breadth of access to the United States as well as the breadth of potential targets, homeland security requires conscious choice in allocating finite resources to address infinite targets; in a word, triage. Triage is embedded in U.S. policy as risk management. Risk management in turn is embodied in U.S. grant programs that apply risk-based rather than pro rata or state-based allocation formulas.

However, risk management entails much more. Risk management is also about favoring security instruments and funding choices that can address multiple risks at once, such as military reaction forces, surge capacities, and push packages with dedicated means of transportation. For example, DHS gives funding priority to regional rather than local hospitals. Risk management is also a paradigm for addressing those scenarios posing the greatest potential for catastrophe, not necessarily the highest probability of occurrence. In the words of the 9/11 Commission's Chair and Vice Chair, "preventing terrorists from gaining access to weapons of mass destruction must be elevated above all other problems of national security." This is the highest priority not because it is certain to occur, but because it will bear the greatest impact on U.S. national security if it does occur.

The corollary should also apply; risk management warrants focus on the targets with the highest probability of attack. That means placing special emphasis on urban areas and especially on New York and Washington, even if the marginal dollar is less well spent than the first dollar spent elsewhere.

Finally, risk management means erring on the side of federal involvement and military involvement to prevent bad scenarios from becoming catastrophic scenarios. Speed is essential, but in acting quickly there is the risk that the United States will overreact and jump the gun.

Thus, an essential ingredient in policy risk management is a public debate over the adoption of a paradigm that recognizes that where WMD terrorism is concerned the federal government should err on the side of response. Alternatively, the public should understand and accept the potential consequences of adopting ad hoc solutions.

(4) Concentric Defense

As homeland security requires a strategy of concentric defense – offense, defense, diplomacy, and response – it also requires a tactical adoption of concentric defense. This concept is geographically embedded in U.S. doctrine. It is reflected in Northern Command's area of responsibility, the PSI, and in efforts by DHS to move the point of cargo inspection overseas.

The concept is an obvious one if one considers the nature of commerce and our imperfect record of interdicting illegal drugs and immigration at the border. Maginot lines do not work against terrorist threats any more than they work against mobile armies.

However, concentric defense is also a policy construct. A comprehensive strategy must not just attack but defend, not only prevent but respond. The conceptual phases of homeland security are summarized in the 2002 Homeland Security Strategy: prevent, prepare, protect, respond, and recover. In short, if we cannot be certain that a particular phase of policy will succeed in deterring the threat, then we must pursue each aspect of policy with vigor and not rely inordinately on offensive operations to address the threat.

Here U.S. policy has done less well. A concentric construct means staying focused on all the homeland security disciplines at once and avoiding the soccer field effect. Law can help provide that steady policy commitment. But ultimately policymakers must hold to a true course. The career engineers at DHS may stay steady on the engine, but the political leadership must remain steady at the helm and not frantically turn the vessel into each approaching wave.

This means that if politicians take the homeland security threat seriously they will have to make political sacrifices that correspond to the nature of the threat. That means placing program funding before tax cuts. Regime implementation, such as the steps necessary to implement the maritime security act, screen aviation cargo, or effectively test for radiation and nuclear signatures at ports of entry, will cost in the range of $5–10 billion each. Obviously, partial implementation, or increasing the number of Sea Marshals, will cost much less. This brings us back to the threat. If one believes that this threat is real, nuclear, and catastrophic, then this is money well spent on societal life insurance.

A president who places homeland security before tax cuts will have additional credibility to also insist on the broad intelligence and military authority needed to push offense and defense beyond our shores. The president who does not do so will send a mixed signal reverberating through the federal, state, and local bureaucracy that homeland security can be done on the cheap, or that the threat is not all that we, or the national security community, imagines. Homeland security requires the country to put its money where its mouth is; the sooner the better.

(5) Appraisal

In no area of national security is the importance of appraisal more evident than in the area of homeland security. First, appraisal is the mechanism for testing the intelligence and policy judgments behind risk management and for ensuring that finite resources are used wisely and as intended.

Second, many homeland security capabilities cannot be tested in the crucible of actual experience. One hopes they never will. In the absence of real-world experience, effective mechanisms of appraisal are essential. These include tabletop exercises, field exercises, and the application of lessons learned from parallel contexts, like Hurricane Katrina.

Third, the framework for appraising homeland security is nascent. As the 9/11 and WMD commissions concluded, congressional oversight of the homeland security function is disjointed. Putting aside institutional shortcomings that may derive from political factors, the structure itself is flawed. By one count, thirty-seven committees or subcommittees have some measure of homeland security oversight. Overlap should be expected, for all the reasons that make national security and homeland security hard to define. Depending on how security is defined, homeland security may implicate virtually every jurisdictional base in the Congress. But with such expansive overlap, institutional responsibility and accountability are lost. Funding mechanisms will cheat toward equitable distribution rather than risk-based distribution. Executive actors may also find congressional oversight a distraction rather than a constitutional opportunity to garner support for vital programs.

Nor is it clear that executive mechanisms of appraisal are filling the void. An inspector general's report alone should not be the mechanism for determining that a wise presidential directive to prioritize potential targets has been implemented in an unrealistic manner.[162] At this time of perpetual crisis, and in the context where policymakers are correctly focused on standing up a homeland security regime, it is unrealistic to assume that they are fully vested in the architecture and function of appraisal. In this area, lessons learned from the long and somewhat eventful history of intelligence oversight may be fruitful. What has worked well? What has proved redundant or unduly subject to politicization?

The intelligence experience offers a fourth additional lesson. Homeland security is arguably the most legally intensive of the national security law fields. There are complex questions of constitutional law involving federalism, the military, privacy, and federal regulation of the private sector. It is no surprise that Northern Command has the largest staff judge advocate's office. What's more, many of these issues are new issues, for which there is no practice or precedent on which to call. That means that lawyers should not just advise on the substance and process of law. They should actively and aggressively appraise the implementation of law for unintended consequences and efficacy. As the DNI is required to report to the president and the Congress each year on the state of intelligence law, homeland security lawyers should identify any statute, regulation, or practice that impedes the ability of their agency to fully and effectively secure the nation. Likewise, policymakers and lawyers should take note from the intelligence experience – law can facilitate response, but legislation marks a beginning of the process, not its conclusion. Homeland security like intelligence ultimately depends on the human factor – leadership and the moral courage to face hard risks and make hard choices.

10 The National Security Lawyer

This book has considered national security law and process in the context of four security threats. First is the threat of attack by nonstate and state-sponsored or supported actors using terrorist means. Overseas, this threat is realized on a daily basis. Within the United States the threat is continuous, but intermittent. The threat of high-explosive attack, like car and truck bombs, targeted suicide bombings, or the sabotage of aircraft, is most likely to materialize. The threat of catastrophic attack with nuclear weapons has the greatest potential impact on our way of life and in terms of human cost. It is in relation to this threat in particular that we need to evaluate and test national security law and process, both because of the potential consequence and because of the focus the enemy has placed on this means of attack.

Second, U.S. constitutional values may ebb and wane in an endless conflict against state and nonstate actors engaged in acts of terrorism or posing the threat of terrorism. In light of the interminable nature of this threat, assertions of presidential authority made *in extremis* may become embedded in U.S. practice and law without a corresponding application of checks and balances. Left outside the reach of effective and independent mechanisms of appraisal, broad assertions of executive authority may in time diminish both the principles of law that define American life as well as the physical security at which they are directed.

Third, sincere policy differences, as well as those that are politically inspired, regarding the nature of the terrorist threat and the corresponding measure of response may result in a zero-sum compromise; that is, a diminution of security or a diminution of law, rather than contextual formulas that advance both at once. If the executive needs broad and rapid authority to engage in intelligence collection – as it does – the better course is not to limit the authority, for fear of misuse, but to increase the opportunities for meaningful internal and external appraisal. Such appraisal will deter misuse, but as importantly, encourage effective use. In this enduring conflict we may exhaust our resources or our principles in a manner that leaves us unwilling or unable to effectively address this century's other certain crises, including the proliferation of weapons of mass destruction to unreliable state actors, the advent of pandemic disease, and environmental degradation and change.

This book has focused on the threat of terrorist attack because this is the threat that today drives the legal debate about the president's constitutional authority. More generally, it drives the purpose and meaning of national security law. It will continue to do so. It is also the threat with the greatest potential to transform U.S. national security, in both a physical and a values sense. The importance of addressing other issues, such as conflict in the Middle East, totalitarian regimes, or pandemic disease, must not be overlooked. Each bears the potential to spiral beyond control resulting in catastrophe at home and overseas. Each of these issues warrants full consideration of the national security instruments and processes described in this book.

In each context, law and national security lawyers may contribute to national security in multiple ways. First, the law provides an array of positive or substantive instruments the president may wield to provide for security. Second, the law provides procedural mechanisms offering opportunities to consider, validate, appraise, and improve policy, as well as ensure its lawful execution. These mechanisms include the horizontal separation of constitutional powers at the federal level, and the vertical separation of powers between the federal government and state government. They are found as well in statute and in internal executive directive.

The most effective means of appraisal are often found through informal practice. Informal contact allows participants to speak with a freedom not permitted or not often found when bearing the institutional mantle of an office or branch of government. Consider the difference in reaction between the counsel that sits down with the policymaker for a discussion and the counsel who requests the policymaker to put down in a memorandum everything that occurred. With informal practice the role of personality and friendship can serve to facilitate information exchange and the frank exchange of views.

Third, in the international context, law provides mechanisms to achieve U.S. national security objectives. This is evident in the context of maritime security, where U.S. law is pegged to an international framework, and effective security requires international as well as domestic participation. In the area of intelligence integration, bilateral and multilateral agreements, like the PSI and bilateral aviation agreements, provide essential mechanisms for identifying intelligence, sharing intelligence, and acting on intelligence.

Fourth, the law reflects and projects American values of democracy and liberty. Values are silent force multipliers as well as positive national security tools. As Lawrence Wright, the author of *The Looming Tower*, and others argue, jihadists like Osama Bin Laden offer no programs or policies for governance, no alternative to Western democracy. They offer only the opportunity for revenge. Rule of law is the West's alternative to jihadist terrorism. Law, and respect for law, offers the structure of democracy, the opportunity for individual fulfillment regardless of sex, race, or creed, and a process for the impartial administration of justice. Sustained commitment to the rule of law in practice and perception will serve as a positive national security tool in curtailing recruitment of the next wave and generation of jihadists.

But law, like homeland security, is an incremental endeavor. It is dependent on sustained action, not rhetoric, and perceptions can be swept aside in a few ill-chosen moments. Law, like this conflict, requires sustained sacrifice and sustained support. Thus, divisive legal arguments should be eschewed, unless they are essential to security and there are no alternative means to accomplish the same necessary security end.

The law may contribute to national security in other ways as well. The law is a source of predictability. Through prediction, it becomes a source of deterrence. If the law is understood to permit the use of force, or the collection of intelligence, then allies and opponents alike may modulate their behavior accordingly.

Law can also be a source of calm and stability at times of crisis, guiding but not compelling decisionmakers to processes of decision that rapidly identify risks and benefits and fix accountability. Rapid decision can be obtained through secrecy and by truncating process; it can also be found through the expectation and practice that process provides. This is evident in the case of the military chain of command. This can be true with the president's national security processes as well.

The law is also a source of continuity. An enduring conflict requires enduring commitment, in values, funding, and sacrifice, and thus unity across party or factional transitions. Where essential policy is embedded in framework statutes, it is less subject to, but not immune from the vicissitudes of momentary political advantage or the policy pressures of immediacy. In a conflict marked by intermittent attacks over years, at least in the United States, law can insulate policy from the loss of public or even official attention. For example, where a tool is dependent on sustained funding and policy commitment, legal mandates can hold bureaucratic focus. And, where policy is embedded in law, intelligence and law enforcement operatives may take greater risks knowing the authority for their actions is documented in law and not dependent on classified authorities or recollections of approval.

At the same time, there is much the law cannot do. Law and process provide an opportunity for success, but do not guarantee result. Leadership, culture, personality, and sometimes good luck are as important as law. A well-crafted emergency response directive does not compel first responders to climb the stairs of a burning building – courage, leadership, and commitment do.

Law is a human endeavor that is dependent on the human factor. We are a nation of laws, but we are also a nation of men and women, or if you like a nation of law and lawyers. It is men and women who write the law, interpret the law, and decide whether to uphold the law. Where national security is at stake, the human influence is manifest. "National security" necessarily involves the application of subjective values and not just security criteria. Further, as considered in Chapter 4, the law is as dependent on theory as it is on black-letter principle, and thus is dependent on human values and choice. Even where the law is clear, the facts rarely are, for the reasons articulated in Chapter 7. The application of fact to law, of intelligence to security, involves human judgment rather than the mechanical review of facts.

Law also involves moral courage. Field Marshal Slim, who served on the Western Front during the First World War and is considered one of the best commanders during World War II, compared physical and moral courage. He described moral courage as "a more reasoning attitude, which enables [a man] coolly to stake career, happiness, his whole future, on his judgment of what he thinks either right or worthwhile." Slim said,

> I have known many men who had marked physical courage, but lacked moral courage. On the other hand I have seen men who undoubtedly possessed moral courage very cautious about taking physical risks. But I have never met a man with moral courage who would not, when it was really necessary, face bodily danger. Moral courage is a higher and a rarer virtue than physical courage.[1]

Most lawyers will not have Field Marshal Slim's opportunity to test the comparative proposition. But they will have their moral courage tested. They will be tested sitting at a Principals Meeting when they have to decide when, whether, and how to speak up. They will be tested when they must step outside their personalities, loud, quiet, or in between, and step into a different role in order to apply the law more meaningfully. The quiet personality will be asked to make public presentations on behalf and in defense of the law. Sometimes the strong personality must sit down for the law, for example, at an interagency meeting where bureaucratic diplomacy may be the order of the day. But minutes later, in the face of the deputy secretary or national security advisor, the lawyer must have the courage to insist on attendance at a necessary meeting. In short, national security law is as contingent on the national security lawyer as it is on the law.

A. NATIONAL SECURITY LEGAL PRACTICE

In a constitutional democracy decisions are intended to be made according to law. That means that sound national security process must incorporate timely and competent legal advice. What form should that advice take?

In some cases, legal review is dictated by statute, as in the case of the Foreign Intelligence Surveillance Act, which requires designated officials, including lawyers, to certify requests for electronic surveillance or physical search before they are submitted to the FISA court. In other cases, the president has directed a specific process of legal review, for example, in areas historically prone to peril, such as covert action. However, the majority of legal advice within the national security process is not required by law or directive, but is the product of practice, custom, and the rapport, if any, between officials and their lawyers.

At the national level the daily participants are generally the same from administration to administration: the attorney general and deputy attorney general; the Office of Legal Counsel within the Department of Justice; and other agencies' general counsels, especially those at Defense, State, CIA, and DHS, as well as the chairman's legal advisor. Of course, in context, senior deputies and alter egos play an equivalent role.

Traditionally, lawyers for the president engaged in national security law have included the counsel to the president and the National Security Council's legal advisor. Practice varies as to the relative role and weight of each and the extent to which other White House lawyers, such as the deputy White House counsel, are involved in national security decision-making, if at all.[2] Depending on administrations, and personalities, the role of the counsel to the vice president has ranged from a defining one to no role at all with respect to national security law.[3]

Other lawyers play central roles as well. The judge advocates general of the military services, for example, are central players in the development of military law and legal policy as well as the application of the law of armed conflict. Within the Department of Justice, the assistant attorney general for national security, the head of the Office of Intelligence Policy and Review, the Office of Legal Counsel, and the assistant attorney general for the criminal division are all central players on issues of intelligence and counterterrorism. Counsel at each of the intelligence community components and those engaged in issues of terrorism asset control and money laundering at Treasury also engage in daily national security practice. Each of these officials is supported by line attorneys who in many cases are the experts in their discipline and serve as the initial (and often) final point of contact for legal advice.

Each president, agency head, and commander will adopt his or her own approach to legal advice, ranging from active engagement with their lawyers and an understanding of the law to avoidance. Some officials do not seek legal advice unless the word "law" is mentioned and then only if it is mentioned four times in the subject line of a memo. Other officials view their lawyers as wide-ranging advisors, officials outside the policy process – nonstakeholders, and thus troubleshooters who may serve in capacity of counselor and not just legal advisors.

Officials and lawyers sometimes refer to lawyers "staying in their lane." But with national security there is rarely a street map. It is not always clear where the lane begins or ends, and whether the intended road is a goat path or an informational superhighway. Some lawyers will operate on a defined track – litigators litigate, Office of Intelligence Policy and Review (OIPR) attorneys process FISA requests (among other things), the AECA lawyer reviews munitions list licenses. However, for more senior lawyers there are rarely set templates outside those dictated by law or directive for how to practice national security law. That means the individual lawyer will define the role as much as he or she will assume it. Moreover, policy officials will ultimately find those lawyers whose style and advice they trust regardless of individual assignments.

Application of national security law involves the rapid review and identification of legal issues embedded in policy options, policy decisions, and policy statements. At the NSC, for example, counsel traditionally coordinate the provision of advice to meetings of the Principals and Deputies Committees, among other tasks, and, where appropriate, attend such meetings to field questions and identify issues. However, this role appears to have varied in texture depending on whether the NSC staff are viewed as facilitators of interagency process or sources of rival legal advice to department general counsel. It also depends on the national security role assumed by the counsel to the president. In addition, NSC counsel provide internal legal advice to the president, national security advisor, and NSC staff as well as review and write memoranda to the president, issue spotting and discussing the legal issues raised. However, these roles are not defined in statute and are, outside the confines of certain narrow spheres, not defined in directive. Rather, these roles are defined by practice and the adoption or modification of past practice by successor officials.

Lawyers serving in defined billets are more likely to find continuity in the form and method of practice, but not necessarily in the substance of practice. For example, the assistant attorney general for the Office of Legal Counsel and his or her deputies generally provide constitutional advice to the executive branch and arbitrate interagency legal disputes, usually through promulgation of formal (often classified) legal memoranda. They are consulted, but are usually less active on daily issues of national security implementation and NSC policy development.

Likewise, line attorneys, as well as programmatic attorneys, are more likely to specialize in particular areas of law and find defined and generally accepted roles. This description might apply, for example, to a line attorney at the State Department who reviews export control licenses, or the attorney at the Treasury Department who reviews financial transactions with foreign states, or a Justice Department lawyer who reviews FISA applications. These lawyers play critical national security roles, but are less likely to address the breadth of national security issues identified in this book. Their lanes *are* relatively clear and defined.

In addition, lawyers serving as agency general counsel, or their equivalent, perform or oversee the performance of myriad tasks generally associated with lawyers, such as drafting legal documents, reviewing legislation, overseeing litigation, and addressing matters of budget, personnel, and contracting. Rule of law and respect for law are often defined by these tasks. Do the lawyers apply the ethics rules with reason, care, and rigor? Are legislative and public document searches conducted in earnest? These everyday tasks help to define constitutional government, involving as they do the interplay between branches of government and between the government and the public.

Harder to define is the role lawyers should take involving matters where there is discretion as to the style of practice, where the lawyer might have a choice between a proactive, active, or reactive role. In role-playing, personality can be as important as intellectual capacity and training. Not every attorney is suited to a process of decision-making that can be rapid and is conducted under stress and often involves the application of law to uncertain or emerging facts. In this context, lawyers must know when to render their best advice and let go of an issue or when to hold an issue and request time for further review, or to buck the issue up the legal line. There is rarely time to double back for a second look. This may be difficult for lawyers who prefer the deliberative and careful speed of appellate work. It may also be difficult for lawyers who prefer practice areas oriented toward black-letter law and absolute answers. In short, national security practice requires a capacity to close on issues and make decisions, identifying nuance and caveats, if necessary.

National security practice also requires a capacity to compartmentalize work. This is true in a security sense. Lawyers operate under multiple constraints regarding what they can say and to whom based on the attorney-client, deliberative process, and state secrets privileges. (A sure way for a lawyer not to be in the right place at the right time is to garner a reputation for indiscretion.) However, by compartmentalization, I also mean an emotional and intellectual ability to move from one issue to another in rapid succession without getting stuck on just one issue. Policymakers must master this same skill. In contrast, subordinates assigned to specific issues are expected to devote their attention to a single policy issue and drive that issue up and down the chain of command.

As in other legal fields, national security lawyers should learn to subordinate matters of ego to the task of meaningfully applying the law. In doing so, they will have ample opportunity to learn the maxim that it is often the messenger who pays the price for the message. How common is the disapproving refrain, "Lawyers!" The refrain might be more aptly addressed – "Legislators!" "Democracy!" or "Benjamin Franklin!" – unless, of course, it is the lawyer who has delayed decision or diluted decision out of undue caution or concern. Lawyers must also appreciate that while steady and faithful application of the law is a hallmark of constitutional government, in most bureaucratic and substantive contexts they are a supporting arm to the policy process. Outside the Department of Justice, success is associated with the policy and not the legal work that supports the policy.

Lawyers are also subject to having their advice tested, as they should. That is part of the national security process and an essential part of internal and external appraisal. Does the lawyer understand the facts? Does the lawyer understand the law? Has the lawyer distinguished between law and legal policy? However, style varies. Where the stakes are high the distinction between understanding, testing, and bullying may be lost. Policymakers have a duty to push. Policymakers do not become policy generals by sitting back and waiting for events to unfold or opportunities to come their way. Boot camp, it turns out, is sound training for national security lawyers. National security lawyers will be tested and pushed, as they should be when national security is at stake. The lawyers will know when a bad idea has encountered a better idea and they must have the courage to adjust their views; but they will also know when they have bent under pressure, knowing the difference between a good faith argument and an inability to hold a line.

The practice of national security law, like many areas of law, requires endurance. However, in private practice the client has usually come to the counsel and now expects hard and constant effort. National security law requires comparable effort, but a different kind of endurance. Lawyers are not always invited into the decision-making room. This reluctance reflects concerns about secrecy, delay, and "lawyer creep" (the legal version of "mission creep," whereby one legal question becomes seventeen, requiring not one lawyer but forty-three to answer). Of course, decisionmakers may also fear that the lawyer may say no to something the policymaker wants to do. Rule of law often depends on the lawyer being in the right place at the right time to render advice. This is achieved by reading agendas, attending staff meetings, and ensuring that they and not the policymaker or the secretariat define what it is the lawyer needs to see.

National security process is never designed to convenience the lawyer. Sometimes it is specifically designed to avoid the lawyer. Endurance means having fresh legs in the middle of the night as well as first thing in the morning. Some officials will wait until the late night or the weekend to move their memos, noting "not available" for a legal clearance. The lawyer avoids such traps by meeting deadlines, negating silent consent, and where necessary by laying out tripwires, alerting the executive secretary of issues they need to see, sending timely e-mail prompting inclusion in discussions, and meeting each policy staff member one-on-one to establish expectations and confidence.

Most important, counsel should gain the support of the principal official engaged. This is done by adding value to the process and articulating for the decisionmaker why lawyers should have a seat at the table (or in the Situation Room, along the wall). Counsel keeps that seat through effective practice that is proactive, entailing the same zeal in overcoming legal and bureaucratic obstacles as they show in identifying them. A lawyer engaged at the advent of policy development is more likely to influence and guide than one that clears the final memorandum to the decisionmaker, where policy advisors have already committed to both the substance of decision and means of execution. Moreover, if the lawyer waits for issues, or is perceived as an obstacle rather than a source of value, the lawyer will find he or she is only contributing to decisions where legal review is mandated and then only as the last stop on the bureaucratic bus route.

Lawyers can advance the application of law in a number of ways. First, by understanding national security process, counsel can better identify where decisions are formed and made and thus where legal input is most useful. Second, by understanding the military and intelligence instruments counsel can better apply the law to fact. For example, military lawyers can hardly apply the principles of proportionality, discrimination, and necessity to targets without having an understanding of the weapons, munitions, and tactics that inform judgments about necessity and proportionality. Likewise, counsel addressing the use of force should understand the qualitative and quantitative limits of intelligence, distinguishing between evidence, inference, and intelligence in the process. Third, counsel must understand bureaucracy, knowing when and how to provide advice in person, via memo, and through e-mail, without losing sight that each written communication is a record no matter how informal, and that tone and demeanor can get lost in e-mail.

Finally, counsel should master and proactively recommend legal methods for overcoming bureaucratic inertia and resistance. Such methods include (a) presidential directives, (b) agency directives, (c) interagency or intra-agency memoranda of understanding, (d) lead agency designations, (e) the conduct of exercises, (f) textual adjustments that defer or eliminate concerns, or (g) just the force of personality or diplomacy. Concerns about the deployment of armed forces in civil context might be addressed through resort to any one of these methodologies or by textually limiting the scope, service, or situation in which the forces might be used. Such limitations might be put in the president's action memorandum, in the executive order, or in the rules of engagement. Alternative process may work as well, such as resorting to biweekly meetings of the agency heads, in an effort to take issues up and over bureaucratic obstacles, or holding weekly lunches of the sort that Mr. Carlucci and Mr. Berger found effective.

Where lawyers are being used to dress policy disagreements up in determinative legal clothing – "my lawyer says this is illegal" – good legal process can allow decisionmakers to focus on the policy issues at hand. Legal issues should be culled from policy agendas and intra- or inter-agency legal meetings held in advance to review options. This allows an opportunity to send issues up the legal chain rather than letting them linger, and possibly sidetracking deliberations. Moreover, just as policymakers forum shop for "can do" lawyers, or perhaps compliant lawyers, lawyers do the same, looking for lawyers who are problem solvers and do not shoot from the hip.

As in other areas of law, preparation is essential. This means reading agendas, consulting with relevant experts on an intra-agency and inter-agency basis, and taking issues up the legal chain of command in advance of meetings so that the lawyer can speak authoritatively when presented with the opportunity to do so. The opportunity may not come again.

Lawyers should also craft, and figuratively or actually, carry walk-about books to address national security issues as they arise. There is no excuse, for example, if the Northern Command staff judge advocate or counsel to the president does not have draft declarations "in the can" to address virtually every homeland security scenario. One purpose of tabletop exercises is to alert policymakers and lawyers to legal obstacles that lie ahead so that lawyers might find the means of circumnavigation before the crisis.

Preparation also entails educating the policymaker. Absent groundwork, the policymaker may respond at the moment of crisis by seeing the law only as something that allows or does not allow the policymaker to do what he wants. Contextual advice built on a foundation already laid is readily absorbed and accepted and will add greater value to the national security mission. A 3 A.M. conference call is no time to explain for the first time the principles of proportionality, necessity, and discrimination in targeting. Nor is the immediate aftermath of a natural disaster or terrorist attack the optimal time to explore for the first time the delicate legal policy issues raised by the deployment of U.S. military personnel in a civil context. In addition, the policymaker will understand in a live situation that the lawyer is applying "hard law" – specific, well established, and sanctioned – and not kibitzing on policy or operational matters.

Advance education also helps establish lines of communication and a common vocabulary of nuance between lawyer and policymaker before the crisis. A policymaker who hears a good brief on civil–military deployment will be sure his or her lawyer fully participates in any subsequent decisional process. In a large and layered bureaucracy, where the lawyer may be less proximate to the decisionmaker, and cannot count on immediate access, the teaching process is equally important in defining roles as well as legal expectations; however, it is more likely to occur through submission of written memoranda.

National security law also entails the application of legal policy; however, lawyers must take care to distinguish between what is law and what is legal policy. The identification of a preferred course as between lawful options is legal policy. The identification of a better argument among available arguments is legal policy. Identification of the long-term and short-term impact of legal arguments is legal policy. For example, will other states assert the same right to act as the United States asserts, and if so, what are the long-term costs and benefits of the United States asserting such authority? If a constitutional argument is legally available to the president, will it nonetheless generate a congressional or public response disproportionate to the benefits of using the argument?

The reality is that many national security law questions are not yes or no questions. Just as many national security policy decisions represent 51–49 judgments, legal judgments may be close calls; legal policy helps to identify the pros and cons of taking alternative positions. This is particularly the case where legal policy is national security policy as well; for example, where foreign reaction to U.S. legal choices may help or hinder alliances, or where reciprocal applications of law may harm U.S. national security.

Finally, lawyers, like policymakers, must return to appraise their work. Has the ground truth shifted in a manner that alters the legal basis for an action in either a permissive or restrictive manner? Has the president's directive been implemented in the manner intended? Do the ROE provide adequate protection and flexibility for U.S. forces? Has process been implemented in a manner that facilitates or that impedes rapid decision or the identification of policy options?

In summary, the national security lawyer must consider not only the substance of the law but also the practice and process of law and the essential decisional skills that bear on the practice of national security law. In the end, however, most senior executive branch lawyers serve at the direction and sometimes discretion of the department counsel, department head, and ultimately the president. Chances are, if the policymaker is not satisfied with the manner, method, or substance of advice he will replace his counsel, seek his reassignment, or work around counsel to work with other lawyers. Whether he is satisfied will not only depend on the performance of the lawyer but also on whether they share common expectations of how to define the duties of the national security lawyer.

B. THE DUTY OF THE NATIONAL SECURITY LAWYER

Academics and practitioners sometimes define the roles and responsibilities of lawyers through identification of the client and the client's interests. Thus, in private context, the ABA Model Rules of Professional Conduct state:

> A lawyer must act with commitment and dedication to the interests of the client and with zeal in advocacy upon the client's behalf.[4]

It is the client who must decide critical questions of strategy[5] and it is to the client to whom the attorney owes a duty of loyalty and confidentiality.[6]

The client-based private model, however, is less apt in identifying and defining the responsibilities of the national security lawyer. To start, in government context, there are differing views on just who (or perhaps what) is the "client." Scholars and practitioners have identified both animate and conceptual candidates, including the president,[7] the agency,[8] the agency head,[9] the public interest,[10] and the Constitution.[11] Consider that there are at least five possible and distinct facets to the president as client alone. At any given time the president may function as chief executive, party leader, commander in chief, the embodiment of the institution of the office of the president, or the president in his personal capacity. Each facet potentially represents distinct interests and responsibilities. While the national security lawyer certainly owes the president dedication and commitment as commander in chief, he does not necessarily owe the president as party leader the same zeal. Indeed, he may be legally barred under the Hatch Act from exercising any zeal at all.

In a related manner, there are differing perspectives, or models, on how national security lawyers should practice law, which reflect but are not necessarily determined by the identification of the "client." In the judicial model,[12] for example, the lawyer is expected to render neutral detached views on the law, as a judge might, ultimately rendering a decision as to what the law is. The advisory model posits that the attorney will render advice on legally available options. The advocacy model, perhaps, is closest in paralleling the private model, with the attorney serving to guide the client to the client's preferred outcomes and then defending the client's actions. It might be said that with the judicial model the attorney works with both hands, presenting both sides of each issue. In the client-based or advocate model, the attorney works with one hand, finding a legal basis for what it is the client wishes to accomplish.

Such models bring structure to consideration of the practice of national security law and may serve as a point of departure in describing the duties of the national security lawyer. However, in the daily mix of practice, most national security lawyers do not relate their conduct back to specific theories of ethical responsibility and conflict of interest analysis, as a government or private practitioner might do in criminal practice. This reflects the nature of most national security practice. The provision of advice regarding the Foreign Assistance Act, for example, does not require identification of the client, but rather the competent official who can authorize use of the authority. This may vary depending on the section of law and internal agency process. When the assistant secretary asks whether the United States can provide aid, the question is not, who is the client? – it is whether the Act authorizes such aid and, if so, subject to what substantive and procedural thresholds.

Likewise, judge advocates in the field do not ask, who is the client? – they ask, which commander has the authority to issue the lawful order to attack?

Even where issues present what look like traditional private legal ethics questions, for example, in cases involving the waiver of a privilege, the question is not resolved through identification of the client – for example, the agency or agency head – but rather through knowledge of the substance of law and process. In the case of executive privilege the answer is the president. In the case of classified information the answer is found in some combination of the originating agency, the DNI, and the president. And in the litigation context, the answer may vary depending on who can ultimately speak for the government on the specific issue presented.

Moreover, attorneys need not resort to ethics or academic models to define their role, when so much of the role is already defined in law, and in particular in the Constitution. First, in Article II the president is charged with taking "Care that the Laws be faithfully executed." Second,

> Before he enter on the Execution of his Office, he shall take the following Oath or Affirmation:
>
> "I do solemnly swear (or affirm) that I will faithfully execute the Office of President of the United States, and will to the best of my ability, preserve, protect and defend the Constitution of the United States."

Third, Article VI requires that "all executive and judicial Officers, both of the United States and of the several States, shall be bound by Oath or Affirmation, to support this Constitution."[13]

As a matter of statute, government officials, including attorneys, also undertake an oath of office tied to the Constitution.

> An individual, except the president, elected or appointed to an office of honor or profit in the civil service or uniformed services, shall take the following oath:
>
> "I, __, do solemnly swear (or affirm) that I will support and defend the Constitution of the United States against all enemies, foreign or domestic; that I will bear true faith and allegiance to the same; that I take this obligation freely, without any mental reservation or purpose of evasion; and that I will well and faithfully discharge the duties of the office on which I am about to enter. So help me God."

This section does not affect other oaths required by law. As is clear from the statutory text, the oath is not exclusive, but is applied in conjunction with other ethical obligations. Thus, in context, attorneys may well have to consider questions pertaining to the identification of the client. A judge advocate, for example, must adhere to his constitutional oath and to applicable bar codes pertaining to the representation of criminal law clients.

The point is that in the private context where academics and practitioners might reasonably debate to whom the attorney owes loyalty, the government attorney takes one oath and that is to the Constitution and not to a client. Further, that oath and the Constitution require faithful application of the law. That starts with faithful application of the Constitution, its structure and its substance, in the common defense of security and liberty.

Finally, the "client," used here to identify the official with authority to decide an issue, as well as the role of the national security attorney, will vary in context. There are more than 40,000 lawyers in the government. Only a fraction of this number practice national security law. In each context, the "client" may be different. Moreover, within each setting the lawyer will (or should) play each role described above: advisor, counselor, advocate, and judge. The practice is also sufficiently contextual that the answer as to which role is appropriate is found not in identifying the client or a particular model of practice, but in the facts. The skill and art is in knowing when and how to play each role.

Consider the following hypothetical, presenting a preemption scenario likely to occur in the future. The president's attorney is asked in the middle of the night to review a prospective target for a missile strike. For reasons of operational security, a "bigot list"[14] is in place. It does not include the attorney general. The target is a suspected WMD weapons facility in a restricted country, but one with which the United States is nominally at peace. The facility is operating under cover as a legitimate commercial enterprise. The target is in play because of intelligence suggesting, but not confirming, that the plant is linked to an Al Qaeda affiliate.

For sound operational reasons, an up or down decision on attacking is needed within two hours, or sooner, to avoid the risk that the enemy will disperse extant WMD weapons. However, it turns out that at the staff level there is disagreement on whether the intelligence linking the target to terrorist actors or even clandestine activities is credible and persuasive. There are also differences of view as to whether additional methods of intelligence gathering may improve U.S. knowledge, although there is general agreement that the target is a hard target and that any disclosure of U.S. interest in the facility could lead to the rapid dispersion of existing WMD stockpiles (if any).

What is the role and the duty of the attorney, and is that role defined by identification of the client or application of a judicial, advocacy, or advisory model of practice?

In the advocate model, the attorney might determine that he or she will defend the president's decision regardless of how the factual dispute is resolved, or for that matter whether it is resolved. Thus, the attorney might advise that so long as the president believes he is defending the country he has the legal authority to do so and counsel will support the decision under U.S. and international law.

In a judicial model, the attorney might ask additional questions. What is the potential for collateral consequences? And, what is the basis for the difference in intelligence opinion? He would then apply the law to the facts as they are known to determine whether a strike is lawful under U.S. and international law. To the extent the attorney believes the target is "unlawful" under U.S. law he would indicate so, and if necessary, advise the president that he could not in good faith approve the target.

Under an advisory model, the attorney might advise the president as to the legal standard and defer to the president's judgment on the application of law to fact. Under the public interest model, the attorney might consider what is in the best interest of the United States or the public. Presumably this interest would revolve around getting the facts right, but also taking all measures necessary to defend the country, erring on the side of security.

The attorney should play all of these roles. First, under any rubric the attorney has a duty to resolve the factual ambiguity. Arguably, under an advocacy model, the attorney might sit back and defer to the president's view of the law and facts and then defend both. However, it is not clear how such inaction would represent zealous or diligent representation. The president would still require knowledge of the facts and the law to faithfully execute his security functions. Moreover, under the advocacy model, even if the attorney were poised to validate the president's judgment, he would still need to know the counterarguments to better represent the president's choice. Thus, the question is how best to do so in a manner that respects the role of the president as commander in chief and chief executive.

The hypothetical also illustrates the potential range of duties, functions, and choices the attorney might (and in my view should) address in a given scenario. The national security lawyer has a duty to guide decisionmakers toward legally available options. In performing this function in a timely and meaningful manner, the lawyer provides for our physical security. In doing it faithfully, based on honest belief on the application of law, he provides for the security of our way of life, which is to say, a process of decision founded on respect for the law and subject to law.

The hypothetical presents threshold questions of authority. Therefore, the attorney must consider whether the president has the constitutional authority to authorize the missile strike. As the president is also, in effect, approving a specific military target while authorizing the initial resort to force the attorney should run through a three-pronged substantive template:

(1) Does the president have the constitutional authority to use force, and is it subject to a statutory overlay? If so, must or should the president consult with the Congress, or notify the Congress in advance?

(2) Is the use of force a lawful exercise in self-defense, anticipatory self-defense, or preemption? Will such an assertion be viewed as controversial? And, what are the legal policy ramifications of U.S. decision?
(3) Is the president's selection of targets and the means and methods of attack consistent with the law of armed conflict as reflected in U.S. and international law?

The attorney should also consider a procedural template:

(1) Who must authorize the use of force?
(2) Must the attorney general be informed? Should the attorney general be informed? If not, or if so, who must/should make that decision?
(3) Is the president aware of the factual dispute? If not, whose duty is it to inform him?
(4) Must the factual dispute be resolved before authorization may be given? If so, how can it be resolved in the timeline presented?

These questions present a mix of fact and law, law and legal policy, as well as substance and process. There are no textbook answers. There are clearly wrong answers. There are as well, as a matter of legal policy, preferred answers. One solution: the lawyer can identify the parameters of the factual dispute and ensure that they are framed and communicated within any decisional documents going to the president. But it is two in the morning. The president has already made his decision, without knowing that the facts are sliding. One solution: the president's lawyer can call the national security advisor and identify the problem and a solution – a conference call with the DNI, national security advisor, and the secretary of defense to determine if the facts are sliding or whether analysts are rehashing judgments already made at the top, without their knowledge. Does the DNI stand by the intelligence and intelligence judgment or not? And if there is any shift in fact or analysis, is the president and the military chain of command aware?

The scenario continues. With the input and concurrence of the attorney general, the DNI, and the secretary of defense, the president decides to authorize the strike. The lawyer now becomes advocate. He clears talking points for use with the Congress, the media, and foreign governments, conscious that the talking points, as opposed to the advice rendered in advance of decision, will shape outside perspectives on the validity of U.S. assertions of authority. As a matter of legal policy, will this be cast in the language of preemption, anticipatory self-defense, self-defense, or under some other rubric? In doing so, he considers what information if any can be disclosed in support of the intelligence link between the target and terrorism. He adds bullets on the legal basis for the strike, not as judge or advisor, reflecting the best arguments on both sides, but as advocate, presenting the arguments in support of action. Bigot list permitting, the lawyer ensures the State Department is generating an Article 51 report to the United Nations identifying the U.S. legal position as one of self-defense.

The strike occurs. The lawyer now shifts to the role of advisor appraising the process. What worked well and what didn't work well? Could the factual dispute have been resolved through alternative process, or was it only identified and forced to the surface through the presentation of decision? Should the president retain case-specific decision authority over comparable strikes, or authorize such strikes in concept in the future and if so subject to what qualifications in policy, law, and legal policy? Is this a question of law, or of command preference that should be dictated by operational need and presidential style?

The hypothetical also illustrates the extent to which the application of national security law and process is dependent on culture, personality, and style. The president can direct legal review of his decisions, but if a national security advisor is not committed to such a review, it will not occur in a meaningful manner, if at all. The process would have failed if the lawyer did not make the call or if the national security advisor would not take the call. In short, it is not the presence of counsel at the NSC, the White House, or the Defense Department that upholds the law. It is the active presence of a president, a national security advisor, and department secretaries who insist on legal input in the decision-making process and lawyers who will place their integrity and careers on the line to provide it.

An indeterminate conflict, of indefinite duration, against unknown enemies and known enemies unseen will put uncommon strain on U.S. national security. It will also put uncommon strain on principles of liberty. If we meet this day's threats without destroying the fabric of our constitutional liberty it will be through the effective and meaningful application of national security law.

The sine qua non for broad national security authority is meaningful oversight. By oversight, I mean the considered application of constitutional structure, executive process, legal substance, and relevant review of decision-making – all of which depend on the integrity and judgment of lawyers. It is lawyers who will help us find the right combination of broad executive authority to defeat terrorism with the considered application of law before action and subsequent appraisal to protect our liberty. So whether one likes law or not, it is central to national security. Lawyers and not just generals will decide the outcome of this conflict.

Lawyers reside at the intersection where physical safety and liberty merge. In this role they are indispensable to good process and should feel a duty to advocate good process. Good process permits the faithful application of the law and the accomplishment of the security objectives. In any given context, the pressure of the moment may encourage short-term thinking and the adoption of process shortcuts. The lawyer alone may be sufficiently detached from the policy outcome to identify the enduring institutional consequences of a particular course of action. So too, the lawyer alone may be familiar, and may feel an obligation to be familiar, with applicable written procedures. Process is substance if it means critical actors and perspectives are omitted from the discussion table.

Good process is not antithetical to timely decisions, operational timelines, or to secrecy. Process must find the right balance between speed and strength, secrecy and input. But process can always meet deadlines. There is no excuse for shortcuts. Process can be made to work faster and smarter. By example, if legal review is warranted, the attorney general alone can review a matter and, if need be, do so while sitting next to the president in the Oval Office.

Third, process should be contextual. The legal and policy parameters for responding to terrorism are different from those for responding to a Balkan crisis. Clandestine and remote military operations against a hidden enemy will dictate different decision processes than NATO air operations against fixed targets, as will the different political and policy parameters of both situations. One has to maintain situational awareness, to find the measure of process and approval that ensures law is applied in a manner that is faithful to constitutional, statutory, and executive dictates *and* that meets operational timelines. Therefore, there will always be some tension as to who should see what when.

Finally, lawyers support and defend the Constitution and not just the policies of their government. It is not clear how a president can faithfully apply the law without faithfully applying the constitutional principles identified in Chapters 3 and 4, including the separation of powers, and checks and balances. Constitutional faith recognizes that the Constitution is a national security document, which in the face of a WMD threat is appropriately read broadly and realistically. Constitutional faith also recognizes that liberty and the rule of law are national security values, which the Constitution is designed to preserve and to protect.

A definition of national security that includes constitutional values makes lawyers schooled in history, law, and ethics essential to the national security process. Being a lawyer in such a process is more than saying yes to a client's goals; it means guiding policymakers not just to lawful outcomes, but to outcomes addressing both aspects of national security by providing for security and preserving our sense of liberty. That is one reason this book places as much emphasis on the role of the lawyer as it does on the content of the law.

There are hard questions ahead in a time of homeland insecurity from which lawyers should not shy. Hamilton observed,

> The violent destruction of life and property incident to war, the continual effort and alarm attendant on a state of continual danger, will compel nations the most attached to liberty to resort for repose and security to institutions that have a tendency to destroy their civilian and political rights. To be more safe, they at length become willing to run the risk of being less free.

It is the national security lawyer's duty to alert policymakers to these tensions. The lawyer's duty is to show all sides to every issue while guiding policymakers and above all the president to lawful decisions that protect our security and our liberty. This is hardest to do when lives are at stake. But the Constitution was not designed to fail, to safeguard our security at the expense of our freedom, nor celebrate freedom at the expense of security. It is designed to underpin and protect us and our way of life. National security lawyers daily demonstrate how it can and must do both.

As a result, we should not begrudge democracy's adherence to law, but continue to find the best contextual process for its meaningful application. In war, and no more so than in addressing a threat where the terrorists' choice of weapons and targets may be unlimited, this means a substance, process, and practice of law that is both security effective and faithful to democratic values.

As Justice Brandeis reminded in *Whitney*,

> Those who won independence believed that the final end of the state was to make men free to develop their faculties, and that in its government the deliberative forces should prevail over the arbitrary. They believed liberty to be the secret of happiness and courage to be the secret of liberty.[15]

The law depends on the morality and courage of those who apply it. It depends on the moral courage of lawyers who raise tough questions, who dare to argue both sides of every issue, who insist upon being heard at the highest levels of decision-making, and who ultimately call the legal questions as they believe the Constitution dictates and not necessarily as policymakers may want at a moment in time. We do not live in a moment in time. We and our children live in perilous times.

Attachments

The Government of the United States

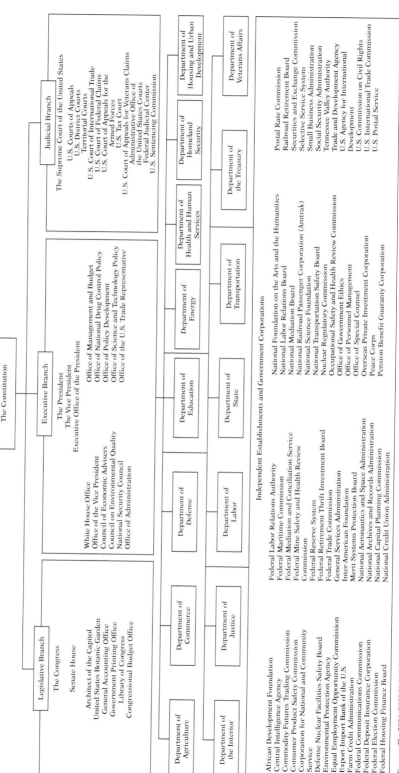

The Constitution

Legislative Branch

The Congress

Senate House

Architect of the Capitol
United States Botanic Garden
Government Accounting Office
Government Printing Office
Library of Congress
Congressional Budget Office

Executive Branch

The President
The Vice President
Executive Office of the President

White House Office
Office of the Vice President
Council of Economic Advisers
Council on Environmental Quality
National Security Council
Office of Administration

Office of Management and Budget
Office of National Drug Control Policy
Office of Policy Development
Office of Science and Technology Policy
Office of the U.S. Trade Representative

Judicial Branch

The Supreme Court of the United States

U.S. Courts of Appeals
U.S. District Courts
Territorial Courts
U.S. Court of International Trade
U.S. Court of Federal Claims
U.S. Court of Appeals for the
Armed Forces
U.S. Tax Court
U.S. Court of Appeals for Veterans Claims
Administrative Office of
the United States Courts
Federal Judicial Center
U.S. Sentencing Commission

Department of Agriculture

Department of Commerce

Department of Defense

Department of Education

Department of Energy

Department of Health and Human Services

Department of Housing and Urban Development

Department of the Interior

Department of Justice

Department of Labor

Department of State

Department of Transportation

Department of the Treasury

Department of Veterans Affairs

Department of Homeland Security

Independent Establishments and Government Corporations

African Development Foundation
Central Intelligence Agency
Commodity Futures Trading Commission
Consumer Product Safety Commission
Corporation for National and Community Service
Defense Nuclear Facilities Safety Board
Environmental Protection Agency
Equal Employment Opportunity Commission
Export-Import Bank of the U.S.
Farm Credit Administration
Federal Communications Commission
Federal Deposit Insurance Corporation
Federal Election Commission
Federal Housing Finance Board

Federal Labor Relations Authority
Federal Maritime Commission
Federal Mediation and Conciliation Service
Federal Mine Safety and Health Review
Commission
Federal Reserve System
Federal Retirement Thrift Investment Board
Federal Trade Commission
General Services Administration
Inter-American Foundation
Merit Systems Protection Board
National Aeronautics and Space Administration
National Archives and Records Administration
National Capital Planning Commission
National Credit Union Administration

National Foundation on the Arts and the Humanities
National Labor Relations Board
National Mediation Board
National Railroad Passenger Corporation (Amtrak)
National Science Foundation
National Transportation Safety Board
Nuclear Regulatory Commission
Occupational Safety and Health Review Commission
Office of Government Ethics
Office of Personnel Management
Office of Special Counsel
Overseas Private Investment Corporation
Peace Corps
Pension Benefit Guaranty Corporation

Postal Rate Commission
Railroad Retirement Board
Securities and Exchange Commission
Selective Service System
Small Business Administration
Social Security Administration
Tennessee Valley Authority
Trade and Development Agency
U.S. Agency for International
Development
U.S. Commission on Civil Rights
U.S. International Trade Commission
U.S. Postal Service

Source: *The 2006–2007 United States Government Manual* (Washington, DC: U.S. Government Printing Office, 2006) at 21.

National Security Council Staff (2005)

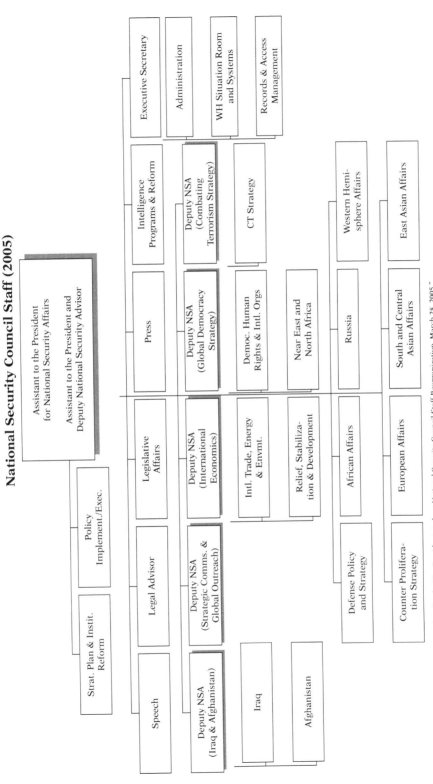

Source: Stephen J. Hadley, "Memorandum for the Vice President et al. on National Security Council Staff Reorganization, March 28, 2005," http://www.fas.org/irp/news/2005/03/nsc-reorg.pdf (accessed January 2007).

The White House
Washington

January 20, 1993

SUBJECT: Organization of the National Security Council

To assist me in carrying out my responsibilities in the area of national security, I hereby direct that the National Security Council system be organized as follows.

A. The National Security Council (NSC)

The National Security Council (NSC) shall be the principal forum for consideration of national security policy issues requiring Presidential determination. The functions, membership and responsibilities of the NSC shall be as set forth in the National Security Act of 1947, as amended, and this Presidential Decision Directive. The NSC shall advise and assist me in integrating all aspects of national security policy as it affects the United States – domestic, foreign, military, intelligence and economic (in conjunction with the National Economic Council). Along with its subordinate committees, the NSC shall be my principal means for coordinating Executive departments and agencies in the development and implementation of national security policy.

The NSC shall have as its members the President, Vice President, Secretary of State and Secretary of Defense, as prescribed by statute. The Director of Central Intelligence and the Chairman, Joint Chiefs of Staff, as statutory advisers to the NSC shall attend NSC meetings. In addition, the new membership of the NSC shall include the Secretary of the Treasury, the U.S. Representative to the United Nations, the Assistant to the President for National Security Affairs, the Assistant to the President for Economic Policy, and the Chief of Staff to the President. The Attorney General shall be invited to attend meetings pertaining to his jurisdiction, including covert actions. The heads of other Executive departments and agencies, the special statutory advisers to the NSC, and other senior officials shall be invited to attend meetings of the NSC where appropriate.

The NSC shall meet as required. The Assistant to the President for National Security Affairs, at my direction and in consultation with the Secretaries of State and Defense and, when appropriate, the Secretary of the Treasury and the Assistant to the President for Economic Policy, shall be responsible for determining the agenda and ensuring that the necessary papers are prepared. Other members of the NSC may propose items for inclusion on the agenda. The Assistant to the President shall be assisted by a National Security Council staff, as provided by law.

B. The NSC Principals Committee (NSC/PC)

An NSC Principals Committee (NSC/PC) is established as the senior inter-agency forum for consideration of policy issues affecting national security. The NSC/PC shall review, coordinate, and monitor the development and implementation of national security policy. The NSC/PC should be a flexible instrument – a forum available for Cabinet-level officials to meet to discuss and resolve issues not requiring the President's participation. The Assistant to the President for National Security Affairs shall serve as Chair. The Assistant to the President for Economic Policy shall be informed of meetings and be invited to attend all those with international economic considerations.

The NSC/PC shall have as its members the Secretary of State (if unavailable, the Deputy Secretary of State or the designee of the Secretary of State); the Secretary of Defense (if unavailable, the Deputy Secretary of Defense or the designee of the Secretary of Defense); the U.S. Representative to the United Nations; the Assistant to the President for National Security Affairs (Chair); the Director of Central Intelligence; the Chairman, Joint Chiefs of Staff; and the Assistant to the President for Economic Policy, as appropriate. The Secretary of the Treasury, the Attorney General or other heads of departments or agencies shall be invited as needed.

The Assistant to the President for National Security Affairs shall be responsible – in consultation with the Secretaries of State and Defense, and, when appropriate, the Assistant to the President for Economic Policy – for calling meetings of the NSC/PC, for determining the agenda, and for ensuring that the necessary papers are prepared.

C. The NSC Deputies Committee (NSC/DC)

An NSC Deputies Committee (NSC/DC) shall serve as the senior sub-Cabinet interagency forum for consideration of policy issues affecting national security. The NSC/DC shall review and monitor the work of the NSC interagency process (including Interagency Working Groups established pursuant to

Section D below). The Deputies Committee also shall focus significant attention on policy implementation. Periodic reviews of the Administration's major foreign policy initiatives shall be scheduled to ensure that they are being implemented in a timely and effective manner. Also, these reviews should periodically consider whether existing policy directives should be revamped or rescinded.

The NSC/DC shall have as its members the Deputy Assistant to the President for National Security Affairs (who shall serve as the Chairman); the Under Secretary of Defense for Policy; the Under Secretary of State for Political Affairs; the Deputy Director of Central Intelligence; and the Vice Chairman, Joint Chiefs of Staff; the Assistant to the Vice President for National Security Affairs; and the Deputy Assistant to the President for Economic Policy, as needed. The Deputy Assistant to the President for National Security Affairs, in consultation with the representatives of the Departments of State and Defense, may invite representatives of other Executive departments and agencies, and other senior officials, to attend meetings of the NSC/DC where appropriate in light of the issues to be discussed. When meeting on sensitive intelligence activities, including covert actions, the attendees shall include the appropriate senior representatives of the Attorney General.

The Deputy Assistant to the President for National Security Affairs shall be responsible – in consultation with the representatives of the Departments of State and Defense, and the NEC, as appropriate – for calling meetings of the NSC/DC, for determining the agenda, and for ensuring that the necessary papers are prepared. The NSC/DC shall ensure that all papers to be discussed by the NSC or the NSC/PC fully analyze the issues, fairly and adequately set out the facts, consider a full range of views and options, and satisfactorily assess the prospects, risks, and implications of each. The NSC/DC may task the interagency groups established pursuant to Section D of this Presidential Decision Directive.

The NSC Deputies Committee shall also be responsible for day-to-day crisis management, reporting to the National Security Council. In this capacity, the group shall be designated the <u>Deputies Committee/CM</u>, for Crisis Management. Any NSC principal or deputy, as well as the Assistant to the President for National Security Affairs, may request a meeting of the Deputies Committee in its crisis management capacity. The Committee also shall focus on crisis prevention – including contingency planning for major areas of concern. While meeting as the Deputies Committee/CM, the group shall be assisted by a small support staff – to provide insitutional memory, develop agendas and record decisions.

D. Interagency Working Groups (NSC/IWGs)

A system of Interagency Working Groups – some permanent, others ad hoc –
is hereby authorized. The NSC/IWGs shall be established at the direction
of the Deputies Committee, which shall also determine the chair of the
NSC/IWG – either departmental or NSC or NEC. In general, foreign policy and defense issues should be chaired at the Assistant-Secretary level by
the Departments of State and Defense, respectively; international economic
issues by the Department of the Treasury or the NEC, as appropriate; and
intelligence, nonproliferation, arms control and crisis management by the
NSC. The IWGs shall convene on a regular basis – to be determined by the
Deputies Committee – to review and coordinate the implementation of Presidential decisions in their policy areas. Strict guidelines shall be established
governing the operation of the Interagency Working Groups, including participants, decision-making path and time frame. The number of these working groups shall be kept to the minimum needed to promote an effective
NSC system.

> [signed]
> William J. Clinton

Source: NSC Hardcopy

Organization of the National Security Council System

National Security Presidential Directive NSPD-1

The White House
Washington

February 13, 2001

MEMORANDUM FOR THE VICE PRESIDENT
    THE SECRETARY OF STATE
    THE SECRETARY OF THE TREASURY
    THE SECRETARY OF DEFENSE
    THE ATTORNEY GENERAL
    THE SECRETARY OF AGRICULTURE
    THE SECRETARY OF COMMERCE
    THE SECRETARY OF HEALTH AND HUMAN SERVICES
    THE SECRETARY OF TRANSPORTATION
    THE SECRETARY OF ENERGY
    ADMINISTRATOR, ENVIRONMENTAL PROTECTION AGENCY
    DIRECTOR OF THE OFFICE OF MANAGEMENT AND BUDGET
    UNITED STATES TRADE REPRESENTATIVE
    CHAIRMAN, COUNCIL OF ECONOMIC ADVISERS
    DIRECTOR, NATIONAL DRUG CONTROL POLICY
    CHIEF OF STAFF TO THE PRESIDENT
    DIRECTOR OF CENTRAL INTELLIGENCE
    DIRECTOR, FEDERAL EMERGENCY MANAGEMENT AGENCY
    ASSISTANT TO THE PRESIDENT FOR NATIONAL SECURITY AFFAIRS
    ASSISTANT TO THE PRESIDENT FOR ECONOMIC POLICY
    COUNSEL TO THE PRESIDENT
    CHIEF OF STAFF AND ASSISTANT TO THE VICE PRESIDENT FOR
        NATIONAL SECURITY AFFAIRS
    DIRECTOR, OFFICE OF SCIENCE AND TECHNOLOGY POLICY
    CHAIRMAN, BOARD OF GOVERNORS OF THE FEDERAL RESERVE
    CHAIRMAN, COUNCIL ON ENVIRONMENTAL QUALITY
    CHAIRMAN, EXPORT-IMPORT BANK
    CHAIRMAN OF THE JOINT CHIEFS OF STAFF
    COMMANDANT, U.S. COAST GUARD
    ADMINISTRATOR, NATIONAL AERONAUTICS AND SPACE ADMINISTRATION
    CHAIRMAN, NUCLEAR REGULATORY COMMISSION
    DIRECTOR, PEACE CORPS

```
DIRECTOR, FEDERAL BUREAU OF INVESTIGATION
DIRECTOR, NATIONAL SECURITY AGENCY
DIRECTOR, DEFENSE INTELLIGENCE AGENCY
PRESIDENT, OVERSEAS PRIVATE INVESTMENT CORPORATION
CHAIRMAN, FEDERAL COMMUNICATIONS COMMISSION
COMMISSIONER, U.S. CUSTOMS SERVICE
ADMINISTRATOR, DRUG ENFORCEMENT ADMINISTRATION
PRESIDENT'S FOREIGN INTELLIGENCE ADVISORY BOARD
ARCHIVIST OF THE UNITED STATES
DIRECTOR, INFORMATION SECURITY OVERSIGHT OFFICE
```

SUBJECT: Organization of the National Security Council System

This document is the first in a series of National Security Presidential Directives. National Security Presidential Directives shall replace both Presidential Decision Directives and Presidential Review Directives as an instrument for communicating presidential decisions about the national security policies of the United States.

National security includes the defense of the United States of America, protection of our constitutional system of government, and the advancement of United States interests around the globe. National security also depends on America's opportunity to prosper in the world economy. The National Security Act of 1947, as amended, established the National Security Council to advise the President with respect to the integration of domestic, foreign, and military policies relating to national security. That remains its purpose. The NSC shall advise and assist me in integrating all aspects of national security policy as it affects the United States – domestic, foreign, military, intelligence, and economics (in conjunction with the National Economic Council (NEC)). The National Security Council system is a process to coordinate executive departments and agencies in the effective development and implementation of those national security policies.

The National Security Council (NSC) shall have as its regular attendees (both statutory and non-statutory) the President, the Vice President, the Secretary of State, the Secretary of the Treasury, the Secretary of Defense, and the Assistant to the President for National Security Affairs. The Director of Central Intelligence and the Chairman of the Joint Chiefs of Staff, as statutory advisors to the NSC, shall also attend NSC meetings. The Chief of Staff to the President and the Assistant to the President for Economic Policy are invited to attend any NSC meeting. The Counsel to the President shall be consulted regarding the agenda of NSC meetings, and shall attend any meeting when, in consultation with the Assistant to the President for National Security

Affairs, he deems it appropriate. The Attorney General and the Director of the Office of Management and Budget shall be invited to attend meetings pertaining to their responsibilities. For the Attorney General, this includes both those matters within the Justice Department's jurisdiction and those matters implicating the Attorney General's responsibility under 28 U.S.C. 511 to give his advice and opinion on questions of law when required by the President. The heads of other executive departments and agencies, as well as other senior officials, shall be invited to attend meetings of the NSC when appropriate.

The NSC shall meet at my direction. When I am absent from a meeting of the NSC, at my direction the Vice President may preside. The Assistant to the President for National Security Affairs shall be responsible, at my direction and in consultation with the other regular attendees of the NSC, for determining the agenda, ensuring that necessary papers are prepared, and recording NSC actions and Presidential decisions. When international economic issues are on the agenda of the NSC, the Assistant to the President for National Security Affairs and the Assistant to the President for Economic Policy shall perform these tasks in concert.

The NSC Principals Committee (NSC/PC) will continue to be the senior interagency forum for consideration of policy issues affecting national security, as it has since 1989. The NSC/PC shall have as its regular attendees the Secretary of State, the Secretary of the Treasury, the Secretary of Defense, the Chief of Staff to the President, and the Assistant to the President for National Security Affairs (who shall serve as chair). The Director of Central Intelligence and the Chairman of the Joint Chiefs of Staff shall attend where issues pertaining to their responsibilities and expertise are to be discussed. The Attorney General and the Director of the Office of Management and Budget shall be invited to attend meetings pertaining to their responsibilities. For the Attorney General, this includes both those matters within the Justice Department's jurisdiction and those matters implicating the Attorney General's responsibility under 28 U.S.C. 511 to give his advice and opinion on questions of law when required by the President. The Counsel to the President shall be consulted regarding the agenda of NSC/PC meetings, and shall attend any meeting when, in consultation with the Assistant to the President for National Security Affairs, he deems it appropriate. When international economic issues are on the agenda of the NSC/PC, the Committee's regular attendees will include the Secretary of Commerce, the United States Trade Representative, the Assistant to the President for Economic Policy (who shall serve as chair for agenda items that principally pertain to international economics), and, when the issues pertain to her responsibilities, the Secretary of Agriculture. The Chief of Staff and National Security Adviser to the Vice President shall attend all meetings of the NSC/PC, as shall the Assistant to the President and Deputy National Security Advisor (who shall serve as Executive Secretary of the NSC/PC). Other heads of departments and agencies, along with additional senior officials, shall be invited where appropriate.

The NSC/PC shall meet at the call of the Assistant to the President for National Security Affairs, in consultation with the regular attendees of the NSC/PC. The Assistant to the President for National Security Affairs shall determine the agenda in consultation with the foregoing, and ensure that necessary papers are prepared. When international economic issues are on the agenda of the NSC/PC, the Assistant to the President for National Security Affairs and the Assistant to the President for Economic Policy shall perform these tasks in concert.

The NSC Deputies Committee (NSC/DC) will also continue to serve as the senior sub-Cabinet interagency forum for consideration of policy issues affecting national security. The NSC/DC can prescribe and review the work of the NSC interagency groups discussed later in this directive. The NSC/DC shall also help ensure that issues being brought before the NSC/PC or the NSC have been properly analyzed and prepared for decision. The NSC/DC shall have as its regular members the Deputy Secretary of State or Under Secretary of the Treasury or Under Secretary of the Treasury for International Affairs, the Deputy Secretary of Defense or Under Secretary of Defense for Policy, the Deputy Attorney General, the Deputy Director of the Office of Management and Budget, the Deputy Director of Central Intelligence, the Vice Chairman of the Joint Chiefs of Staff, the Deputy Chief of Staff to the President for Policy, the Chief of Staff and National Security Adviser to the Vice President, the Deputy Assistant to the President for International Economic Affairs, and the Assistant to the President and Deputy National Security Advisor (who shall serve as chair). When international economic issues are on the agenda, the NSC/DC's regular membership will include the Deputy Secretary of Commerce, a Deputy United States Trade Representative, and, when the issues pertain to his responsibilities, the Deputy Secretary of Agriculture, and the NSC/DC shall be chaired by the Deputy Assistant to the President for International Economic Affairs for agenda items that principally pertain to international economics. Other senior officials shall be invited where appropriate.

The NSC/DC shall meet at the call of its chair, in consultation with the other regular members of the NSC/DC. Any regular member of the NSC/DC may also request a meeting of the Committee for prompt crisis management. For all meetings the chair shall determine the agenda in consultation with the foregoing, and ensure that necessary papers are prepared.

The Vice President and I may attend any and all meetings of any entity established by or under this directive.

Management of the development and implementation of national security policies by multiple agencies of the United States Government shall usually be accomplished by the NSC Policy Coordination Committees (NSC/PCCs). The NSC/PCCs shall be the main day-to-day fora for interagency coordination of national security policy. They shall provide policy analysis for consideration by the more senior committees of the NSC system and ensure timely responses to decisions made by the President. Each NSC/PCC shall include representatives from the executive departments, offices, and agencies represented in the NSC/DC.

Six NSC/PCCs are hereby established for the following regions: Europe and Eurasia, Western Hemisphere, East Asia, South Asia, Near East and North Africa, and Africa. Each of the NSC/PCCs shall be chaired by an official of Under Secretary or Assistant Secretary rank to be designated by the Secretary of State.

Eleven NSC/PCCs are hereby also established for the following functional topics, each to be chaired by a person of Under Secretary or Assistant Secretary rank designated by the indicated authority:

Democracy, Human Rights, and International Operations (by the Assistant to the President for National Security Affairs);

International Development and Humanitarian Assistance (by the Secretary of State);

Global Environment (by the Assistant to the President for National Security Affairs and the Assistant to the President for Economic Policy in concert);

International Finance (by the Secretary of the Treasury);

Transnational Economic Issues (by the Assistant to the President for Economic Policy);

Counter-Terrorism and National Preparedness (by the Assistant to the President for National Security Affairs);

Defense Strategy, Force Structure, and Planning (by the Secretary of Defense);

Arms Control (by the Assistant to the President for National Security Affairs);

Proliferation, Counterproliferation, and Homeland Defense (by the Assistant to the President for National Security Affairs);

Intelligence and Counterintelligence (by the Assistant to the President for National Security Affairs); and

Records Access and Information Security (by the Assistant to the President for National Security Affairs).

The Trade Policy Review Group (TPRG) will continue to function as an interagency coordinator of trade policy. Issues considered within the TPRG, as with the PCCs, will flow through the NSC and/or NEC process, as appropriate.

Each NSC/PCC shall also have an Executive Secretary from the staff of the NSC, to be designated by the Assistant to the President for National Security Affairs. The Executive Secretary shall assist the Chairman in scheduling the meetings of the NSC/PCC, determining the agenda, recording the actions taken and tasks assigned, and ensuring timely responses to the central policymaking committees of the NSC system. The Chairman of each NSC/PCC, in consultation with the Executive Secretary, may invite representatives of other executive departments and agencies to attend meetings of the NSC/PCC where appropriate.

The Assistant to the President for National Security Affairs, at my direction and in consultation with the Vice President and the Secretaries of State, Treasury, and Defense, may establish additional NSC/PCCs as appropriate.

The Chairman of each NSC/PCC, with the agreement of the Executive Secretary, may establish subordinate working groups to assist the PCC in the performance of its duties.

The existing system of Interagency Working Groups is abolished.

- The oversight of ongoing operations assigned in PDD/NSC-56 to Executive Committees of the Deputies Committee will be performed by the appropriate regional NSC/PCCs, which may create subordinate working groups to provide coordination for ongoing operations.

- The Counter-Terrorism Security Group, Critical Infrastructure Coordination Group, Weapons of Mass Destruction Preparedness, Consequences Management and Protection Group, and the interagency working group on Enduring Constitutional Government are reconstituted as various forms of the NSC/PCC on Counter-Terrorism and National Preparedness.

- The duties assigned in PDD/NSC-75 to the National Counterintelligence Policy Group will be performed in trie NSC/PCC on Intelligence and Counterintelligence, meeting with appropriate attendees.

- The duties assigned to the Security Policy Board and other entities established in PDD/NSC-29 will be transferred to various NSC/PCCs, depending on the particular security problem being addressed.

- The duties assigned in PDD/NSC-41 to the Standing Committee on Non-proliferation will be transferred to the PCC on Proliferation, Counterproliferation, and Homeland Defense.

- The duties assigned in PDD/NSC-35 to the Interagency Working Group for Intelligence Priorities will be transferred to the PCC on Intelligence and Counterintelligence.

- The duties of the Human Rights Treaties Interagency Working Group established in E.O. 13107 are transferred to the PCC on Democracy, Human Rights, and International Operations.

- The Nazi War Criminal Records Interagency Working Group established in E.O. 13110 shall be reconstituted, under the terms of that order and until its work ends in January 2002, as a Working Group of the NSC/PCC for Records Access and Information Security.

Except for those established by statute, other existing NSC interagency groups, ad hoc bodies, and executive committees are also abolished as of March 1, 2001, unless they are specifically reestablished as subordinate working groups within the new NSC system as of that date. Cabinet officers, the heads of other executive agencies, and the directors of offices within the Executive Office of the President shall advise the Assistant to the President for National Security Affairs of those specific NSC interagency groups chaired by their respective departments or agencies that are either mandated by statute or are otherwise of sufficient importance and vitality as to warrant being reestablished. In each case the Cabinet officer, agency head, or office director should describe the scope of the activities proposed for or now carried out by the interagency group, the relevant statutory mandate if any, and the particular NSC/PCC that should coordinate this work. The Trade Promotion Coordinating Committee established in E.O. 12870 shall continue its work, however, in the manner specified in that order. As to those committees expressly established in the National Security Act, the NSC/PC and/or NSC/DC shall serve as those committees and perform the functions assigned to those committees by the Act.

To further clarify responsibilities and effective accountability within the NSC system, those positions relating to foreign policy that are designated as special presidential emissaries, special envoys for the President, senior advisors to the President and the Secretary of State, and special advisors to the President and the Secretary of State are also abolished as of March 1, 2001, unless they are specifically redesignated or reestablished by the Secretary of State as positions in that Department.

This Directive shall supersede all other existing presidential guidance on the organization of the National Security Council system. With regard to application of this document to economic matters, this document shall be interpreted in concert with any Executive Order governing the National Economic Council and with presidential decision documents signed hereafter that implement either this directive or that Executive Order.

[signed: George W. Bush]

cc: The Executive Clerk

Source Notes
Source: NSC hardcopy
Approved for release: March 13, 2001
Transcription and HTML: Steven Aftergood

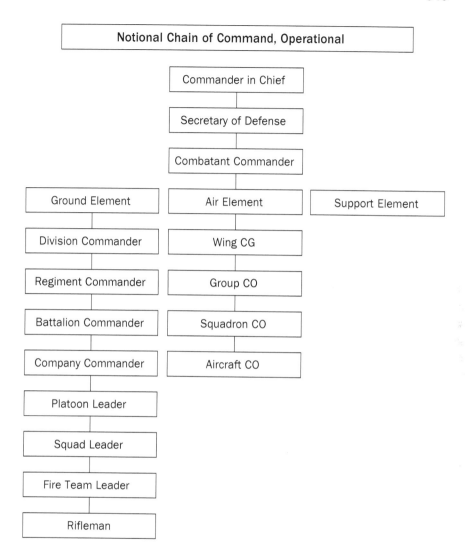

Notional Chain of Command, Operational

Homeland Security Council Staff (2005)

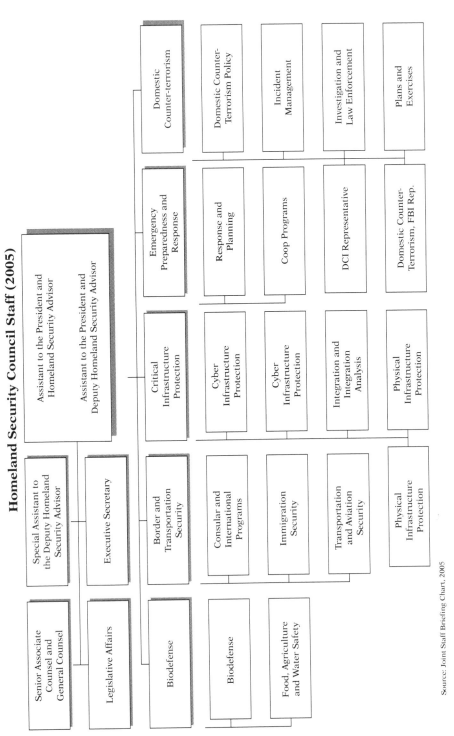

Source: Joint Staff Briefing Chart, 2005

Notes

1. Perilous Times: Describing the Threat

1. A note on terminology: John Brennan, a former head of the Central Intelligence Agency's (CIA's) Counterterrorism Center and the interagency Terrorist Threat Integration Center (now the National Counterterrorism Center), points out that linking terrorism with jihad "unwittingly transfers the religious legitimacy inherent in the concept of jihad to murderous acts that are anything but holy." (John Brennan, "We've Lost Sight of His Vision," *The Washington Post*, February 26, 2006).

   The problem with "terrorist" is that it reaches too far, covering a genre or generalized set of tactics that can describe the environmental extremist that burns down a SUV dealership as well as the Al Qaeda operative intent on blowing up New York. Former Representative and 9/11 Commission Vice Chairman Lee Hamilton tells the story of former Deputy Secretary of Defense Richard Armitage leaving a meeting and bemoaning that "We can't even agree on who we are fighting." Hamilton points out that in one newspaper he counted eight different terms to describe the terrorist opponent, including "terrorists," "Islamists," and "Al-Qaeda affiliates." (Lee Hamilton, the Landon Lecture, Kansas State University, March 29, 2005. Available at http://www.mediarelations.K-state.edu/WEB/News/NewsReleases/hamiltontext305.html.)

   Accepting Brennan's point, I have chosen "jihadist" in a value-neutral manner, so as to delink terrorism from the adjective "Islamic." "Terrorist" falls short as well because it is too general a term for the focus I wish to apply to those persons, organizations, and movements that are committed to engaging in mass casualty incidents, potentially using WMD. "Jihadist" is also the term in present use by the intelligence community as reflected in the declassified portions of the 2006 National Intelligence Estimate on Iraq.

2. In the 1990s, Osama Bin Laden was referred to within the intelligence community and U.S. government as Usama; hence the acronym UBL on many documents. I have opted for the more current, and some argue more accurate, transliteration of OBL. There is also debate as to whether the correct transliteration is Ladin or the more frequent Laden. Likewise, Al Qaeda is presented multiple ways as well.

3. Arnaud de Borchgrave, "Iran Scores in World War," Commentary, *The Washington Times*, August 24, 2006.

4. Joseph Ellis, "Finding a Place for 9/11 in American History," *The New York Times*, January 28, 2006.

5. "Calculating the New Global Nuclear Terrorism Threat," IAEA Press Release, November 1, 2001. Available at http://www.iaea.org (accessed November 6, 2006). For reports of trafficking on nuclear material and know-how, visit the IAEA website. The reader can find additional and accessible information on the websites for the Council on Foreign Relations http://www.cfr.org and the Center for Strategic and International Studies http://www.csis/ among other sites.

6. Department of Homeland Security Daily Open Source Infrastructure Report for 27 December 2006, available at http://www.dhs.gov/ (visited January 2007) citing to Richard Willing, "Nuclear Traffic Doubles Since '90s," *USA Today*, December 26, 2006 (the report notes an increase in the number of scams as well).

7. *Youngstown Sheet & Tube Co. et al. v. Sawyer*, 343 U.S. 579, at 634 (1952)(Justice Jackson, concurring).

8. *United States v. Katz*, 389 U.S. 347, at 358 (1967).

9. *Youngstown*, at 641 (Justice Jackson, concurring).

10. Consider the theory of a unitary executive. The theory is derivative of the separation of powers, with emphasis on *separation*; because each branch is independent of the others, each branch is entitled to reach its own views as to what the law is, without interference from the other branches. For sure, the president as chief executive may, acting in good faith, interpret the law and direct the executive branch to follow his interpretation. But the theory's premise that the executive is therefore free to ignore the views of the other branches is pernicious, and ignores 200 years of constitutional practice starting with John Marshall's statement that it is the province of the Supreme Court to say what the law is. Moreover, the theory can elevate the separation of powers to a pedestal not intended, placing the executive's legal determinations beyond the reach of the Constitution's other interlocking checks and balances. The Constitution recognizes that a foundational shared obligation is for each branch to uphold liberty through oversight of the other branches. Similarly, providing for the common defense is a responsibility of all branches of government.

2. The Meaning of National Security

1. *The Federalist Papers*, No. 8: Hamilton, "The Effects of Internal War in Producing Standing Armies and Other Institutions Unfriendly to Liberty."

2. *See*, Mark R. Shulman, "The Progressive Era Origins of the National Security Act," 104 Dick. L. Rev. 289 (2000). Shulman identifies references to the term in college debates dating to the 1790s. As Shulman's article and others point out, the phrase "national security" has a long history, but did not become part of the daily vocabulary of national decision-making and process until the twentieth century.

3. 18 U.S.C. app. 1.

4. President George W. Bush, National Security Presidential Directive 1, "Organization of the National Security Council System," February 13, 2001.

5. "A National Security Strategy for a New Century," (Washington: The White House, December 1999, released January 2000).

6. President Clinton's comparable directive, "Organization of the National Security Council" did not define "United States national security," but included equally expansive language drawn from the National Security Act of 1947: "The NSC shall advise and assist me in integrating all aspects of national security policy as it affects the United States – domestic, foreign, military, intelligence and economic." Presidential Decision Directive 2, January 20, 1993.

7. "*Definitions*. For purposes of this order: (A) 'National security' means the national defense or foreign relations of the United States." President William J. Clinton, Executive Order 12958, "Classified National Security Information," April 20, 1995.

8. "A collective term encompassing both national defense and foreign relations of the United States. Specifically, the condition provided by: a. a military or defense advantage over any foreign nation or group of nations; b. a favorable foreign relations position; or c. a defense posture capable of successfully resisting hostile or destructive action from within or without, overt or covert." *DOD Dictionary of Military Terms*, as amended through August 8, 2006. Available at http://www.dtic.mil/doctrine/jel/doddict/ (accessed November 7, 2006).

9. *New York Times Co. v. United States*, 403 U.S. 713, 719 (1971)(Justice Black, concurring).

10. Ibid., at 727 (Justice Brennan concurring).

11. H. Lasswell, *National Security and Individual Freedom*, at 51 (New York: McGraw-Hill, 1950).

12. Walter Lippman, *U.S. Foreign Policy: Shield of the Republic*, at 50–51 (Boston: Little, Brown, 1943).

13. Frederick Tipson, "National Security and the Role of Law," at 10 in *National Security Law*, John Norton Moore, Frederick Tipson, and Robert Turner, Eds. (Durham: Carolina Academic Press, 1990, 1st Ed.).

14. Academics and commentators, less bound than executive bureaucracies by the correlation between mission statement, budget and policy reach, define national security both broadly and narrowly. *See, e.g.*, Joseph Romm, *Defining National Security: The Nonmilitary Aspects* (1993); Robert Kaplan, "The Coming of Anarchy," *The Atlantic Monthly* (Feb. 1994); *Walter Lippman, U.S. Foreign Policy: Shield of the Republic* 51 (1943).

15. *Temperature Trends in the Lower Atmosphere: Steps for Understanding and Reconciling Differences*, U.S. Climate Change Science Program, April 2006, available at http://www.climatescience.gov/library (accessed November 2006); Andrew Revkin, "Federal Study Finds Accord on Warming," *The New York Times*, May 3, 2006; See also, "Stern Review on the Economics of Climate Change," 30 October 2006 available at http://www.hm-treasury.gov.uk/independent_reviews/stern_economics-climate (accessed November 24, 2006); Bill McKibben, "The Coming Meltdown," *The New York Review of Books*, vol. 53, Num. 1, January 12, 2006; Jim Hansen, "The Threat to the Planet," *The New York Review of Books*, Vol. 53, Num. 12, July 13, 2006; Philip Boffey, "The Evidence of Global Warming," *The New York Times*, July 4, 2006.

16. *Ginsberg & Sons Inc. v. Popkin*, 285 U.S. 204, 208, 76 L.Ed. 704, 52 S. Ct. 322 (1932).

17. Justice Clark stated in *Youngstown* (at 662), "where Congress has laid down specific procedures to deal with the type of crisis confronting the president, he must follow those procedures in meeting the crisis; but in the absence of such action by Congress, the president's independent power to act depends upon the gravity of the situation confronting the nation."

18. *United States v. Nixon*, 418 U.S. 683 (1974).

19. *In re: Grand Jury Subpoena, Judith Miller*, 397 F.3d 964 (D.C. Cir. 2005).

3. National Security law

1. 50 U.S.C. 1701, et seq.

2. See e.g., E.O. 12139 "Exercise of Certain Authority Respecting Electronic Surveillance," May 23, 1979; E.O. 12949 "Foreign Intelligence Physical Searches," February 9, 1995.

3. John Lehman, "Getting Spy Reform Wrong: Sept. 11 Commission's Proposals Were Turned into Bureaucratic Bloat," *The Washington Post*, November 16, 2005.

4. Quoted in, Thom Shanker, "Study is Said to Find Overlap in U.S. Counterterror Effort," *The New York Times*, March 18, 2006.

5. Jane Mayer, "The Hidden Power," *The New Yorker*, July 3, 2006.

6. "Congress as 'The Broken Branch,'" Interview with Norman J. Ornstein and Thomas E. Mann, *The Washington Post*, October 11, 2006.

7. *Public Papers of the Presidents of the United States*, Administration of Jimmy Carter 1978, "Foreign Intelligence Surveillance Act of 1978, Statement on Signing S. 1566 into Law, October 25, 1978."

8. But see, Gary J. Bass, "Are Democracies Really More Peaceful?" *The New York Times Magazine*, January 1, 2006.

9. Chief Justice John G. Roberts interview with Brian Lamb, C-SPAN, as quoted in "Today," *The Washington Post*, September 18, 2006.

10. The federal judiciary is often dubbed the least democratic branch of government because its life-tenured members are appointed and not subject to election. However, in the national security context the judiciary is in some regards the most transparent branch, with judges explaining their national security decisions in writing and in (usually) public opinions.

4. Constitutional Framework

1. For a list and description of the leading national security law cases *see* Michael Reisman and James Baker, *Regulating Covert Action*, Suggested Readings, (New Haven: Yale University Press, 1992). These cases include: *Paquette Habana*, 175 U.S. 677 (1900); The Prize Cases, 67 U.S. (2 Black) 635 (1862); *Dames & Moore v. Regan*, 453 U.S. 654 (1981); *Chicago and Southern Airlines, Inc. v. Waterman Steamship Corp.*, 333 U.S. 103 (1948); *Department of Navy v. Egan*, 484 U.S. 518 (1988); *United States v. Nixon*, 418 U.S. 683 (1974); *Totten v. United States*, 92 U.S. 105 (1875); *United States v. Snepp*, 444 U.S. 507 (1980); and the detainee line of cases, including *Hamdan* 126 S.Ct. 2749 (2006), *Rasul* 542 U.S. 466 (2004), and *Hamdi* 542 U.S. 507 (2004).
2. *See*, "Placing of United States Armed Forces under United Nations Operational or Tactical Control," Office of Legal Counsel, Department of Justice, Memorandum for Alan J. Kreczko, Special Assistant to the President and Legal Advisor to the National Security Council, May 8, 1996. Available at http://www.usdoj.gov/olc/hr3308.htm.
3. "No Senator or Representative shall, during the Time for which he was elected, be appointed to any civil Office under the Authority of the United States, which shall have been created, or the Emoluments whereof shall have been encreased during such time;" Article I, Section 6.
4. Section 5(b), The War Powers Resolution, P.L. 93–148 (1973), 50 U.S.C. §§1541–1548.
5. Ibid., Sec. 3.
6. *Curtiss-Wright Export Corp. v. United States*, 299 U.S. 304, 312 (1936).
7. Ibid., at 320.
8. See, *Restatement of the Law Third*, The American Law Institute, *The Foreign Relations Law of the United States*, Vol. 1, pp. 72–73.
9. *Youngstown*, ibid., at 587 (Justice Black concurring).
10. Ibid., at 643–44 (Justice Jackson concurring).
11. Ibid., at 654.
12. Ibid., at 662 (Justice Clark concurring).
13. Ibid., at 610–11 (Justice Frankfurter concurring).
14. Ibid., at 629 (Justice Douglas concurring).
15. Ibid., at 653 (Justice Jackson concurring).
16. Ibid., at 682 (Justice Vinson dissenting).
17. Ibid., at 634 (Justice Jackson concurring).
18. Ibid., at 641.
19. Ibid., at 593 (Justice Frankfurter concurring).
20. Ibid., at 635–36 (Justice Jackson concurring).
21. *Dames & Moore*, at 933–934.
22. *Hamdan v. Rumsfeld, Secretary of Defense, et. al*, Slip Opinion, at 26, June 29, 2000.
23. *Youngstown*, at 634.
24. *Sierra Club v. Morton*, 450 U.S. 727, 732 (1972).
25. *See*, *Flast v. Cohen*, 392 U.S. 83 (1968)(taxpayer standing); *Schlesinger v. Reservists to Stop the War*, 418 U.S. 208 (1974)(citizen standing).
26. War Powers Resolution, Sec. 2.
27. The lead cases in this area are: *United States v. Reynolds*, 345 U.S. 1 (1953); *United States v. Nixon*, 418 U.S. 683 (1974); *Totten*, and *Doe*. See also, *Kasza v. Browner*, 133 F.3d 1159 (9th Circuit 1998), and *Tash Hepting v. AT&T Corporation*, 439 F. Supp. 2d 974 (2006) addressing a suit against AT&T arising out of the Terrorist Surveillance Program discussed in the next chapter. The lower court's opinion includes an accessible discussion of the state secrets privilege. At the time of publication, this case was pending review before the 9th Circuit.
28. *Reynolds*, at 11. The accident report was eventually released. To learn the rest of the story, *see* Barry Siegel, "The Secret of the B-29: A Daughter Discovers What Really Happened," *The Los Angeles Times*, April 19, 2004. *See also*, Scott Shane, "Invoking Secrets Privilege Becomes a More Popular Legal Tactic by U.S.," *The New York Times*, June 4, 2006.
29. *Nixon*, at 710.
30. The Classified Information Procedures Act (CIPA), P.L. 96–546, Sec. 1 (1980), 18 U.S.C. App.
31. *See*, *El-Shifa Pharmaceutical Industries Company v. United States*, 2003 WL 1342179 (Fed. Cl)

32. *Youngstown*, at 635.
33. "Disclosure of Grand Jury Matters to the President and Other Officials," Memorandum for the Attorney General from Acting Assistant Attorney General Walter Dellinger, September 21, 1993. Available at the DOJ/OLC website.
34. The Clinton Administration subsequently sought an express national security exception to the grand jury secrecy rule. However, it was not until after 9/11 that Congress included an exception in the PATRIOT Act, discussed in Chapter 5.
35. *Youngstown*, at 635 (Justice Frankfurter concurring).
36. Intelligence Authorization Act of 1991, P.L. 102–88, S. Rep. No. 102–85, at 42.
37. At the time he signed the Intelligence Authorization Act of 1991 into law, President Bush advised the chairmen of the congressional intelligence committees that as a practical matter he could not foresee a circumstance where he would withhold notification to the Congress for more than forty-eight hours after initiation of a covert action. See discussion in Chapter 6.
38. *See*, James E. Baker, "LBJ's Ghost: A Contextual Approach to Targeting Decisions and the Commander in Chief," 4 *Chi. J. Int'l Law* 407 (Fall 2003).
39. Charlie Savage, "Bush Challenges Hundreds of Laws, President Cites Powers of his Office," *The Boston Globe*, April 30, 2006; *See also*, "Presidential Authority to Decline & Execute Unconstitutional Statutes," Memorandum for Abner Mikva, Counsel to the President, November 2, 1994. Available at the DOJ-OLC website.
40. Dana Milbank, "Bush's Fumbles Spur new Talk of Oversight on Hill," *The Washington Post*, December 18, 2005; Susan Milligan, "Congress Reduces its Oversight Role, Since Clinton a Change in Focus," *The Boston Globe*, November 20, 2005.
41. Jane Mayer, "The Hidden Power," *The New Yorker*, July 3, 2006. Indeed, there is some indication that the secretary of state was not informed either.
42. A. Whitney Griswold, "The Basis of a Rule of Law," *Liberal Education and the Democratic Ideal*, Yale University Press (1959).

5. Electronic Surveillance: Constitutional Law Applied

1. *See*, Geoffrey Stone, *Perilous Times: Free Speech in Wartime* (W. W. Norton, 2004).
2. *See*, Robert L. Benson, *The Venona Story*, Center for Cryptologic History, National Security Agency (1996) and additional background available at http://www.nsa.gov/history/ (accessed October 2006); see also, National Security Agency, Resources from the Federation of American Scientists at http://www.fas.org/irp/nsa/ (accessed June 2006).
3. CRS 13 quoting Vol. 2, page 12. S.Rep. No. 95-604(I), 1978 U.S.C.C.A.N. 3904-9.
4. *Final Report of the Select Committee to Study Gov't Operations with Respect to Intelligence Activities*. S.Rep. No. 94-755, at 314–15 (1976).
5. 50 U.S.C. §403–4a. The Director of National Intelligence was added to this section in 2004. See, §104A of the "Intelligence Reform and Terrorism Prevention Act of 2004," P.L. 108–458.
6. 50 U.S.C. §413.
7. By negative legislative history, I mean the absence of a legislative response to an executive interpretation of the law. See, *Willenbring v. Neurater*, 48 M.J. 152, 174 (1997).
8. *See*, Memorandum for the Secretary of State and the Secretary of Defense from President Truman, "Communications Intelligence Activities," October 24, 1952, available at http://jya.com/nas102452.htm. (accessed October 23, 2006).
9. *Totten, Administrator v. United States*, 92 U.S. 105, 106 (1876).
10. Ibid, at 106.
11. *Tenet et al. V. Doe et Ux*, 544 U.S. 1, 8 (2005).
12. *C. & S. Air Lines v. Waterman S. S. Corp.*, 333 U.S. 103, 111 (1948): "The President, both as Commander in Chief and as the Nation's organ for foreign affairs, has available intelligence services whose reports are not and ought not to be published to the world. It would be intolerable that courts, without the relevant information, should review and perhaps nullify actions of the Executive taken on information properly held secret." This language, of course, might pertain to a number of circumstances including questions of standing, justiciability generally, and state secrets claims.

13. *See, e.g., Nixon, Reynolds, Egan,* as well as *CIA v. Sims,* 471 U.S. 159 (1985), and *Snepp v. United States,* 444 U.S. 507 (1980). For a summary of cases relevant to national security law and the intelligence function see "Suggested Readings" in *Regulating Covert Action.*

14. *Olmstead v. United States,* 277 U.S. 438 (1928).

15. *Katz v. United States,* 389 U.S. 347, 351 (1967).

16. Consider the Court's statement: "To read the Constitution more narrowly is to ignore the vital role that the public telephone has come to play in private communication." Ibid., at 352.

17. Ibid., at 353, 359.

18. Ibid., at 258, quoting *Beck v. State of Ohio,* 379 U.S. 89, 96 (1964).

19. *See,* Title 18 U.S.C. Chapter 119.

20. *See,* Title 18 U.S.C. Chapter 206. A pen register is defined as "a device or process which records or decodes dialing, routing, addressing, or signaling information transmitted by an instrument or facility from which a wire or electronic communication is transmitted, provided however, that such information shall not include the contents of any communication." 18 U.S.C. §3127(3).

21. A trap or trace device "means a device or process which captures the incoming electronic or other impulses which identify the originating number or other dialing, routing, addressing, and signaling information . . . provided however, that such information shall not include the contents of any communication." 18 U.S.C. §3127(4).

22. Where one party to a conversation consents to its monitoring, for example, when a witting actor calls an unwitting actor to elicit incriminating statements or admissions during a telephone conversation.

23. 18 U.S.C. §2518(6).

24. For a discussion of probable cause and the Fourth Amendment generally *see* a *Katz; Brinegar v. United States,* 338 U.S. 160, 175–76 (1949); and *In re Sealed Case Nos. 02-001, 02-002,* 310 F.3d 717 (For. Int. Sur. Ct. of Rev. 2002).

25. *Brinegar,* at 175–76.

26. 18 U.S.C. §3123(a)(1).

27. *See, e.g., In re Application of the United States for an Order for Prospective Cell Site Location Information on a Certain Cellular Telephone, F. Supp. 2d_,* 2006 WL 3016316 (S.D.N.Y. October 23, 2006)(addressing and upholding the application of pen register authority to disclose cell site location and therefore track the location of the subject).

28. *United States v. United States District Court for the Eastern District of Michigan, Southern Division, et. al.; Lawrence Robert 'Pun' Plamandon et al., Real Parties in Interest,* 407 U.S. 297 (1972). The case is known colloquially as "the Keith Case" after the presiding district court judge.

29. Ibid. at 321–22. "We emphasize . . . the scope of our decision. As stated at the outset, this case involves only the domestic aspects of national security. We have not addressed and express no opinion as to, the issues that may be involved with respect to activities of foreign powers or their agents . . . Moreover, we do not hold that the same type of standards and procedures prescribed by Title III are necessarily applicable to this case."

30. Ibid., at 320.

31. *Report to the President by the Commission on CIA Activities Within the United States,* Washington: GPO, June 1975 (Rockefeller Commission Report), available at http://history-matters.com/archive/church/rockcomm/html/Rockefeller (accessed November 2006); by the United States Senate Select Committee to Study Governmental Operations with Respect to Intelligence Activities (Church Committee). Sections of the Committee's fourteen reports are available online, including "Alleged Assassination Plots Involving Foreign Leaders, An Interim Report" (1975), which can be found at http://history-matters.com/archive/church/reports (accessed November 2006); Recommendations of the Final Report of the House Select Committee on Intelligence, House Report No. 94-833 (Washington: GPO, 1976) (Pike Committee).

32. Henry R. Appelbaum, "In Memoriam: Vernon Walters – Renaissance Man," *Studies in Intelligence* at https://www.cia.gov/csi/studies/vol46no1 (accessed October 2006).

33. *See*, Letter from Attorney General Eliot Richardson to Lt. Gen. Lew Allen, Director National Security Agency, October 1, 1973, available at The National Security Archive, "Wiretap Debate Déjà Vu." George Washington University, http://www.gwu.edu/~nsarchiv/NSAEBB/NSAEBB178/index.htm (accessed September 16, 2006). (Although the Attorney General stated "I will communicate with you further on this in the near future," it is not clear from the unclassified record as to what subsequent guidance was provided.)
34. Memorandum for the President, From Philip Buchen, "Legislation on Electronic Surveillance for Foreign Intelligence Purposes," March 15, 1976. National Security Archives.
35. *Alleged Assassination Plots*, at 285.
36. This is tragically illustrated with reference to the NSA interception of communications on 9/10/01 stating among other things "Tomorrow is zero hour" and "The Match begins tomorrow." The communications were not translated and disseminated until 9/12/01. "Justice may probe leaked pre-9/11 intercepts," CNN.com. http://archives.cnn.com/2002/US/06/20/911.warning (accessed October 10, 2006). Allen Lengel and Dana Priest, "Investigators Concluded Shelby Leaked Messages," *The Washington Post*, August 5, 2004. Mary Lawton, the first director of the Office of Intelligence Policy and Review, illustrated this point with reference to a surveillance operation conducted over a weekend that recorded a murder by the target of a family member. The tape was not reviewed until the following Monday.
37. DNI Negroponte quoted in Arnaud de Borchgrave, "Network of Danger Zones," *Washington Times*, September 30, 2006. The NSA is reported to consume 650 million intercepts worldwide per day, only a fraction of which are reviewed by analysts. Michael Hirsh, "The NSA's Overt Problem: So Many Conversations, So Few Clues to the Terrorist's Chatter," *The Washington Post*, January 1, 2006.
38. See generally the documents available at National Security Archives.
39. For a helpful research site on the Act, visit Federation of American Scientists, "Foreign Intelligence Surveillance Act," (http://www.fas.org/irp/agency/doj/fisa/index.html. (last accessed September 19, 2006).
40. *Public Papers of the Presidents of the United States*, Administration of Jimmy Carter 1978, "Foreign Intelligence Surveillance Act of 1978, Statement on Signing S. 1566 into Law, October 25, 1978.
41. 50 U.S.C. §1804(a)(4)(A).
42. 50 U.S.C. §1801(b)(2).
43. *In re: Sealed Case No. 02-001*, United States Foreign Intelligence Surveillance Court of Review, November 18, 2002.
44. 50 U.S.C. §1842 (b)(2)
45. A roster for the FISC and the Court of Review can be found at http://www.fas.org/irp/agency/doj/fisa/court2006.html.
46. 50 U.S.C. §1805(f)(2)
47. 50 U.S.C. §1809.
48. 18 U.S.C. §2511(2)(f). The references are to Chapter 118 and 206 of Title 18.
49. *But see*, Correspondence between Daniel Bryant, Assistant Attorney General, Office of Legislative Affairs, and James F. Sensenbrenner, Jr., Chairman, Committee on the Judiciary, U.S. House of Representatives, July 26, 2002; August 26, 2002; and September 20, 2002. http://www.fas.org/irp/news/2002/10/doj101702.html
50. Letter from William E. Moschella, Assistant Attorney General, Office of Legislative Affairs, to Speaker Dennis Hastert, April 28, 2006, available at Federation of American Scientists, "Foreign Intelligence Surveillance Act," (http://www.fas.org/irp/agency/doj/fisa/index.html.
51. The annual FISA reports are available on the FAS FISA site.
52. Hon. Royce Lamberth, "The Role of the Judiciary in the War on Terrorism," speech to the University of Texas Alumni Association, April 13, 2002, available at http://www.pbs.org/wgbh/pages/frontline/shows/sleeper/tools/lamberth.html (accessed November 2006). *See also, In Re: Sealed Case Nos. 02-001, 02-002*, The Foreign Intelligence Surveillance Court of Review, 310 F.3d 717 (2002); but see, Interim Report on FBI Oversight in the 107th Congress by the Senate Judiciary Committee: FISA Implementation Failures,

Senator Patrick Leahy, Senator Charles Grassley, Senator Arlen Specter, February 2003, available at http://www.fas.org/irp/congress/2003_rpt/fisa.html (accessed July 2003); Report to Congress on Implementation of Section 1001 of the USA PATRIOT Act, Office of the Inspector General, Department of Justice, March 8, 2006 (reporting on complaints received, overruns, and overcollections involving electronic surveillance). Available at http://www.usdoj.gov/oig/special/s0603/index.htm.

53. See wiretap reports at www.uscourts.gov/library/statistical reports.html (viewed November 14, 2006). The statistics do not indicate what percentage, if any, of the orders are subsequently challenged by suppression motions and what percentage of suppression motions are sustained.

54. Jim McGee and Brian Duffy, "Someone to Watch Over Us," The Washington Post Magazine, June 23, 1996.

55. The Washington Post Magazine; In Re: Sealed Case, footnote 15, noting that "the primary proponent of procedures that cordoned off criminal investigators and prosecutors from those officers with counterintelligence responsibilities was the deputy counsel of OIPR... He [subsequently] left the Department and became the Legal Advisor to the FISA court."

56. 50 U.S.C. §1805(c)(1)(D).

57. See e.g., Final Report, Attorney General's Review Team on the Handling of the Los Alamos National Laboratory Investigation, May 2000, (the Bellows Report), declassified version available at FAS website, Ibid.; The 9/11 Commission Report: Final Report of the National Commission on Terrorist Attacks Upon the United States (New York: W. W. Norton, 2004), at 271–276.

58. Court of Review, at 10. "Memorandum to: Assistant Attorney General Criminal Division, et al., From The Attorney General, Subject: Procedures for Contacts Between the FBI and the Criminal Division Concerning Foreign Intelligence and Foreign Counterintelligence Investigations," July 19, 1995, available at FAS website.

59. Although originally given a sunset date (a date-specific limitation on the duration of the amendment) this segment of the PATRIOT Act became permanent law in 2005.

60. The Uniting and Strengthening America by Providing Appropriate Tools Required to Intercept and Obstruct Terrorism Act, USA PATRIOT Act, P.L. 107-56, October 25, 2001, §203.

61. In Re all matters submitted to the Foreign Intelligence Surveillance Court, 218 F. Supp. 2d 611 (2002).

62. Court of Review, at 729.

63. Ibid., at 735.

64. Ibid., at 746.

65. James Risen and Eric Lichtblau "Bush Lets U.S. Spy on Callers Without Courts," The New York Times, December 16, 2005.

66. "The NSA Program to Detect and Prevent Terrorist Attacks: Myth v. Reality," at 2, U.S. Department of Justice, Office of Public Affairs, January 27, 2006.

67. See, Tash Hepting v. AT&T Corporation citing to press reports and statements about an alleged "second NSA program in which BellSouth Corp, Verizon Communications Inc and AT&T were alleged to have provided telephone calling records of tens of millions of Americans to the NSA.... The article did not allege that the NSA listens to or records conversations but rather that [the companies] gave the government access to a database of domestic communications records that the NSA uses 'to analyze calling patterns in an effort to detect terrorist activity.'"

68. Eric Lichtblau and David Sanger, "Administration Cites War Vote in Spying Case," The New York Times, December 20, 2005.

69. Charlie Savage, "Wiretaps Said to Sift All Overseas Contacts," The Boston Globe, December 23, 2005.

70. Douglas Jehl, "Spy Briefings Failed to meet Legal Test, Lawmakers Say," The New York Times, December 21, 2005.

71. Risen & Lichtblau, note 65.

72. For a detailed exposition of some of the arguments that might be made see e.g., Department of Justice, "Legal Authorities Supporting the Activities of the National Security Agency Described by the President," January 19, 2006, available at www.findlaw.com (accessed November 2006); letter to Congress from fourteen constitutional scholars and former government officials, February 2, 2006, available at www.findlaw.com. (accessed January 2006). Clearly, a lawyer briefing the president or national security advisor would not have the opportunity to cover all of the substance contained in these lengthy opinions. The critical national security law skill is determining the essential information to brief in the allocated time.

73. "Where is the Courage to Walk Away?" *Marine Corps Times*, Opinion, August 22, 2005.

74. R. Jeffrey Smith, "Worried CIA Officers Buy Legal Insurance," *The Washington Post*, September 11, 2006.

75. Letter from the Attorney General to Senator Patrick Leahy, Chairman of the Committee on the Judiciary, United States Senate, and Senator Spector, Ranking Minority Member, January 17, 2007 (as posted on *The New York Times* website and accessed January 18, 2007).

76. *See*, Eric Lichtblau and David Johnston, "Court to Oversee U.S. Wiretapping in Terror Cases," *The New York Times*, January 18, 2007; Dan Eggen, "Court Will Oversee Wiretap Program," *The Washington Post*, January 18, 2007.

6. National Security Process

1. *The Federalist Papers*, No. 8: Alexander Hamilton, "The Effects of Internal War in Producing Standing Armies and Other Institutions Unfriendly to Liberty."

2. The military term of art for a chain of command where each level of command reports to a single superior up to the president, thus defining responsibility for making decisions and accountability for the subsequent conduct of operations. See, The Principles of War, *U.S. Army Field Manual 100-5*: "Unity of command means that all the forces are under one responsible commander. It requires a single commander with the requisite authority to direct all forces in pursuit of a unified purpose." There are a number of books discussing problems with a dual chain of command for political and military decisions during the Iraq war, see e.g., Michael R. Gordon & Bernard E. Trainor, *Cobra I: The Inside Story of the Invasion and Occupation of Iraq* (Pantheon: 2004).

3. The Goldwater-Nichols Department of Defense Reorganization Act of 1986, Pub. L. No. 99-433, discussed in Chapter 8.

4. To the extent the president is addressing the structure and composition of his own *immediate* staff within the Executive Office of the President, as a matter of separation of powers doctrine, he is free to do so as he sees fit without congressional direction. So too, the president can determine with whom he meets. Thus, Congress provided that the chairman and DCI may, subject to the direction of the president, attend and participate in meetings of the NSC. In the words of Frank Carlucci, "The genius of the legislation is that it creates a structure that's totally flexible." Forum on the Role of the National Security Advisor, Woodrow Wilson International Center for Scholars, Washington, D.C. April 12, 2001. A transcript is available at http://webcast.rice.edu/speeches/20010412secadv.html (accessed October 27, 2005).

5. Compare, for example, the relative styles of Gen. Hayden, William Webster, George Tenet, and William Casey.

6. President George W. Bush, National Security Presidential Directive 1, "Organization of the National Security Council System," February 13, 2001.

7. President William J. Clinton, Presidential Decision Directive 2, "Organization of the National Security Council," January 20, 1993.

8. *See, Armstrong v. Executive Office of the President*, 90 F.3d 553(D.C. Cir. 1996), cert. denied, 520 U.S. 1239 (1997).

9. NSPD-1 lists as regular Principals Committee attendees the secretary of state, the secretary of the treasury, the secretary of defense, the chief of staff to the president, and the APNSA. The DCI (now DNI), the chairman of the Joint Chiefs of Staff, the attorney general, and the director of the Office of Management and Budget are listed as attendees for meetings pertaining to their responsibilities. The NSPD includes additional members, such as USTR and Commerce, when international economic issues are on the agenda. The directive also states that the president's chief of staff and the national security advisor to the vice president shall attend all meetings of the committee, as will the deputy national security advisor, who serves as executive secretary. The counsel to the president shall attend any meeting, in consultation with the APNSA, he deems appropriate. PDD-2 establishing the PC for the previous administration included comparable membership, but also included the U.S. representative to the United Nations, but did not include the chief of staff to the vice president. In practice, members of the Principals Committee and the Deputies Committee may choose not to attend a particular meeting, and officials who are not designated members of these committees will often attend when needed.

10. NSPD-1.

11. "Forum on the Role of the National Security Advisor," comments of Samuel R. Berger,

12. *See, e.g.*, Memorandum for Condoleeza Rice, From Richard A. Clarke, "Presidential Policy Initiative/Review – The Al Qida Network," January 25, 2001, requesting "a Principals level review on the al Qida network." Available at http://www.gwu.edu/ñsarchiv/nsaebb/nsaebb147/index.htm (accessed November 2006).

13. Put directly, it may not be an efficient use of the president's time to participate in meetings developing policy options until those options are sufficiently defined for decision. Moreover, at the policy development stage, policymakers may alter the manner of their input in the presence of the president by toning down criticism of alternate views or seeking to anticipate the president's own view and arriving there first.

Typically, following a decision-making Principals Meeting, the president will be briefed orally (usually by the assistant to the president for national security affairs, a.k.a. the national security advisor), or in writing using either an information or action/decision memorandum. By volume, the majority of presidential decisions are likely to be made in writing; however, much of the most significant work occurs in meetings with the national security team, or with select members from the team, meaning in practice the national security advisor.

14. *See* http://www.fas.org/irp/offdocs for a list of presidential directives and online access to publicly available directives.

15. The statutory language is important because it precludes military officers from serving in the position of executive secretary to the council. It also serves as a legal basis, (i.e., distinction,) for the executive secretary to testify before the Congress regarding the budgetary needs of the NSC as an institution, whereas neither the executive secretary nor NSC staff generally will testify before the Congress on policy matters.

16. Senior directors are, in theory, equivalent in grade to departmental assistant secretaries, without of course having been through the confirmation process. But that is like saying a member of the Senior Executive Service (SES) is equivalent to a general. Only a general is a general, as only generals and soldiers well know. Personality and background also play a large part in determining just where a member of the NSC staff fits into the government.

17. *See*, Jim Rutenberg and David Sanger, "Overhaul Moves White House Data Center into Modern Era," *The New York Times*, December 19, 2006.

18. Under President Nixon and President Ford, the professional staff numbered fifty and under President Carter, thirty five. John Tower, et al., *Report of the President's Special Review Board*, II-4 (1987)(Tower Commission Report).

19. *See*, C. Northcote Parkinson, *Parkinson's Law, and Other Studies in Administration* (Cutchogue, New York: Buccaneer Books, 1957).

20. At the outset of his first administration, President Clinton announced a 25 percent reduction in the size of the White House staff including the NSC staff; however, this directive was implemented with a series of lawful, but creative methods to find slots that did not

count against the personnel cap, such as career training programs and certain details from agencies. In the Bush Administration, some functions previously assigned to the NSC, like public health, are now handled by the Homeland Security Staff, also located within the Executive Office of the President.

21. One test of this balance is the amount of travel performed by the NSC staff independent of the president's and national security advisor's own travel. An NSC staff that has time to travel apart from presidential missions may be moving away from its core mission of advising and assisting the president.

22. This is essential, because in most cases it must be done on faith where the written views of Principals are not attached to presidential memos. Therefore, NSC staff are constrained in sharing drafts of presidential memoranda with agencies, which could become subject to FOIA requests as agency records retained by agencies. Unlike national security agencies, the National Security Council is not subject to the Freedom of Information Act (FOIA). *Armstrong v. Executive Office of the President*, 90 F.3d 553 (D.C. Cir. 1996).

    Further, records in agency possession are subject to a different quantum of constitutional review when possible claims of executive privilege are evaluated in response to congressional requests for documents. In short, agency personnel tend to be less sensitive (or zealous depending on how one looks at it) about protecting the president's deliberative process than White House lawyers are. In fairness, participants in the presidential decision-making process might well be less candid if they knew their views, particularly in draft, would become public knowledge. Participants might eschew the controversial option with an eye toward the public's response.

    For a remarkable appreciation of the potential subtle influence of public disclosure on internal advice, see General George Marshall's response to George Washington's and Robert E. Lee's biographer, Douglas Southall Freeman. Asked by Freeman in 1942 whether he was "putting away anywhere any memoranda of these tremendous days," Marshall had an aide respond, "My policy has been not to do this, for two reasons:

    In the first place it tends to cultivate a state of mind unduly concerned with possible investigations, rather than a complete concentration on the business of victory. Further, it continually introduces the factor of one's own reputation, the future appreciation of one's daily decisions, which leads I feel, subconsciously to self-deception or hesitations in reaching decisions."

    Quoted in *The Papers of George Catlett Marshall*, Vol. 3, at 207–08, (Baltimore: The Johns Hopkins University Press, 1991). Readers can judge for themselves whether future and present advisors to presidents have adhered to the Marshall norm.

23. The Executive Office of the President comprises the president's immediate staff offices. A list of the constituent parts is found at http://www.whitehouse.gov/government/eop.html (accessed November 13, 2006); however, this list does not include the NSC staff, which is, in fact, part of the EOP. The EOP staff occupies the West Wing, the Old Executive Office Building, the New Executive Office Building, as well as other outlying buildings in the neighborhood of the White House and elsewhere. The president's most immediate senior advisors serve in the White House Office. The staff has grown from the days prior to the Second World War when the State, War, and Navy Department's occupied the Old Executive Office Building (OEOB). On the eve of Pearl Harbor, it is to the OEOB that Japanese diplomats came to call on Secretary of State Cordell Hull.

24. The OLC website includes a number of opinions on the subject.

25. National Security Advisors Forum. However, Brezinski also noted that some foreign governments, especially authoritarian governments, perceive statements emanating from the NSC staff and White House as more authentic expressions of presidential commitment than statements originating with the State Department.

26. 5 U.S.C. §§7321–7326, 5 U.S.C. §7301 note; see also, "Hatch Act for Federal Employees," U.S. Office of Special Counsel. Available at http://www.osc.gov/ha_fed.htm. (Viewed November 14, 2006).

27. For example, an active duty military officer serving as the APNSA or a DAPNSA would be subject to the limitations applicable to active duty military officers.

28. Glenn Kessler, "Rice Bucks Tradition with Pre-Election Appearances," *The Washington Post*, November 4, 2006; Glenn Kessler, "Rice Hitting the Road to Speak, National Security Advisor's Trips to Swing States Break Precedent," *The Washington Post*, October 20, 2004.

29. In the Clinton Administrations it was the National Security Council Legal Advisor's responsibility to uphold, and if necessary, enforce the Hatch Act. In Frank Carlucci's view, it is the chief of staff's role and not the national security advisor's to raise domestic political factors. National Security Advisors Forum.

30. 9/11 Commission Report, at 132.

31. Ibid., at 132.

32. I was asked to brief the president on a 10 to 15-page memorandum I had written under the national security advisor's signature. I noticed immediately that the president had highlighted the document throughout, stuck post-its at certain passages and covered the document with marginal notes. The depth of the questioning was consistent with the paperwork.

33. Jane Mayer, "The Hidden Power," *The New Yorker*, July 3, 2006.

34. The president may, of course, do this in an anticipatory manner, as in the case of authorizing U.S. forces to respond in self-defense.

35. *See* J. Baker, "When Lawyers Advise Presidents in Wartime: Kosovo and the Law of Armed Conflict," *Naval War College Review*, Winter 2002.

36. In this way, for example, the sometime maligned war powers reports that are required by the War Powers Resolution within 48 hours of a triggering event, but are considered by some as ministerial, can serve a useful procedural function, even if the events reported on have been carried in the media for the proceeding 48 hours. Sincerely addressed, the reporting elements cause executive officials to consider issues such as the duration of stay and the potential for reinforcement at the outset of a deployment and to articulate their best judgments, at least internally, in a manner they are willing to put in writing to the president. This can result in a lowest-common denominator consensus external product, but it also can generate timely consideration of difficult policy issues within the executive branch that otherwise might initially be avoided. For a further discussion of this line of argument, see Chapter 8.

37. Ralph Wetterhahn, *The Last Battle*, at 97–99 (New York: Plume, 2001).

7. Intelligence

1. *See, Intelligence in the War of Independence*, Central Intelligence Agency, undated (on file with the author and available from the Office of Public Affairs, CIA); P. K. Rose, "The Founding Fathers of American Intelligence," Center for the Study of Intelligence, Central Intelligence Agency, 1999 available at https://www.cia.gov/csi/books/940299/art-1.html (accessed November 2006).

2. Stephen F. Knott, *Secret and Sanctioned: Covert Operations and the American Presidency* (New York: Oxford University Press, 1996).

3. Although in a context where oversight was informal and conversational, I am skeptical of advocates on either side of this issue who argue in absolutes.

4. *See, Secret and Sanctioned*, and *Regulating Covert Action*.

5. *E.g.*, Joseph E. Persico, *Roosevelt's Secret War: FDR and World War II Espionage* (New York: Random House, 2001).

6. This is not the conventional wisdom, which posits that the CIA director was demoted.

7. *See*, Federation of American Scientists website.

8. *See*, The 9/11 Commission Report, pp. 419–423; *The Commission on the Intelligence Capabilities of the United States Regarding Weapons of Mass Destruction, Report to the President of the United States*, Washington: U.S. Government Printing Office, 2005, pp. 337–341.

9. Intelligence Reform and Terrorism Prevention Act of 2004, P.L. 108–458, December 17, 2004, §102(b)(Intelligence Reform Act).

10. National Security Act of 1947, as amended, Section 103(a). 50 U.S.C. §403–3.

11. Intelligence Reform Act, §102(f)(4).

12. Intelligence Reform Act, §§104A (d)(1)-(4).

13. National Security Act, §103(d)(5). This language was amended in 2004 to "perform such other functions and duties related to intelligence affecting national security as the president or the Director of National Intelligence may direct." Intelligence Reform Act, at §104(d)(4).

14. Intelligence Reform Act, §1016. See also, Executive Order 13388, "Further Strengthening the Sharing of Terrorism Information to Protect Americans," October 25, 2005.

15. For a reference to known and in some cases declassified or summarized presidential national security directives see, Federation of American Scientists, Intelligence Resource Program, http://www.fas.org/irp/offdocs/direct.htm (accessed October 25, 2006).

16. *Foreign and Military Intelligence*, Book 1, at 425, *Final Report of the Select Committee to Study Governmental Operations with Respect to Intelligence Activities* (Washington: GPO, 1976).

17. See *Regulating Covert Action*, at 69–71, 126–7.

18. In January 2007, the House established a Select Intelligence Oversight Panel of the Committee on Appropriations, with membership drawn from the Appropriations Committee and three members from the Permanent Select Committee on Intelligence. In theory, the subcommittee is intended to better integrate and fuse the authorization and appropriations functions, a process previously addressed by having members of the Select Committee on Intelligence serve concurrently on the Appropriations and Armed Services Committees. See, H. Res. 35, January 9, 2007.

19. In 1995, the position of Associate Director for Military Support, filled by an officer of flag rank, was created to ensure a military perspective was available to the DCI (and subsequently the director of the CIA) and to facilitate the provision of intelligence to the Defense Department and in particular the military joint forces commander.

20. Section 103A(c)(1) and (3). Note the different constitutional treatment of these provisions. Where Congress has express constitutional authority to raise armies etc., and thus in its view can directly regulate the number of officers on active duty serving in designated billets, the Congress's authority to determine the qualifications of the president's immediate advisors is less direct. *Myers v. United States*, 272 U.S. 52(1926).

21. In general, strategic intelligence informs national policy and plans, whereas tactical intelligence is directed to specific policy implementation or military operations and plans. Likewise, strategic warning focuses on identifying trends and the emergence of threats to policymakers, whereas tactical warning focuses on specific incidents. *See, e.g.,* the *DOD Dictionary of Military and Associated Terms* online for the Department's definitions.

22. *Congressional Research Service*, "Director of National Intelligence: Statutory Authorities," April 11, 2005, p. 2; Commission on Roles and Capabilities of the Intelligence Community, p. 45, available at http://www.access.gpr.gov/intelligence/int/pdf/report.html (accessed 14 March 2006).

23. The National Security Strategy of the United States of America, March 2006, states: "First, our intelligence must improve: The President and the Congress have taken steps to reorganize and strengthen the U.S. intelligence community. A single, accountable leader of the intelligence community with authorities to match his responsibilities, and increased sharing of information and increased resources, are helping realize this objective." At 24. Available at http://www.whitehouse.gov/nsc/nss/2006 (Accessed November 2006).

24. For a review of the intelligence community visit the ODNI website at http://www.dni.gov/. See also, Daniel B. Silver (updated and revised by Frederick Hitz and Shreve Ariail) "Intelligence and Counterintelligence," in Moore and Turner, *National Security Law*; Jeffrey Richelson, *The U.S. Intelligence Community*, 4th Ed., (Boulder, CO: Westview Press, 1999).

25. A more bureaucratic definition might include information relevant to national security derived from intelligence sources and methods.

26. See the ODNI website for descriptions of the six basic intelligence sources or disciplines: Signals Intelligence (SIGINT), Imagery Intelligence (IMINT), Measurement and Signature Intelligence (MASINT), Human-Source Intelligence (HUMINT), Open-Source Intelligence

(OSINT), and Geospatial Intelligence. I also recommend, Frederick P. Hitz, *The Great Game: The Myth and Reality of Espionage* (New York: Alfred A. Knopf, 2004).

27. Originally codified in Section 103(d)(1) (50 U.S.C. §403-3) of the National Security Act, now found in section 104A(d)(1) of the Intelligence Reform Act, 50 U.S.C. §403-4a.

28. Some methods of intelligence collection necessarily will have an effect both at home and abroad, such as the interception of a communication as discussed in Chapter 5, which may have both an overseas and domestic nexus.

29. *See, e.g.,* Surveillance Court of Review.

30. Patrick Radden Keefe, "Big Brother and the Bureaucrats," *The New York Times*, August 10, 2005.

31. For an uncommon look into the mix of intelligence collection directed at a particular tactical and strategic question, *see*, Remarks by George Tenet, Director of Central Intelligence, at Georgetown University, February 5, 2004. http://www.cia.gov/cia/public_affairs/speeches/2004/tenet_georgetownspeech_02052004.html

32. *See, Williamson v. United States*, 512 U.S. 594 (1994).

33. *See* De Borchgrave, "Network of Danger Zones," and Hirsh, "NSA's Overt Problem,"; Former Deputy Director and Acting Director of Central Intelligence John McLaughlin has said, "In the Cold War, we struggled to get data. Today, the problem is that there is too much data – more than we can handle." Quoted in David Kaplan and Kevin Whitelaw, "Remaking U.S. Intelligence," *U.S. News & World Report*, November 13, 2006. Kaplan and Whitelaw report that 30% of the imagery collected by U.S. agencies goes unexamined and that many of the 50,000 IC analytical reports per year go unread by critical policymakers.

34. Kevin Whitelaw, "The Eye of the Storm," *U.S. News & World Report*, October 29, 2006.

35. For an unclassified look at an NIE summary *see*, Declassified Key Judgments of the National Intelligence Estimate 'Trends in Global Terrorism: Implications for the United States dated April 2006, available at David Sanger, "Study Doesn't Share Bush's Optimism on Terror Fight," *The New York Times*, September 27, 2006, available at http://www.nytimes.com/2006/09/27/ (accessed November 2006).

36. 50 U.S.C. §§403-1 and 403-3, as amended by the Intelligence Reform Act.

37. E.g., the Counterintelligence and Security Enhancements Act of 1994, Pub. L. 103–359, 50 U.S.C. 401 note. See also, Michael J. Woods, "Counterintelligence and Access to Transactional Records: A Practical History of USA PATRIOT Act Section 215," 37 *Journal of National Security Law and Policy*, Vol. 1 (2005).

38. "Report on the Covert Activities of the Central Intelligence Agency," Sept. 30, 1954 (Doolittle Committee).

39. Covert action is one of the five intelligence functions along with collection, analysis & dissemination, liaison, and counterintelligence. R. Gates, "The CIA and Foreign Policy," *Foreign Affairs*, Winter 1987/88, (Vol. 66, No. 2, 1987), p. 216.

40. For an historical overview, *see*, G. Treverton, *Covert Action: The Limits of Intervention in the Postwar World* (New York: Basic Books, 1987); and, M. Reisman and J. Baker, *Regulating Covert Action* (New Haven: Yale University Press, 1992).

41. In addition to the president's constitutional authority, covert action was undertaken pursuant to §102(d)(5) of the National Security Act, "it shall be the duty of the Agency, under the direction of the National Security Council . . . (5) to perform such other functions and duties relating to intelligence affecting the national security as the National Security Council may from time to time direct." Church, Foreign and Military Intelligence, at 131; Reisman & Baker, *Regulating Covert Action*, p. 118.

42. 22 U.S.C. §2422 (repealed).

43. 50 U.S.C. §413b(e)(2006).

44. 50 U.S.C. §§413b(e)(1)(2)(3) and (4)(2006).

45. *Senate Report No. 102-85*, "Legislative History, Intelligence Authorization Act of 1990," P.L. 102–88, p. 235.

46. For a discussion of the etymology of the phrase "national security" *see*, M. Shulman, "The Progressive Era Origins of the National Security Act," *104 Dick. L. Rev. 289* (Winter 2000).

47. 50 U.S.C. §413b(a)(2006).

48. 50 U.S.C. §413b(c)(1)(2006).

49. 50 U.S.C. §413b(c)(2)(2006).

50. 50 U.S.C. §413b(c)(3)(2006).

51. Senate Report 102-85, at 233, quoting the text of a letter sent to the Chairmen of the Senate and House Intelligence Committees. "Dear Mr. Chairman: I am aware of your concerns regarding the provision of notice to Congress of covert action.... I anticipate that in almost all instances, prior notice will be possible. In those rare instances where prior notice is not provided, I anticipate that notice will be provided within a few days. Any withholding beyond this period will be based upon my assertion of authorities granted to this office by the Constitution." For an example of an instance when a president might withhold notification occurring before these provisions were enacted see, S. Turner. "Covert Common Sense: Don't Throw the CIA out with the Ayatollah," *The Washington Post*, Nov. 23, 1986.

52. *Senate Report No. 102-85*, "Legislative History, Intelligence Authorization Act of 1990," P.L. 102-88, p. 234.

53. President Ronald Reagan, *National Security Decision Directive 286, Approval and Review of Special Activities*, October 15, 1987.

54. 50 U.S.C. §413(a)(1)(2006).

55. 50 U.S.C. §413(a)(2006), as amended by the Intelligence Reform and Terrorism Prevention Act of 2004, P.L. 108–458 §1071(a)(Y).

56. President William J. Clinton, Presidential Decision Directive (PDD) 2, "Organization of the National Security Council," January 20, 1993, para. A.

57. 50 U.S.C. §513b(a)(5)(2006).

58. *The 9/11 Commission Report, Final Report of the National Commission on Terrorist Attacks Upon the United States*, New York: Norton, 2004, p. 132. See also, R. Posner, "The 9/11 Report: A Dissent," *The New York Times Book Review*, August 29, 2004.

59. September 18, 2002 Testimony before Senate and House Select Committees on Intelligence.

60. 50 U.S.C. §413b(f)(2006).

61. 50 U.S.C. §413b(a)(1).

62. This is a citation to the Chief of Mission Statute, which states: "Under the direction of the President, the chief of mission to a foreign country – (1) shall have full responsibility for the direction, coordination, and supervision of all Government executive branch employees in that country...; and (2) shall keep fully and currently informed with respect to all activities and operation of the government within that country, and shall insure that all Government executive branch employees in that country...comply fully with all applicable directives of the chief of mission...." Of course, "consistent with" is not specific as to the actual modalities and measure of detail involved.

63. Intelligence Reform Act at §102A(K), 50 U.S.C. 403–1; and §104A(f), 50 U.S.C. §403–4a.

64. *See, e.g.*, Scott Shane, "C.I.A. Role in Visit of Sudan Intelligence Chief Causes Dispute Within Administration," *The New York Times*, June 18, 2005.

65. Memorandum of Disapproval for the Intelligence Authorization Act, Fiscal Year 1991, November 30, 1990, Public Papers of the Presidents of the United States, 1990, Book II, July 1 to December 31, 1990, at 1729–30 (GPO: Washington, 1991).

66. A list of bilateral treaties is found in the note to 18 U.S.C. §3181. A list of multilateral treaties directed at international terrorism can be found at http://www.un.org/News/dh/latest/intreatterror.htm (accessed November 14, 2006).

67. See *Valentine et al. v. United States ex rel. Neidecker*, 299 U.S. 5 (1936).

68. For a list see Conventions Against Terrorism at http://www.unodc.org/unodc/terrorism_conventions.html (accessed November 2006).

69. *E.g. Collins v. Loisel*, 259 U.S. 309, 316 (1922); *Peters v. Egnor*, 888 F.2d 713, 717 (10th Cir. 1989); 18 U.S.C. §3184.

70. *E.g. United States v. Lui Kin-Hong*, 83 F.3d 523, 524 (1st Cir. 1996) (per curiam) (reversing grant of bail to Hong Kong bribery suspect); *In re Mitchell*, 171 F. 289, 289 (S.D.N.Y. 1909)(bail, but suspect to return to the Tombs at end of civil trial affecting overall situation).

71. *Neely v. Henkel*, 180 U.S. 109, 122 (1901) (Harlan, J.); *Melia v. United States*, 667 F.2d 300, 302 (2d Cir. 1981); Fed. R. Crim. P. 54(b)(5); Fed. R. Evid. 1101(d)(3).

72. 18 U.S.C. §3181(b).

73. *See* generally, *Ker v. Illinois*, 119 U.S. 436 (1886); *Frisbie v. Collins*, 342 U.S. 519 (1952); *Toscanino v. United States*, 500 F.2d 267 (2d Cir. 1974); and *United States v. Alvarez-Machain*, 504 U.S. 655 (1992). The doctrine is discussed in Reisman & Baker, *Regulating Covert Action*, pp. 128–30.

74. *Toscanino*, ibid.

75. *United States Attorney's Manual*, Section 9-15.000, available at http://www.usdoj.gov/usao/ eousa/foia-reading-room/usam/title9/15mcrm.htm (accessed November 2006).

76. *See*, *Regulating Covert Action*, at 129 and 194.

77. William K. Rashbaum and Raymond Bonner, "As 3 Nations Consulted, Terror Suspect Eluded Arrest," *The New York Times*, July 29, 2005, at A8.

78. Compare, for example, the government's comments regarding Maher Arer, Karen DeYoung, "Gonzales Revisits Deportation Remarks," *The Washington Post*, September 22, 2006.

79. *See*, *United States v. Yunis*, 681 F. Supp. 896 (D.D.C 1988); *United States v. Yunis*, 681 F. Supp., 909 (D.D.C. 1988); and *United States v. Yunis*, 867 F.2d 617 (D. C. Cir. 1989).

80. "Memorandum of Understanding Between the Government of the United Kingdom of Great Britain and Northern Ireland and the Government of the Hashemite Kingdom of Jordan Regulating the Provision of Undertakings in Respect of Specified Persons Prior to Deportation." August 10, 2005. *Online*. Available: http://newsvote.bbc.co.uk/mpapps/ pagetools/print/news.bbc.co.uk/1/hi/uk/4143214.stm (accessed 10 March 2006).

81. V. Blum. "Gaining a Foothold in Guantanamo: Defense Lawyers Want Access to Every Detainee – and Say in Prisoner Transfers." *Legal Times*, March 28, 2005.

82. *See, e.g., Khaled El-Masri v. Tenet*, 437 F. Supp. 2d 530 (E. D.Va., 2006). *See also*, Dana Priest, "Wrongful Imprisonment: Anatomy of a CIA Mistake," *The Washington Post*, December 4, 2005.

83. *Report of the Events Relating to Maher Arar*, Commission of Inquiry into the Action of Canadian Officials in Relation to Maher Arar, September 18, 2006, at 13–15. Available at http://www.ararcommission.ca/eng/index.htm (accessed November 2006). *See also*, Katherine Shrader, "CIA is Probing Mistaken 'Renditions,'" Philadelphia Inquirer, December 28, 2005.

84. Nick Wadhams, "U.N. Says Human Rights Violators Cite U.S." *The Washington Post*, October 24, 2006.

85. For a rendering of the story *see*, *Regulating Covert Action*, at 50–52.

86. Convention Against Torture and Other Cruel, Inhuman or Degrading Treatment or Punishment, 23 I.L.M. 1027 (1984) as modified, 24 I.L.M 535 (1985). See also, 18 U.S.C. §2340A, implementing the Convention in U.S. law.

87. Rome Statute of the International Criminal Court, 37 I.L.M. 999 (1998), Articles 7 and 8. The United States is not a party to the International Criminal Court.

88. *See*, "U.S. Treatment of Terror Suspects and U.S.-EU Relations," Mary Crane, Ed., Council on Foreign Relations, December 6, 2005 at www.cfr.org; Craig Whitlock, "Europeans Investigate CIA Role in Abductions," *The Washington Post*, March 13, 2005.

89. *Ker v. Illinois*, 119 U.S. 436, 444 (1886).

90. *See*, *Regulating Covert Action*, at 66–67. French agents set off two explosions, the first to scare away the crew, the second to sink the vessel. A photographer returned to the vessel after the first explosion to save his equipment and was killed by the second explosion. Postscript: In July 2005, a report written by Adm. Pierre Lacoste, at the time of the incident the head of French foreign intelligence, was published in France. In the report, Lacoste states that French President Mitterand had approved the operation, notwithstanding his denials at the time, and had done so using the vague and euphemistic language identified in the Church Committee report on U.S. assassination plots in the 1960s. "I asked him if he was authorizing me to execute the project of neutralization. He gave his agreement, stressing the importance that he attached to the nuclear tests. The authorization was sufficiently explicit." Quoted in Charles Bremner, "Mitterand Ordered Bombing of Rainbow Warrior, Spy Chief Says," *The Times*, July 11, 2005.

91. See the ODNI website for an updated list.

92. *9/11 Commission*, at 358.
93. Ibid., at 132.

8. Use of Military Force

1. In my view the "law of armed conflict" and "law of war" are interchangeable. *See, e.g.*, DOD Dictionary of Terms, "Law of War: That part of international law that regulates the conduct of armed hostilities. Also called the law of armed conflict." This is the approach taken by a majority of commentators. While admittedly burdensome as a prosaic term, I prefer the law of armed conflict, because it reflects the application of this body of law (although not necessarily every element of it) to "combat," and not just to what participants in domestic "war power" debates will recognize as an elusive category of hostilities known as "war." Many scholars and practitioners also refer to the "law of armed conflict" as "international humanitarian law." *See, e.g.*, Francoise Bouchet-Saulnier, *The Practical Guide to Humanitarian Law* (Lanham, MD: Rowman & Littlefield, 2002). I do not take issue with this as descriptive nomenclature. The law of armed conflict is international, humanitarian, and law. However, the term is not generally accepted as interchangeable with the Law of Armed Conflict. In part, this reflects a traditional division in the law between the methods and means of warfare falling under the rubric of "law of armed conflict," and Hague Convention limitations on the means and methods of force, on the one hand, and the treatment of civilians and combatants, falling under the rubric of "humanitarian law," and generally the Geneva Conventions, on the other hand. For some, the distinction takes on substantive importance where, for example, scholars and practitioners incorporate within the term "humanitarian law" concepts that may not be generally accepted by governments as encompassing part of the law of armed conflict.
2. Authorizing the president "to use all necessary and appropriate force against those nations, organizations, or persons he determines planned, authorized, committed, or aided the terrorist attacks that occurred on September 11, 2001, or harbored such organizations or persons, in order to prevent any future acts of international terrorism against the United States by such nations, organizations or persons."
3. The operative authorization is found in Section 3: "The President is authorized to use the Armed Forces of the United States as he determines to be necessary and appropriate in order to – (1) defend the national security of the United States against the continuing threat posed by Iraq; and (2) enforce all relevant United Nations Security Council resolutions regarding Iraq."
4. *See*, Eugene V. Rostow, "'Once More Unto the Breach': The War Powers Resolution Revisited, 21 *Valparaiso Univ. Law Rev*. 1, at 6, Fall 1986.
5. Ibid., at 21.
6. William Howard Taft, "The Presidency, Its Duties, Its Powers, Its Opportunities and Its Limitations," pp. 85–86, New York, Charles Scribner's Sons (1916). Note that this offense-defense distinction was argued by the plaintiffs in *Campbell v. Clinton*, 203 F.3d 19 (D.C.Cir. 2000), "Here there can be no question that the Executive's initiation of offensive military attacks against other sovereign nations 'typically' or 'often' are concluded before two years have elapsed." Reply Brief for Plaintiffs-Appellants, August 2, 1999.
7. *See*, Letter from Walter Dellinger, Assistant Attorney General, Office of Legal Counsel to Senators Dole, Simpson, Thurmond, and Cohen, September 27, 1994, regarding "the lawfulness of the president's planned deployment of United States military forces to Haiti." "Finally, after examining the circumstances, nature, scope and duration of the anticipated deployment, we determined that it was not a 'war' in the constitutional sense."
8. *See*, Louis Fisher, *Presidential War Power* (Lawrence: University Press of Kansas, 1995).
9. The War Powers Resolution, P. L. 93–148, Sec. 2 (c); 50 U.S.C. §§1541–1548.
10. See, *Campbell v. Clinton* ("Appellants fail because they continued, after the votes, to enjoy ample legislative power to have stopped prosecution of the 'war.'")
11. That is not to say that OLC always holds for the president; however, where the office is inclined to steer the president away from an option as outside the law, White House lawyers

are equally likely to steer OLC away from a definitive written product, preferring to convey advice orally or in summary fashion within policy memoranda.

12. "Instances of Use of United States Armed Forces Abroad, 1798–1989," *Congressional Research Service*, December 4, 1989, edited by Ellen Collier. See also, *Background Information on the Use of U.S. Armed Forces in Foreign Countries 1975 Revision*, Foreign Affairs Division, Congressional Research Service, Committee on International Relations, (Washington: Government Printing Office, 1975).

13. In the case of World War I the Congress declared war against Germany and Austria–Hungary; in the case of World War II Congress declared war against Japan, Germany, Italy, Bulgaria, Hungary, and Romania.

14. *See*, George Kennan, *Russia and the West Under Lenin and Stalin*, (Boston: Little, Brown, 1960).

15. Followed by more than ten years of enforcement of No Fly Zones over Northern and Southern Iraq. *See*, UNSCRs 687 and 688 (2001).

16. *See, e.g.*, Jacob Javits, *Who Makes War* (New York: Morrow, 1973).

17. President Richard Nixon, "Veto of the War Powers Resolution," October 24, 1973, Public Papers of the Presidents, 1973, at 893–895.

18. By personal recollection, the NSC legislative affairs office tallied approximately fifty sessions with members of Congress prior to the commencement of air operations.

19. The War Powers Resolution, Section 4.

20. The Resolution does not define "equipped for combat." For some time the executive branch applied an informal rule of thumb that "equipped for combat" meant armed with crew-served weapons. However, this presented an absurd hair-trigger as crew-served weapons, like machine guns and mortars, are organic to most ground units, whether or not those units anticipate hostile circumstances or are engaged in routine training or deployments.

21. Letter from the president to the Speaker of the House of Representatives and the president Pro Tempore of the Senate, September 24, 2001. This and other war powers letters are available at http://www.whitehouse.gov/news/releases.html (accessed November 1, 2006).

22. War Powers Resolution, Sec. 8(a)(1).

23. Abraham Sofaer, "The War Powers Resolution," U.S. Department of State Bulletin, November 1988. Current Policy No. 1107.

24. After *Chadha*, in which the Supreme Court held a one-house legislative veto was unconstitutional on among other grounds the absence of presentment to the president, section 5(c) is generally recognized as violating the presentment clause. Section 5(c) purports to require the president to withdraw U.S. armed forces "at any time" the Congress directs by concurrent resolution. Unlike joint resolutions, concurrent resolutions are not presented to the president for signature and do not therefore become law. Section 9 of the Resolution contains a "separability clause" stating that if any provision of the resolution is held invalid the remainder of the resolution shall not be affected.

25. *See*, Congressional Record, June 7, 1995, H5655–66, H55662–64 quoting letters from Presidents Ford, Carter, and George H. W. Bush.

26. While deciding the case on standing, District Judge Paul Friedman seemed to signal disagreement with the government's substantive argument noting, "While neither the defeat of the House concurrent resolution [which would have purported to authorize military force] nor the passage of the Appropriations Act [specifically funding Kosovo air operations] constitutes an 'authorization' within the meaning of the War Powers Resolution, congressional action on those measures is relevant to the legislative standing analysis." Footnote 9. *Campbell v. Clinton*, 52 F.Supp.2d 34, 44 n. 9 (DDC 1999).

27. The United States continuously flew combat sorties over the northern and southern Iraq no fly zones from the end of the 1990–1991 Gulf War until the second Iraq war. However, the executive branch took the view that such no fly zones were authorized pursuant to P.L. 102–1, a view conveyed to the Congress throughout this period in reports required by statute every sixty days on the implementation of the Iraq cease-fire. P.L. 102–1 stated expressly that it served as authorization for the purposes of the War Powers Resolution. With respect to Lebanon, the executive branch took the view that U.S. Marines deployed to

Lebanon were not engaged in hostilities until the barracks bombing in October 1983. The Congress subsequently passed a Joint Resolution authorizing the continued deployment of Marines to Beirut as well as a date certain for their withdrawal.

28. *Youngstown*, at 879–880.

29. *See Campbell*, (D.C. Cir. 2000) as well as *Raines v. Byrd*, 117 S. Ct. 2312 (1997).

30. *Campbell*, ibid., at 23 (D.C. Cir. 2000).

31. *See, Ginsberg & Sons, Inc. v. Popkin*, 285 U.S. 204, 208, 76 L. Ed. 704, 52 S. Ct. 322 (1932).

32. The president's inherent constitutional authority to permit troops to remain in hostilities for more than sixty/ninety days may raise a different set of foreign affairs issues than are raised by the decision to initially deploy armed forces. Moreover, Congress's authority to suspend or terminate hostilities, based on Art. I, Section 8, is not necessarily as extensive as its authority to make war. For example, the decision to terminate hostilities may more deeply implicate presidential authority in the area of foreign affairs. By eighteenth-century standards, the termination of a war would necessarily involve the president's treaty-making authority, as under international law declared wars were terminated pursuant to treaty. By further example, it is not hard to imagine that a decision not to enter a conflict would have a very different foreign relations impact than a decision to withdraw halfway through; the latter would more likely break an alliance or rupture relations with third countries left stranded, thus implicating the president's authority in the area of foreign relations, in addition to his authority as commander in chief and chief executive.

33. *See*, for example, Laws and Customs of War on Land, October 18, 1907 36 STAT 2277 (hereinafter Hague Convention IV); Convention for the Amelioration of the Condition of the Wounded and Sick in Armed Forces in the Field, August 12, 1949, 6 UST 3114 (1950) (hereinafter Geneva Convention I); Convention for the Amelioration of the Condition of Wounded, Sick and Shipwrecked Members of the Armed Forces at Sea, August 12, 1949, 6 UST 3316 (1950) (hereinafter Geneva Convention II); Convention Relative to the Treatment of Prisoners of War, August 12, 1949, 6 UST 3316 (1950) (hereinafter Geneva Convention III); Convention Relative to the Protection of Civilian Persons in Time of War, August 12, 1949, 6 UST 3516 (1950) (hereinafter Geneva Convention IV).

34. Shabtai Rosenne, *Practice and Methods of International Law*, p. 55 (Oceana Publications: New York, 1984).

35. Restatement of Foreign Relations Law Third, at 381 (St. Paul: American Law Institute, 1987).

36. The literature and commentary are extensive. For an overview, see Turner and Moore, *Regulating Covert Action*.

37. The French text of the Charter is also authoritative and references the word "aggression" in lieu of "armed attack."

38. For background on the ICJ, its status, and the status of its opinions in international law, *see* Statute of the International Court of Justice. 1945 U.S.T. Lexis 199, 3 Bevans 1153 (1945). There is extensive commentary on the ICJ's exercise of jurisdiction in the Nicaragua case including in many leading textbooks on international law and in the *American Journal of International Law*.

39. *See*, Imanuel Geiss, Ed., *July 1914: The Outbreak of the First World War* (New York: W. W. Norton, 1967).

40. The rebels were led by William Lyon Mackenzie, a newspaper publisher and sometime Member of Parliament deeply enmeshed in Canadian disputes between Upper and Lower Canada as well as the Tory Party and Reform movement at the time. Mackenzie eventually fled to New York State where he was tried in 1839 for violating U.S. neutrality laws. He was sentenced to a $10 fine and eighteen months in jail. He was pardoned after twelve months. Following passage of an Amnesty Act, he returned to Canada and was once again elected to the Parliament. See, Dictionary of Canadian Biography, at http://www.biographi.ca/EN/showBioPrintable.asp?BioID=38684.

41. *The Papers of Daniel Webster, Diplomatic Papers*, Volume 1, 1841–1843. Letter to Fox 24 April 1841.

42. *Restatement Third*, at 382.

43. As discussed in the previous chapter, the 9/11 Commission revealed that the United States was pursuing the same objective through parallel intelligence means.

44. The doctrine was also advanced in multiple public appearances by the president and his senior advisors. See for example, President Bush's Graduation Speech at West Point on June 1, 2002. Available at www.whitehouse.gov.

45. *2002 Strategy*, at 15 and 5.

46. Ibid., at 15.

47. *1999 Strategy*, at 3, 8, 21, and 28.

48. President Bush Outlines Iraqi Threat, Remarks by the president on Iraq, Cincinnati Museum Center, October 7, 2002. (Available at www.whitehouse.gov).

49. Ron Suskind, *The One Percent Doctrine* (New York: Simon & Schuster, 2006) at 62.

50. *2006 Strategy*, at 6.

51. Office of the Press Secretary, Briefing by Tony Snow, July 10, 2006. Available at www.whitehouse.gov/news/releases.

52. President George Bush, Commencement Address at the United States Military Academy, Mitchie Stadium, West Point, New York, May 27, 2006.

53. Defense Secretary John Reid: 20th-Century Rules, 21st Century Conflict, Ministry of Defense, 3 April 2006. Available at http://www.britainusa.com/secions/articles_show_nt1.asp?d=0&=41072&L1=&L2=&a=41586. (accessed April 24, 2006).

54. Anthony Faiola, "In Japan, Tough Talk About Preemptive Capability," *The Washington Post*, July 11, 2006.

55. Bruce Wallace, "U.S. Is Japan's Nuclear Shield, Rice Says," *The Los Angeles Times*, October 19, 2006.

56. *Restatement Third*, ibid., at 383.

57. The reference is to Hugo Grotius, *The Law of War and Peace* (1625).

58. UN Security Council Resolutions are accessible on the UN website, http://un.org/docs/sc/.

59. See, William H. Taft and Todd F. Buchwald, "Preemption, Iraq, and International Law," 97 *American Journal of International Law* 557 (July 2003).

60. *See, e.g.*, President Clinton's speech to the UN, September 21, 1999 ("By acting as we did, we helped to vindicate the principles and purposes of the U.N. Charter, to give the U.N. the opportunity it now has to play the central role in shaping Kosovo's future. In the real world, principles often collide, and tough choices must be made. The outcome in Kosovo is hopeful.")

61. *See* UNSCRs 1239 (14 May 1999), 1203 (24 October 1998), 1160, 1199.

62. Sean Murphy, *Humanitarian Intervention: The United Nations in an Evolving World Order* (Philadelphia: Univ. of Penn. Press, 1996). Murphy points out that the great power motives were less beneficent than presented at the time, a recurring theme throughout his examples.

63. *Final Report of the Prosecutor by the Committee Established to Review the NATO Bombing Campaign Against the Federal Republic of Yugoslavia*. Available at http://www.un.org/icty/pressreal/nato061300.htm (Accessed November 6, 2006).

64. Statement by U.N. Secretary General Kofi Annan in New York, 24 March 1999, SG/SM/6938 available at http://www.un.org/News/Press/docs/1999/sgsmxxxx.doc.htm (visited 3/5/07).

65. W. Michael Reisman, "Unilateral Act and the Transformation of the World Constitutive Process: The Special Problem of Humanitarian Intervention," 11 *European Journal of International Law* 15 (2000).

66. Steven Weisman, "Powell Says Rapes and Killings in Sudan Are Genocide," *The New York Times*, September 10, 2004.

67. Acting under Chapter VII in August, 2006, the Security Council authorized the United Nations Mission in Sudan (UNMIS) "to use all necessary means as it deemed within its capabilities:... to protect civilians under threat of physical violence...." (See, UNSCR 8821). However, UNMIS has been woefully under-resourced and has not had the capabilities to fulfill this mission, again reflecting a lack of political willful rather than legal authority.

68. ...and such use of force is consistent with international law, or the United States is otherwise prepared to act outside international law, or articulate a new customary rule law.

69. *See*, ICTY Opinion.
70. Title 18 of the US Code establishes U.S. criminal jurisdiction over war crimes committed by or against members of the U.S. armed forces or U.S. nationals. Note that 18 USC §2441's substantive prohibitions derive meaning through cross-reference to the Geneva Conventions, among other international norms. At the same time, the Code as amended by the Military Commissions Act of 2006 reserves to the president the authority to interpret the meaning of the Law of Armed Conflict. U.S. jurisdiction to enforce the LOAC is also found in the Uniform Code of Military Justice (UCMJ). See, for example, Articles 2, 18, and 21, Uniform Code of Military Justice, 10 USC §§802, 818, and 821. Jurisdiction to punish violations of the LOAC is also exercised through application of the punitive articles of the UCMJ, as in the case of William Calley, who was convicted after the My Lai massacre of 22 counts of murder under Article 118 of the UCMJ. *United States v. Calley*, 22 CMA 534 (1973).
71. U.S. Const. Art II, §3.
72. DOD Joint Publication 3-0, Doctrine for Joint Operations (Sept 10, 2001); DOD Law of War Program, Department of Defense Directive 2311.01E, para. 4.1 (May 9, 2006).
73. The cartridges were first manufactured in Dum Dum, India. For a description of the horrific effect of these types of cartridges on charging infantry, see the description of the Battle of Omdurman in Mark Urban, *Generals*, at 192 (London: Faber and Faber, 2005).
74. *See, e.g.*, Lionel Beecher, "The Campaign to Ban Cluster Bombs," *Council on Foreign Relations*, November 21, 2006; "Red Cross Steps up Campaign Against Cluster Bombs," *USA Today*, November 7, 2006; "Norway Plans Talks on Cluster-Bomb Ban," *Washington Times*, November 18, 2006.
75. See, Article 37.2 of Protocol I.
76. Article 23 (f), Hague Convention No. IV, 1907.
77. Some illustrative definitions follow.

Necessity

That principle which justifies those measures not forbidden by international law which are indispensable for securing the complete submission of the enemy as soon as possible. (*Law of War Handbook*, International and Operational Law Department, Judge Advocate General's School, U.S. Army, 2005, at 164.)

Military Objective

Attacks shall be limited strictly to military objectives. In so far as objects are concerned, military objectives are limited to those objects which by their nature, location, purpose or use make an effective contribution to military action and whose total or partial destruction, capture or neutralization, in the circumstances ruling at the time, offers a definite military advantage. (Protocol I to the Geneva Conventions of 1949 (1977) 1123 U.N.T.S. 3, Art. 52.2)

In case of doubt whether an object which is normally dedicated to civilian purposes, such as a place of worship, a house or dwelling or a school, is being used to make an effective contribution to military action, it shall be presumed not to be so used. (Protocol I, Art. 52.3)

When objects are used concurrently for civilian and military purposes, they are liable to attack if there is a military advantage to be gained in their attack. ("Military advantage" is not restricted to tactical gains, but is linked to the full context of a war strategy, in this instance, the execution of the Coalition war plan for liberation of Kuwait). (Desert Storm, After Action Report, at 0–11.)

Military objective is a component of military necessity. Once a commander determines he or she has a military necessity to take a certain action or strike a certain target, then he or she must determine that the target is a valid military objective. The current definition of military objective is found in GP I, article 52(2). (*Law of War Handbook*, Ibid., at 165–66).

Discrimination or Distinction

Requires combatants to distinguish between military targets and civilian objects and persons.

Basic Rule

Parties to the conflict shall at all times distinguish between the civilian population and combatants and between civilian objects and military objectives and accordingly shall direct their operations only against military objectives. (Article 48, Protocol I)

In the conduct of military operations at sea or in the air, each Party to the conflict shall, in conformity with its rights and duties under the rule of international law applicable in armed conflict, take all reasonable precautions to avoid losses of civilian lives and damage to civilian objects. (Protocol I, Article 57.4)

Indiscriminate attacks are prohibited. Indiscriminate attacks are:

(a) those which are not directed at a specific military objective;

(b) those which employ a method or means of combat which cannot be directed at a specific military objective; or

(c) those which employ a method or means of combat the effects of which cannot be limited as required by this Protocol. (Protocol I, Art. 51.4)

There is a necessity for distinguishing between combatants, who may be attacked, and noncombatants, against whom an intentional attack may not be directed, and between legitimate military targets and civilian objects. (Department of Defense, Final Report to Congress: Conduct of the Persian Gulf War, (1992).

The principle of distinction is sometimes referred to as the 'grandfather of all principles,' as it forms the foundation for much of the Geneva tradition of the law of war. The essence of the principle is that military attacks should be directed at combatants and military targets, and not civilians or civilian property. GP I, article 48 sets out the rule. (*Law of War Handbook*, at 166)

Proportionality requires that loss of life and damage to property incidental to attacks must not be excessive in relation to the concrete and direct military advantage expected to be gained.

With respect to attacks, the following precautions shall be taken:

(a) those who plan or decide upon an attack shall:

. . . (iii) refrain from deciding to launch any attack which may be expected to cause incidental loss of civilian life, injury to civilians, damage to civilian objects, or a combination thereof, which would be excessive in relation to the concrete and direct military advantage anticipated. (Protocol I, Article 57.2)

The test to determine if an attack is proportional is found in GP I, article 51(5)(b). Note: This principle is only applicable when an attack has the possibility of affecting civilians. If the target is purely military with no known civilian personnel or property in the vicinity, no proportionality analysis need be conducted. (*Law of War Handbook*, at 166).

Now consider the principles applied on a sample Rules of Engagement Card used during the First Gulf War/Desert Storm.

ALL ENEMY MILITARY PERSONNEL AND VEHICLES TRANSPORTING THE ENEMY OR THEIR SUPPLIES MAY BE ENGAGED SUBJECT TO THE FOLLOWING RESTRICTIONS:

A. Do not engage anyone who has surrendered, is out of battle due to sickness or wounds, is shipwrecked, or is an aircrew member descending by parachute from a disabled aircraft.

B. Avoid harming civilians unless necessary to save U.S. lives. Do not fire into civilian populated areas or buildings which are not defended or being used for military purposes.

C. Hospitals, churches, shrines, school, museums, national monuments, and any other historical or cultural sites will not be engaged except in self-defense.

D. Hospitals will be given special protection. Do not engage hospitals unless the enemy uses the hospital to commit acts harmful to U.S. forces, and then only after giving a warning and allowing a reasonable time to expire before engaging, if the tactical situation permits.

E. Booby traps may be used to protect friendly positions or to impede the progress of enemy forces. They may not be used on civilian personal property. They will be recovered or destroyed when the military necessity for their use no longer exists.

F. ...

G. Avoid harming civilian property unless necessary to save U.S. lives. Do not attack traditional civilian objects, such as houses, unless they are being used by the enemy for military purposes and neutralization assist in mission accomplishment.

H. Treat all civilians and their property with respect and dignity. Before using privately owned property, check to see if publicly owned property can substitute. No requisitioning of civilian property, including vehicles, without permission of a company level commander without giving a receipt....

I. ...

J. ...

REMEMBER

1. FIGHT ONLY COMBATANTS.
2. ATTACK ONLY MILITARY TARGETS.
3. SPARE CIVILIAN PERSONS AND OBJECTS.
4. RESTRICT DESTRUCTION TO WHAT YOUR MISSION REQUIRES.

(From, *Rules of Engagement (ROE) Handbook for Judge Advocates*, Center for Law and Military Operations, Judge Advocate General's School, U.S. Army, Charlottesville, VA (2000)).

For additional illustrative definitions and discussion of these terms, as well as proportionality and military objective, see for example, W. Hays Parks, *Air War and the Law of War*, 32 AF L Rev 1 (1990); William J. Fenwick, *The Rule of Proportionality and Protocol I in Conventional Warfare*, 98 Mil L Rev 91 (1982). See also Protocol Additional to the Geneva Conventions of Aug 12, 1949, and Relating to the Protection of Victims of International Armed Conflicts, Dec 12, 1977, 16 ILM 1391, art 48–58 (1978) (hereinafter Additional Protocol I); Chapter 8, "The Law of Targeting," *Annotated Supplement of the Commander's Handbook on the Law of Naval Operations* (Oceans Law and Policy Dept 1997). *Operational Law Handbook 2002*, ch 2, International and Operational Law Department, The Judge Advocate General's School, U.S. Army.

I am not aware of an authoritative statement by the United States as to which textual provisions and operational elements of the law of armed conflict reflect customary international law. However, in public statements and filings before the ICTY the United States has stated that those provisions relating to the methods and means of warfare are customary in nature, and therefore, binding on states that are not party to the Protocol.

78. In one such instance, for example, overhead photographs showed a company-sized formation of Taliban military personnel attending a funeral. The media broadcast the photos, which launched a debate as to why the United States had held off on an air strike. Outside the photo frame was a village. There followed a story that the commander had deferred a strike out of concern that the net military gain would be overtaken by the potential for collateral casualties in the village and the negative impact on the local population of striking what might have been a funeral, albeit a "military" funeral. (October 5, 2006). See also, Moshe Yaalon, "The Rules of War," *The Washington Post*, August 3, 2006 (the writer, a retired Lieutenant General who served as Chief of Staff of the Israeli Defense Forces, 2002–2005, describes "one of countless examples" where commanders selected a smaller munition that would destroy only the top floor of the target building because commanders knew a larger bomb would endanger forty families in the vicinity. The decision was taken on policy grounds. As it turned out, in the case Yaalon cites, the terrorists were meeting on the ground floor and the cell lived to fight another day.)

79. *New Wars, New Laws? Applying the Laws of War in 21st Century Conflicts*, David Wippman and Matthew Evangelista eds. (Ardsley, New York: Transnational Publishers, 2005); Michael Reisman and Chris Antoniou, *The Laws of War: A Comprehensive Collection of*

Primary Documents on International Laws Governing Armed Conflict (New York: Vintage, 1994).

80. On the policy value of reciprocal treatment see, Milt Bearden, "When the CIA Played by the Rules," *The New York Times*, November 4, 2005; See also, James E. Baker, "LBJ's Ghost: A Contextual Approach to Targeting Decisions and the Commander in Chief," 4 *Chi. J. Int'l L* 407 (Fall 2003); "When Lawyers Advise Presidents in Wartime: Kosovo and the Law of Armed Conflict," 55 *Naval War Coll Rev* 11 (Winter 2002).

81. *See, e.g.,* President George W. Bush, Address to the Nation (Mar. 19, 2003), available online at http://www.whitehouse.gov/news/releases/2003/03/20030319-17.html (visited Sept 13, 2003) (condemning Iraqi use of human shields in the Second Gulf War); Judith Miller, "War in the Gulf: the Arabs; Neighboring Allies Outraged by Iraqi Violence in Kuwait," *The New York Times* 8 (Feb 23, 1991) (discussing Arab reactions to the use of human shields in the First Gulf War). See, for example, Melissa Healy, "Pentagon Details Abuse of American POWs in Iraq; Gulf War: Broken Bones, Torture, Sexual Threats Are Reported. It Could Spur Further Calls For War Crimes Trial," *The Los Angeles Times* 1 (Aug 2, 1991).

82. Major General J. N. Mattis, US Marines Commanding General, 1st Division (REIN), *Commanding General's Message to All Hands* (Mar 2003) available online at http://www.usni.org/resources/Iraq/mattis_USMC_to_all_hands.htm (visited Sept 6, 2003).

83. Reconnaissance by fire is a method of searching out the enemy by firing on suspected positions and thus drawing return fire, helping to identify the location and perhaps the strength of the opponent.

84. *See* C. B. Shotwell, "Economy and Humanity in the Use of Force: A Look at the Aerial Rules of Engagement in the 1991 Gulf War," 4 *USAFA J Leg Stud* 15, 17–20 (1993) (citing numerous sources supporting the view that contrary to the conventional wisdom of the time, bombing of civilian populations during World War II did not break the morale of civilian communities, but rather strengthened their resolve to fight against their enemies).

85. Thanassis Cambanis, "In Arab World, Zarqawi Tactics Bred Disgust," *The Boston Globe*, June 12, 2006; "Poll: Jordanians Classify Al Qaeda as Terrorists," *Jerusalem Post*, January 6, 2006.

86. Headquarters, Department of the Army, Counterinsurgency, Field Manual 3-24, Marine Corps Warfighting Publication No. 3-33.5, 15 December 2006, at 1–25 available at http://usacac.arm.mil/CAC/Repository/Materials/COIN-FM3–24.pdf (accessed January 2007).

87. *See* Geoffrey Best, *War and Law Since 1945*, 115–23, 253–66 (Oxford: Clarendon, 1994) (explaining how the protection of civilian life was a major international concern behind the Geneva Conventions and "has become the driving concern of contemporary IHL development"); W. Michael Reisman and Chris T. Antoniou, eds, *The Laws of War* 80–93 (Vintage 1994) (citing numerous international laws governing the protection of civilians during wartime); *Department of the Army Field Manual; The Law of Land Warfare* 3 (Dept of the Army 1956) (noting that two of the three purposes of the "law of land warfare" are directed toward such an end; the law of land warfare is inspired by the desire to diminish the evil of war by protecting "both combatants and noncombatants from unnecessary suffering" and "[s]afeguarding certain fundamental human rights of persons who fall into the hands of the enemy, particularly prisoners of war, the wounded and sick, and civilians . . . "). Major Lisa L. Turner & Major Lynn G. Norton, *Civilians at the Tip of the Spear*, 51 AF L Rev 1, 76–82 (2001) (explaining the provisions of the Geneva Conventions intended to protect civilians).

88. Hassan Fattah and Steven Erlanger, "Israel Attacks Beirut Airport and Sets Up Naval Blockade," *The New York Times*, July 13, 2006.

89. *See*, for example, Human Rights Watch, *Civilian Deaths in Nato Air Campaign*, Summary (February 2000), available online at www.hrw.org/reports/2000/nato (visited Sept 13, 2003) (implying that large numbers of civilian deaths resulted from questionable targeting and munition decisions); Human Rights Watch, *New Figures on Civilian Death in Kosovo War* (Feb 7, 2000), available online at www.hrw.org/press/2000/02/nato207.htm (visited Sept 13, 2003) (alleging that "'[a]ll too often, NATO targeting subjected the civilian

population to unacceptable risks'" and suggesting that illegitimate targeting and munition decisions resulted in large numbers of civilian deaths).

90. *See* Protocol I art 57, §4; *Annotated Supplement to the Commander's Handbook on the Law of Naval Operations* 8-2 Oceans Law and Policy Dep't, The United States Naval War College, (1997) (cited in note 18).

91. 10 U.S.C. §162(b).

92. *See*, Baker, "LBJ's Ghost" and "When Lawyers Advise Presidents."

93. *See*, *The Last Battle*.

94. *See*, Graham Allison, *Essence of Decision: Explaining the Cuban Missile Crisis* (Boston: Little, Brown, 1971).

95. *See*, Eliot A. Cohen, *Supreme Command: Soldiers, Statesmen and Leadership in Wartime* (Free Press, 2002); Baker, "LBJ's Ghost," and Wesley Clark, *Waging Modern War* (New York: Public Affairs, 2001)(taking issue with the operation of the chain of command through the Chairman).

96. Collectively this chain of command is known as the National Command Authorities (NCA); however, former Secretary of Defense Donald Rumsfeld banished the term in the interest of clarity. In lieu of the amorphous NCA, Department of Defense personnel were instructed to indicate which official in the chain of command authorized an action. Further, combatant commanders were no longer referred to as CinCs. There is only one commander in chief to whom combatant commanders report through the Secretary of Defense. Whether or not this is the stuff of secretarial decision, clarity serves a useful military purpose. This takes on constitutional significance when a military operation or target is undertaken pursuant to the president's constitutional authority, or internal directive requires the Secretary's approval. Nonetheless, the military ship can turn slowly; NCA and CINC will likely persist in the vernacular of national security process as well as law (e.g., 10 U.S.C._ "The CinC's Initiative Fund" available to unified commanders for unexpected operational expenditures).

97. For example, while deployed for training at Camp Lejuene a Marine Battalion would remain within the administrative command of the Commandant of the Marine Corps; however, once assigned to an operational unit, the battalion would fall under the operational command of the relevant unified commander.

98. 10 U.S.C. §151(d).

99. H. R. McMaster, *Dereliction of Duty: Lyndon Johnson, Robert McNamara, the Joint Chiefs of Staff, and the Lies That Led to Vietnam* (New York: HarperCollins, 1997).

100. According to media accounts, the president has approved the creation of a tenth combatant command with geographic responsibility for Africa. See, Jeff Schlogol, "Africa Command Plans Approved by Bush, DOD Officials Confirm," *Stars and Stripes*, December 30, 2006. Combatant responsibility for Africa currently resides with European Command, Central Command, Pacific Command, and Special Operations Command depending on the region and function in question. *See*, Unified Command Plan available at http://www.defenselink.mil/specials/unifiedcommand/ (accessed January 2007).

101. This text is quoted directly from the command websites. The mission statements may be amended from time to time and may have been since this text was first set. See, http://www.defenselink.mil/sites/u.html. or visit the Combatant Command websites directly.

102. *See*, *Univ. of Chicago Journal of International Law*, Vol. 4, Fall 2003 on "The Role of the Lawyer in War;" Frederic Borch, *Judge Advocates in Combat: Army Lawyers in Military Operations from Vietnam to Haiti* (Washington: Office of the Judge Advocate General and Center of Military History, 2001).

103. "The Role of the Lawyer," ibid.

104. Paul Watson, "NATO Takes Security Helm," *The Los Angeles Times*, October 6, 2006.

105. H.R. 3308, May 8, 1996, Office of Legal Counsel Memorandum for Alan J. Kreczko, Special Assistant to the president and Legal Advisor to the National Security Council from Walter Dellinger, available at the OLC website.

106. *See*, Article 92 UCMJ as well as *United States v. New*, 55 MJ 95 (2001) and *United States v. Dearing*, 63 MJ 478 (2006).
107. "War is too important to be left to the generals."
108. Max Hastings, "Behind the Revolt – The Generals' View: To the Micromanager Goes the Blame," *The Washington Post*, April 26, 2006.
109. General Tommy R. Franks, *Briefing on Military Operations in Iraq* (Mar 22, 2003), available online at http://www.centcom.mil/CENTCOMNews/transcripts/20030322.htm (visited Sept 8, 2003).
110. Report of the DoD Commission on Beirut International Airport Terrorist Act, Oct 23, 1983 (Dec 20, 1983) available online at http://www.ibiblio.org/hyperwar/AMH/XX/MidEast/Lebanon-1982–1984/DOD-Report/ (visited Sept 8, 2003) (hereinafter Long Commission Report) (discussing circumstances and aftermath of terrorist attack on the U.S. compound in 1983).

9. Homeland Security

1. I use the phrase preventive diplomacy to distinguish the concept from public diplomacy, which in U.S. practice equates to public relations, a necessary part of preventive diplomacy, but only one of the full array of tools available to address the root causes of terrorism, including foreign and economic assistance provided by governmental and nongovernmental organizations. For background on Foreign Assistance and Economic Assistance see, Buchwald and Matheson, "U.S. Security Assistance and Related Programs," Chap. 27 in *National Security Law*, Turner & Moore.
2. The Department of Defense and military doctrine distinguish homeland defense from homeland security. In the military lexicon, "defense" is the physical "protection of the US sovereignty, territory, domestic population, and critical defense infrastructure against external threats and aggression, or other threats as directed by the president. The Department of Defense is responsible for homeland defense." Homeland security is defined as "a concerted national effort to prevent terrorist attacks within the United States, reduce America's vulnerability to terrorism, and minimize damage and recover from attacks that do occur. The Department of Homeland Security is the lead federal agency for homeland security." "Strategy for Homeland Defense and Civil Support," Department of Defense, June 2005, at 5.

   Three points emerge. First, the Department's and military's definition and perception of their roles are subject to presidential direction and amendment. This is critical, because in its present distillation the definition of "security" is oriented toward terrorism and not the broader range of manmade and natural emergencies encompassed within the homeland security rubric.

   Second, however the terms are bureaucratically defined, the Department does not feel direct responsibility for that portion designated "security" rather than "defense." However, the distinction between defense and security are not clear in the middle gray of homeland security incidents.

   Therefore, like much else with homeland security, consideration and reconsideration of the manner in which agencies define their roles are critical. Are there gaps, for example, between what DHS defines as its areas of lead responsibility and those areas that DOD defines as its lead areas of responsibility, and if so, are those gaps filled by other agencies like HHS?
3. Lawrence Wein, "Face Facts," op-ed contributor, *The Washington Post*, October 25, 2006. Letters to the Editor, Sunday October 29, 2006, from among others, John Agwunobi, M.D., Assistant Secretary for Health, HHS. Ceci Connolly, "U.S. Plan for Flu Pandemic Revealed," *The Washington Post*, April 16, 2006.
4. *See*, The National Strategy for Pandemic Influenza, November 1, 2005 and related documents at PandemicFlu.gov (accessed November 12, 2006).
5. *See*, Newt Gingrich, "The Only Option is to Win," *The Washington Post*, August 11, 2006; Graham Allison, "Nuclear Terrorism the Gravest Threat Today," *Wall Street Journal*

Europe, July 14, 2003; John Arguilla, "In the Fight Against Terrorism, The Long War Is the Wrong War: Sooner or Later, Terrorists Will Get, and Use, WMD," July 16, 2006, *San Francisco Chronicle*; Sam Nunn, "Nuclear Pig in a Poke," *Wall Street Journal*, May 24, 2006.

6. "The Terrorism Index: A Survey of the U.S. National Security Experts on the War on Terror." March 8-April 21, 2006. Available at www.americanprogress.org (viewed June 29, 2006).

7. Harold D. Lasswell, "The Garrison State," *American Journal of Sociology*," Vol. 46, Issue 4 (Jan. 1941), 459.

8. *See, e.g.*, Donald Rumsfeld, in a Press Conference at NATO Headquarters, Brussels, Belgium, Thursday, June 6, 2002, available at:http://www.defenselink.mil/transcripts/2002/t06062002_t0606sd.html

9. Recall the rush for duct tape after Secretary Ridge recommended keeping a supply on hand in February 2003. In Connecticut, one eager person covered his house in duct tape. The duct tape soon threatened the man's supply of fresh air as well as the goodwill of his neighbors.

10. Quoted in *Catastrophic Terrorism: Imminent Threat, Uncertain Response*, at 32 (Cantigny Conference Series, McCormick Tribune Foundation 2001).

11. See, the Sixth Amendment to the Constitution and *Duncan v. Louisiana*, 391 U.S. 145 (1968).

12. See the Terrorism Act of 2000, Schedule 8, Part II, as amended by the Terrorism Act of 2006, Part 2, Sections 23–25. Available at http://www.opsi.gov.uk/Acts/acts2000/00011-u.htm (accessed November 2006). Compare, among other U.S. laws, 8 U.S.C. §1226a "Mandatory detention of suspected terrorists; habeas corpus; judicial review," and 18 U.S.C. Appendix Rule 5, "Initial Appearance."

13. Richard A. Posner, "We Need our Own MI5," *The Washington Post*, August 15, 2006.

14. For a range of statistical data, *see The National Strategy for Homeland Security*, Office of Homeland Security, July 2002 (available at http://www.whitehouse.gov/homeland/book/nat_strat_hls.pdf); U.S. Customs and Border Protection, "Fact Sheet," on the Container Security Initiative, September 30, 2006 as well as other CSI related briefing sheets on securing U.S. ports (available at www.dhs.gov, visited November 2006); "Secure Seas, Open Ports: Keeping our waters safe, secure and open for business," Department of Homeland Security, June 21, 2004 (at www.dhs.gov visited November 2006); see also, "Preventing Nuclear Smuggling: DOE Has Made Limited Progress in Installing Radiation Detection Equipment at Highest Priority Seaports," *Government Accountability Office*, GAO-375, March 31, 2005 (available at www.gao.gov visited November 2006); the Northern Command website also provides some homeland statistics at http://www.northcom.mil/about_us/history.htm.

15. Alan Sipress, "Computer System Under Attack," *The Washington Post*, October 6, 2006.

16. Executive Order 13228, October 8, 2001.

17. As amended, the Council members include the president, the vice president, the secretary of the treasury, the secretary of defense, the attorney general, the secretary of health and human services, the secretary of transportation, the secretary of homeland security, the director of the Federal Emergency Management Agency, the director of the Federal Bureau of Investigation, the director of national intelligence, and the assistant to the president for homeland security. As noted later, the chairman of the Joint Chiefs of Staff is a statutory advisor to the HSC.

18. The secretary of state, the secretary of agriculture, the secretary of the interior, the secretary of energy, the secretary of labor, the secretary of commerce, the secretary of veterans affairs, the administrator of the Environmental Protection Agency, the assistant to the president for economic policy, and the assistant to the president for domestic policy "shall be invited to attend meetings pertaining to their responsibilities."

19. The chief of staff to the president, the chief of staff to the vice president, the assistant to the president for national security affairs, the counsel to the president, and the director of the Office of Management and Budget "are invited to attend any Council meeting."

20. P.L. 107–296 (2002).

21. 6 U.S.C. §494.

22. 6 U.S.C. §493.

23. 6 U.S.C. §496.

24. Subject of course to specific funding limitations and restrictions. The State Department authorization acts, for example, limited the number of State employees that could be seconded to other agencies at any one time. On my watch, this argument quickly removed CIA's legal objection to the detail of CIA personnel to serve on the NSC staff, which staff, of course, advised and assisted the NSC to which the DCI was a statutory advisor. Of course, policy and personnel officers may sometimes persuade their lawyers to make legal arguments to shield policy or fiscal objections, because a legal prohibition, if appropriately raised, is not subject to appeal up the policy chain of command.

25. The converse is not the case. The reference is to the principal deputy national security advisor.

26. Walter Pincus, "Hayden's Hands-On Style Changes Tone at CIA," *The Washington Post*, December 28, 2006.

27. Homeland Security Presidential Directive-1, "Organization and Operation of the Homeland Security Council," October 29, 2001, as amended. Available at Federation of American Scientists.

28. Remarks of the Staff Judge Advocate, Northern Command, at the Judicial Conference of the United States Court Appeals for the Armed Forces, May 17, 2006.

29. http://www.fema.gov/about/index.shtm (visited January 2007).

30. "A 'Cutter' is a Coast Guard vessel 65 feet in length or greater, having adequate accommodations for crew to live on board. Larger cutters (over 180 feet in length) are under control of Area Commands (Atlantic Area or Pacific Area). Cutters at or under 180 feet in length come under control of District Commands." For a list of cutters in the Coast Guard inventory see http://www.uscg.mil/datasheet/index.shtm (accessed November 11, 2006). See also, various GAO reports on modernizing the Coast Guard, including "Status of Deep-Water Fast Response Cutter Design Efforts," June 15, 2006. Stephen Barr, "Coast Guard's Response to Katrina a Silver Lining in the Storm," *The Washington Post*, September 6, 2005. Ted Sherman, "Coast Guard Issues SOS," *Atlanta Journal-Constitution*, November 25, 2005.

31. The figure is difficult to fix because statistics are kept of the general outline of the seacoast, usually described as the coastline, and more detailed measure of the seacoast, usually referred to as the shoreline. Oddly enough, the length of the coastline is usually given as 95,000 miles by Homeland Security officials. The National Oceanographic and Atmospheric Administration figure is 88,633 as of 1975. Of course, with climate change and other variables the actual length of the shoreline may, in fact, vary from year to year; however, unlike the number of containers that enter the United States each year, this does seem a figure on which responsible officials and cartographers ought to be able to agree.

32. Government Accountability Office, "Federal Food Safety and Security System: Fundamental Restructuring is Needed to Address Fragmentation and Overlap," at 11, GAO-04–588T, March 30, 2004.

33. *See*, for example, PDD-56 "Managing Complex Contingency Operations," May 1997; and, Presidential Decision/NSC-27 "Procedures for Dealing with Non-Military Incidents," January 19, 1978. Available at the Federation of Americans Scientists website.

34. *See* NRP, available at the DHS website. See also, testimony of Brigadier General Broderick, and Robert Stephan, assistant Secretary for Infrastructure Protection, Department of Homeland Security, before the Senate Homeland Security and Governmental Affairs Committee, February 10, 2006.

35. Bureau of Justice Statistics. http://www.ojp.usdoj.gov/bjs/lawenf.htm (visited 8/17/06).

36. http://www.official-doucments.co.uk/document (visited August 17, 2006).

37. The phrase comes from Dick Clarke and Randy Beers. For first responder statistics see: U.S. Department of Justice, Bureau of Justice Statistics, Law Enforcement

Statistics available at http://www.ojp.usdoj.gov/bjs/lawenf.htm (accessed November 3, 2006); U.S. Fire Administration, Fire Departments, available at http://www.usfa.dhs.gov/statistics/departments/ (accessed November 3, 2006).

38. "DoD Announces Certification for WMD-CST Teams in Four States," Department of Defense press release No. 706-06 July 25, 2006.

39. 6 USC §361.

40. Fact Sheet: National Incident Management System (NIMS), U.S. Department of Homeland Security, available at http://www.dhs.gov/dhspublic/display?theme=43&content=3421&print=true (accessed July 7, 2004). The NIMS was released on March 1, 2004 and is available on the DHS website.

41. Catastrophic Terrorism, Cantigny Conference, at 36.

42. John Miller (Assistant Director of the FBI, Op-Ed Contributor) "Law Enforcement, American Style," *The New York Times*, September 14, 2006.

43. For a description of the NCIC see, http://www.fas.org/irp/agency/doj/fbi/is/ncic.htm (accessed November 3, 2006). Among other things, the NCIC includes a "Terrorist File" within its categories of individuals covered as well as persons who have committed or have been identified with committing an offense in a foreign country that would be a felony in the United States.

44. Dan Eggen and Spencer Hsu, "U.S. Responded to Plot with Speed, Secrecy," *The Washington Post*, August 13, 2006. ("Senior officials at the Virginia State police knew about the British investigation, according to police spokeswoman Corinne Geller, though she declined to elaborate. In New York, officials said they learned about the British probe several weeks ago and were told early last week – by British contacts – that arrests were imminent. The city police department has an extensive intelligence operation, including officers assigned to Scotland Yard and other locations overseas.") Mary Beth Sheridan, "Localities Operate Intelligence Centers to Pool Terror Data," *The Washington Post*, December 31, 2006.

45. David Wood, "'Interoperability' Issue still Bedevils Emergency Response," *Newhouse.com*, March 2, 2006.

46. Karen DeYoung, "Five Years Later: The Bureaucratic Front A Fight Against Terrorism – and Disorganization," *The Washington Post*, August 9, 2006; Karen DeYoung, "In Arizona, Officials Share Data the Old-Fashioned Way," *The Washington Post*, August 9, 2006; Ronald K. Noble, "All Terrorism is Local, Too," *The New York Times*, August 13, 2006.

47. Statement of Robert S. Mueller, III, Director of the Federal Bureau of Investigation, Before the House Appropriations Subcommittee on Science, the Departments of State, Justice and Commerce, and Related Agencies, September 14, 2006. There were 44 Legat offices in 2001. As of September 2006, the FBI has 167 agents and 111 support personnel assigned to 57 Legat offices and 13 sub-offices. Among the new Legat locations are Baghdad, Kuala Lumpur Malaysia, Sana'a Yemen, and Freetown, Sierra Leone.

48. The first ten amendments to the Constitution, ratified in 1791, comprise the Bill of Rights.

49. *See* Amendment II and Article 1, Section 8, Clauses 15 and 16.

50. *See*, *Jacobsen v. Commonwealth of Massachusetts*, 197 U.S. 11 (1905) ("Although this court has refrained from any attempt to define the limits of that power, yet it has distinctly recognized the authority of a state to enact quarantine laws and 'health laws of every description;' indeed, all laws that relate to matters completely within its territory which do not be their necessary operation affect people of other states. According to settled principles, the police power of a state must be held to embrace, at least, such reasonable regulations established directly by legislative enactment as will protect the public health and the public safety." At 25.)

51. Article VI, paragraph 2. See, *Holland v. Missouri*, 252 U.S. 416 (1920).

52. *Crosby v. National Foreign Trade Council*, 530 U.S. 363, 372–373 (2000). Preemption also arises in the context of federal jurisdiction where the existence of a substantial question of federal law or a conflict with federal law may serve to preempt a state cause of action and cause removal of an issue into federal court. *See e.g.*, *Grable & Sons Metal Products v. Darue Engineering & Manufacturing*, 545 U.S. 308 (2005); *McHahon v. Presidential Airways*,

410 F.Supp.2d 1189 (2006); *Nordan v. Blackwater Security Consulting*, 382 F.Supp.2d 801 (2005).

53. *See e.g.*, Conditions of Contract, www.delta.com. Stating that carriage is subject to the rules and conditions of the Warsaw Convention (Convention for the Unification of Certain Rules Relating to International Transportation by Air). See, *El Al Israel Airlines v. Tseng*, 525 U.S. 155 (1999).

54. 10 U.S.C. §12405.

55. In like manner, Title 49 of the United States Code provides (1) that "the United States Government has exclusive sovereignty of [the] airspace of the United States;" (2) "a citizen of the United States has a public right of transit through the navigable airspace;" and, (3) assigns to the Administrator of the FAA responsibility for plans, policy, and regulations for the use of the navigable airspace necessary "to ensure the safety of aircraft and the efficient use of airspace." Although the statute does not state so expressly, the statute is fairly read to occupy the field.

56. *Crosby v. National Foreign Trade Council*, 530 U.S. 363, 372–373 (2000).

57. For a clear and succinct review of preemption doctrine as well as an application of natural preemption in foreign affairs context *see*, *Crosby v. National Foreign Trade Council*, 530 U.S. 363 (2000) (holding a Massachusetts statute prohibiting state contracting with companies doing business with the military government of Burma, with certain specified exceptions, unconstitutional under the Supremacy Clause, because it would inter alia serve as an obstacle to the accomplishment of Congress's effort to devise a comprehensive multilateral strategy to impose sanctions on the military government of Burma. The federal Burma law was passed three months after the Massachusetts Burma law, but did not expressly preempt the latter.)

58. As discussed, the Stafford Act and Insurrection Act provide for cost-sharing formulas as well as time limitations on the use of military assets.

59. *National Strategy for Homeland Security*, Office of Homeland Security, July 2002. Available at www.whitehouse.gov.

60. Homeland Security Strategy, at 13.

61. Ibid., at 8.

62. *See*, http://www.stratcom.mil/organization-fnc_comp.html (accessed November 3, 2006).

63. *See*, http://www.northcom.mil (accessed November 2006).

64. In April 2006 the United States and Canada signed an updated NORAD Agreement including within NORAD's mission a maritime surveillance and early warning mission. www.norad.mil/newsroom/news_releases.

65. For references to Gen. Ralph Eberhart's characterization of the authority delegated to the Commanding General of Northern Command in 2001 and as modified in 2003 see "New Procedure Targets Civilian Jets," *The Associated Press*, October 3, 2003; "Generals Can Now Shoot Down Airliners," *Telegraph*, September 28, 2001.

66. "Northcom Gets Helping Hand," *Colorado Springs Gazette*, October 17, 2006.

67. Northern Command SJA brief.

68. Latin for "power of the county." See also, Bonnie Baker, "The Origins of the Posse Comitatus," *Air & Space Power Journal*, November 1999. Available at www.airpower.maxwell. af.mil (accessed November 2006)(arguing that a second impetus behind the Act was the western expansion of the United States).

69. 18 U.S.C. §1385.

70. 10 USC §375.

71. DOD Directive 5525.5, January 15, 1986, "DoD Cooperation with Civilian Law Enforcement Officials." Enclosure 4 (E4), paragraph E4.1.3.

72. *United States v. Hartley*, 796 F.2d 112, 114 (5th Cir., 1986). See also, *United States v. Prado-Montero*, 740 F.2d 113 (1st Cir. 1984, cert. denied 105 S.Ct. 441, 527 (1984).

73. *Hartley*, at 115, citing cases from 4th, 5th, 9th circuits as well as state court cases.

74. Department of Defense Directive 5525.5, "DoD Cooperation with Civilian Law Enforcement Officials, January 15, 1986, Enclosure 4.

75. See, 10 U.S.C. §§371–374.

76. 18 U.S.C. §382.

77. 18 U.S.C. §831.

78. E.O. 12804, (May 5, 1992).

79. E.O. 10730 (September 24, 1957) and E.O. 11,118 (September 10, 1963).

80. Domestic Operational Law Handbook for Judge Advocates, Center for Law and Military Operations, Judge Advocate General's School, Charlottesville, Virginia, (2001), at 56, citing *Alabama v. United States*, 373 U.S. 545 (1963).

81. Section 1076 of the Department of Defense Authorization Act of 2007, P.L. 109–364.

82. 42 U.S.C. §5122 et seq. (1974).

83. 42 U.S.C. §5170.

84. 42 U.S.C. §5170a.

85. 42 U.S.C. §5170a.

86. 42 U.S.C. §5170b.

87. 42 U.S.C. §5191.

88. For further background on homeland security see Stephen Flynn, *American the Vulnerable* (New York: Harper Collins, 2004). Also, visit the following websites. www.cfr.org; www.csis.org; and Center for Health and Homeland Security, http://www.umaryland.edu/healthsecurity/

89. For background on the A.Q. Khan network *see* Esther Pan, "Nonproliferation: The Pakistan Network," Backgrounder, Council on Foreign Relations, February 12, 2004, available at http://www.cfr.org/publication/7751/ (viewed November 13, 2006).

90. Thomas Friedman, "A Choice for the Rogues," *The New York Times*, August 2, 2006.

91. *See*, Congressional Research Service, "Cruise Missile Proliferation," Christopher Bolkcom and Sharon Squassoni, July 3, 2002. Available at, www.fpc.state.gov and at fas.org/irp/crs.

92. Anthony Shadid, "Israel, Hezbollah Vow Wider War," *The Washington Post*, July 15, 2006.

93. 22 U.S.C. §2751 et seq., (Chapter 39); the Export Administration Act of 1979, P.L. 96–72.

94. See, E.O. 12923 (June 30, 1994); E.O. 13222 (August 17, 2001).

95. 50 U.S.C. §1701.

96. The substantive threshold has been interpreted broadly by successive administrations. Hence the authority has been used for among other purposes to prohibit the importation of Krugerrands into the United States in an effort to isolate and influence the apartheid government of South Africa.

97. For three prominent examples, *see*, the Iran Nonproliferation Act, P.L. 106–178; the Iran-Iraq Arms Nonproliferation Act, 50 U.S.C. Note; and, the Cuban Liberty and Democratic Solidarity (Libertad) Act of 1996 (Helms-Burton Act), 22 U.S.C. §§6021–6091.

98. For more information go to http://www.wassenaar.org/ (viewed November 11, 2006).

99. For more information go to http://www.australiagroup.net/ (viewed November 11, 1006).

100. For more information *see*, http://www.mtcr.info/english/index.html. For a list of the membership of each arrangement as well as a description of their mandates, visit the Department of State website at www.State.gov. For a further description of the PSI, see Remarks of the President on Weapons of Mass Destruction Proliferation, at the National Defense University, February 13, 2004, at www.whitehouse.gov.

101. For more information *see*, http://www.nuclearsuppliersgroup.org/testo_home.htm (viewed November 11, 2006).

102. 1968 entered into force 1970. A list of the parties can be found at Treaties in Force at http://www.state.gov/s/l/treaties/c15824.htm.

103. Convention on Prohibitions or Restrictions on the Use of Certain Conventional Weapons Which May be Deemed to be Excessively Injurious or to Have Indiscriminate Effects, 19 I.L.M. 1523 (1980).

104. Convention on the Prohibition of the Development, Production and Stockpiling of Bacteriological (Biological) Weapons and on Their Destruction, 26 U.S.T. 583 (1972).

105. A description of this program can be found at the website of the United States Enrichment Corporation, www.usec.com.

106. *See*, Sec. 1501(b) of the National Defense Authorization Act for Fiscal Year 1997 (Public Law 104–201; 50 U.S.C. 2362 note. There are also numerous websites providing descriptions and commentary on the Nunn-Lugar program.

107. Quoting from the CTR homepage at http://www.defenselink.mil/pus/ctr/accomplish.html (accessed November 11, 2006).

108. *See* http://usinfo.stat.gov/products/pubs/proliferation/.

109. Consider, for example: (1) the tension between U.S. and multilateral interests in non-proliferation, as reflected in the PSI, and the parallel interests of participant states in unilateral economic interests, as reflected by Australia's apparent decision to enter the uranium enrichment market; (2) the competing interest in fully funding Nunn-Lugar while not creating market incentives for proliferation activities; (3) the commercial and security trade-offs between U.S. interests in leading the PSI at the same time that the United States is the world's number one arms merchant; and, (4) the variance in U.S. policy (including "carrots" and "sticks") offered to Libya, Iran, and North Korea to terminate their nuclear weapons programs. Of course, there are rational policy explanations behind each tension, such as the necessity of maintaining a viable defense arms industry for U.S. needs by permitting certain sales overseas. At the same time the United States sends mixed signals as to where its priorities lie.

110. 9/11 Public Discourse Project, *Final Report on 9/11 Commission Recommendations*, December 5, 2005, at 4. Available at www.9-11pdp.org.

111. Raymond Bonner, "Call to Enrich Uranium in Australia Stirs Debate," *The New York Times*, August 2, 2006.

112. As envisioned by the Rome Treaty, Article 98 permits Parties and non-Parties to reach bilateral agreements that Parties will not surrender the citizens of non-Parties to the ICC or cooperate in their investigation and prosecution.

113. Recollection of the author of comments made by Senator Mansfield while serving as U.S. Ambassador to Japan in 1985.

114. Henry Kissinger, "China: Containment Won't Work," *The Washington Post*, June 13, 2005.

115. In terms of volume, Canada and Mexico remain our largest trading partners. United States International Trade Commission, U.S. Trade Balance, by Partner Country 2005. http://dataweb.usitc.gov (accessed November 2006).

116. *See e.g.*, Stephen Cohen, "Economic Impact of a West Coast Dock Shutdown," January 2002, at brie.berkeley.edu/publications/ships%202002%20final.pdf (accessed November 2006); "The Economics of Cargo Screening," Port Technology International at www.porttechnology.org.

117. Pam Zubeck, "Coordination Against Terror," *Colorado Springs Gazette*, October 25, 2005. Statistics vary depending on how exactly the figure is calibrated. See, e.g., Secure Seas, Open Ports, June 21, 2004 placing the number of recreational boaters in the United States in 2003 at 79 million.

118. Fact Sheet: A Day in the Life of Homeland Security, June 19, 2003, available at http://www.dhs.gov/xnews/releases/press (accessed November 2006); "9/11: Five Years Later: Post-9/11, U.S. Coast Guard Makes Port Security a Top Priority," NY1 News, at www.ny1.com/ny1/content/index.jsp?&aid=61721 (accessed November 2006).

119. Observations on Agency Performance, Operations and Future Challenges, Statement of Stephen Caldwell, Acting Director Homeland Security and Justice Issues, Government Accountability Office, June 15, 2006, at 33.

120. See note 5.

121. United Nations Convention on the Law of the Sea, 21 I.L.M. (1974).

122. Law of the Sea; for definitions of the operative terms see Articles 3 and 33.

123. Under international law, a ship has the nationality of the nation in which it is registered and under whose flag it sails. (In some circumstances a vessel may be registered in one state and flagged in another, but that is not the norm.) As a result, and in general, the law of the flag state is the law applicable on board a vessel. "Flag of convenience," such as those associated with Panama or Liberia, is a term used to describe vessels owned by persons in one country, but registered and flying the flag of another country. As the term

suggests, this is usually done for purposes of convenience, including obtaining the benefits of relaxed labor laws, shipping laws, and for tax purposes. The state of convenience
gains the benefit of registry fees and commercial status.

In theory, the flag state nation is supposed to have a "genuine link" to the vessel in
question. In addition, the flag state is responsible for "exercising effective authority and
control over the ship in administrative, technical and labor matters," including those necessary to provide for the safety of the ship and to adhere to international standards (i.e.,
IMO rules).

Generally, when a vessel is on the high seas it is immune from boarding or search absent
the consent of the flag state and in some cases the master of the vessel. In addition, "a
warship or clearly-marked law enforcement ship may board a ship . . . if there is reason
to suspect that the ship is engaged in piracy, slave trade, or unauthorized broadcasting;
is without nationality; or though flying a foreign flag or refusing to show its flag, is in fact
of the same nationality as the warship or law enforcement ship." The PSI is an effort to
further define and expand the basis on which states might lawfully board foreign vessels,
either as a matter of flag state consent, or through the evolution of customary international law through practice.

In general, vessels in a coastal state's territorial sea are subject to the coastal state's
jurisdiction as if they were on the land territory of the state, excepting, for example, certain sovereign immune vessels and vessels engaged in innocent passage. Vessels in a coastal state's contiguous zone and exclusive economic zone are subject to
varying degrees of coastal jurisdiction and inspection as well. See, *Restatement of
the Law Third*, as well as the Law of the Sea Convention, including Articles 3, 33,
and 56.

124. Secure Seas, Open Ports.

125. John F. Frittelli, "Maritime Security: Overview of Issues," Congressional Research Service,
December 5, 2003, at 5.

126. John Mintz, "15 Freighters Believed to be Linked to Al Qaeda," *The Washington Post*,
December 31, 2002.

127. *But see*, among other reports, "Cargo Security: Partnership Program Grants Importers
Reduced Scrutiny with Limited Assurance of Improved Security," The General Accountability Office, March 2005 (suggesting gaps in the coverage and capacity of the Customs
Trade Partnership Against Terrorism Program (CTPATP) even at the small number of
ports currently included within the program). Among other things, CBP does not have
the manpower necessary to fully screen and uphold the program overseas – one more area
where resources are insufficient to meet mission requirements in an area where there is
general policy agreement on necessity.

128. *See*, the CBP website and DHS websites for various fact sheets on securing U.S. ports, at
http://www.cbp.gov/newsroom/fack_sheets/2006 (accessed August 10, 2006).

129. Government Accountability Office, "Preventing Nuclear Smuggling: DOE Has Made Limited Progress in Installing Radiation Detection Equipment at Highest Priority Seaports,"
GAO-05-375, March 31, 2005. Available at http://www.gao.gov (accessed November 2,
2006).

130. *See* IAEA website generally. Also, Eric Lipton, "Testers Slip Radioactive Materials Over
Borders," *The New York Times*, March 28, 2006; Bryan Bender, "A Pledge to Track Uranium
Fades," *The Boston Globe*, July 17, 2006.

131. *Public Health Security and Bio-terrorism Preparedness and Response Act of 2002*, June 12,
2002 107–188.

132. For a list of grant programs and funding allocations by state see http://www.dhs.gov/
xopnbiz/grants/.

133. Note how the question of preemption is treated: "Nothing in this section or section 363
[the Secretary's quarantine powers in time of war] or the regulations promulgated under
such sections, shall be construed as superseding any provision under State law . . . except
to the extent that such a provision conflicts with an exercise of Federal authority under
this section or section 363."

134. *9/11 Public Discourse Project* http://www.9-11pdp.org visited March 23, 2006. The Project "graded" five separate preparedness areas – adequate radio spectrum for first responders (F), establishment of a unified incident Command System (C), allocation of homeland security funds based on risk (F), critical infrastructure risks and vulnerability assessment (D), and private sector preparedness (C). However, the Project noted that the first and third grades could change with the passage of legislation addressing the problems identified. Of course, as the GAO has demonstrated, the passage of legislation is not equivalent to capacity.

135. Geoff Fein, "Katrina Showed Need for Rapid Damage Assessment, Improved Communications," *Defense Daily*, July 27, 2006.

136. Press conference with officials from Homeland Security, the Environmental Protection Agency, and the Departments of Health and Human Services, Energy, Transportation, and Defense, Washington, D.C. August 31, 2005. Available at http://www.dhs.gov/dhspublic (visited 9/1/05).

137. The public health field was pioneered at the turn of the last century by cities like Minneapolis and New York. The nation's 450,000 public health care workers are roughly divided in thirds at the federal, state, and local level.

138. 42 U.S.C. §264.

139. This is reflected in executive statements about accomplishments and goals in this area. See e.g., HHS Fact Sheet: Biodefense Preparedness: Record of Accomplishment, April 28, 2004, at www.hhs.gov/news/press/2004pres.

140. In the private realm, the American Bar Association and Castigny Conference Series have run a series of forward leaning conferences.

141. *General Accountability Office*, "HHS Bioterrorism Preparedness Programs: States Reported Progress but Fell Short of Program Goals for 2002," February 10, 2004, GAO-04-360R.

142. Eric Lipton, "Bid to Stockpile Bioterror Drugs Stymied by Setbacks," *The New York Times*, September 18, 2006.

143. *See*, Michael Greenberger, "The Threat of Smallpox: Eradicated but not Erased: A Review of the Fiscal, Logistical, and Legal Obstacles Impacting the Phase I Vaccination Program," available at the University of Maryland Law School website.

144. Statement of Brigadier General Matthew Broderick, Director for Operations Coordination, U.S. Department of Homeland Security, Before the U.S. Senate, Homeland Security and Governmental Affairs Committee, February 10, 2006.

145. Ibid.

146. Bruce Rolfsen, "USAF Predator Cleared for Domestic Relief Ops," *Defense News*, September 11, 2006.

147. Ibid.; Geoff Fein, "Katrina Showed Need for Rapid Damage Assessment, Improved Communications," *Defense Daily*, July 27, 2006.

148. Pam Zubeck, "Coordination Against Terror," *Colorado Springs Gazette*, October 26, 2005, quoting Daniel Goure, Vice President of the Lexington Institute think tank.

149. Pam Zubeck, "NorthCom Official Lists Katrina Lessons," *Colorado Springs Gazette*, October 22, 2005.

150. DOD Directive 5525.5.

151. Ibid., *Cantigny Conference*, at 20. In 1999 a young Marine shot an innocent civilian shepherd along the Southwest border while providing military assistance to civil authorities enforcing U.S. counternarcotics laws.

152. Department of Defense Strategy for Homeland Defense and Civil Support, June 2005, at iii.

153. Christopher Lee, "Crowded ERs Raise Concerns on Readiness," *The Washington Post*, September 28, 2006.

154. Charlie Savage, "US Sees Insurers as Possible Tool in Terror Fight," *The Boston Globe*, February 22, 2005.

155. Direct bureaucratic responsibility for this task resides with the Private Sector Office, Department of Homeland Security. Visit, http://www.dhs.gov (private sector office). Of

course, the responsibility is ultimately shared by the president, the Congress, state and local authorities, as well as private sector leaders, including corporate CEOs, industry associations, and chambers of commerce. See, Stephen Flynn and Daniel Prieto, "Neglected Defense: Mobilizing the Private Sector to Support Homeland Security," March 2006, Council on Foreign Relations. Available at http://www.cfr.org/publications/10475/neglected_defense.html.

156. Jennifer Steinhauer, "Governors Resist Shifting Authority over Guard," *The New York Times*, August 15, 2006; David Broder, "Governors Wary of Change on Troops," *The Washington Post*, August 6, 2006.

157. Eric Berger, "Perry Says Disaster Plan Flawed," *Houston Chronicle*, April 4, 2006.

158. Tom Roeder, "NorthCom Chief says Attack not Inevitable," *Colorado Springs Gazette*, October 6, 2006.

159. *9/11 Public Discourse Project*, at 1. There is no question this is a hard and expensive problem, but unlike other homeland security problems, this is one that can be solved with effort, money, and testing, and then taken off the "to do" list.

160. *See*, William Langewieche, *The Outlaw Sea: A World of Freedom, Chaos, and Crime* (New York: Nine Point Press, 2004).

161. Dana Shea and Frank Gottron, "Ricin: Technical Background and Potential Role in Terrorism," Congressional Research Service, February 4, 2004; "Insurgents Suspected in Mass Poisoning of Iraq Police," *The Australian*, October 11, 2006. http://www.theaustralian.news.com.au/printpage (accessed October 31, 2006). *Germs* argues that America's introduction to bioterrorism occurred in 1984 with a domestic attack using Salmonella by the followers of a religious cult figure named Rajneesh. Judith Miller, Stephen Engelberg, William Broad, *Germs: Biological Weapons and America's Secret War* (New York: Simon & Schuster, 2001).

162. The reference here is to the 2006 DHS Inspector General's report indicating that in response to the president's direction in HSPD-5 that DHS identify potential terrorist targets in the United States the resulting list included everything from a petting zoo and popcorn factory to national landmarks like the Golden Gate Bridge.

10. The National Security Lawyer

1. Peter de la Billiere, *Supreme Courage: Heroic Stories from 150 Years of the Victoria Cross*, at 24 (London: Little, Brown (2004).

2. During the Clinton Administration the legal advisor reported to the national security advisor, and operated independently from, but in coordination with, the counsel to the president, the president's senior legal advisor. During the Bush administration the legal advisor reported directly to the counsel. The role of the legal advisor in this latter function has varied from administration to administration depending on, among other factors, the personality of participants and the extent to which the office is perceived by agencies as facilitating national security process, as John Norton Moore has argued for a long time, or as a source of potential rival legal advice.

3. *See*, Jane Mayer, *New Yorker*.

4. American Bar Association, Model Rules of Professional Conduct. Rule 1.3 Diligence – Comment. Available at http://www.abanet.org/cpr/mrpc (viewed 9/12/06).

5. Rule 1.2.

6. Rule 1.6.

7. *See*, Nelson Lund, The President as Client and the Ethics of the "President's Lawyers," 61 *Law & Contemp. Probs.* 61 (Winter 1998); Steven Calabresi, "The President, The Supreme Court, and the Constitution: A Brief Positive Account of the Role of Government Lawyers in the Development of Constitutional Law," 61 *Law & Contemp. Probs.* 61 (Winter 1998).

8. The literature is varied on this subject, but if there is a default answer it appears to be "the employing Agency," but that makes no sense, if for example, the lawyer is seconded to the National Security Council or is a judge advocate on rotation outside his service or the Department of Defense.

9. *See, e.g.,* Rule 1.13, *Model Rules of Professional Conduct for Federal Lawyers*, The Federal Bar Association, 1990. "Government lawyers are often formally employed by a Federal Agency but assigned to an organizational element within the Federal Agency. Unless otherwise specifically provided, the Federal Agency, not the organizational element is ordinarily considered the client. The Federal Agency acts through its authorized officials ... the head of the organization is subject to being overruled by higher agency authority." In other words, the Agency Head is the client. The Rules note: "The FBA is not empowered to discipline members or enforce these Rules. However, the FBA encourages Federal Agencies to adopt rules ... based on these Rules ... "

10. *See,* Jesselyn Radack, "Tortured Legal Ethics: The Role of the Government Advisor in the War on Terrorism," 77 *U. Colo. L. Rev.* 1 (Winter 2006); Steven K. Berenson, "Public Lawyers, Private Values: Can, Should, and Will Government Lawyers Serve the Public Interest?" 41 *Boston Col. L. Rev.* 789 (July 2000).

11. Although the Constitution is arguably subsumed within the concept of public interest scant attention is paid in the scholarly literature to the national security lawyer's responsibility to uphold and defend the Constitution as the source of ethical duty. But see, Randolph Moss, "Executive Branch Legal Interpretation: A Perspective from the Office of Legal Counsel," 52 *Admin. L. Rev.* 1303 (Fall 2000) citing to the Constitution as one of a number of sources of ethical responsibility.

12. *See e.g.,* Moss.

13. The meaning of "Officer" is addressed in *Morrison v. Olson,* 487 U.S. 654 (1988) and *Buckley v. Valeo,* 424 U.S.1 (1976).

14. The list of persons authorized to have access to the information. The term originates with the list kept by General Eisenhower's staff of persons needing to know the date, time, and place of the D-Day landings.

15. *Whitney v. California,* 274 U.S. 357, 375 (1927) (Justice Brandeis concurring).

Index